The Age of Humanism and Reformation

A. G. DICKENS

The Age of Humanism and Reformation

EUROPE IN THE
FOURTEENTH, FIFTEENTH
AND SIXTEENTH CENTURIES

Prentice-Hall, Inc., Englewood Cliffs, New Jersey

Library of Congress Catalog Card Number: 74-39361

3 - 28 - 73

P   0-13-018606-6
C   0-13-018614-7

10   9   8   7   6   5   4   3   2   1

Acknowledgements: Art on pp. 46, 60, 72, 95, 103, 115, 125, 129, 145, 148, 156,
167, 168, 173, 176, 189, 205, and 222 is reproduced with the permission of The
Bettman Archive, Inc.; on pp. 22, 23, 24, 25, 31, 33, 112, 113, 114, 117, 135, 185,
and 191, with the permission of Scala Fine Art Publishers, Inc.; and on pp. 10,
120, and 202, with the permission of Scala-Alarni.

Prentice-Hall International, Inc., London
Prentice-Hall of Australia, Pty., Ltd., Sydney
Prentice-Hall of Canada, Ltd., Toronto
Prentice-Hall of India Private Ltd., New Delhi
Prentice-Hall of Japan, Inc., Tokyo

Contents

Illustrations, vii
Preface, ix

ONE

Humanism in Italy

1. The Early Humanists and Petrarch, *3*
2. Humanism and Art in the *Quattrocento, 14*
3. The Educators and Lorenzo Valla, *24*
4. Medicean Florence and Platonism, *30*

TWO

States and Nations
in Early Modern Europe

1. The Complexities and the Common Background, *37*
2. France, England, and Burgundy, *47*
3. The Iberian Peninsula: Overseas Exploration, *59*
4. Central and Eastern Europe, *70*

THREE

High Renaissance Europe

1. Europe and the Italian Wars, *87*
2. The Wars to the Death of Julius II, *91*
3. War and Diplomacy, 1513–1530, *100*
4. Art and Letters in Italy, *108*
5. Humanism in Northern Europe, *128*

FOUR

Reformation and Counter Reformation

1. Luther and Zwingli, *143*
2. Lutheranism and Politics, *157*
3. Calvin and the Reformed Churches, *164*
4. The Two English Reformations, *172*
5. Catholic Reform and Revival, *182*

FIVE

The Later Sixteenth Century

1. Spain and Philip II, *195*
2. England under Elizabeth I, *204*
3. The French Civil Wars, *216*
4. The Revolt of the Netherlands, *228*
5. Social and Intellectual Change
   in the Sixteenth Century, *240*

Postscript, 253

Genealogies, 261

Reading Lists, 269

Index, 281

Illustrations

Portrait of Petrarch, *10*
Italy in about 1494 (map), *15*
Pazzi Chapel, *22*
Maltesta Temple, *22*
Sacrifice of Isaac, the Baptistery Doors, *23*
S. Francesco in Gloria (Sassetta), *24*
Madonna with Child (Masaccio), *25*
Conferma della Regola (Ghirlandaio), *31*
Primavera (Botticelli), *33*
Printer's trademark, *46*
France and Burgundy c. 1500 (map), *48*
Ferdinand and Isabella, *60*
Expansion of Europe in about 1530 (map), *66*
Jacob Fugger, *72*
Savonarola preaching, *95*
Portrait of Charles V, *103*
Military invention (Da Vinci notebook), *110*
Bizarre faces (Da Vinci notebook) *111*
Dying Slave (Michelangelo), *113*
Pietà (Michelangelo), *114*
Reading Room, the Laurentian Library (Michelangelo), *115*
School of Athens, Stanza della Segnatura (Raphael), *116*
Tempesta (Giorgione), *117*
Niccolò Machiavelli, *120*
Baldassare Castiglione (Raphael), *125*
Scanning device (Dürer), *129*
Erasmus (Matys), *135*
Tetzel's Indulgence campaign, *146*
Title page, *To the Christian Nobility*, *148*
The Swiss Confederation (map), *154*
Zwingli, memorial portrait, *156*
Cartoon, Luther, Calvin and the pope, *167*
Calvinist iconoclasm, *169*

Title page, *The Historie of the Reformation*, *173*
Thomas Cranmer, *176*
Ignatius Loyola before Pope Paul III, *185*
The Council of Trent, *189*
St. Ildefonso (El Greco), *191*
Europe in 1555 (map), *197*
Philip II (Titian), *202*
Elizabeth Queen, *205*
Queen Elizabeth's signature, *205*
The Massacre of St. Bartholomew, *222*
The Low Countries (map), *230*

Preface

While stressing the immense significance of thought, art, and religion in the legacy of early modern Europe, this survey is based upon the conviction that the higher values cannot be explained without some detailed political narrative and analysis. The book will have served its main purpose if it helps readers to distrust many familiar simplifications, and to think harder than ever about the complex interactions between all these various aspects of human struggle and endeavor.

As with all such surveys, my debts to fellow-historians remain too numerous to list. Yet in particular I must thank my friend Maurice Ashley for helpful criticisms of detail, and Mrs. Dorothy Carr for her invaluable work on the bibliography. Without the indefatigable help of my secretary Miss C. L. Hawker I could not at present continue writing alongside my other numerous duties. And both for assiduous checking of the text and for ideas concerning the illustrations I am greatly indebted to several members of my publisher's staff.

A. G. D.

The Age of Humanism and Reformation

ONE

Humanism in Italy

1. The Early Humanists and Petrarch

Over a century after the publication of Burckhardt's classic volume *The Civilisation of the Renaissance in Italy (1860),* we obstinately continue to speak of "the Renaissance," yet we most variously define the nature and the effects of this rebirth. The differences remain so profound that we are tempted to expunge the very word from our terminology, or else to use it merely as a colorless term to cover that period of Western civilization stretching from the fourteenth to the seventeenth century. The present book will not seek to impose order upon this unruly scene by any dogmatic redefinition of "Renaissance." On the other hand, it must be prepared to define and handle the term "humanism." Moreover it will recognize the phenomena which passed under that label as truly dynamic, since they ushered in further changes even more fundamental to modern Western civilization. In this account we shall take the view that modern Western history had its chief origins within a developing set of ideas. The ground must hence be cleared by explaining the origins, character, and progress of humanist classical studies which aimed at a deeper understanding of Greek and Roman civilization. As our enquiry unfolds, we shall be drawn beyond this somewhat restricted program of revival; we shall find ourselves trying to evaluate its effects upon original literature, upon both political and scientific thought, upon the art, architecture, and social manners of Europe.

Some of the simplifications of contemporary pride one may now rapidly dismiss. The new humanism was wrongly depicted by enthusiasts as an enlightenment overcoming a "Middle Age" of darkness. Marsilio Ficino *(1433-99)* was not a *better* philosopher than St. Thomas Aquinas *(d.1274).* In terms of creative literature, Petrarch *(1304-74)* excelled the other early humanists, but even he was not a profounder or more technically accomplished poet than Dante *(d.1321),* whom in fact both he and his friend Boccaccio *(1313-75)* held in veneration. The valid contrast does not lie between a "medieval" rudeness and a "modern" sophistication. The artistry and realism of the Icelandic prose-sagas perfected in the thirteenth century need not fear comparison with any parallels, ancient or modern. The medieval French poet Jean de Meung *(d.1305)* has been called the Voltaire of his age; he was highly irreverent in his attitudes toward romance, superstition, monasteries, feudalism, popes, and kings. Geoffrey Chaucer *(d.1400)* translated Petrarch, yet was hardly touched by humanism. Nevertheless he can boast a subtle humor and humanity, a creative imagination scarcely existent in the neo-classical literature of fifteenth-century Florence. It is important to realize that the humanist classical revival came upon an age when the vernacular literatures of Europe were independently reaching new levels of achievement. And somewhat similarly, when humanist concepts invaded the fields of painting and sculpture, they inherited the elaborate techniques developed by so-called "gothic" painters and sculptors throughout recent centuries. Humanism did not enter a static world; it was not required to breathe and grow in a cultural vacuum. The attempt to imitate Latin and Greek literature could even prove stultifying in some minds. Despite some creative achievements like Petrarch's poem *Africa,* the significance of early humanism does not lie in any direct rivalry with the vernacular literatures; rather does it lie in a process of fusion with those literatures, in the steady stimulus which humanism gave to fresh social and cultural values uncharacteristic of the earlier Middle Ages.

In our own century the word humanism is used in a variety of senses little related to those agreed upon by historians of civilization. As applied to the period now under consideration, it implies a creative study of Greek and Roman civilization. The humanists desired to know the Ancient World as it had really existed, to divest it of the veils swathed about its forms by the Christian centuries, to understand its higher values for their own sake. At first with mediocre success, they tried to emulate its creations. Some of them believed that through apprenticeship they or their successors might come to surpass the ancients and so add a new glory to the history of man. In fourteenth- and fifteenth-century Italy, humanist studies were known by the sober terms *studia humanitatis* and *studia humaniora:* they chiefly comprised grammar, rhetoric, history, poetry, and moral philosophy, all based upon an analysis of leading ancient authors. But not until 1490 do we encounter the actual word *umanista,* which had by then become university slang for a teacher of the *studia humanitatis.*

Cultural history abhors violent revolutions: the novelty of the humanist movement, however genuine, can easily be misconceived. The early humanists were born not merely amid flourishing vernacular literatures but as heirs to earlier, less sophisticated modes of classical study. Medieval Europe, culturally united by the Latin tongue, had never wholly lost contact with the thought and the art of the Ancient World. The so-called Carolingian Renaissance of the ninth century had sought a recovery of Roman art and literary style. In twelfth-century Chartres there had flourished a famous school of classical literature. The figure of Vergil, a folk-hero among the Italian peasants, had become in Dante's great poem the revered spokesman of all pre-Christian wisdom. Alongside western Europe, linked closer by the Crusades, stood Byzantium, the metropolis of that Eastern Empire which encapsulated the heritages of both Greece and Rome. In architecture and the plastic arts, survivals from the Ancient World remained numerous. The "gothic" schools of painting which attained their first peaks in Giotto *(d.1336)* and Duccio *(d.c.1340)* were in large part the offspring of Byzantine mosaic and painting. Many well-preserved monuments of ancient architecture enshrined their message in forms easier to comprehend than those of literature. In Italy there stood many Greek and Roman temples; in Rome and Ravenna the magnificent late-classical churches and baptistries have been in continuous use to our own day. Eleventh- and twelfth-century Italy could produce churches like S. Miniato al Monte at Florence, where the light, polychrome, classical forms might still pardonably be mistaken for creations of some fifteenth-century humanist architect. In Italy gothic architecture reigned but briefly, and it was deeply modified by native Romanesque notions. Even in Provence there remain Romanesque churches which boast a wealth of would-be classical detail. Yet any deep understanding of the spirit of Roman art and letters could scarcely have arisen from any Western people save the Italians, who alone could without absurdity regard the Romans as their ancestors, the past of Rome as their own past, enshrined upon their own soil.

There had also occurred rebirths of ancient thought quite distinct from those which we label humanist. The scholastic theology and philosophy of Albertus Magnus *(d.1280)* and Thomas Aquinas sprang from a grandiose design to salvage and Christianize the great heathen Aristotle. Thomism deeply pervaded the writings of Dante. Disputes between its admirers and its critics dominated many universities until the sixteenth century, but it was finally accepted by the Papacy as normative for Catholic philosophy and theology. The enthusiasm and corporate spirit of the humanists owed much to the fact that they were consciously reacting against all forms of scholastic philosophy, reacting against what they regarded as hair-splitting metaphysical systems irrelevant to real human needs. Modern enthusiasts for scholasticism have treated humanist thought as superficial and undeserving of the term philosophical. It is indeed true that few humanists were interested in studies of Being or metaphysics; true again that they did not attempt encyclopedic works, those verbal cathedrals of the schoolmen which claimed to cover and to systematize all knowledge of God, man, and the universe. The humanists distrusted such aspirations as naïve, their results as unverifiable. Without renouncing Christianity, the thinkers of the humanist mainstream saw man as a comprehensible being standing midway between God and the lower orders of nature. Not unlike the *philosophes* of the eighteenth century, they saw darkness being dispelled and the way back to the Ancient World likely to prove also—at least for a future generation—the way forward into a glorious future. In practice they concerned themselves with a philosophy of man, a limited objective compared with those of the scholastic thinkers. While they drew methods and examples from ancient writers, they strove to think in a manner relative to the needs and welfare of modern men. They abandoned the encyclopedic approach and wrote a host of more modest, more specialized treatises on politics, diplomacy, war, social life and manners, education, the arts, history, grammar, and rhetoric. However nonmetaphysical, these works would seem also worthy to be called philosophy. The common denominator might well be regarded as a historical, a comparative attitude of mind. Even Aristotle ceased to be a junior partner of the Almighty and became like other thinkers a child of history. Again, while they hoped to attain new approaches to Christianity, the humanists enormously increased the secular content of thought and literature. Once for all, learning had emerged from the cloister and the academic lectureroom to rejoin the human mainstream.

By what date can we detect the beginnings of this change of attitude toward the Ancient World? Undoubtedly they antedate the work of Petrarch, so long accepted as the founder of humanism. Around 1300 recognizable groups of humanists were meeting at Padua, Verona, Vicenza, Venice, Milan, Florence, and Naples. The earliest of these circles gathered at Padua around the distinguished judge Lovato dei Lovati, and after his death in 1309 continued under the leadership of his nephew. Most of Lovato's original poetry has been lost, but enough remains to reveal the sensitive enthusiasm with which he sought to recapture the Latin style of the ancients. Significantly he wrote a treatise on Seneca's tragedies, concentrating upon their meters, the unfamiliar character of which had hitherto impaired interest and understanding. The work of these early Paduans was soon eclipsed by that of Albertino Mussato *(d.1329),* who corresponded with scholars in other cities and unlike Lovato became known throughout most of Italy. He defended poetry against puritanical theologians, wrote verses inspired by Ovid and Horace, compiled a Vergilian epic on a modern theme and histories based upon Livy, Caesar, and Sallust. Closely following the model of Seneca, Mussato wrote in 1314 the tragedy *Ecerinis:* it concerned the former tyrant Ezzelino da Romano, the theme having some topical reference to the quarrel between Padua and the aggressive Can Grande della Scala, lord of Verona. For this patriotic piece Mussato was publicly crowned with laurel by the Paduans, an event which caused the exiled Dante to dream of similar honors in Florence. Soon afterwards in Vicenza, Ferreto dei Ferreti was writing histories which can be taken as beginning the gradual transition from the medieval chronicler to the would-be classical historian.

While at Padua the devotees sought to write original literature in the ancient spirit and forms, at Verona there flourished during the first three decades of the fourteenth century an activity of equal significance: the discovery and critical examination of classical manuscripts. This study derived from the riches of the cathedral library, which contained among others the manuscripts of the long-ignored poet Catullus. Here Giovanni de Matociis reordered the confused biographies of the *Historia Augusta* and discovered that there were two Plinys. Meanwhile the chancellor of Can Grande della Scala at Verona was Benzo d'Alessandria, who like Petrarch and Poggio in later days travelled about Italy systematically transcribing and collating manuscripts. More independently, during the 1320s the leading humanist of Florence, Geri d'Arezzo, wrote extensively in Latin prose and verse. Though only six epistles and a dialogue have survived, these suffice to show how faithfully he followed ancient models, how completely he had rejected the rhetoric admired by Dante's contemporaries in order to achieve a hitherto unequalled simplicity and elegance. When in 1395 Petrarch's successor Coluccio Salutati *(d.1406)* looked back at the origins of the movement, he singled out as its leading founders Albertino Mussato and Geri d'Arezzo.

What influences and social backgrounds promoted these tendencies in the Italian cities? The latter had long been among the most sophisticated urban communities of Europe, and some like Florence, Venice, and Milan were among her largest and wealthiest. In many of them not only vernacular poetry but also Latin rhetoric, grammar, and composition had already flourished—and been turned to political uses—throughout the thirteenth century. These cities contained not merely a few learned clerics but also large groups of educated laymen emancipated from those pangs of con-science which so many clerical lovers of pagan literature had suffered throughout the Middle Ages. When young men no longer dreamed that hell-fire would be their reward for delighting in the story of Dido, then the secure reign of classical humanism had begun! But an examination of the leading figures in these groups reveals a more specific and consistent influence. Apart from some professional grammarians, the majority of the known leaders were judges or lawyers. In Italy this meant that they were assiduous students of the Roman legal codes, men whose daily work involved the adaptation of ancient law to modern circumstances. Ancient Rome had survived also in the reception of her law by princes and magistrates, and the interpretation of ancient legal texts was an activity by no means remote from the textual analysis of ancient literature.

The rise of humanism cannot be rigidly tied to political or economic conditions in these cities; it was not always associated with periods of trading prosperity, with republicanism as opposed to autocracy, with politi-cal enlightenment, or with pacific attitudes. Many Italian towns, it is true, could boast ancient traditions of civic independence, freedom of thought, multilateral trade and intercourse. On the other hand, in many of them centuries of faction were now giving place to the rule of despots. In 1318 the Carrara family assumed the lordship of Padua. Verona throughout this period was ruled by the powerful della Scala, who during the reign of Can Grande *(1312-29)* captured Vicenza and defeated the Paduans. During the fourteenth century Bologna was disputed between the native family of Pepoli, the Visconti of Milan and the popes. Milan had fallen in 1278 under the rule of the Visconti, who were destined to be succeeded in 1450 by the equally masterful Sforza.

Yet Florence and Venice, the two greatest of the Italian cities, both preserved to a large degree their ancient republican constitutions. The mercantile and manufacturing city of Florence fell under the control of the Medici in 1434, but even then retained the forms and much of the spirit of her republican past. She also gallantly defended her freedom against Milan and other enemies, though in the fifteenth century she did not scruple to conquer Pisa, Cortona, and Leghorn. Other cities tended to fear Florence even more than they feared the Visconti ogre in Milan. The case of Venice had become even more anomalous. Hitherto a great maritime power ruthlessly engaged in exploiting weak Byzantium and crushing her rival Genoa, Venice found in the growing insecurity of the eastern Mediterranean a strong incentive to turn to the acquisition of a land-empire. The party advocating this policy pointed out the obvious advantages of acquiring both fertile farmlands and the direct control of the Alpine passes. These counsels triumphed by the early years of the fifteenth century. Beginning in 1405 with the capture of Vicenza, Padua, and Verona—to which cities she admittedly accorded a high measure of internal self-government—Venice by the mid-century ruled Lombardy as far west as the River Adda. In short, to equate oligarchic, expansionist republicanism with political liberty, freedom of thought, and cultural creativity seems at best a simplification and at worst an outright error. The foreign policies of Florence and Venice were scarcely calculated to restore the old Italian civic spirit, while their rivals the Visconti argued with some plausibility that their own personal rule in Milan could contribute more to the freedom of Italy than could any confused republic. Again, it would be comforting for modern democrats to believe that all the greatest art and scholarship flourished under republican patronage. This notion is patently untrue of the period 1300 to 1600; this wishful thinking springs perhaps from a mistaken tendency to identify the cultured Italian princes of that age with those very different dictators of our own century, half-educated demagogues thrown up by the explosion of weak democracies.

In these earlier stages the humanists proved slow to grasp the predominant role of Greece, as opposed to Rome, in the thought and art of ancient times. At first the paucity of good linguistic training proved a formidable barrier. Before 1300 the Greek language had been known to very few Western scholars: the main exception was the Flemish Dominican and friend of Aquinas, William of Moerbeke *(d.1286)*, who translated works by Aristotle and his commentators. Only one area of western Europe could produce teachers of Greek: Calabria, the *Magna Graecia* of ancient times, where several monasteries had continued to follow the Greek rule. The cultivated Robert of Anjou, king of Naples *(d.1343)*, attracted translators from this area to his court and set them to work on Galen and other Greek authors. To his court also came the Calabrian Barlaam, who instructed a number of Italians. At this early stage, however, Greek studies failed to spread rapidly throughout Italy and the West. Despite personal contacts, Barlaam failed to impart much Greek to Petrarch, and the latter remained convinced to the end of his life that the Romans had improved upon the Greek achievement and thus given birth to a superior culture. His friend Boccaccio became unusual among contemporary Florentine men of letters when he acquired a somewhat sketchy knowledge of Greek from the Calabrian teacher Leontius Pilatus. The Italian humanists began substantially to acquire this part of the ancient heritage when in 1396 Manuel Chrysoloras, already the most distinguished scholar of Byzantium, was appointed to teach Greek at Florence. The Florentine government secured his highly successful services by the offer of a house and an initial five-year contract at 150 florins a year, later raised to 250. By the time of his death at the Council of Constance in 1415, numerous Italians were equipped to continue and extend his teaching. His Italian career proved timely. Already occupied in large part by the Ottoman Turks, the doomed Byzantine Empire had handed on Chrysoloras like a living torch of Hellenic culture.

Enough has been said to indicate that Petrarch (Francesco Petrarca) cannot accurately be called the father of humanism, however often he has been accorded this title. Even so, he was the first writer of genius to partake in the humanist revival. He avoided much reference to his predecessors, while ensuring that posterity should cherish his own complex personality alongside his works. To this day he exercises a spell which makes his less cautious admirers hasten to justify his every inconsistency and foible. Petrarch's early background was one of exile and struggle. Life made him a wanderer and a free-lance, but perhaps even under settled circumstances his restless temperament would never have allowed him to settle within the civic frame accepted by so many later Florentine humanists. His father, a minor legal official, had been expelled from Florence along with Dante and took refuge in Arezzo, where Francesco was born. Finding meager employment in Italy, in about 1313 the father took his family to Avignon, where the popes had been living for a decade under French tutelage. After studying the classics at Carpentras nearby, the young Petrarch obeyed his father's wish by undergoing several years of legal education both at Montpellier and at Bologna. Lacking any prospect of a substantial inheritance, he then took minor orders and received patronage from two prelates of the Colonna family. After his father's death in 1326 he lived chiefly at Avignon, but in 1333 he undertook a long journey to Paris, Ghent, Liége, and Cologne, meeting scholars and copying ancient manuscripts. Meanwhile he met Laura, the respectable married lady who was to inspire his finest Italian verse, yet without ever becoming a close friend.

On returning to Italy Petrarch transacted legal business for the rulers of Verona; he also recorded his emotions on surveying the ruins of Rome, abandoned by the popes, depopulated and pitiful. By 1337 he had returned to Avignon and entered upon a period of solitary studies at Vaucluse, where he communed with the mountain scenery in a mildly romantic spirit. While he continued to idealize the shadowy Laura, he begat a son and a daughter upon some obscure concubine. The platonic love divorced from physical passion and balanced by a generally satirical attitude toward womankind, these features belong to the literary cleric of the later Middle Ages; they contrast with that easy and courteous exchange of minds between educated men and women observable in later days.

In 1341, when the first drafts of his Latin epic *Africa* had been circulating for a couple of years, Petrarch travelled south to Naples and

Portrait of Petrarch
SCHOOL OF BELLINI
Galleria Borghese, Rome

returned thence to Rome, armed with magniloquent testimonials from King Robert. At Rome he gratified an old ambition by receiving on the Capitol the poet's laurel crown. From this point he attained a European celebrity, was courted by the great and swam upon the rising tide of cultural snobbery. He accepted the hospitality of the ruling despot in Parma, but when in 1347 Cola di Rienzo led a popular revolution in Rome, Petrarch threw himself into it with enthusiasm. Such, however, was the spirit of the age that the Gonzaga of Mantua, the Malatesta of Rimini and the Visconti of Milan continued to salute the poet who had not only supported Rienzo but had stigmatized despots in his ode to Italy and in his epistles to the Emperor. For his part Petrarch became during his later years quite closely associated with the Visconti, even though the rest of the world recognized the cruelty and corruption of their rule. At one stage, in a spirit one might indulgently call unrealistic, he gave vent to much rhetoric concerning liberty, calling upon all the politicians—Rienzo, the despots, the Emperor, the Pope—to establish the blessings of freedom throughout Italy. At least Petrarch had one consistent aim. Emancipated from the petty localism of Italian politics, he stood among the first Italians who thought upon a national scale. And in fairness it might be added that, as in Machiavelli's day, it was possible to believe that Italian independence and a measure of freedom might be won and maintained by some powerful prince—or even as Dante had wanted to believe by an emperor from across the Alps—rather than by the high walls and republican valor of the few remaining "free" cities.

Despite his admiration for Rienzo, Petrarch cannot be credited with anything resembling modern democratic sentiments. Though lacking any personal claim to aristocratic origins, he was outspoken in his contempt for the uneducated and the vulgar. Yet like Dante before him, he did much to make the feudal and urban aristocracies value cultural achievement and admit men of genius to something like social equality. His relations with the Church evince a characteristic individualism. By any standards, Petrarch must be called a Christian. He revered and loved St. Augustine, while his equal attraction to Cicero arose in no small part from the conviction that Cicero was a forerunner of Christianity, one whose Stoic doctrines harmonized with the Gospel. Though he wrote a *canzone* to the Virgin, Petrarch despised saint-cults and relics. Though he devoted some energy to combatting heresy, his attitude to dogma was liberal for his day. Outside the central truths of the Christian religion he allowed much freedom of judgment. From a passage of Augustine he derived the notion that the obscurity of the Scriptures is useful, since it permits different minds to detect different truths. Yet for the evangelical and mystical approaches he showed little feeling: he ignored St. Francis, and like Cicero he saw the universe as man-centered, as fashioned by God for the welfare of the human race. He helped to formulate that high concept of the cosmic dignity of man which Erasmus was to maintain and Luther to denounce.

Petrarch's distaste for the philosophy of the university schoolmen was boundless; he was interested neither in Aquinas nor in the current battles between the Realists and the Nominalists. As sources of religious truth he rested content with the Bible and the early Fathers.

> If in old age we cannot escape from the schools of dialectic because we played in them as boys, then we should not blush to go on playing hopscotch, or ride a hobby-horse, or let ourselves be rocked in a cradle. . . . there is nothing more unpleasant than an elderly logic-chopper. If he starts spitting out syllogisms, I advise you to run away and tell him to argue with Encheladus.[1]

The business of philosophy was neither to create refined metaphysical abstractions, nor even to discover the secrets of the physical universe, but to teach men how to live:

> For what, pray, will it profit to have known the nature of beasts, birds, fishes and snakes, but to be ignorant of, or to despise the nature of man—why we are born, whence we come and whither we go.

Both the private thought and the teaching of Petrarch interlaced a craving for civilized pleasures with constant reflections upon mortality. His self-cultivation was balanced by a delight in friendship, his austere moralism by charity toward human weakness. He could not share that harsh doctrine of Aquinas and Dante which saw the eternal expiation of hell as a monument to the glory and justice of God. Petrarch's emphasis upon a moral philosophy having practical relevance to life in the world may be ranked among his most positive contributions to humanism, even though his own Christian–Stoic solution did not attract all his successors. This apart, his special place in the rise of humanism derives from the fact that his literary genius transcended mere conscientious classical scholarship. He did not need to grovel before the ancient Greeks and Romans. As the greatest contemporary poet in the Italian tongue, he derived no more from Latin literature than from the medieval Provençal and Italian poets, whose work he continued and developed. Even in his Latin poems and treatises, his relationship with his ancient models remained far from slavish. He deprecated over-dependence on the ancient philosophers. He adored Cicero, yet derived elements of style from Seneca and even Augustine, thereby offending the purists of later days. And while the systematic study of rhetoric became a legitimate task of humanism, Petrarch scorned the mere rhetorician who had nothing of substance to say.

[1] A giant buried by Jupiter under Mount Etna.

Despite his misanthropic and clerical moods, the mind of Petrarch affords the strongest impression of breadth in time and space. He applied a splendid historical and topographical sense to the study of ancient Rome. One of his many great letters attempts a thumbnail political sketch of all the lands of Europe from England to Cyprus. Ever curious to survey new landscapes and human customs, this wanderer was never in exile; he was at home even in the lonely mountain regions shunned by commoner spirits for another three centuries.

> We see overhanging the lakes, the airy and snow-crowned Alps, a most welcome spectacle in summer, the woods touching the stars, the streams complaining amid the hollows of the rocks, the rivers falling thunderously from the high mountains, and wherever you turn, there rises the sound of birds and water-springs.

It remains hard to speak with precision on the development of Petrarch's thought and style throughout his long literary career. Had he lived a century and a half later he would doubtless have committed his works to printed and dated editions. In fact he lived in the age of manuscripts and he kept on correcting and amplifying his work over many years, so that a mature reflection can easily appear in a much earlier work. A landmark seems to appear in 1348, the year of the Black Death, when Laura and many others of his friends passed from the scene. Though Petrarch did not fulfil his impulse to retire to a hermitage, the element of gravity seems now to increase, and the poems he wrote *in morte di Madonna Laura* are deeply religious in tone. Meanwhile he kept his independence from ecclesiastical, civic, and academic chains. Despite pressure from Boccaccio, he refused the rectorship of the recently founded university of Florence and would not go back to assume his patrimony and citizenship. He visited Rome, returned again for a time to Provence, invited the Emperor Charles IV to intervene in Italy in the interest of his Visconti friends. In 1362 he was living in Padua and the following year visited Venice to donate his library to the Republic. Finally he retired to a villa at Arquà in the Euganean Hills, and there one July morning in 1374 he was found lying dead.

The author who called Petrarch "the first modern man" made a crude but almost pardonable tribute to a reflective, companionable, above all independent spirit. At all events we have recalled Petrarch's personality with a detail we can accord to only two or three figures of early modern Europe. Doubtless Luther will demand as much attention, and to attempt a comparison between these two would indeed form a searching academic exercise. Thomas Mann did likewise with Goethe and Tolstoy, as representing the opposite sides of a yet more modern world. Who better than Petrarch and Luther could fulfil a like function for the period commonly called "Renaissance and Reformation"?

2. Humanism and Art in the *Quattrocento*

"What is it to be a Florentine, except to be both by nature and law, a Roman citizen?" This was a saying of Coluccio Salutati, Petrarch's correspondent and idolatrous disciple, who was chancellor of Florence—one of the few permanent high officials of the Republic—from 1375 until his death in 1406. It was Salutati's duty to use his eloquence in the defence of Florentine liberties against the Visconti, the Papacy and other foes. Gian Galeazzo Visconti himself admitted that Salutati's letters were worth more than a thousand horsemen. This public task and the chancellor's active encouragement of the younger classical scholars arouse in us greater interest than his own heavy and sententious Latin works. With him there began in the city a great half-century of humanism in which constitutional rule, intellectual enlightenment, and artistic creation achieved a rare balance. And even when from 1434 Florence fell increasingly under the dominance of the Medici, the momentum of this cultural advance scarcely slackened.

The precise relationship between politics and culture in this new Periclean age continues to be disputed. Dr. Hans Baron has pointed to a fresh phase of humanism developing around 1400 in large measure as a patriotic response to the aggressive threats of the Visconti despot in Milan. The independent spirit of men like Salutati, Niccoli, Bruni, and Poggio Bracciolini changed the ambivalent attitudes of Petrarch into a true reverence for the ideals of republican Rome, a rejection of lingering monastic ideals, and a sturdy call to the values of the active life. More recently, Dr. George Holmes has suggested that this Florentine response did not arise purely from the Visconti threat but rather from a whole series of crises, beginning with the bloody struggle waged in 1375-78 against the Papacy. Conversely, he also points to the fructifying influences exerted in later decades by the close contacts of Florentines like Bruni and Poggio with the papal court. In 1377 this court returned to Rome from Avignon, but almost immediately there broke out the Great Schism, which saw two and finally three popes competing for recognition by the European powers. Though the Council of Constance *(1414-18)* ended the Schism—and incidentally burned the Bohemian heresiarch John Huss—it failed to initiate any general reform of the Church. During this prolonged papal crisis, and indeed later on under Pope Eugenius IV *(r.1431-47)*, Florence stood in a position of "friendly superiority" over Rome, her humanists enjoying exceptional rewards and prestige in this dual environment.

Narrow and simple explanations will not suffice to account for Florentine civic humanism. It may be seen as the development of an old tradition dating back not merely to the immediate predecessors of Petrarch but in some sense to Brunetto Latini *(d.1294)*, whom his ungrateful pupil Dante

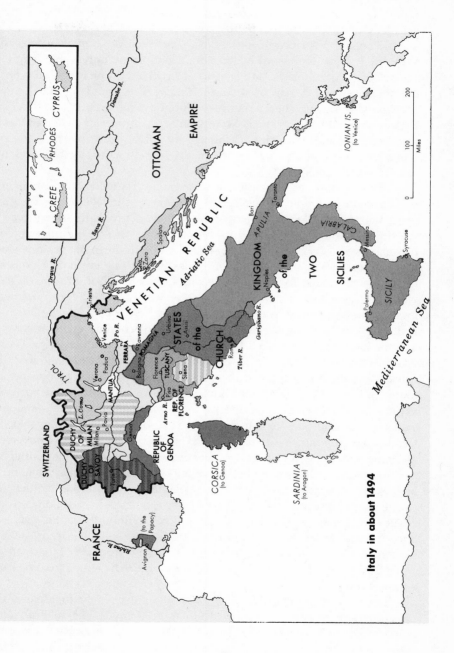

Italy in about 1494

relegated to the Inferno on a charge of homosexuality, but who in real life cultivated rhetoric for civic ends and was an early enthusiast for Cicero. However we regard the Florentine *genius loci,* we cannot explain a continuity of four centuries by reference to the political events of any given decade. One may point to a population alert, skilled, and practical at all its levels, capable of brief religious revivals yet relatively emancipated from superstition. Dante apart, the Florentines had played only a minor role in the evolution of scholastic and mystical Christianity. The medieval schools did not closely affect their lives, for their university, founded in 1349, never dominated the established patterns of Florentine intellectual life. It is hard to penetrate more deeply than did the sixteenth-century art-historian Vasari who attributed the Florentine achievement to the spirit of criticism, and remarked that the air of Florence made "minds naturally free and not content with mediocrity."

The greatness of Florentine scholarship and art does not admit of a predominantly economic explanation. Florence was indeed one of the most populous and most productive cities of medieval Europe. Its strength lay in the organization and output of its cloth industry and in the international preeminence of its hard-headed bankers, who had been art patrons since the days of Giotto. Even when the popes resided at Avignon, Florentine financiers continued to handle their widespread financial interests. Meanwhile the consolidated state debt offered an attractive field for investment. In 1338 the population was estimated at some 90,000, a vast figure for a medieval city. Not long afterwards, however, an economic and demographic recession set in: aggravated by warfare, plague, internal labor problems, competition from English and French cloth, it continued well into the fifteenth century and in 1450 the population was thought to number no more than 50,000. Civic humanism and great art therefore did not arise upon a curve of material prosperity. The desire to find social–economic explanations continues to our day unabated, one writer arguing that the trend from commerce to industry favored culture, another conversely ascribing this same culture to the tendency of some patrons to withdraw from industry! Perhaps the most which may confidently be said along these lines is that, even in relative economic decline, Florence lacked neither the public nor the private wealth to further her established aspirations toward beauty and learning. This large yet close-knit community found a style at once internally pervasive yet strongly local: one could hardly mistake a Florentine picture of the *Quattrocento* as coming from any other source, while by contrast the contemporary art of nearby Siena seems to come from a past century.

The three major figures of Florentine humanism in the first half of the fifteenth century were Leonardo Bruni *(c.1370–1444),* Poggio Bracciolini *(1380–1459),* and Leon Battista Alberti *(1404–72).* All three had close links with the Petrarchan tradition, particularly through their patrons, Salutati and the wealthy antiquarian Niccolò Niccoli *(d.1437).* Yet their differences seem as striking as their kinships, and their works progress outside the narrow bounds of the *studia humanitatis.* Bruni came to Florence from the subject-city of Arezzo and soon obtained instruction in Greek from Chryso-loras, who nourished in his pupils not merely a linguistic discipline but also a broad enthusiasm for Greek thought and letters. In later life Bruni repaid this debt by a series of valuable Latin translations from the Greek classics. Through the influence of Salutati he secured in 1405 the office of secretary at the papal court. After serving four popes and attaining prosperity, he returned to Florence in 1415 and devoted himself to literary work, especially to his monumental *History of the Florentine People.* He became chancellor in 1427 and on his tomb in Santa Croce lies his recumbent effigy in marble, clad by order of the Signoria in a Roman toga, and holding the *History* in his right hand.

In this work of genuine research Bruni departed from the outlook of Villani and the other city chroniclers. With rational regard to the sources, he disproved the legends that Florence had been founded by Caesar, destroyed by the Goths, and recolonized by Charlemagne. On the other hand, his treatment of internal party struggles was sketchy, while he imagined the twelfth-century Romanesque Baptistery to have been an ancient temple of Mars. More important, his history has a strong ideological content; he exalted the virtues of republicanism and believed that the decline of ancient Rome sprang from its acceptance of imperial rule. Likewise he censured the traditional pride of the Florentines in their friendships with emperors, kings, and popes. In addition, he produced something more than a municipal history, for this was one of the humanist works which took an independent view of the periodicity of Western civilization. In Bruni's view, while the decadence of civilization had arisen from the autocracy of the Roman Emperors, its revival by the Italian cities had once again become possible when Charlemagne removed the seat of Empire north of the Alps. Not every element in this scheme commended itself to Bruni's contemporaries. Only a few years later Flavio Biondo in his *Decades of History (1439-50)* dated Europe's collapse from the barbarian invasions, selecting as crucial the sack of Rome by the Goths. Nevertheless both Bruni and Biondo established the basic notion of a "Middle" Age, a period of cultural darkness separating ancient Rome from the recent revival.

Leonardo Bruni may also claim a place in the process whereby educated and witty ladies came to play important roles in Italian court-life. In his little treatise *On the Study of Literature (c.1405)* he admittedly places Christian morals first in the training of women, who do not need to cultivate the rhetorical arts for purposes of academic or forensic argument. Yet other-wise, he would make them entirely familiar with the world of classical literature. History should take first place, as affording wisdom and moral examples. With the ancient orators and poets every educated woman must show herself thoroughly familiar; poetic harmony and rhythm appeal to the deepest instincts of her nature. On the whole, the poets are also full of moral examples, the unchaste conduct of Venus and Dido being too obviously fictional to make demoralizing impressions. Indeed, asks Bruni, can one say as much for certain disturbing passages in the Bible? All this may doubtless be regarded as cautious pioneering aimed at the very few; yet ere long a more daring feminism appeared. By the early sixteenth century there was a notable proliferation of "bluestockings," while in both Spain and Italy a few university chairs were then held by women.

Even more than those of Bruni, the life and writings of Poggio exude the very essence of *Quattrocento* humanism. Born a Florentine, he emerged from the circle of Salutati and Niccoli to become a papal clerk and later, like Bruni, a secretary in the papal curia. Though he never lost touch with his native city, a great part of his long life was spent in the Roman court, which in his letters he depicts as a very paradise for classical scholars. As the years passed this Roman branch of humanism began to outshine the Florentine headquarters; a writer in 1438 could think of only two leading humanists who were not members of the papal court. Poggio nevertheless returned to serve as chancellor at Florence from 1453 to 1458; he also wrote a *History of the Florentine People,* which covered the period 1352–1455 and was influential, though unprinted until 1715. His most important services to classical scholarship date from his early and middle years. To him more than to any other individual was due that great addition to the corpus of ancient writings made during the first four decades of the century. In 1407 he visited Monte Cassino to search for manuscripts and while attending the Council of Constance in 1415–17 he made three journeys across the Alps to Cluny, St. Gallen, Cologne, and other ancient cathedrals and monasteries famous for their libraries. He thus brought to light some "lost" orations of Cicero and the complete text of Quintilian's *Education of the Orator,* hitherto known in mutilated versions. Such discoveries involved far more than a pedantic addition of details. For example, Quintilian soon began to rival Cicero as the guide to rhetoric and composition.

Hailed as a hero in the saga of discovery, worthily renowned as a versatile author, Poggio showed distinct limitations both as a man and as a scholar. His taste and elegance we may see in the beautiful new script which he developed from Carolingian models. On the other hand he could be mean and malicious, though his liking for scabrous anecdotes, often anticlerical in character, appears all too normal in a papal official of that day. His Greek was never more than mediocre, while as a historian he was Bruni's inferior in all save his Latin style. Here Poggio's talent lay in the depiction of character and in graphic reporting, a fine example being his account of the martyrdom at Constance of the heretic Jerome of Prague.

Leon Battista Alberti was like Petrarch far more than a practitioner of the *studia humanitatis,* even though such studies lay at the center of his work. Athlete, poet, painter, musician, social theorist, above all an architect, he wrote treatises on ethics, religion, sociology, law, mathematics, and the natural sciences. For a historian seeking to grasp the full potential of humanism Alberti might seem even more significant than Petrarch. Reversing the tendency to abandon the vernacular languages, he wrote some of his works in Italian, yet his outlook derived in all essentials from the Florentine humanist tradition. His books on sculpture and painting received direct inspiration from the practice of those arts in Florence, while his famous treatise *Of the Family* reflects the fascinating panorama of Florentine society. From Petrarch he inherited his emphasis on Stoic rectitude and will power, his dislike of scholasticism. More consistently than Petrarch, he demanded social action as opposed to cloistered virtue.

The illegitimate offspring of a leading Florentine family grown wealthy in the wool trade, Alberti rejected a business career to pursue a life of learning. Even so, he proclaimed that knowledge is desirable only for the sake of man. As a social thinker he condemned the violent factions which occasioned such bloodshed and made Italian city-dwellers live in fortified tower-houses. He pleaded for a firm yet human administration of the law, for imprisonment which should be reformative and not retributive. He had a vision of the State as designed—whether along republican or princely lines—to act purely in the interest of its individual citizens. He proclaimed that by the application of reason and will every man can achieve his full potential; that man is born to exploit nature and to seek happiness. Alberti's doctrine of the golden mean counsels a calm freedom from both passion and materialism, yet it opposes the extremism of those who seek to inhibit all natural emotions.

Exalting the role of the family in society, Alberti advocated the need both for good sexual relations and for true companionship between man and wife. On the other hand, he did not stand among the advanced feminists of the age: the family is to remain under patriarchal rule, with no question as to the source of authority. In matters of religion, he discarded the conservatism of Petrarch. Often genuflecting toward Christianity, he nevertheless mingled it with both the wisdom and the phraseology of the ancient pagans, even referring to "temples" and "the gods." By implication he seems to embrace a spirit of toleration akin to that of Voltaire: while men must clearly punish offenses against men, Alberti would leave God to punish offenses against God.

At the age of twenty Alberti wrote a Latin comedy so exact in its mimicry as to deceive a learned sixteenth-century editor into publishing it as a genuine work of the comic poet Lepidus. Nevertheless his relationship with the classics became anything but servile. His famous work on architecture *De Re Aedificatoria* has an unoriginal aesthetic theory based on that of Vitruvius (*first century* B.C.): that a series of mathematical harmonies should underlie a good building, from which nothing can be subtracted or added without ruining the whole. More important, Alberti proposes to build planned towns wherein the needs of the government, the Church, and the private citizen are carefully considered, yet if necessary subordinated to the town-plan as a whole. Again passing beyond Vitruvius, he sets forth a splendid vision of the social nature of architecture, and of the architect's contribution to the well-being of mankind. Characteristically, Alberti sought to make practice match precept, and he became the first of the learned polymaths who actually designed and erected buildings in accordance with their theories. His actual buildings make a stylistic advance on those of his great Florentine predecessor Filippo Brunelleschi *(1379-1446)*. Though the latter's dome of Florence Cathedral was a superb piece of engineering, it remained gothic in method and spirit. Nevertheless in 1419, while Alberti was still a boy, Brunelleschi had begun the city's first classical building, the Foundling Hospital, with its Corinthian columns and semicircular arches, its Roman pediments and terracotta medallions. This building and Brunelleschi's Pazzi Chapel of 1430 were based upon a study of ancient architecture, yet they remained half-classical in both outlook and detail, owing much to local Romanesque works like the basilica of San Miniato and the Baptistery.

Alberti's scholarship was of a much more rigorous type than that of Brunelleschi. He measured the proportions of Roman buildings and gave meticulous study to the detail of the classical "orders." More important, Alberti remained unsatisfied with the mere introduction of ancient motives; he sought to plan a building which, while not a mere copy of any one ancient building, was profoundly Roman in spirit. His masterpiece is his church of S. Francesco at Rimini, more suitably known as the Malatesta Temple, since it forms a monument to that proud, amoral tyrant Sigismondo Malatesta *(d.1468)* and his mistress Isotta. The west facade takes the form of a Roman triumphal arch, while along the sidewalls are sarcophagi to commemorate the humanists of the Malatesta court. Within there occur in rich profusion the initials and symbols of Sigismondo and Isotta, together with the superb marble reliefs by the Florentine Agostino di Duccio, the quintessence of all fifteenth-century sculpture. For the great merchant Giovanni Rucellai, Alberti designed a Florentine palace with its three superimposed "orders," Doric on the ground floor, Ionic above, and Corinthian uppermost, a daring combination destined to attract imitators. It was Rucellai who put his name in large letters on Alberti's new facade for S. Maria Novella, and who made the complacent comment on his building exploits:

> All these things have given me, and are giving me, the greatest
> satisfaction and the sweetest feelings, since they do honour to the
> Lord, to Florence and to my own memory.

With Alberti and his patrons we seem to have moved decisively out of the clerical Middle Ages.

Pazzi Chapel
BRUNELLESCHI
Sta. Croce, Florence

Malatesta Temple
ALBERTI
S. Francesco, Rimini

So far as concerns painting and sculpture, there survive no recognized works from Alberti's own hand to put alongside his theoretical writings. In the latter his emphases are all upon scientific realism and illustration: he would have the painter instructed in all relevant forms of knowledge, especially poetry, history and mathematics. History painting which conveys exactly the emotions arising from great events: this is the highest and hardest branch of the art. Alberti was fully aware of the great mental effort by which the Florentine artists were already conquering the problems of perspective, and he invented a net which the artist could place between himself and his subject, and on which he could mark the outlines observable through it. Realizing that the painter must also construct imaginary scenes, he also supplied an elaborate theory of perspective. In this field he had also been preceded to some extent by Brunelleschi as well as painters like Uccello; they were in fact now entering a new realm untraversed scientifically either by ancient or by medieval artists.

The work of Alberti illustrates the extent to which humanist thought and scholarship were fused with the art of the *Quattrocento.* The dominant characteristics of this period were a realism which can reasonably be called "scientific," and a replacement of didactic symbolism by human emotion and personality. The real forerunner of humanism in the art of painting did not date from ancient times. Giotto *(d.1337),* a contemporary of the earliest humanists, had taken a quite independent step toward these ideals. The solidity of his figures and the profundity of his feeling caused men of the fifteenth century to look back upon him as a great pioneer in the revival of the arts. More than any other artist, Giotto had ensured that, for centuries to come, the human figure with the religious message would form the core of Italian art. Nevertheless Giotto cannot be claimed as a humanist painter. He has not absorbed the anatomical knowledge of the Ancient World; his landscapes are merely symbolic and make no advance toward a science of perspective. After his death Florentine painting made no progress in these respects until it began to fall under the influence of realistic sculpture as practiced under classical inspiration by Ghiberti *(1378–1455)* and by Donatello *(c.1386–1466).* As long ago as 1260 when Niccolo Pisano completed his pulpit for the Pisan Baptistery, Italian sculptors imitating ancient Roman sarcophagi had begun to liberate themselves from gothic forms, yet the next leap forward was not made until the first years of the fifteenth century. In 1404, the year of Alberti's birth, Donatello was already assisting Ghiberti with the famous reliefs for the doors of the Baptistery at Florence; from the 1420s he displayed his immense versatility and inventiveness by a long series of commissions executed in Florence, Pisa, Rome, Siena, and Prato. Donatello also worked intermittently in Padua, where he constructed his equestrian statue of Gattamelata, the first to rival its ancient Roman equivalent on the Capitol Hill. The figures of Donatello can express joy and abandonment, as in his organ loft in the Cathedral Museum of Florence

Sacrifice of Isaac
GHIBERTI
Baptistery Doors, Florence

with its procession of dancing children. But in the greatest of his works there lies a heroic tension contrasting starkly with the placidity of saints in medieval art, and looking forward to the masterpieces of Michelangelo. Pious tradition is finally discarded in favor of the most rigorous observation of models in the studio.

The genius who did more than any other to extend this new classicism to the art of painting was Masaccio, whose short working life fell well within the central period of Donatello's long career. Masaccio died in 1428 at the age of 27, having been independently active for only six years. In advance of Alberti's theory of perspective he had absorbed the mathematical rules of that science; his figures were endowed with a solidity of form, a massive grandeur derived from both ancient and very recent sculpture. While the Sienese painters lingered amid sweet archaisms, those of Florence entered with Masaccio upon a world which decisively abandoned gothic concepts. These Florentine conquests were disseminated throughout northern Italy by other intellectual artists, men of truly scientific temper, masters of space and of the human form; by Mantegna *(1431–1506)* in Padua and Mantua, by Piero della Francesca *(c.1416–92)* in Arezzo and Urbino.

Even before 1400 the painter Cennino Cennini and the Florentine biographer Filippo Villani (writing *c.1376–1404)* had begun to exalt the role of the artist in society. The latter asserts that "according to the view of many intelligent people" painters were in no way mental inferiors in comparison with masters of the liberal arts, "for the latter obtain by study and book-learning what their arts require, while painters rely solely on the high intelligence and tenacious memory which manifest themselves in their art." This attitude was promoted by the classical scholars, who doubtless gained from Pliny an exaggerated concept of the status of the artist in ancient

S. Francesco in Gloria, SASSETTA.   Collezione Berenson, Florence

Rome, but who could point with greater effect to his genuinely high status in ancient Athens. Yet there occurred no very sudden or universal change of values. Michelangelo and Leonardo were perhaps the first artists regarded by their admirers as possessing godlike qualities, and even in their time Castiglione had to protest against the neo-feudal snobs who thought the graphic arts "mechanical and inappropriate for a gentleman."

3. The Educators and Lorenzo Valla

From the first the humanist program implicitly demanded changes in the pattern of school and university education, though comprehensive theory and its systematic application were not forthcoming until the early decades of the fifteenth century. The specific influences at work were neither Plato nor Aristotle, but rather Plutarch's tract on the upbringing of children, Cicero on the training of the orator, above all Quintilian's *Education of the Orator,* the full text of the last being rediscovered by Poggio in

Madonna with Child
MASACCIO
Palazzo Vecchio, Florence

1417. These ancient authors had in fact envisaged no mere specialist training: for Cicero and Quintilian the orator was the full man, endowed not only with the arts of expression but with all the deeper graces of integrity and wisdom. Of all the works of Antiquity those of Cicero and Quintilian fused most readily with Christian morals. To achieve this fusion was the object of that famous sequence of humanist educators from Vergerio *(Of Honest Manners, c.1402)* to Erasmus *(d.1536)* and Juan Luis Vives *(d.1540)* in the sixteenth century. From the work of these men sprang a lasting ideal of liberal education, one which has ever since dominated the schools of the privileged classes in Western countries.

> We call those studies "liberal" which are worthy of a free man; those studies by which we attain and practise virtue and wisdom; that education which calls forth, trains and develops those highest gifts of body and mind which enoble men, and which are rightly judged to rank next in dignity to virtue alone. For to a vulgar temper gain and pleasure are the sole aims of existence, to a lofty nature, moral work and fame.

These are the words of Vittorino da Feltre *(d.1446),* the younger friend of Vergerio who both implemented and extended his ideas. In 1423 Vittorino was called from the chair of rhetoric at Padua to instruct the children of Gianfrancesco Gonzaga, Marquis of Mantua. Establishing his school in a sumptuous villa, he set the tone of the place by renaming it *La Giocosa.*

Here the young Gonzagas were joined not only by aristocratic schoolfellows but by a group of poorer pupils, boarded, taught, and where necessary clothed free of charge. In the course of twenty years Vittorino gained a remarkable ascendancy over the Marquis, allayed his family quarrels, taught his daughter Cecilia to read the Gospels in Greek before she was eight, trained the heir Ludovico to become one of the most admirable rulers and patrons of the century. Despite the frescos at the *Giocosa* depicting children at play, despite the desire to make the young enjoy learning, there was nothing permissive about the curriculum or the methods. That a century later humanist education was so successfully adapted by the Jesuits need occasion no surprise. Everything in the syllabus was calculated with a view to its moral effect, every pupil observed, every slack or unpleasing habit duly checked and rectified. Vittorino indulged in no romantic sentimentality concerning the natural goodness of the child: only when the system had done its transforming work could the pupil be relied upon to choose virtue and discipline.

One should not dismiss the *Giocosa* as a mere school for children, since it afforded a better and fuller training in the classics than any available at a university, at least until the foundation in 1442 of the humanist-dominated University of Ferrara. Again, it did not cultivate rhetorical tricks and frills. Vittorino's pupils were made to cultivate a plain style and to study the classics for their actual subject matter: Pliny for his natural history and Ptolemy for geography. They learned everday Latin speech by knowing Terence and Plautus. In the pages of Livy and Plutarch the heroes of ancient Rome—safer examples than those of recent Italian history—indicated to future rulers and commanders the paths of civic duty and heroism. Solemn and martial music in the Dorian mode was thought not only to stimulate desirable emotions but to arouse interest in mathematics. Above all, the end-product of education must not be the crabbed scholar. Games and martial exercises were compulsory, and in the summer months they were continued in greater comfort by a migration to the hill-country above Lake Garda. Careful dieting, clothing, and exercise replaced the unhygienic disorder of old-fashioned places of education. Vittorino made no original contribution to the education of women; but the daughters of the house did work in his school, and Vittorino even championed one of them when her father sought to marry her off to a worthless young Montefeltro. (When the latter was providentially murdered she cheerfully entered a religious house.)

Equal in renown to Vittorino was his friend Guarino da Verona *(d.1460),* who had emerged from a conventional early education by studying with humanists in Padua and Venice. Taken in 1403 to Byzantium by a Venetian official, he entered the household of Chrysoloras, who had recently returned from Italy and had a fine establishment with a garden reaching down to the Bosphorus. There in the heart of the doomed Byzantine Empire, Guarino spent nearly five years in Greek studies, having access to manuscript collections which dwarfed those in Italy. On his return he worked in Bologna, where he met Poggio and Bruni, and in 1412 the city of Florence invited him to the chair of Greek formerly occupied by Chrysoloras. Subsequently he conducted a school of his own in Venice and served as a civic professor of rhetoric in his native city of Verona. In 1429 the Marquis Niccolò d'Este summoned Guarino to Ferrara, where he made famous the school centered upon Leonello, heir to the Marquisate. After his succession, Leonello obtained for the school an Imperial charter as a university in 1442, and here its true founder Guarino finished his life in great honor. During his later years he delivered professorial lectures in the morning, while during the rest of the day he tutored the students of his own boarding house. "How often," recalled one of these students, "did we keep at work until midnight, and then, fired with determination to excel, begin again long before daylight." So long as Guarino was educating the young prince, he took care to stress outdoor exercise. But the new university was less centered upon the court; it fostered to a lesser degree the "balanced" life of the aristocrat, and it aimed chiefly at the training of the professional man—the secretary, the diplomat, the teacher, the princely, municipal or ecclesiastical official. Indeed, mature men frequently joined the classes alongside the youths.

Guarino methodized linguistic education even more minutely than had Vittorino da Feltre. His pupils passed through three stages, called elementary, grammatical, and rhetorical. The rules of syntax and style were conveyed dogmatically without the logical argumentation of the medieval ι̧rammarians; examples drawn from the best Greek and Latin authors clinched every point. Guarino wrote little except teaching manuals, but his ideals were presented in a tract of 1459 by his son Battista. The latter, recalling his father's Byzantine training, insisted that "without a knowledge of Greek, Latin scholarship is in any significant degree quite impossible." Apart from this important emphasis, the work of Guarino laid the foundations for a wide expansion of humanist education, for his system could be operated with passable success by disciples of far less intellect and scholarly experience.

We should underestimate the historical legacy of the early humanist educators, and that of Guarino in particular, if we envisaged them as the esoteric teachers of elite groups in a few of Italy's most advanced courts and cities. Directly and indirectly, many thousands of students soon became exposed to their influence, which crossed the Alps around the mid-century and embraced many circles in the German universities. Humanism inspired the schools managed by the Brethren of the Common Life in the Netherlands and the Rhineland. By the end of the fifteenth century Colet and others had naturalized its ideals in England. Even where no independent humanist school flourished, such methods could be grafted on to the *trivium*, the arts course with which the student at a medieval university had always begun his career. However diluted by pedagogues of lesser learning and ruder manners, the essentials of humanist teaching swept through clerical, aristocratic, and bourgeois society. The great work of Burckhardt has perhaps unduly conditioned us to wonder at the hot-house flowers of humanism. Should we not rather compare it with a new graft upon an old tree, one which slowly transformed the shape and flavor of the fruit?

However pious the Christian sentiments of the great majority of these popularizers, the subject matter and the implicit values of humanism remained markedly secular. Independently of its influence there had existed intellectual rebels like Marsiglio of Padua *(d.1342)*,[2] and it was natural enough that a few men of this stamp should seize upon humanism as a critical solvent, rather than as a system to be fused with that of official Christianity. Ancient philosophers propounded challenging moral standards; linguistic scholarship enabled men to dispute the authenticity of ancient documents, and indeed, to deduce new meanings from the Scriptures themselves. The early and middle decades of the fifteenth century produced at least one such revolutionary and learned mind, a natural successor to Marsiglio, armed with even sharper weapons.

Unlike so many of the leading humanists, Lorenzo Valla *(c.1407-57)* was not a Florentine by birth or by adoption, though he spent some time in Florence during the early twenties. A Roman with many relatives in the papal service, he failed at first to obtain office in the curia, and went to lecture *(1430-33)* on rhetoric in the university of Pavia. Here he may have been influenced by the example of the Lombard humanists, who now criticized scholastic philosophy much more fiercely than did the Florentines. In 1431 Valla published his first important work, the dialogue *On Pleasure,* in which he rejected Stoicism and defended Epicureanism. The speakers were real persons, including Poggio, Bruni, and Niccoli, while the enthusiastic disciple of Epicurus was none other than Valla's friend Antonio Beccadelli, *alias* Panormita, already notorious for his collection of clever pornographic verse, *Hermaphroditus (1425).* The relaxation of standards in Italy may be measured by the fact that Panormita's work was dedicated to Cosimo de' Medici and a copy sent to the archbishop of Milan, who later recommended its author for the post of official historiographer at Milan. In his dialogue Valla makes Panormita defend the thesis that the highest good is pleasure *(voluptas).* Civic life, laws, art, even the virtues themselves have as their aim utility: men's actions are—and should be—calculated with regard to the likelihood of the resultant pleasures and pains. Bruni advocates Stoicism, yet Panormita dismisses as irrational this heroic and self-abnegating ideal; he rejects the whole notion that moral values exist for their own sake. We should rather concentrate on the effort to diminish the suffering and increase the enjoyment of this transient life. In conclusion, Niccoli is made to criticize both Stoics and Epicureans for their neglect of

[2]See below, p. 40.

Christian doctrines, yet even he suggests that Epicureanism is nearer than Stoicism to Christianity.

One can hardly doubt that Valla himself leaned toward this latter position. Beneath the urbane surfaces, he was here advancing a serious viewpoint which could carry a humanist far beyond the cautious attitudes of Petrarch. In other places he seems to look forward to the doubts and the criticisms of the sixteenth century. He also anticipated one of Luther's themes by a tract on free will and predestination, in which he stresses the inscrutable mystery of the divine mind in its relation to men. Our limited intelligences cannot for a moment pretend to reconcile God's omnipotence with man's alleged free will, and our salvation must depend not on human effort but on God's mercy alone. Having here attacked Boethius *(d.c.524)*, that much-read forerunner of the medieval philosophers, he proceeded in other writings to assail the whole tradition of scholastic philosophy and theology with an acute and ruthless radicalism that in later days appealed both to Erasmus and to Luther. Yet in the last resort his trend is distinctly Lutheran and not Erasmian, for he considers man powerless to influence his own salvation, and he places upon God the whole responsibility, God being the creator of all minds and inclinations.

Learned Italians of this period enjoyed a remarkable freedom to speculate, but Valla had special inducements to speculate at the expense of the Papacy. From 1436 to 1447 he lived under the protection of King Alfonso I of Naples, who had quarrelled bitterly with Pope Eugenius IV. About 1440 Valla wrote his famous denunciation of the Donation of Constantine, the grant of spiritual and temporal rule over the Western Empire allegedly made by that emperor to Pope Sylvester I. The document had in fact been forged in the eighth or ninth century: it already lay under suspicion, and Valla's attack could not claim to be wholly original. Even so, it was one of the triumphs of humanist literary and historical criticism, and it included for good measure a general assault on papal claims and powers. In later days it rendered great service to Luther and many other enemies of the Papacy, its impact strengthened by the fact that Valla came to be widely regarded as the greatest of all teachers of Latin style. With the advent of printing his textbook *On the Elegances of the Latin Language* passed through innumerable editions, and Erasmus, who epitomized the work at the age of eighteen, said that one must take account of it as of the nails and fingers of one's hands.

The work of Valla did not immediately stimulate a new wave of opposition against the Papacy. Among the notable developments of the mid-fifteenth century were the physical recovery of Rome and the recourse of numerous scholars to the patronage of Nicholas V *(r.1447–55)*. While some educated Italians detested the functions of the Papacy as then exercised, few if any desired its abolition; by mundane considerations it remained a lucrative and prestigious Italian institution. Its humanist critics were too often antiheros, "career men" responsive to the claims of patrons, the popes included. Having perpetrated these attacks, Valla himself returned to Rome with the new pontificate of 1447, and he was duly taken into the curia, where he rose to the office of Apostolic Secretary. The triumph of humanism over tradition could hardly have found more vivid illustration. Curialist scholars like Poggio and Valla quarrelled with one another over money and patronage; the most richly comic episode of all occurred when the hardened and worldly Poggio charged Valla with impiety and heresy. Yet at this stage changes developed within the structure of humanist studies that were not closely connected with the thought of either Poggio or Valla. Chief among these was a revival of interest in metaphysics, especially in the thought of Plato and the neo-Platonists.

4. Medicean Florence and Platonism

In 1434 Cosimo de' Medici returned from exile and ousted from power the group of families led by his enemies the Albizzi. In the years which followed he became the real ruler of Florence, though without assuming the trappings of monarchy or altering the republican façade of government. Doubtless the significance of the year 1434 used to be exaggerated by historians. It is true that Cosimo established a revised electoral process calculated to guard against the choice of an unfavorable *Signoria,* yet in all other respects it was not the machine of state which changed, but only its controller and its beneficiaries. With an easy familiarity and an unpretentious manner Cosimo cultivated the populace; he spent his ample fortune in building churches, monasteries and libraries. He carefully managed the public finances and avoided taxing the poor: above all, he pursued a cautious peace policy and was aided in this design by internal quarrels within the kingdom of Naples and by the continuing weakness of the papacy. Milan alone remained dangerous, but in 1440 Duke Filippo Maria's invasion of Florentine territory suffered a crushing defeat at Anghiari.

On Cosimo's death in 1464 there were renewed attempts by Florentine malcontents and exiles to displace the Medici, but they were overcome by his ailing yet popular son Piero, who died five years later, leaving power to Cosimo's twenty-year-old grandson Lorenzo, later entitled the Magnificent. In 1478 a desperate group of plotters headed by the Pazzi family sought to murder Lorenzo and his brother Giuliano at mass in the Cathedral, while Archbishop Salviati was to seize the government. In the event only Giuliano fell to the assassins and amid an orgy of retribution the Medici rode higher than ever upon popular esteem. This affair led to the hanging of the archbishop, a consequent papal interdict upon the city, and a war against the Pope and Naples. That Lorenzo managed in due course to make his

Conferma della Regola: left, Lorenzo the Magnificent
DOMENICO DEL GHIRLANDAIO
Sta. Trinità, Florence

peace with these powers was due to the incapacity of the Neapolitans and to the chance that a Turkish fleet happened to capture Otranto.

Like his grandfather before him, Lorenzo realized that the main peril to the Italian states lay in the dynastic claims of France, even though the problems of the French kings did not as yet permit them to undertake an actual invasion of Italy. Milan and Naples were in fact the two powers directly threatened, and it was not difficult to persuade them of the need for circumspection. In particular the Sforza, who had recently succeeded the Visconti in Milan, felt the weakness of their own claims; and when in 1480 Ludovico Sforza took control over the heir to the duchy, his young nephew Gian Galeazzo, he was naturally eager to bolster his usurped position by winning friends. Lorenzo de' Medici thus came to occupy the center of a triple alliance of Florence, Milan, and Naples, an alliance whose primary intent was to avoid giving excuses for intervention to France or to any other non-Italian state. The theory of a "balance of power" so freely applied by historians to the period after 1494—and thence to many phases of modern European history—has in fact its beginnings during this previous half-century. Indeed Guicciardini in the final draft *(1536)* of the opening passages of his great *History of Italy* writes explicitly that Lorenzo "sought with every care that Italian affairs should be maintained as it were balanced *(bilanciate)*, so that they should not incline either to one side or the other." As we shall observe, this admirable arrangement began to collapse before Lorenzo's early death, but so long as he lived there seemed a fair chance of avoiding disaster.

Despite the great expansion of humanist studies both throughout Italy and beyond the Alps, Florentine art and letters under Medici patronage deserved to be accorded pride of place throughout the Western world. Even more powerful than his grandfather, openly honored as a ruler by the princely houses of Europe, Lorenzo found it increasingly hard to maintain the pose of a good republican; this change was bound to affect the political and cultural climate of Florence. Less initiative lay with the patriciate and the citizen body as a whole, and it was natural enough that the old republican emphasis upon the heroic and active political life should give way to a cult of the interior life. In any event, the humanism of Petrarch and Poggio had delivered its message, and a shift of attention to other aspects of the Ancient World was likely to occur around the mid-century. When this shift came, it did not take the form of a reaction toward medieval contemplative ideals, but rather found nourishment in the works of Plato and the neo-Platonists, whose thought had never been totally obscured from medieval eyes by the dominance of Aristotle. In some measure this shift had been mediated by St. Augustine and by Boethius, both old favorites with clerical and pious readers. In the writings *(c.500* A.D.*)* attributed to Dionysius the Areopagite, Christianized Platonism had supplied a scheme of thought to St. Bernard, the Victorines[3] and other philosophical mystics of the Middle Ages. Again, thanks to a readily available Latin translation, Plato's *Timaeus* had furnished innumerable scholars with a poetical, imaginative but wildly unscientific picture of the universe.

Despite all these earlier continuities, Medicean Platonism may be regarded as beginning with the visit in 1438-39 of the Byzantine scholar Gemistus Plethon to the Church Council held at Florence. Cosimo de' Medici was so impressed with Plethon's teaching that he not only resolved to set up a Platonic Academy but educated Marsilio Ficino, the amiable son of his physician, to lead in the revival. By the late seventies Ficino had translated all Plato's dialogues, and had written not only a commentary on the *Symposium* but his own chief original work *The Platonic Theology.* Ficino's house near the Medici villa at Careggi became the center of a

---

[3] A house of canons formed in Paris in 1113 and famous for several eminent scholars.

loosely-knit but enthusiastic group, including both professional scholars from many parts of Italy and cultured members of the leading Florentine families. It was not a teaching university and did not closely resemble the European academies of later times; certainly it included men whose thought did not march closely with that of Plato as understood by modern scholarship. Even the enthusiastic Ficino accepted the role of reconciler between Platonism and Christianity, while like so many of his predecessors he saw his hero through the eyes of Plotinus and the neo-Platonist mystics of the second and third centuries of the Christian era.

The aspect of Platonism most dwelt upon by Ficino and his disciples was the sharp division between matter, which is evil, and spirit, which is God-given and led on by divine love to find its way back to a mystical contemplation of its maker. On the one hand is spiritual love, of which all beauty is an emanation; on the other, there are the base fleshly loves which it is our duty to combat with the higher part of our being. These notions were to leave numerous imprints upon European art and letters, not least upon Elizabethan literature in England. Many students of the period have first encountered them in the wonderful speech assigned to Bembo in the closing passages of Castiglione's *Book of the Courtier*. They inspired artists, and breathe through the *Primavera* and the *Birth of Venus* by Sandro Botticelli *(1444–1510),* greatest of the Florentine painters in Lorenzo's circle.

Primavera
Botticelli
Galleria Uffizi, Florence

The same concepts continued to form the doctrinal backbone of Michelangelo's sonnets. Yet apart from Ficino, the only creative mind in the Academy itself was that of the young nobleman Pico della Mirandola *(1463-94),* who was not satisfied to remain a mere Platonist but learned Hebrew, Aramaic, and Arabic, and who saw a guide to the Christian mysteries in the Cabbala, the system of Jewish theosophy and biblical interpretation by means of ciphers.

Devotees might regard the Platonist movement as a high sublimation of humanism; critics might see it as an alien influence forcing back into philosophical abstractions the hitherto practical and constructive spirit of humanist thought. Perhaps it is best defended by reference to its influences upon imaginative art and literature, for alongside Platonism a more traditional humanism continued even in Medicean Florence. The clever but superficial Angelo Poliziano ("Politian," *1454-94),* tutor of Lorenzo's children and a familiar figure at Careggi, brought the imitation of Roman literature to a pitch of perfection unattained by men of earlier generations like Salutati and Poggio. And that Platonism did not cramp its devotees seems indicated by Lorenzo's own Italian poems. In these we may doubtless detect undertones of the Platonic dichotomy between flesh and spirit, yet in the main they should be seen as a stage in the great tradition of vernacular poetry stretching back to Petrarch, to Dante, to the lyrical poets of thirteenth-century Provence and Italy.

In the most famous of his carnival songs Lorenzo bewails the swift passage of youth and proclaims the need to live life to the full. These lines read like a premonition. At the height of his fame, having just sent off his son Giovanni as a cardinal to Rome, Lorenzo retired to Careggi and awaited his death, which came in April 1492. Among his last visitors was the admired Dominican preacher Girolamo Savonarola, who summoned Lorenzo to repentance and gave him his blessing. This event was specifically recorded by Poliziano, an eyewitness, but a rival story arose to the effect that Savonarola urged Lorenzo to restore liberty to Florence, and on his refusal consigned him to die under the divine wrath. This story happens to be untrue: it was invented by Savonarola's hagiographers after the friar's martyrdom, for they wanted to recount a career consistently devoted to a republicanism which rejected the Medici. Even so, the confrontation at Lorenzo's deathbed has a quality dramatic enough: it symbolizes the end of the Medicean idyll and the opening of a harsher, altogether more tragic and fanatical period. Yet before we can proceed to this Italian sequel, we must first cross the Alps and observe the trends of a world less culturally advanced yet distinguished by outstanding political and social vitality, a world which by Lorenzo's time had already begun to assimilate humanism.

TWO

States and Nations
in
Early Modern Europe

1. The Complexities and the Common Background

Historians of fifteenth- and sixteenth-century Europe, especially those observing the continent from outside, sometimes seek to impose simple patterns upon a diverse and unruly scene. In an effort to give the wood a precise shape, they miss some altogether vital differences between the trees. A good example occurs in the phrase "the rise of the modern nation-state," which would be the conventional title for this present chapter. Yet even if we selected the three favorable examples, France, Spain, and England, their dissimilarities both within and since this period might well seem far more impressive than their points of resemblance. Meanwhile in Germany and in Italy no nation-state in fact emerged, though some of the component states of each were advancing in power and efficiency. Again, it would be more than difficult to devise any common formula applicable to Poland, Bohemia, Hungary, Scotland, the Swiss Confederation. The story of the Habsburg territories remains obstinately individual; so does that of the aborted Burgundian state, which threatened to revive the old Middle Kingdom of Lotharingia, but which on the fall of Charles the Bold in 1477 was partitioned between France and the Habsburgs.

Just as diverse as the stories of all these states are the psychological factors of state-loyalty and patriotism. England had boundaries dictated by geography, a government centralized and effective since the Norman Conquest, subjects whose long-standing chauvinism had been shaped by sustained warfare against France. Well before 1400 England's constitutional development had begun to show individual features. To its unique common law had been added elements of representative government, including by the middle of the fourteenth century a compact House of Commons, a body to be taken seriously by kings and magnates. On the other hand, throughout most of the fifteenth century the kings of France were still engaged in the elementary task of conquering marginal provinces, while many of their subjects stood prepared to throw in their lot with England or with Burgundy. In Italy the psychological factors remained still more complex. The fickle attitudes toward the popes displayed by the Roman populace—and also by the nobility of the Campagna—defies logical analysis. By contrast we have already noticed that both Florentines and Venetians maintained an aggressive civic patriotism while also unctuously regarding themselves as defenders of Italian liberty. Venice systematically annexed neighboring city-states and to her own ultimate peril called in foreign adventurers to break the resistance of rival Italian powers. Within the resultant Venetian Empire a citizen of a subject-city might have three loyalties: to country, state, and city. The early sixteenth-century Vicentine historian Luigi da Porto exalts Italians as opposed to non-Italian barbarians. At the same time he speaks of Vicenza as *mia patria*. Yet he regards the Venetians as his legitimate overlords, even though, when Venice seemed to be conquered, he and his fellow Vicentines stood prepared without shedding tears to accept the overlordship of the king of France or else that of the Emperor. Even those supposed rationalists the Florentines present some curious anomalies. In 1513 Machiavelli emotionally appealed for the liberation of Italy from the barbarian invaders, forgetting perhaps that four years earlier he had expressed apprehension that France and the Emperor might stop attacking his enemy Venice!

Under the largely nominal rule of the Holy Roman Emperor an equally complex network of loyalties existed among the Germans. After his accession in 1519 the Emperor Charles V called upon the German princes in the name of the common Fatherland to reject French intrigues and subsidies. He spoke also of the "liberty and freedom" of the "German nation." Meanwhile the King of France appealed to these princes to defend their German liberties by opposing their Emperor. As a Habsburg Charles was in fact a supranational dynast, Duke of Burgundy since 1506, King of Spain since 1516, and commanding the loyalties of a civil and military officialdom drawn from all his peoples. Flemish by birth and mother-tongue, he failed to reside in his German lands for very long periods. As he grew old, he accepted whole-heartedly the ideals of Spain, the kingdom to which he ultimately retired on his voluntary abdication in 1555–56. Within the component states of the Holy Roman Empire, loyalty to territorial princes often blended uneasily with a sentimental yet tenacious allegiance to the Empire. Perhaps the most deeply felt loyalty of all was that of the German citizen to his own walled town, as island of ordered life amid an ocean of insecurity. Meanwhile, if the Habsburg Emperor spoke of a German nation, Martin Luther, entering into the heritage of a nationalism already preached by the German humanists, did more than any man to create a national culture by the vitality of his German Bible and by the implied or overt appeals to German patriotism in his other vernacular writings. Nevertheless in Germany as in Italy the rising tide of national feeling failed to create a functioning national state until late in the nineteenth century.

In Spain a complex of regional loyalties survived the partial union of Aragon and Castile accomplished in 1469 by the marriage of Ferdinand and Isabella. The constitutions, estates, and customs of the two kingdoms remained separate. For long afterwards a Spanish national pride, stimulated by crusade against Islamic powers and by overseas conquest, did little to obliterate a jealous adherence to regional liberties. Spanish patriotism was directed with growing strength toward the person of the monarch, that sacred being whose horse no other man could bestride and whose discarded mistresses no one might presume to marry. Contrasting with Spain an area which dynastic accident brought under Spanish rule, we may witness during the later sixteenth century the birth of a nation based upon dramatically opposite ideals. This process occurred in the minds of the Netherlandish people around 1560, during the earliest years of their revolt against the overlordship of Philip II.

All in all, only an observer prone to accept slogans and lacking sensitivity for the European mental climate could claim to observe simple, homogeneous continental trends during the fifteenth and sixteenth centuries. Modern Europe has produced many diverse national cultures, diverse types of state, diverse political systems and philosophies: hence its perennial fascination and fruitfulness. If by some miracle a sixteenth-century conqueror had hammered it into a single state, and if his successors had gradually reduced it to a more or less homogeneous culture, then the peoples of Europe might have lived on balance more securely ever since. Yet in that event the story we are telling in this book would have been quite immeasurably duller, and far less significant for the spiritual future of the human race.

Conversely, however, the rise of the European state should not be envisaged purely as a series of individual episodes. There existed during these centuries certain common factors, demographic, economic, and above all ideological: a disturbed and shifting background which intensified both the domestic and the external problems of the European states. The bubonic plague of 1348, known as the Black Death, began by diminishing the population of most countries by something like one-third, and during the following two centuries it recurred several times upon a lesser but still serious scale. The extent to which its ravages disrupted the trading and agrarian relationships of European society has often been exaggerated, yet allied with long periods of destructive warfare in France and elsewhere it contributed to popular misery and unrest. Affected, though to a debatable extent, by these catastrophes, feudalism continued to disintegrate on the manorial level, where serfs increasingly commuted their labor services for money rents and free laborers exploited the shortage of labor to gain higher wages. For different reasons, in England, France, and other Western areas feudalism also declined upon the military level, as the old feudal host, long insufficient for waging distant or prolonged warfare, yielded place to new modes of recruitment, such as those arranged by military contractors, who raised contingents and hired them to kings for hard cash.

In regard to the common ferment of ideas, we have already reviewed the rise of Italian humanism, the spread of which into other countries—and into the middle strata of society—will soon engage our attention. Yet in addition there had developed since the early fourteenth century some ideological solvents of a still more corrosive character, in particular those applied to the Church and the Papacy. With its popes long resident at Avignon, its national churches manipulated by secular rulers, its universities and religious Orders discussing theological novelties and even heresies, its most devout minds turning toward a personal and inward religion, fourteenth-century Catholicism faced challenges even more formidable than those which confronted the secular states. In his notorious book *The Defender of the Peace (1324)* Marsiglio of Padua *(d.1342)* based his frank antipapalism and anticlericalism not merely upon ecclesiastical abuses but upon broad philosophical principles. He would have forced the priesthood to surrender their enormous juridical and political powers, together with most of their wealth, in order to become what God intended them to be: physicians of the soul. Marsiglio regards episcopacy as a human invention, since Scripture does not mention the institution of bishops by Christ. Likewise the Papacy wields power over western Europe merely as a result of its bestowal by the Emperor Constantine; even this much Marsiglio acknowledged merely because in his day Constantine's Donation had not yet been exposed as a forgery. In spiritual matters he places the authority of a General Council of the Church above that of the pope, while in all the affairs of this world the secular State should rule over laity and clergy alike, both being equally its subjects. Marsiglio became a servant and champion of the Emperor Lewis IV in the latter's bitter struggle against the French-influenced papacy at Avignon. In this service one of his colleagues was another famous figure, the Nominalist philosopher William of Occam *(d.1349)*, who maintained similarly heterodox views concerning the nature and functions of the priesthood. Such opinions scarcely involved fundamental religious dogma, yet they contained implications portentous for both Church and State. They did not die with their authors; indeed, they were to recover a vigorous life during the Conciliar Movement[1] and during the Protestant Reformation. For example Thomas Cromwell, the lay minister who managed Henry VIII's revolt against Rome, personally financed an English translation of Marsiglio's *The Defender of the Peace*.

[1] See pp. 42–43 below.

Of the earlier theological threats to orthodoxy, the most profound and far-reaching were those made by the eminent Oxford teacher John Wycliffe *(d.1384)*, who went so far as to announce that all legitimate lordship should depend upon divine grace, and that sinful churchmen should hence be stripped of their property by the State. Wycliffe also taught that papal claims to authority had no real basis in Christ's recorded teaching, and that the legitimacy of the pope's acts depended alone on their conformity with Scripture. Upon the theological front he anticipated during his last years several of the doctrines taught by the Protestant Reformers of the sixteenth century. He castigated the worship of saints and pilgrimages to their shrines; he called for the translation of the Bible into English, a task soon completed by his disciples Nicholas of Hereford and John Purvey. Above all, he denounced the doctrine of transubstantiation, which had been made obligatory by the Lateran Council of 1215 and afterwards refined by the Christian-Aristotelian metaphysics of Aquinas. Wycliffe denied its central affirmation: that in the mass the "substance" (the underlying permanent reality) of the bread and wine was changed on consecration into the "substance" of the body and blood of Christ, only the "accidents" (outward appearances) of bread and wine remaining.

In England the immediate affects of the Wycliffite heresy remained limited. Repressed by the Lancastrian kings, it inspired an underground and largely proletarian movement of dissent, which had no chance of seizing control of the English Church, but nevertheless survived to merge with the continentally-inspired Protestantism of the 1520s. As will appear, the most active heirs of Wycliffe were the Bohemians, who under the leadership of John Huss *(c.1369–1415)* adopted certain of Wycliffe's doctrines and used them not only for religious purposes but also to promote a new Bohemian nationhood. The rest of the heresies which affected late medieval Europe had only a limited scope. Of these by far the most interesting was the already ancient sect of the Waldensians, seated in the valleys of Savoy and Piedmont, but having offshoots in other parts of Italy and in due course capable of establishing tenuous links with the Hussites.

With the later Protestant Reformation in mind, we may tend to overestimate the potential of these older heresies, none of which was well placed to explode across large areas of Europe. There lurked more insidious dangers to authority among the clerics themselves, for in the careers of men like Occam, Wycliffe, and Huss the critical spirit of the universities applied itself not only to ideas but to institutions. In numbers and in public influence few if any sectors of late medieval society grew so swiftly as did the universities, and nowhere else could daring ideas be ventilated with such freedom. Alongside but not generally within the universities, there developed types of spirituality containing quite different seeds of change. The Franciscan movement had infused into Catholicism a spiritual gaiety and gentleness, a sense of God-in-nature which tended to outmode the grim law-giving outlook inherited from the earlier Middle Ages. The greatest religious personality in fifteenth-century Italy was St. Bernardino of Siena *(d.1444)*, whose missions indicate that the spirit of St. Francis had by no means evaporated amid the divisions besetting the Franciscan Order after its founder's death in 1226. Meanwhile in northern Europe another gospel of gentleness and heartfelt religion appeared in the "new piety" *(devotio moderna)*, which invited lay men and women to emulate, even amid the affairs of this world, those high devotions hitherto limited to the more austere religious Orders. Descended from the German mystics of the earlier fourteenth century, the *devotio* centered upon the lower Rhineland and the Netherlands, having its chief monument in the *Imitation of Christ (c.1418)*, attributed then to Gerson but in modern times to Thomas à Kempis. With the rise of printing in the later fifteenth century, the appeal of this book expanded more swiftly than ever: a host of editions came not only from the northern presses but also from those of Spain and Italy. For the *Imitation* a role may be claimed in the prehistories of both Protestant and Catholic Reformations. The legacy of the *devotio moderna* and of similar spiritual movements presented an ambivalent spectacle to official Catholicism. Instilling deep fervor and seldom occasioning disobedience, they nevertheless took little account of popes, Councils, canon law, and saint worship. Though they often attracted clerics, they did not revolve primarily around the priesthood and the sacraments. Moreover they invited adventurous minds into unfathomable seas; they involved experiment with psychological states which might well present categorical commands at variance with the policy of the Establishment.

No survey of the fifteenth-century background could avoid referring to the Conciliar Movement, even though any serious account of its vicissitudes would occupy inordinate space and end by contributing relatively little to our account of these early phases of modern Western civilization. The lamentable Great Schism *(1378-1417)*, let alone the need for reform, led inevitably to the widespread conviction that a General Council, perhaps a Council in more or less permanent session, might cure the crisis facing the Church. The Council of Constance *(1414-18)* did not only depose all three popes and install a new one in Martin V. It also declared in unambiguous terms that, like all other men, the pope was obliged to obey a General Council "in matters of faith, the extinction of the Schism and the reform of the Church in head and members." Moreover Catholic Christendom in general accepted this revolutionary work of its assembled prelates and doctors. The Council of Basle *(1431-49)*, despite its airing of notions even more radical, ended in anticlimax. During its later years it fell into exhaustion and divisions. It had faced a host of intractable problems: a determined papalist reaction under Eugenius IV, the intrigues of secular politicians, new movements of schism, and the intransigence of the Bohemian heretics.

Finally the Papacy began to recover some genuine prestige from its negotiations at Ferrara and Florence *(1438-39)* with the Greek Orthodox Church. In 1460, soon after he became Pope as Pius II, Aeneas Sylvius Piccolomini, the former liberal humanist, the repentant devotee of Venus, the one-time conciliar enthusiast, felt able to declare heretical every appeal to a General Council. Taunted by his Bohemian and German critics with this change of front, he responded in all sincerity with the words, "Reject Aeneas; accept Pius."

In the Church the principle of monarchy had now triumphed over that of parliamentary government, yet history was to prove this triumph dearly bought. Even within Catholicism Roman autocracy has been repeatedly reinforced by crises, yet to this day it has never found universal acceptance as a norm. Moreover the failure of the restored Papacy to execute the reforms demanded by the Councils was bound to generate further movements of protest, even of secession. The Conciliar Movement had lost its energy, its cohesion, its prestige, yet it had left Church, Papacy, and society at large with some ineradicable attitudes, attitudes which rendered impossible a return to the days of the great medieval popes. In particular Europe had to reckon with a large, fast-growing group of intellectuals—still mainly clerics—who had missed their chance yet abandoned not a jot of their critical spirit. Half a century later the early Reformation years were to show that the monarchy of popes, the lordship of bishops, and the secular ambitions of kings were by no means the only factors governing the evolution of organized Christianity. Below these grandiose figures a host of smaller people were arguing and planning in the growing cities and universities: an educated clerical proletariat, a bureaucracy of humanists and jurists, a *bourgeoisie* out to control its local churches; and already in their hands was a wholly new weapon for dissident intellectuals—the art of printing.

In this survey of change during the later Middle Ages we have still to discuss a factor of paramount importance: the growth in the number, size, wealth, and sophistication of cities. No development so deeply modified feudal society, together with its religious and social attitudes. Throughout the twelfth and thirteenth centuries kings and other rulers had readily chartered innumerable towns in return for money, yet no one can have realized the immensity of the changes this process was furthering. Throughout these same centuries urban growth had already been strongly stimulated by the development of seaborne trade. The Near East had been opened up by the Crusades, the chief beneficiary of which proved to be Venice, the *entrepôt* between Asia and the overland route across the Alpine passes to central and northern Europe. Venetian and Genoese galleys, later joined by those of Spain, traded along the Atlantic coasts. In Bruges and in London they met the ships of the Hanseatic cities, which similarly dominated the Baltic and the northwestern ports. Meanwhile, as the plains of eastern Europe were colonized, a deep belt of walled towns replaced the primitive settlements of earlier days. The great mineral resources of Bohemia, Hungary, and the Tyrol entered upon a phase of more intensive exploitation. The old cities of Italy did not merely provide industrial experience and fine craftsmanship. They also provided financial enterprise and method, together with a contemptuous rejection of the old ecclesiastical prohibitions against interest-taking. In the thirteenth century, banking houses had appeared in Siena and Florence; they were soon lending large sums to the kings of France and England. Venice and Florence stimulated their international trade by issuing gold coinages, and in due course their examples were followed not only in France, England, and Flanders, but also in Poland and Hungary. On the other hand, bills of exchange, which avoided the risky transport of bullion, first developed in the Burgundian fairs and were already multiplying rapidly around 1300. In European economic life the dominant and revolutionary process of the fourteenth century, and still more of the fifteenth, was the rise of a sophisticated capitalism. This was not only a capitalism of commerce and banking but a capitalism of large-scale industry which lured men from the countryside to swell the urban proletariats. In the countryside itself the attitudes of landlords and peasants were modified by the growing ascendancy of the merchants and financiers, the lenders of money, the nonfeudal, nonmilitary classes which soon extended their influence outside the towns. Even here the profit motive transformed in varying degrees the former custom-ridden manorial economy.

At once the creatures and creators of this economic growth, the cities naturally fostered secular, independent, and even—among the unprivileged classes—democratic attitudes. The cities attained a striking degree of internal cohesion, yet they can hardly be idealized as oases of calm within the tumultuous feudal world. Most of all in cultivated Florence, conspiracies, accusations, executions, and sentences of exile succeeded one another with appalling frequency. Almost everywhere there developed tensions between the merchant-capitalists and urban-patriciates on the city councils and the unprivileged burghers, and again between the masters organized in their trade guilds and the wage-earning industrial workers who faced ever-decreasing chances of promotion to mastery. The lines of demarcation were by no means identical at all times and places. Not everywhere did there appear movements as militant as those which disrupted the Flemish industrial cities, especially Bruges, Ghent, and Ypres. Here the first crisis came as early as 1302, when at Courtrai the Flemish workers vanquished Philip IV of France, who had taken sides with their patrician enemies. Not until eighty years later did an army of French and Flemish nobles crush the popular movement at the battle of Roosebeke. And it so happened that in this same year 1382 the great merchants of Florence recovered power following a short-lived control of the commune by the wage-earning class. Into these already-existent patterns of urban specialization and the development of capitalism must be fitted the great movement of humanism and the plastic arts with which we began our account of modern Europe. To be sure, the fourteenth century was also an age when so many Italian city-states surrendered their liberties to tyrants and city bosses, yet we have already observed that this cultural advance did not closely or invariably depend upon political liberties. Evil princes could patronize superb art, while the conflicting medley of Italian states continued to stimulate political thought. The sturdy tradition of the artist-craftsman, the love of letters in professional and pedagogic circles, these phenomena could not be neglected by princes or by big businessmen avid for prestige. Whichever of the three most intensive areas of European urban culture we regard—Italy, the Netherlands, southern and central Germany—the triumphs of art and letters seem based upon a complex fusion of agencies, not upon the creativity of any one class nor upon any one type of power structure.

Of the many ideological and technological developments arising from the late-medieval cities, the most potent was the art of printing from movable type. It arose not from among the Italian artists but from among the technicians of the German cities, men who were simultaneously inventing or improving clocks, astrolabes, and weapons demanding a mechanical imagination and a degree of precision in metal work unattained by medieval craftsmen. Late in the fourteenth century block books had been made, each page being printed from a carved wooden block, yet these involved almost as much labor as manual copying. The crucial advance lay in the invention of metal letters which could be rapidly assembled, used thousands of times in a press, and then broken up to be reassembled for the next text. According to a sixteenth-century tradition the original inventor was Laurens Janszoon Coster of Haarlem *(d.1440)*, but if so the idea did not first prosper in the Netherlands, but in Mainz with Johann Gutenberg *(d.1468)*. A goldsmith of patrician family, Gutenberg appears to have been involved in printing as early as 1438, though his first known work, an indulgence proclamation, dates from 1454. Already with Gutenberg, and especially in his two magnificent Bibles, printing became not merely an industrial craft but an art in its own right; and within a very few years books were produced which for beauty or legibility have never been excelled. From the mid-fifties Peter Schöffer, the most original of Gutenberg's immediate successors, made some striking advances: for example, he printed in colors, used lead spacing between the lines, and cast Greek types.

From this stage printing firms appeared swiftly in Bamberg, Strassburg, Nuremberg, and Cologne, then in innumerable German, Netherlandish, and Swiss cities. With the encouragement of Louis XI of France, German printers cooperated in 1470 with the French scholar Guillaume Fichet to operate a press in the Sorbonne, its first production being an edition of the letters of the Italian humanist Barzizza. No mere technician but also a

The trademark of Jodocus Badus
Ascensius, the printer of Paris,
showing an early printing press
(1520)

translator and man of letters, William Caxton was printing English books in
Bruges by 1474 and two years later he came home and founded the first
English press in Westminster. Known quite justly as "the German art,"
printing was taken by Germans into Italy during the sixties, and by the end
of the century there existed presses in over seventy Italian towns. Venice
alone had now some 150 such businesses, amongst which that founded by
the dedicated humanist Aldus Manutius *(d.1515)* was beginning to achieve a
Europe-wide primacy. The humanists had not invented printing, yet in the
work of such great publishing houses their taste, their connections, and
their literary labors at once enlarged and dignified the functions of the
press. The Reformation was soon to open new mental and social areas to its
influence. Yet this stirring situation cannot reasonably be described either
in terms of technological materialism or in terms of pure ideas: from the
first the contributions of the printers became inextricably mingled with
those of the scholars and men of religion. While the historical effects of
printing remained enormous, the invention did not in itself generate world-
shaking ideas. Technical inventions did not alone reshape politico-ecomonic
structures; still less did they create the thoughts of Marsiglio, Valla, Machiavelli, Erasmus, Luther, and Montaigne. Even so, this rapid diffusion of ideas
in standardized form was a new factor in human history: it amplified the
forces of change rather than those of conservatism. During the half-century
between the invention of printing and 1500 some 36,000 separate book titles
were issued, and while an average edition probably numbered about 1000

or even less, some editions are known to have doubled or trebled that figure. As we observe the flood rising still higher in the decades after 1500, we need no longer envisage the typical reader as the cathedral canon with his edition of St. Augustine, or as the courtly scholar with his Aldine volumes of the Greek and Latin classics. A large vernacular literature was now in print and the common man was becoming involved more deeply than ever before in a swift-changing world of ideas. Yet before we describe this world, it would seem reasonable to survey the individual states and nations of Europe as they moved forward into what we now call the modern history of the West.

2. France, England, and Burgundy

Immeasurably destructive in some areas of France, the Hundred Years War might well be placed among the more stupid dynastic struggles of European history. Nevertheless its closing phases were attended by certain creative effects for both participants and for Europe as a whole. When in 1415 the ambitious English King Henry V renewed hostilities and against heavy odds won the battle of Agincourt, there followed five years of disaster for France. By 1419 Henry had conquered all Normandy: he then overran much of the Île de France and in May 1420 he concluded the Treaty of Troyes with the Duke of Burgundy and Queen Isabella of France. Accepted by the Paris *Parlement*[2] and the States-General, this treaty gave him the Princess Catherine in marriage and recognized him as heir to the crown of France in succession to her imbecile father Charles VI. As regent, he took formal possession of Paris, while south of the Loire the Dauphin Charles (later Charles VII) maintained French defiance. In southwestern France Henry V naturally continued to rule the rich and extensive territories of Guienne, inherited from his Angevin ancestors.

Almost equally formidable were the obstacles presented to French unity by the Dukes of Burgundy, who were affording such powerful aid to the English. This situation dated from the mid-fourteenth century, when King John of France had created for his youngest son Philip a semi-independent duchy in this great province of eastern France. John's lack of wisdom became apparent when Philip espoused the heiress of Flanders and then married two of his children into a family which ruled much of the northern Netherlands. Henceforth his power lay in the Netherlands even

---

[2]The *Parlement* of Paris was a court staffed by lawyers that had sprung from the King's Council in the thirteenth century. It still retained the right not merely to register the royal edicts but also to delay their registration by remonstrating against them. It had no resemblance to the English Parliament, the closest equivalent of which was the States-General. The *Parlement* of Paris was in no sense a representative institution, most of its members having purchased their offices and made them hereditary. In several newly-acquired provinces the kings erected provincial *Parlements* with similar functions.

France, c. 1500

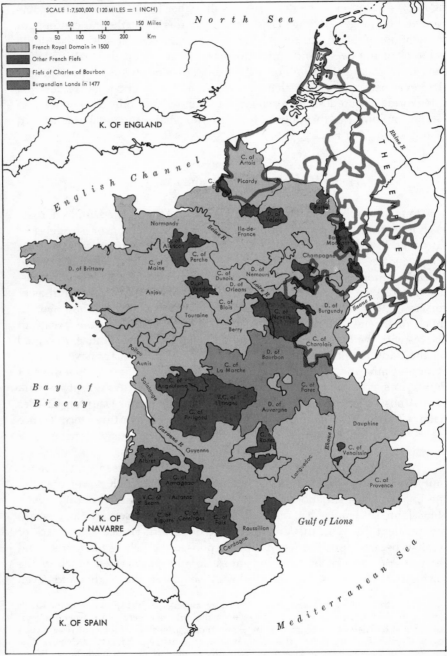

SCALE 1:7,500,000 (120 MILES = 1 INCH)

0   50   100   150 Miles
0   50   100   150   200 Km

French Royal Domain in 1500
Other French Fiefs
Fiefs of Charles of Bourbon
Burgundian Lands in 1477

North Sea

K. OF ENGLAND

English Channel

THE EMPIRE

Rhine R.

C. of Artois

Picardy

C. of
E

D. of
Valois

Normandy

Seine R.

Ile-de-France

Barois
Mouv

D. of
Alençon

C. of
Perche

C. of
Maine

C. of
Dunois

D. of
Nemours

Champagne

D. of Brittany

D. of
Vendome

D. of
Orleans

Loire R.

Saône R.

Anjou

C. of
Blois

C. of
Nevers

D. of
Burgundy

Touraine

Berry

C. of
Charolais

Poitou

D. of
Bourbon

Aunis

C. of
La Marche

Saintonge

C. of
Angouleme

C. of
Foret

Bay of
Biscay

V.C. of
Limoges

D. of
Auvergne

Dauphine

Garonne R.

C. of
Perigord

C. of
Rodez

Rhone R.

C. of
Venaissin

Guyenne

S. of
Albret

C. of
Provence

Languedoc

C. of
Armagnac

V.C. of
Bearn

Astarac

K. OF
NAVARRE

C. of
Bigorre

C. of
Comminges

C. of
Fois

Roussillon

Gulf of Lions

Cerdagne

K. OF SPAIN

Mediterranean Sea

more than in Burgundy. Instead of drawing the rich Flemish cities into the orbit of France, the successive Dukes of Burgundy found Bruges and Brussels more attractive than Dijon as residences and seats of government. That they became wealthier than the kings of France depended on the enormous textile industries of Ghent, Bruges, and Ypres. Since the Burgundian state centered increasingly upon the Low Countries, in the long run it contributed powerfully toward the emergence of a Netherlandish nation. Meanwhile the dukes could not afford to tie their policy to that of their French cousins. On the contrary they were forced to place the utmost emphasis upon friendship with England, which supplied the raw wool to their populous and turbulent weaving towns.

In the first years of the fifteenth century a feud had developed in France between Duke John the Fearless of Burgundy and his cousin Louis Duke of Orléans, youngest brother of King Charles VI. On every issue these two princes stood opposed, and the murder of Orléans by John in 1407 merely rendered the divisions more acute. The partisans of Orléans, called Armagnacs after their first leader Bernard Count of Armagnac, naturally pursued revenge, while in 1418, even as the English overran Normandy, the Burgundians massacred some of the Armagnac leaders. The survivors nevertheless retained control of the Dauphin Charles, and in August 1419 they treacherously murdered Duke John of Burgundy during a parley arranged on the bridge at Montereau. Hence John's heir Philip (later entitled "the Good") became a vigorous ally of Henry V, and the Burgundian-Netherlandish state a formidable third force in the Anglo-French struggle. Relics of this pattern have never wholly disappeared from the politics of northwestern Europe. The Netherlands continued to be the focal point of English foreign policy—a glance at the map helps to show why—and in recent times the freedom of both Holland and Belgium from French, and later from German control has remained a cardinal principle for British statesmen.

In August 1422 the victor of Agincourt suddenly died, yet his brother John Duke of Bedford proved a successor of equal ability in his role as regent of France. Though weakened by the scheming of his cultivated but irresponsible brother Humphrey Duke of Gloucester, Bedford repeatedly vanquished the forces supporting the Dauphin and built up an effective administration in Normandy. There followed an episode showing that alongside the growth of sophisticated humanism in Italy, momentous events could arise in Northern Europe from the general belief in miracles, sanctity, and witchcraft. In May 1429 the peasant-girl Joan of Arc inspired her countrymen to relieve the besieged city of Orléans. In July she brought the Dauphin to Rheims and had him crowned as Charles VII. Yet at this stage the brute political facts resumed their ascendancy. Despite some minor successes, Joan failed to take Paris and fell captive to the Burgundians when attempting to relieve Compiègne. Duke Philip sold her to the English and after numerous examinations by a French ecclesiastical tribunal Joan was found guilty of sorcery and heresy. Shortly before her burning at Rouen in May 1431, Bedford had his young nephew Henry VI crowned King of France in Paris, yet he could not break the military stalemate. At the Congress of Arras in 1435 the ambassadors of Charles VII refused to concede the French crown, even though they stood prepared to leave the English in possession of both Normandy and Guienne. The key to the situation remained with Philip of Burgundy, who now felt that after so many years of warfare he had decently fulfilled his obligation to avenge his father's murder. At Arras Philip concluded a hard bargain with Charles VII, under which Charles not only sought his forgiveness for the murder of his father, but ceded to Philip various towns and counties in eastern and northeastern France. Philip then abandoned the English.

Following the Arras Congress and the death of Bedford in the same year, the English position in France steadily deteriorated. Despite able leadership and their formidable longbows, the English had owed much of their success to the divisions between Frenchmen and to the support of Burgundy. The withdrawal of the latter now exposed the flank of Normandy to French attack, while in April 1436 the loss of Paris deprived the lengthy Norman perimeter of its central bastion. And though Bedford's firm administration had at first kept Normandy tolerably loyal, the English now found themselves struggling to maintain the morale of their scattered garrisons amid a hostile population. In Guienne the situation remained for many years wholly different. There the Plantagenet kings had ruled the Gascons for three centuries, while the prosperity of the winegrowers and of the merchants of Bordeaux depended on the wine fleet which sailed annually for England. So long as they maintained command of the sea and manned their line of fortresses from Bayonne to Blaye, the English could scarcely be ousted from southwestern France.

While Joan of Arc had inspired French patriotism and exploded the myth of English invincibility, the prosaic labors of the reconquest were organized by the civil servants and generals of Charles VII, later called "the Well-Served." Theories of autocratic monarchy based on Aristotle and on Roman law had attracted many Frenchmen during the later fourteenth century, but the time had now come to translate mere theory into administrative, fiscal, and military facts. Charles's military ordinances of the 1440s gave birth to a professional standing army of 12,000 men, stronger than the English in that increasingly important arm, artillery. Not only great magnates but bourgeois councillors brought their gifts to the royal service. The vast majority of Frenchmen still belonged to agrarian communities, yet the growing wealth of trading and manufacturing cities demanded more political recognition and opportunities of service. Though hereditary nobles still held the military commands, they had to yield a measure of influence to the merchants and lawyers, who by slow stages were modifying the structure of medieval society. That the new forces were backed by an adequate treasury owed much to townsmen like Jean Bureau, treasurer of France and keeper of the King's fortresses and artillery, and Jacques Cœur, the merchant prince who built his superb house at Bourges, served on many diplomatic missions, revived the mercantile marine, and arranged the loans which enabled Charles VII to reconquer Normandy. With the aid of Jacques Cœur, Charles restored a sound currency, abolished many tolls, revived the fairs of Lyons, and signed trade treaties with Scotland, Denmark, Aragon, and Venice. As with the other resurgent monarchies, financial reforms underlay all military and governmental achievement. Townsmen and peasantry might sigh for peace and the rule of law, but to gain those blessings they had first to groan under the weight of arbitrary taxation. The land-tax known as the *taille* became a permanent impost. Charles organized the system of district tax officers called *élus*, who operated everywhere except in those more fortunate provinces where the local estates had managed to retain legal control over taxation. The King also set up the office known as the *État Général des Finances* to coordinate the royal revenues; likewise the auditing body, the *Chambre des Comptes*. The "new monarchy" in France arose in the later years of Charles VII, even though in later times it was his son Louis XI who won recognition alongside Henry Tudor and Ferdinand of Aragon as one of the "three wise men" of Christendom.

The reforms of Charles bore military fruits after the brief peace *(1444-49)* following the Truce of Tours. Both before and after this interlude the English ruling class showed itself bitterly divided, for medieval monarchy functioned well only under a king of mature age and strong personality. The feuds which developed during the minority of Henry VI far exceeded his curative powers when he came of age. Unfitted for kingship in fair times or foul, Henry might have become an adequate head for some small religious house. He inherited the periodic insanity of his French grandfather, and by a supreme irony this heritage hastened the collapse of England's French empire, even that of her domestic peace. At the Truce of Tours a marriage was arranged between him and the French King's niece Margaret of Anjou, a princess of striking beauty and virile temper. Henry fell completely under her dominion, yet she failed to grasp the niceties of English politics. Since the Duke of Bedford's day the English war effort had been hampered by a group of councillors leaning toward peace and economy. Indeed, since 1433 stringency at home in England had meant financial starvation for the forces abroad, and a field army could not, like mere scattered garrisons, live off the French countryside. The crisis came in 1449 when the Queen's favorite minister Suffolk broke the truce by an unprovoked raid into Brittany: Charles VII at once declared war. Suffolk's rival the popular Duke of York having been sent to Ireland, no prestigious commander remained to defend Normandy, and the French found themselves amazed at the ease of their own successes. Rouen fell, betrayed from within, and after a few weeks little remained save Caen, Cherbourg, and Harfleur. In April 1450 a relief army despatched from England suffered obliteration at Formigny.

In England the anger of the nation failed to evoke better leadership. While Suffolk was banished—and murdered by sailors on his way abroad— Margaret and Henry continued to rely upon Somerset and other incompetent ministers, excluding York from power. As expected, the French now turned southward, and in 1450 attacked Guienne in force. This province, still in large part loyal to its ancient ruling family, should have presented them with a far tougher proposition, yet though the Gascons fought back they received no help from England. Some local lords helped the invaders, and by the end of 1451, the French forces stood in full occupation. Back in England, amid ever-mounting indignation, York and his allies constrained the King and Queen to dismiss Somerset, but they evaded their promises, and sought to withdraw attention by sending a new force to Guienne under John Talbot, earl of Shrewsbury, the last survivor from the famous captains of Henry V. Landing near Bordeaux, Shrewsbury recaptured it with the aid of the citizens and proceeded to overrun the Bordelais. His triumph proved short-lived. On 17 July 1453 with far more gallantry than sense, he hurled his force on the French positions at Castillon and after a bloody struggle was defeated and slain. With Castillon the long story of the great English provinces in France came to an end and Europe recognized the justice of the French victory. Even the Burgundian chronicler Waurin rejoiced in the fact that Guienne had followed Normandy into the hands of the French. On the mainland, he concluded, Calais alone rests in English hands, and "may God be willing that it too be brought back."

The victories of Formigny and Castillon cemented the foundations of the reformed French state, even though Burgundy, Brittany, and some other outlying provinces remained independent. For England the immediate results were hardly less significant. These appalling failures ruined the credit of the monarchy, divided the nobles, and led almost immediately to civil strife. The feudal host, unsuited to prolonged foreign warfare, had long been replaced by forces which noblemen or knights recruited and then indentured to the service of the king. Yet now brought home from France, these retinues were admirably fitted to promote internal conflict and private warfare. For England the dark sequels of continental empire thus included some thirty years of intermittent civil war. On the other hand, the English remained fortunate in that they were compelled to abandon the exhausting attempt to conquer the far larger French nation. As it would now appear, England's destiny lay across and beyond the Atlantic Ocean; to follow that destiny meant leaving continental Europe. Even military success might have entailed a merging of her culture with that of France—an episode which would have marred the self-confidence of her overseas expansion and the integrity of the great literature she was to produce in the next two centuries.

Yet this transfer of English energies did not occur instantly. Albeit for brief periods, Edward IV, Henry VII, and Henry VIII all took fine armies into France, and imbued with the notion of France as hereditary foe, Tudor Englishmen proved slow to understand the new menace of their day: the Habsburg combination, enriched by the Netherlands and the New World, spearheaded by the formidable infantry of Spain.

The last years of Charles VII *(d.1461)* were saddened by quarrels with his son, whose factious conduct met a just reward when he succeeded to the throne as Louis XI. Only a few years after his accession Louis had to face a rebellion headed by his own brother and by the heir to the Duchy of Burgundy, Charles the Bold. At Péronne in October 1468 Louis actually fell into the power of Charles, an enterprising prince who studied the old chronicles of Lotharingia and sought to re-create that middle kingdom overshadowing both France and the Holy Roman Empire. The population of the heavily urbanized Burgundian dominions may now have approached six million, as large as that of Castile, half as large again as that of England. Charles the Bold also made every effort to acquire the Angevin claim to the kingdom of Naples. A great maritime empire stretching from the North Sea to the central Mediterranean might hence have been added to his firm grip upon the land route from Venice to Bruges, thus giving him a strategic and economic control over Europe. His father and grandfather had constructed the framework of the Burgundian state, the lands and populations of which were admittedly varied, yet no more disparate than those from which the Habsburgs, and later the Hohenzollerns, were to build major powers. Moreover, the plan was no mere dynastic or geopolitical dream, for the merchants of eastern France, the Rhineland, and the Netherlands were quick to appreciate the economic advantages of a large trading area under a common administration and with a common coinage.

Escaping the clutches of Charles the Bold, King Louis XI understandably set himself to ruin this dangerous rival, who soon afforded him opportunities by displaying a lack of patience, of diplomatic subtlety, even of military competence. The rise of Burgundy had already alarmed her Rhenish neighbors and the now independent cantons of Switzerland. These having formed an alliance with Louis, Duke Charles in 1475 occupied the Duchy of Lorraine; and in the following year he treacherously massacred the defenders of the town of Granson near Lake Neuchâtel. He thus aroused the active hostility of the Swiss, whose great phalanxes of pikemen had long specialized—equally with the English archers, whom they never met in battle—in the annihilation of conventional armies led by unimaginative aristocrats. All the Swiss now needed was a paymaster, and such they found in the wily King Louis, aided by the dispossessed Duke of Lorraine. Two days after the fall of Granson a large force from the Swiss Confederation arrived on the scene. Charles sought to withdraw to a plain where he could use his cavalry, but on 2 March 1476 the withdrawal became a rout. Striving to retrieve his reputation, the Duke soon collected a new force and besieged Morat. Here on 22 June a more equal battle developed, yet the Swiss outflanked the Burgundian troops, whose obstinate courage merely increased their casualties. Charles withdrew into solitude and his friends feared for his reason, but around midwinter he was roused from his gloomy torpor by the news that the young Duke René of Lorraine had recovered Nancy. Assembling a third army, Charles would have retaken this scantily-garrisoned capital, had not the Swiss sent 20,000 men to its relief. Attacking them with foolhardy courage on 5 January 1477, Charles perished in the *mêlée*. With him there disappeared that middle state which would have reshaped the history of western Europe.

Having left the Swiss to accomplish the hard and bloody work, Louis XI hastened to collect the benefits. This task proved by no means simple. The heir of Charles the Bold was his daughter Mary, a young woman of nineteen whom Louis wanted as wife for his son the Dauphin, even though the latter was seven years of age and already betrothed to an English princess. Louis would not compromise by allowing her marriage to some French nobleman, for he had no intention of setting up a powerful rival. With tolerable legality he could detach some of the Burgundian lands, notably the Duchy of Burgundy itself, which lapsed to him as its suzerain after the offenses of Charles the Bold. Legally speaking, it was otherwise with Flanders and Artois, and with the County of Burgundy called Franche Comté. These lands had never belonged to France, yet for the time being Louis occupied them. Arriving at the frontier of Flanders, he found himself faced by the hostility of the Flemish cities. These formidable communes had hated Charles the Bold, yet they had no desire to see him replaced by an astute French master. Consequently they ensured that his heiress Mary married Maximilian of Habsburg, son of the Emperor Frederick III. When, however, Mary died still young in 1482, Maximilian found himself with small financial resources and dubious rights in the Netherlands, except as guardian to their infant son Philip. He therefore resolved to come to terms with Louis, who preferred to partition the Burgundian lands rather than to arouse popular and foreign resistance by attempting a wholesale conquest. Risking an English reaction—in fact nullified by the death of Edward IV—Louis agreed to marry his heir to Maximilian's daughter, on condition that Artois and Franche Comté should be reserved for her dowry.

In the event, the gains of Louis proved disappointing, for the Habsburgs not only won control over Flanders and the other Netherlandish possessions but contrived to avoid delivering Artois and Franche Comté to France. Enough of the Burgundian state had remained to prevent France from reaching her "natural" frontier the Rhine. Meanwhile by their famed policy of dynastic marriage the Habsburgs, collectors of territories rather than true state-builders, had incorporated some wealthy and populous provinces into their immense but ramshackle collection. Their position in the Netherlands made them for the first time a power in northwestern Europe, for the title of Holy Roman Emperor had hitherto brought them no effective authority in northern Germany or on the lower Rhine. As for France, she had still to face a menacing neighbor on her eastern frontiers, yet she retained one signal advantage. The former Burgundian dukes, French by origin, had been able to manipulate many French noble families, not to mention the restive citizens of Paris. The Habsburgs on the other hand could pursue no such intrigues. Their future conflicts with the French crown were to draw Frenchmen together in loyalty, not to tear them apart in rebellion. About this same time the cause of internal order also benefited from the death in 1481 of the last head of the house of Anjou, which meant that great domains in Anjou, Maine, and Provence reverted to the crown.

Meanwhile Louis XI was using every weapon—marriage, imprisonment, even torture—to discipline the French nobility. A miser, a cynic, and a tyrant, he was capable of freakish impulse, yet in general he was infinitely devious and calculating. He nevertheless deserved better of ordinary Frenchmen than his moralizing biographers have been inclined to concede. Far-sighted economic planning could sometimes take precedence over his more immediate political motives. He allowed trade with the Low Countries even when the latter were at war with him. To ensure a favorable trade balance he allowed free fairs at Lyons, Caen, and Rouen. He introduced silk weaving to diminish the heavy import of silk from Italy, and on restoring trade with England he organized in London what amounted to a trade exhibition of French products. He had prophetic ambitions to strengthen French shipping by navigation laws and to form a great national company for overseas trade. He established a network of posting services; his couriers transformed French communications and brought Brussels within fifty hours of Paris. Behind the pitiless scheming and the acts of tyranny, Louis was an idealist after his fashion, an ancestor of the French state of Richelieu and Colbert.

By the time Louis died *(1483)* the common people of England also had ample reason to pray for strong and undivided government. The Wars of the Roses had arisen thirty years earlier out of the disastrous situation obtaining at the end of the wars in France. In 1453 the English nobility were back at home, full of suspicions and recriminations, while the recent birth of an heir to the throne presaged the continuance of Queen Margaret's influence. The struggle, which by the spring of 1455 developed into open warfare, has conventionally been regarded as a dynastic clash between the families of York and Lancaster. Both were descended from sons of Edward III, the former arguing a case by hereditary right, the latter a claim based on long possession of the crown, confirmed by Parliament. This simplification of the issue found its image in the famous scene during which members of the two parties chose the white and the red roses as their respective badges, though some five years of warfare occurred before the Duke of York actually claimed the throne. In the feudal kingdoms there was no novelty in the spectacle of an opposition forcibly backed by "reforming" magnates of royal blood and the higher nobility. In England this pattern had long ago developed under Edward II and again under Richard II; it had become ever more clearly distinguishable since the death of Henry V. Yet in order to account in full for the tragic events following 1453 one must point to fissures extending much more deeply into English society.

In every region of England divisive social conditions favored the development of a long and bitter series of struggles. Already we have referred to the private armies of liveried retainers supported by men of rank and substance. In periods of peace they had been all too frequently employed to settle personal disputes by force or blackmail. Major affrays, even small private wars, had proved not uncommon throughout the half-century before the Wars of the Roses. But the deepest trouble arose from the corruption rather than from the defiance of the law. Even popular songs satirized the extent to which legal decisions were settled by the intimidation or bribery of witnesses and jurymen. The very complexity of the English legal system, the great number of competing courts and jurisdictions, afforded exceptional opportunities to wealthy and unscrupulous litigants. Many of these problems, especially that of livery and maintenance, had been the frequent subject of parliamentary legislation, yet in the absence of a strong royal executive Parliament could supply no effective redress. Indeed, many members of the House of Commons were themselves agents of the contending magnates. Such evils, always endemic in feudal society, became most characteristic of the fifteenth century. There spread a sophisticated gangsterism which even decent men had to practice by way of self-defense, a disease incurable by any physician other than a resolute and single-minded king.

From the outset of the Wars of the Roses the Duke of York was popular among the flourishing townsmen of the southern counties, while the Lancastrian monarchy of Henry VI and Queen Margaret found its chief backers among the great nobles and churchmen of the less developed northern counties. Since several of the battles resulted in massacres of defeated leaders, the period weakened the baronage in a most literal sense. By contrast the towns took little direct part and only for very short periods did hostilities become so intensive as to hamper their growing prosperity. The resultant change of social balance, together with the growing popular demand for order, steadily prepared the way for the emergence of a national leader endowed not only with military fortune but also with that steady political application which alone could gather the fruits of victory. A century ago the historian J. R. Green hailed Edward IV as the first of these "new monarchs," and his claim seems not wholly without substance. This son of Richard Duke of York seized the crown in 1461, soon after his father's defeat and death in battle at Wakefield, and he ruled with no little success until his death in 1483. His quarrel with the Earl of Warwick, hitherto his chief supporter, led to a short-lived restoration of Henry VI in 1470-71, but after this interruption Edward's personal ascendancy became stronger. He, and for that matter his brother and successor Richard III, anticipated some of those attitudes and methods more often associated with the Tudor monarchs. They pursued every measure, including the extortion of forced loans from the wealthy, in order to augment the revenue of the crown. They utilized the services of obedient middle-class administrators, and they promoted in the Court of Chancery an equity-jurisdiction which supplemented the rigid methods of the Common Law. They began the policy of establishing regional councils to control the distant and restive areas of Wales and northern England. They managed parliaments with skill and fraternized with the rich merchants of London: Edward invested in trading ventures and was literally a merchant-king. Yet all things considered, there remained differences between the rule of Edward and that of the first Tudor king, Henry VII, differences which sprang from personal character. Edward was a pleasure-loving profligate with impulsive flashes of energy, Henry a man of business, an administrator of ruthless efficiency whose attention never wandered, a ruler admirably fitted to subordinate to his own Council all the overlapping and hitherto ill-governed organs of state. The difference of touch, the contrast of personality, might be well exemplified by the respective matrimonial affairs of the two monarchs. Edward provoked feuds and risked his throne by an unwise marriage to Elizabeth Woodville, an attractive widow whose person he had failed to secure by dishonorable advances. But when his turn came Henry married the heiress of the rival House of Lancaster, so uniting the white and red roses. On her death, with even colder calculation, he planned for obvious political ends to marry the insane daughter of Ferdinand and Isabella of Spain.

In order to preserve the Yorkist dynasty Edward should have learned from the recent past; he should have provided for the legal succession of his brother Richard, an experienced soldier and administrator. Instead, when in 1483 Richard found himself merely protector of Edward's twelve-year-old son, he succumbed to the obvious temptation. He assumed the crown and is generally believed to have murdered both Edward's sons in the Tower of London. His lack of scruple and his need for increased taxation soon made Richard unpopular. An extensive plot among both the old and the new nobility ended in the recall from exile of Henry Tudor, Earl of Richmond, a member of the House of Lancaster with a poor hereditary claim to the crown, his obscure Welsh grandfather having married the widow of Henry V. In August 1485 the rivals met at Bosworth, where Richard, betrayed even on the battlefield, died fighting. As the battle ended, Henry found Richard's crown lying unheeded in a thorn-bush and thereupon placed it upon his own head. Both the discovery and the gesture did not lack a significant symbolism.

The purposeful and clear-headed rule of Henry VII deserves study in far greater detail than we can here attempt, since he has become—alongside Louis XI and Ferdinand of Aragon—a prime exemplar of the "new" European monarchy. He not only anticipated but improved upon the counsels of Machiavelli, since he avoided that lurid notoriety which had ruined Richard III and was to ruin Machiavelli's own model, Cesare Borgia. By military and diplomatic skill he repressed the plots and invasions concerted by Yorkist claimants to the throne. And whereas many laws against retainers had already reached the statute book, Henry actually enforced them and did not fear to strike at the most powerful offenders. In his later years, with the aid of his agents Empson and Dudley, he built up a vast fortune and went down to popular history as a miser-king. With a parliamentary rather than a hereditary title, he sought by all possible means to legitimize the Tudor dynasty both in English and in foreign eyes. His own marriage to Edward's daughter Elizabeth of York gave his descendants a firm genealogical claim and a splendid theme for propaganda. Henceforth the Tudor mission could justly be depicted as the healing of the old feud, the coming of a new dawn after a night of bloodshed and division. By naming his eldest son Arthur, Henry likewise showed his grasp of myth and tradition: it was a reminder of that Arthurian legend which promised England fortune and wealth with the coming of another Welsh prince to her throne.

With an eye to continental prestige and the support of another rising power, he married Arthur to Katherine of Aragon, daughter of Ferdinand and Isabella. On Arthur's early death he kept the princess in England until he could arrange for her marriage to his second son Henry. With equally far-reaching results, he married his daughter Margaret to James IV of Scotland, thus taking the first step toward the union of the two crowns a century later. Even more clearly than Edward IV, he perceived that England was no longer in essence a feudal kingdom and that the wealth and power of the monarchy depended upon the growth and taxable capacity of the merchant classes. He thus signed numerous commercial treaties, notably with the Habsburg government in the Netherlands. His political wisdom also showed itself in negatives, in his refusal to undertake enterprises which might have attracted lesser men but which lay beyond his limited resources. He controlled the Irish Parliament, but did not seek to strip the tribal chieftains of their powers. He left the old feudal families a large share in the government of northern England. He took an army to France to help his ally the Duke of Brittany, yet without fighting he speedily signed the Treaty of Etaples *(1492)* by which the King of France bribed him heavily to return home. While he suffered no great sums to leave England for Rome, his attitude to the Church remained conventional. At this time Lollardy, a forerunner of Protestantism descended from Wycliffe, was on the upgrowth in England, but Henry continued to lend the authority of the Crown to its extirpation. On one occasion he troubled to convert a Lollard at the stake before piously burning him. Less conventionally, Henry did support the explorations of John and Sebastian Cabot (who in 1497 reached Labrador, thinking themselves in China), but he made no sustained effort to break the

Spanish-Portuguese monopoly in the New World. All this cautious moderation did not pass unadmired, yet by the time of Henry's death in 1509 the younger generation of Englishmen had become bored by his fiscalism and by his pacific attitudes toward the continental powers. After a quarter of a century the blessings of peace, internal and external, were too often taken for granted.

3. The Iberian Peninsula: Overseas Expansion

It would be misleading to regard the Middle Ages of Spain as a period of savage crusade, ending in 1492 with the fall of the Arab kingdom of Granada. Apart from this one small area with its mountain frontiers, the Christian reconquest had been largely completed as long ago as 1266. Since that time both sides had preserved something of the old liberal outlook: the great bulk of medieval Spaniards were not fanatical crusaders, racists, or worshippers of monarchs. Moors and Jews flourished under Christian rule much as the Christian Mozarabes had flourished under the Caliphs in the golden tenth century of Cordova. In Toledo there stands a church which in the thirteenth century was used by all three religions, by Christians on Sunday, Jews on Saturday, and Moslems on Friday. In Granada 200 years later could be found many Moslems of Spanish blood. Intermarriage had been common during the earlier Middle Ages and many eminent Moors had Christian mothers. Medieval Spain, as its spectacular buildings still testify, was a melting-pot of cultures where at one time or another Byzantine, French, Flemish, Lombard, and Moorish artists and craftsmen all flourished. Its literature often displays a profound humanity unexcelled by that of any medieval people. The nobles and even the common people enjoyed liberties incompatible with the demands of absolute monarchy. In a word, the harsh characteristics of sixteenth-century Spain should not be regarded as a mere inheritance from a crusading Middle Ages; rather were they a complex reaction, which occurred during the period 1470 to 1550 and differentiated the "new monarchy" in Spain from its mundane equivalents in France and England. Having once formed a bridge between Christendom and Islam, Spain now became a frowning Catholic fortress.

From an economic viewpoint the nation had everything to lose by pursuing a policy of racism and intolerance. The centuries of intermittent campaigns and raids had left more than walled towns and monumental castles: at least in Castile they had also left a distaste for arable farming, a pursuit in any case limited by the paucity of good land among these arid plateaux. The Moors of Valencia were Europe's leading experts in the techniques of irrigation, a science to which their Christian conquerors would have been wise to accord the highest priority. Again, the ablest businessmen and industrialists were Jews, and when in 1484–87 those of Barcelona emigrated in large numbers the municipal authorities openly bewailed the impending ruin of the city. In her new-found fanaticism Christian Spain thenceforth gradually destroyed the non-Christian and nominally Christian communities without taking adequate measures to preserve, let alone to extend, their economic functions. Behind this development lay many forces: an intensified Catholic piety, a fanciful doctrine exalting "purity of blood," and finally an import of American bullion which concealed the decline of agriculture and industry behind a deceptive façade of gold and silver. Insofar as it was communicated by individuals, the spirit of persecution derived chiefly from a small group of enthusiasts headed by the pious and able Queen Isabella of Castile, whose dark childhood memories included those of the Moorish and Jewish influences besetting the monarchy of Castile under her eccentric half-brother Henry IV.

The marriage of Isabella with Ferdinand of Aragon in 1469 united the policies of two branches of the house of Trastámara, but it did not achieve a constitutional union of the two kingdoms, let alone the destruction of that strong regional separatism which has marked Spanish history even to our own times. Each state retained its separate laws, institutions, army, coinage, and taxation. Customs barriers continued along their common frontiers, and until a later period there were no arrangements for the mutual extradition of criminals. It has been surmised that Castile might have been linked with Portugal more easily than with Aragon. In 1469 the two Spanish kingdoms

Ferdinand and Isabella
from a rare sixteenth-century print

stood back-to-back rather than face-to-face. In itself the "Crown of Aragon" formed a complex federal state. It comprised not only the kingdom of Aragon, but those of Valencia and the Balearic Islands: most important of all, it included the county of Catalonia with its great but now declining port of Barcelona. Since the Black Death the total population of these lands numbered considerably less than one million. Together they constituted a Mediterranean naval and trading power, pointing toward the Levant and confronting the Turkish and Arab states. This orientation was stressed when the kings of Aragon inherited Sicily, and again in later years, when Ferdinand replaced another branch of his family in the kingdom of Naples.

By contrast Castile, with Seville, Cadiz, and its northwestern ports stood ready to rival Portugal as an Atlantic power, and at length to become the greatest colonizing state of the sixteenth century. In terms of wealth and population Castile could claim to be the second monarchy of Europe. Isabella had over five million subjects, of whom more than a tenth were *hidalgos,* nobles exempt from torture, taxation, and imprisonment for debt. Castile's economic weakness lay in an inadequate wheat crop, her strength in weapon manufacture and in her huge but government-pampered sheep-farming organization, the *Mesta.* In the constitutional sphere there appear further disparities between Castile and Aragon. The Cortes of the former met in three separate chambers: clergy, nobility, and commons; they exercised important controls over taxation, but little influence upon policy and law-making. For fourteen years *(1483-97)* the monarchs did not even trouble to summon them. The Cortes of Aragon had four chambers, since here the greater nobles were divided from the lesser. They enjoyed far greater legislative functions, and they elected a Justiciar, an official of high standing charged with the duty to guard against all breaches of the constitution. This Aragonese spirit of independence—also expressed in the claim of the nobles to renounce their allegiance—suffered few setbacks until the time of Philip II. Even so, in neither Castile nor Aragon could the Cortes assemble without the royal summons, and for this reason alone they could not impose day-to-day restraints upon the royal policies. The strongest executive organ in Spain was the Council of Castile, from which Ferdinand and Isabella removed the feudal magnates, setting up a compact, efficient body of three nobles, one prelate, and eight professional lawyers. As with the multi-purpose Privy Council of Tudor England, its functions were not purely administrative, for it drafted legislation and could act as a summary court of law. As yet the Council of Castile and the several other royal councils were not centralized in a capital but continued in true medieval fashion to accompany the persons of the monarchs.

Under Ferdinand and Isabella Spanish opinion already displayed a pronounced monarchical trend. With surprising equanimity it accepted the appointment of royal *corregidores,* who resided in the cities, managed their business affairs, sought ways to enhance taxation, and controlled relations between Moslems and Christians. In 1476 the crown reorganized the Castilian *Hermandad,* an association of cities for law enforcement, having its own courts and police force. Again, between 1487 and 1499 the crown annexed the masterships of the three immensely rich and influential military-religious orders of Calatrava, Alcantara, and Compostella. Papal confirmation of this last action came several years afterwards. As time passed the royal manipulation of churchmen and their properties attained an omnicompetence unsurpassed by any German Lutheran prince of later days. Needless to add, the crown appointed all the bishops and many other high ecclesiastics, including the heads of the main religious orders. As their colonies developed across the Atlantic the Spanish monarchs sought permission from Rome to set up a patriarch who would have been in effect an American pope under their own management. Even the Spanish pontiff Alexander VI, who so generously divided the extra-European world between Spain and Portugal, refused this demand. In short, nowhere did the Papacy pay more heavily than in Spain for the state's enforcement of doctrinal orthodoxy. And when in 1503 Ferdinand conquered the kingdom of Naples, his direct military hold upon Rome itself became almost irresistible.

The prime instrument of this church-state collaboration was the Spanish Inquisition, the only institution with powers extending throughout the whole of Spain. Though the Inquisition had operated in Italy and elsewhere since the early thirteenth century, the Spanish Inquisition dates effectively from 1479, when Ferdinand began to organize it after obtaining papal permission. He intended it chiefly to deal with those notoriously wavering new Christians: the *Conversos* and the *Moriscos,* respectively the converts from Judaism and Islam. Its officers were all crown-appointees who blandly identified religious orthodoxy with loyalty to the state, and punished offenders against either. They were answerable to no other courts, not even to those of the pope. The code of the Inquisition was astutely revised in order to give little chance of escape to the accused, who commonly received a life sentence even in the event of his submission. Needless to add, this remarkable body had most effective procedures for seizing the estates of its victims for the use of the Crown. The chief personality behind its development was Tomás de Torquemada, who served as Grand Inquisitor from 1483 until his death in 1498. In earlier years he had been Isabella's confessor and did much to encourage her well-meaning severity. During his period of office he probably burned about 2000 persons: he also overcame the well-founded economic fears of the monarchs, when in 1492 he persuaded them to offer the Jews a choice between baptism or exile. Seeing them prepared to allow Jewish emigrants to sell their possessions, Torquemada circumvented this generosity by prohibiting all Christians from having any communications with the Jews. By this simple device, the latter were forced to leave most of their belongings in the hands of the Inquisition. About 800,000 families are thought to have emigrated, and the blow to Spain's economy was probably heavier than those sustained in later years through the expulsion of the *Moriscos*. And it would seem mistaken to minimize the inhumanity of Torquemada by claiming that he represented Spanish public opinion, since the hatred of the laity of all classes compelled him to move about the country with a huge bodyguard. Three protests against his activities were carried to Rome, yet to the end he retained the full confidence of his sovereigns. Yet one claim at least can be made in his favor: that the prisons of the Inquisition were not only more capacious but more salubrious than those of the state or of the bishops.

At the time of Torquemada's death the leading figure of the Spanish Church was Francisco of Jiménez de Cisneros (Ximenes, *1436-1517*), formerly an ascetic Observantine friar and confessor to the Queen, but now archbishop of Toledo. Like the Inquisition, this great ecclesiastic formed a monument to the integration of Church and State. He was also chancellor of Castile and after the death of Isabella in 1504 he withstood the tensions which threatened for years to break the recent union between the two kingdoms. When Ferdinand himself died in 1516, Ximenes as regent of Castile handed on the heritage to the young Charles I—later the Emperor Charles V—who unlike his grandfather Ferdinand was the unchallenged heir to Castile as well as to Aragon. The primate was no mere Torquemada. A munificent patron of learning, he founded the University of Alcalá (Latin: *Complutum)* from his own funds, and he endowed the *Complutensian Polyglot,* begun in 1502 and printed 1514-17. This latter, a multilanguage edition of the Bible in six folio volumes, owed much to the work of Jewish converts, whose scholarship gave Spain such advantages in the study of Hebrew and Aramaic. Ximenes, who also compelled cathedral chapters to reserve places for learned clergy, did much to create the last progressive circle of biblical and classical humanists to flourish in Spain. In more traditional vein he initiated reforms among the lax Spanish religious orders and he deserves a place among the early founders of the Catholic Reformation. It cannot be claimed that he modified the persecuting and racist policies of Isabella. At the conquest of Granada the Moors had been promised freedom of worship, costume, and education, together with their own law courts and an exemption from additional taxes. Yet in 1499 Ximenes, provoked by their reluctance to accept Christianity, embarked upon a policy of forcible reconversion. A resultant Moorish revolt then gave him the excuse not only to cancel the liberal peace treaty but in 1502 to decree the expulsion of all who should refuse baptism. And while in fact the immediate banishments were not very numerous, he had begun a process which ruled out both tolerant coexistence and peaceful integration. Deliberately reviving the spirit of crusade, in 1509-10 he led expeditions across the Mediterranean, conquering Oran, Algiers, and Tripoli.

Though Spain failed to establish a secure colony in North Africa, these campaigns were only a part of her expansionist enterprise. Ferdinand himself was vastly more interested in Italy than in the schemes of Ximenes to found a Christian African empire. In 1500 he agreed with France to partition the kingdom of Naples on the plea that under its weak ruler it was fast becoming a prey to the Turk. We shall soon describe how he then quarrelled with the French and drove them from Neapolitan territory by the end of 1503. In these hard-fought Italian campaigns the "Great Captain" Gonsalvo de Cordova perfected the Spanish infantry, arming it with the long pikes which were to give it command of the battlefields of Europe for well over a century. Having also annexed Roussillon and Cerdagne, Ferdinand completed Spain's Pyrennean frontier by plotting with Pope Julius II to wrest Spanish Navarre from its rightful king. In 1511 the Holy League headed by Ferdinand and Julius declared Navarre to be an ally of their enemy France. Spanish Navarre having been occupied in 1513, Julius then issued bulls which transferred it to Ferdinand. After Isabella's death the latter had in fact taken the precaution of marrying Germaine de Foix, granddaughter of a former king of Navarre, and claiming through her a hereditary right to the little kingdom. Exploits such as this enabled Machiavelli to rank Ferdinand alongside Cesare Borgia as the very type of ruthless prince demanded by the conditions of the age.

Amongst the dynastic marriages arranged by Ferdinand and Isabella, two acquired exceptional importance in European history, and both were originally aimed at the encirclement of France. To one we have already alluded—that between their daughter Katherine of Aragon and the future Henry VIII of England. This union led to the prolonged involvement of England with Spanish policy, then to Henry's suit for nullity and to the English schism from Rome. These later events were of course unpredictable, but hindsight enables us to see that the failure in Rome of Henry's suit was to be ensured by Spain's military control of the Papacy, a control established thirty years earlier. Another outcome of Katherine's marriage to Henry was the strict Catholic devotion of her daughter Mary Tudor, a true descendant of Isabella and a persecutor who finally steered to ruin the Catholic cause in England. The second fateful marriage took place in 1496 and united the Emperor Maximilian's son Archduke Philip with Juana, the mentally deranged daughter of Ferdinand and Isabella. Their son Charles, born in 1500, was to succeed his grandparents in 1516 as Charles I of Castile and Aragon. Yet with the early death of Archduke Philip in 1506, Charles also became heir to his other grandfather Maximilian, on whose demise in 1519 he succeeded to the vast Habsburg and former Burgundian lands. Thereupon he duly secured election as Charles V to the office of Holy Roman Emperor. His fantastic agglomeration of territories had many economic connections but no political links except a monarch. Europe had seen no such phenomenon since the time of Charlemagne, and it was to dominate European political history until 1556, when Charles abdicated and divided his Empire between his brother Ferdinand and his son Philip.

To contemporaries the conquests of Ferdinand and Isabella in Africa and along the Pyrennees seemed far more important than their patronage of the Genoese Christopher Columbus, first of the many navigators who began to add the transatlantic dimension to the civilization of the west. The ancient Romans had not been a seafaring nation, and while the Vikings of the tenth century reached the American mainland, they lacked the resources to pursue colonization so far afield. Their successors the medieval European nations gradually developed the techniques necessary for oceanic travel, yet in the first place they naturally turned eastward to the known wealth of the Levant, to the homeland of their religion, now held captive by the Saracen and the Turk. Since 1381, when Venice had destroyed the Genoese fleet, the eastern trade which developed in the wake of the Crusades had become a Venetian monopoly. But Venice was an Adriatic and east-Mediterranean power, unfitted to break out into the Atlantic. Her limitations remained when, after capturing Byzantium in 1453, the Turks hampered her trade with the Levant. Even on the oceanic coasts of Europe the prevailing west winds and the adverse Gulf Stream discouraged attempts at a direct east-west crossing of the Atlantic. The essential preliminary was the southward exploration of the African coasts, which would enable European sailors to take advantage of both the Equatorial Current and the trade winds moving from Africa toward the West Indies and Brazil. The Genoese had paved this way southward, and the Portuguese followed under the active patronage of Prince Henry the Navigator *(d.1460)*. Technical advances also promoted the enterprise. The new fifteenth-century carrack with its small foremast and lateen sail aft had sailing qualities superior to those of its predecessors, while the Portuguese improved the compass derived from China and the astrolabe derived from the Arabs. Prince Henry formed a large collection of charts and books on exploration, and set up a committee specifically to organize Portuguese trade with Africa. This small kingdom, hitherto somewhat of a backwater, suddenly developed an intelligence, a boldness of spirit, an ability to think and plan upon a global scale. These qualities, reinforced by a ruthless desire for high and rapid profits, enabled Portugal initially to take the lead in a European expansion which soon dwarfed that of the Crusades.

Encouraged by the yield of the slave trade and by hopes of reaching India, the Portuguese discovered the Azores and the Cape Verde Islands in 1445, then began planting colonies along the African coast. In 1452 a bull of Nicholas V, confirmed four years later by the Spanish pope Calixtus III, authorized Henry to enslave the natives of newly discovered countries. Hence Europeans became deeply involved in the inhuman traffic hitherto largely the perquisite of Moslem traders. From the first, quasi-religious motivation blended seductively with greed. Recording that Prince Henry received a fifth of the slaves as his personal share, his chronicler noted that "he had much joy on account of their salvation, for otherwise they would have been destined to perdition." When in later days the Portuguese penetrated deep into the Congo basin, a considerable Christian culture arose in some areas: Negroes were ordained as priests and in 1518 Dom

Expansion of Europe, in about 1530

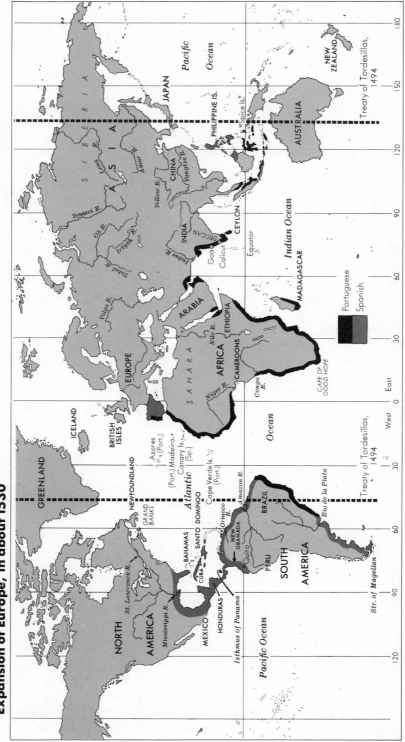

Portuguese
Spanish

Eurico, the son of a Negro ruler, visited Rome to be ordained bishop by the pope. In 1486 Bartholomew Diaz rounded the Cape, called "of Good Hope" by his optimistic sovereign John II of Portugal. He was followed in 1498 by Vasco da Gama, who crossed the Arabian Sea and reached southern India at Calicut. From 1501 the Portuguese were delivering spices brought back by this route to Antwerp, and thus they undercut the trade pursued by Venice along the traditional routes. Moreover they attacked Moslem shipping with fierce efficiency, closing the Red Sea passage to India and so starving the Venetian trade not far from its source of supply. For their part the Venetians did not scruple to finance Turkish attacks upon the Portuguese, yet the latter triumphantly fought off all threats. They ended by constructing immense chains of trading posts and settlements, centered from about 1510 upon Goa and surviving intact until the Dutch overran them in the seventeenth century. To crown these amazing exploits, Fernan de Andrade reached Canton in 1517, and three years later the Emperor of China was receiving Portuguese ambassadors.

Spanish oceanic exploration began somewhat later and its marked differences from that pursued by the systematic Portuguese arose in part from the personality of its founder. Despite his worldly ambitions, Columbus was an Italian visionary of Jewish origins, lured into the wholly unknown by a theory. But he could scarcely claim this theory was original, and he did not set sail to discover a "new" continent. Roger Bacon *(d.1292)*, Pierre d'Ailly *(d.1420)*, and (in 1474) the Florentine astronomer Paolo Toscanelli had surmised with confidence that the eastern shores of Asia lay directly across the Atlantic. Armed with the writings of d'Ailly and Toscanelli, Columbus applied to John II of Portugal, but found that ruler more interested in opening up the eastern routes. When he approached Ferdinand and Isabella, they were disturbed by the financial drain of the Granada campaign and they hesitated to become involved with Columbus; the more so since his demands included the office of viceroy in all the lands to be discovered and a tenth part of the gold and other treasures accruing from the voyage. Nevertheless in April 1492 they agreed to back his expedition and in August he left Palos with three carracks, provisions for a year, and a polite letter from his sovereigns to the Khan of Cathay. On this first voyage he landed in the Bahamas, in Cuba, and in Hispaniola. The following year he crossed again, finding Jamaica and other islands.

Ferdinand now required international recognition of Spanish claims, particularly in view of the predatory ambitions of the Portuguese. Apart from claiming the Canary Islands, he had hitherto agreed not to infringe their enterprises, and at this moment it was by no means difficult to arrange an advantageous line of demarcation, especially since a Spanish pope was now available as intermediary. Alexander VI thus issued a series of four bulls, which in effect divided all newly discovered lands between Spain and Portugal, the boundary being an imaginary line one hundred leagues west of the Azores and Cape Verde Islands. To the west of this line Spain would enjoy a monopoly. But after direct negotiations between the two powers, this division was modified in 1494 by the Treaty of Tordesillas, which shifted the line some 270 leagues further west, and thus allowed the Portuguese later on to claim Brazil. Four years later Columbus on his third voyage reached and explored the Venezuelan coast, but he was not in fact the first to reach the American mainland, for in 1497 the Cabots had landed near the mouth of the St. Lawrence. Already Columbus had revealed his inadequacies as governor of the new colony of Hispaniola, and having been removed from office he died in 1506, still believing that he had discovered an archipelago off the coast of Asia. Before 1500 intelligent observers began to question this assumption and to speak of a "new world," yet even when in 1513 Balboa crossed the isthmus of Panama, many people still supposed that he had merely reached an inland sea of the Asian continent. The falsity of this hypothesis became widely evident after 1517, when Andrade investigated some actual islands off the east coast of Asia. The final proof came in 1519-22 with Magellan's tragic voyage of circumnavigation, which was completed by only one of his five ships.

By this time the imperial enterprise of the Spaniards had begun to unfold upon a scale at least comparable with that of their Portuguese rivals. In 1519 Hernan Cortés left Cuba to conquer the rich but politically divided Aztec empire of Mexico. His rapid success derived as much from his cunning appreciation of the native psychology as from military daring—or from the terror inspired by a European cavalry charge. By 1522-23 Cortés was triumphantly building Mexico City upon the site of the former Aztec capital. Far to the south, across the mighty ramparts of the Cordillera, Francisco de Pizarro set out in 1530 with 180 men and 27 horses to conquer the Inca Empire, where an unwarlike people worked soft metals, lacked the wheel, and had only the llama as beast of burden. By luck and treachery, Pizarro and Almagro were able at the outset to capture the ruling Inca, and thenceforth to face only a demoralized opposition. Dependent upon seaborne supplies, they erected in 1535 the entirely new capital of Lima, close by the sea.

Already the facts of geography had begun to shape the history of European civilization in the New World. These facts had thrust the emissaries of the Iberian nations into Central and South America. In Brazil the Portuguese found enough to occupy their energies, already taxed by the demands of their Afro-Asian Empire. The Spaniards, on the other hand, did seek in later centuries to move northward from Mexico, yet they encountered strong European opponents in the Caribbean, and on land the still more daunting barrier of the deserts now in the southwestern United States. That North American geography thus resisted the Spaniards proved a fateful circumstance for the whole future of the human race.

Significant also for Western men was the encounter of Europeans with civilizations which owed nothing to Christianity or Islam. While both religious enthusiasts and sub-Christian adventurers lauded exploration as a means to spreading the faith, certain others drew a distinctly secular moral. Antonio Galateo of Ferrara *(d.1517)* cried, "All glory to those brave men . . . who dared to entrust themselves to the unexplored and limitless ocean, to penetrate nature's huge, empty spaces. They have taught us that nothing is impossible to man." To sixteenth-century intellectual life geographical discovery contributed vastly less than did ancient literature. But already in the first generation the discovery of non-Christian cultures suggested to Thomas More some critical thoughts upon the behavior of so-called Christian states. In later days such cultures drew Montaigne and a few of his contemporaries toward a far more daring relativism: these thinkers examined traditional European values in a manner impossible to men in the little Catholic Europe of the Middle Ages.

The initial effects of the early waves of European expansion upon the native populations were often unfavorable and sometimes starkly tragic. Despite enlightened Franciscan missionaries, despite the outspoken championship of native rights by a few idealists like Bishop Las Casas *(d.1566)*, within forty years of the arrival of Cortés perhaps nine-tenths of the native Mexican population had died as a result of European epidemics and the hardships of forced labor. Admittedly the native regime replaced by the Spaniards in Mexico was also grossly inhumane, yet its continuance could not have resulted in genocide upon this scale. Sixteenth-century Europeans were ill-equipped to undertake the tutelage of less developed or less warlike peoples. The medieval Church had made slow progress in taming men separated by a very few generations from barbarian ancestors. Indeed, by encouraging crusades and stressing the duty to combat and enslave the infidel, certain churchmen had helped to degrade the great expansion of the sixteenth century. For centuries, trade with extra-European areas had followed closely in the wake of "religious" warfare. But the moral failures of the expansion derived as much from individual greed as from the defects of contemporary teaching. For the individual participant, overseas trade and colonization were desperate gambles, with early death a more likely reward than high fortune: inevitably they attracted the more aggressive and the less scrupulous elements of the population. Needless to add, the first half-century is not the whole story, and on the American continent history can place obvious credits alongside the debits. Even against the early disasters in Mexico and Peru, it can set the emergence from the ruins of some remarkable hybrid cultures. Meanwhile in North America a still vaster continent with a sparse indigenous population allowed Europeans to initiate the greatest of all their overseas experiments at a lower initial cost in human suffering, yet a cost which in due time was to be enormously multiplied by the horrors of the African slave-trade.

4. Central and Eastern Europe

Counterbalancing the decline of the land routes to Asia and the advances of the Ottoman Turks into the Balkans, the European economy developed important growth sectors upon its eastern and northeastern frontiers. During the fifteenth and sixteenth centuries there issued from the great seigneurial estates of Poland and Prussia increasing consignments of grain: in return the coarse textiles of England and the Netherlands went to clothe the serfs on those same estates. Meanwhile the merchants of the Hanseatic League occupied whole quarters of some Baltic and Russian cities, from which a growing volume of timber, metals, and naval stores came to the West. These two centuries, and still more the seventeenth, were Baltic as well as Atlantic centuries. By 1600 Sweden's great wealth of iron and copper was about to help her become an empire-building power. To the south of the Baltic, colonization was proceeding among the forests and marshes of the less populated states of Germany. From among these states Brandenburg-Prussia was also destined to arise as a major power, one created not merely by the able Hohenzollern dynasty but by improving landlords, laborious serfs, and foreign colonists, among whom Dutch pioneers and Huguenot craftsmen came to play prominent parts. Further south still, the mines of Saxony and Bohemia were booming from the years around 1500 and drawing workers from all over Europe.

During the fifteenth century the most dynamic organization of the northeastern world was the Hanseatic League. Its operations were based upon two facts of life: that merchants held power within all major medieval cities, and that merchants trading over large areas of Europe needed mutual support and protection. The League sprang from a long series of shifting alliances. Its solid nucleus lay in the Baltic port of Lübeck and the nearby North Sea port of Hamburg. In the fourteenth century the League's Baltic organization turned upon Wisby, while its western outposts lay at Cologne and Bruges. By 1370 it had defeated the Danes and wrested from them the control of the Sound, the gateway to the Baltic, together with the neighboring fisheries. Sometimes its power extended even to the preservation of merchant-oligarchies in member-cities. When in 1374 a democratic movement overthrew the city government at Brunswick, the League used economic sanctions to force the citizens to restore the old ruling class. The Emperor treated the Hansa with great respect, while the menacing union of the three Scandinavian kingdoms in 1397 was weakened in 1450 by the withdrawal of Sweden. Even so, the later fifteenth century saw a measure of decline in power of the League. The native English merchants not only wrested the trade of their own country from the Germans' grasp, but by the time of Henry VII were pursuing a lively commerce of their own with Flanders, Scandinavia, and the Baltic. Again, internal rivalries grew within the Hansa when its Netherlandish members, encouraged by the Dukes of Burgundy, broke out of their appointed zone and sought to rival the Baltic cities in the trade on that sea. Around 1450 this tilt of the balance toward the western cities was powerfully aided by the inscrutable decision of the herring-shoals, hitherto based on the western Baltic, to migrate and reassemble off the coast of Holland. Needless to add, after 1500 the rise of Atlantic commerce began to increase the strength of the ports along the western approaches to Europe. These tendencies all weakened the power and cohesion of the Hanseatic League, while the Germans as a whole steadily failed to evolve a centralized nation-state, within which a league of cities might have been refashioned as a weapon to protect German trade and overseas interests. In actual fact there occurred a notable growth of power on the side of the individual German princes, a development which boded ill for civic liberties and for any free association of cities.

In southern Germany the tendency to association had always been weaker, and the political influence of the cities did not correspond with their wealth and number. In 1488 a group of south German princes, knights, and cities formed the powerful Swabian League, an order-keeping body which was to play a prominent part in crushing the subversive movements of the 1520s. Yet this was in essence a princely rather than an urban organization; its purposes, constitution, and policies show no real resemblance to those of the Hanseatic League. Admittedly the southern cities were more culturally advanced, more diversified in their social character and economic activities. In 1500 they stood at what could still be regarded as the hub of Europe. They were intimately linked with Venice to the south of the Alpine passes; with the Swiss, the French, and even the Portuguese to the west; with the Lower Rhineland, the Netherlands, the Hanseatic cities to the north; with the Danube valley to the east. In Alsace both Strassburg and Schlettstadt became major centers of humanism; while Nuremberg formed a metropolis of metalworkers and artists, and Augsburg could claim to be the birthplace of modern international banking. In the late fifteenth and early sixteenth centuries, two of the several Augsburg finance houses began to achieve a special preëminence. The Fuggers based their position not only upon their superb network of offices throughout Europe but upon Imperial patronage, since they were able to advance enormous loans to the expansionist Habsburgs in return for the future output of silver mines in the Tyrol and of copper mines in Hungary. Their rivals the Welsers financed more normal trading and industrial ventures, but like the Fuggers they maintained branches from Lisbon to Vienna and Danzig, from Antwerp to Rome. The relations of such firms transcended all state frontiers, divided the European economy into spheres of interest and even derived profits from the Indulgence system of the Catholic Church. In the wars of the Reformation period the Fuggers twice saved the Emperor by their loans, and later on they did not hesitate to remind him of the fact in blunt language. Yet the bankers were hated from the first by almost every other element in the German

Jacob Fugger "the Rich" with his
chief accountant Matthäus Schwarz.
Note the filing cabinets showing the
names of major cities where the main
offices of the firm were located.

nation, while their very intimacy with great ruling houses proved in the long
run their undoing. For all their skill and strength they could not force
emperors and kings to repay their loans. But before the decline came, the
Welsers did indeed marry one of their daughters to a Habsburg archduke!

In contrast with these meaningful economic and social changes, the
political structure of the Empire remained a world in trance. While some of
the component principalities had begun their own processes of moderniza-
tion, none of them was nearly strong enough to unite the nation by
conquest. While the Imperial office itself remained elective—and at some
vacancies became the object of serious bargaining—in actual fact a Habsburg was elected on every occasion from 1438 on. The Empire had already
received its most durable constitution at the hands of another dynasty. The
Emperor Charles IV of the house of Luxemburg has deservedly been called
the greatest sovereign of the fourteenth century, and his Golden Bull of
1356 was bitterly slandered by that famous phrase of Lord Bryce, who wrote
of Charles that "he legalised anarchy and called it a constitution." On the
contrary, the Golden Bull did much to protect Germany from the intermittent chaos which might so easily have followed the death of each Emperor.
The functions of the seven Electors were in substance settled by this
document for the long life yet remaining to the Empire. The lay Electors
were four in number: the King of Bohemia, the Count Palatine, the Duke of

Saxony, and the Margrave of Brandenburg. Among the princes who had failed to reach this magic circle, perhaps the most important were the Dukes of Bavaria and the Landgraves of Hesse. Of the very numerous ecclesiastical rulers, whose lands covered about one-sixth of Germany, only the archbishops of Mainz, Cologne, and Trier (Trêves) belonged to the College of Electors; of these Mainz enjoyed seniority, with the right to summon the Electors to Frankfurt and to crown there each new Emperor.

The *Reichstag* or Imperial Diet met so frequently during the fifteenth century that the procedures and the representation then became largely settled. During this period and henceforth it met in three colleges or chambers: that of the Electors; that of the Princes of the Empire, spiritual and lay; and (after 1489) that of the Imperial Cities, which were not ruled by princes but dependent immediately upon the Empire. The list of cities thus admitted to direct membership showed some fluctuations, but by the end of the century about sixty-five had established permanent claims. Some were small and could not pursue independent policies; others like Nuremberg, Augsburg, and Strassburg had the wealth and manpower to raise considerable forces and to build almost impregnable fortifications. Collectively the cities did not carry much weight in the Diet, though they paid large sums in Imperial taxation. Even in the College of Princes, which included many petty rulers, attention was paid to the relative importance of each member and the majority view did not necessarily secure adoption. The collected decisions of a Diet, duly accepted by the Emperor, were promulgated as its "Recess" *(Reichsabschied),* but even his chief court, the Imperial Chamber, had no ready means of executing them within the territories of a recalcitrant prince or city. Likewise the military and fiscal organization of the Empire remained sketchy. Each Elector, prince, or city owed a levy of men to the Imperial army, yet except at the height of the Turkish peril, the call was so often neglected that the resultant force proved derisory. In fact the army and treasury of the Suabian League were usually stronger in the early sixteenth century than those of the Empire. The latter's weakness was also reflected by the success of another regional organization for law keeping, the *Vehm* of Westphalia, a curious body which resembled a secret society. Its mysterious courts were conducted by bodies of initiates, and they executed summary justice even in capital cases.

In many country areas where no strong prince had unquestioned authority, public order remained minimal, even by medieval standards. Among the chief offenders stood the Imperial knights, independent but impoverished and unrepresented in the Diet. Rulers over a village or two, many of them exacted harsh tolls, openly plundered travellers, and waged private wars against one another. The many-spired city of merchants, scholars, and craftsmen; the robber-baron in his castle on the crag—these were the antitheses of German society. Like the knights, the peasantry lacked political representation. Both their rulers and their feudal lords steadily eroded their judicial rights and privileges, often replacing Germanic by Roman law, which discriminated with such weight and precision against the lower orders of society. By way of contrast, the German universities flourished during the decades around 1500, when humanism derived from Italy extended its hold upon their masters and students, even though it lacked the heavy endowments attracted by the older subjects. Though they largely invented German nationalism and emerged from their historical studies loudly proclaiming Germanic virtues and victories, these well-travelled scholars could hardly be called insular. By the same token the expanding universities were less and less purely concerned with the training of clerical theologians and philosophers. Droves of German students passed southward to Bologna and other schools of Roman law, and they duly returned to claim good livings as judges or officials in the pay of rulers and cities. Though many of these jurists were also prominent in classical studies, some humanist writers like Wimfeling and Brant denounced the practitioners of Roman law as bloodsuckers and foes of German freedom. The overthrow of lawyers also figured prominently among the demands made by rebellious peasants and artisans: this occurred in 1491–92 during a revolt against the Abbot of Kempten; again in the larger Alsatian rising of 1493. Yet meanwhile most of the plans propounded for constitutional and legal reform in the Empire came from above; little heed was paid to the grievances of that grumbling beast of burden, the peasant.

During the long but inglorious reign of Frederick III *(r.1440–93)* projects of reform foundered upon the Emperor's marked lack of interest. Not only did he fail to repress the feuds of princes and knights, but he refused to attend meetings of the Diet, even when urgently pressed by its members. While his prestige as Emperor sank to abysmal depths, and while he relinquished the German Church to papal exploitation, Frederick showed a lively concern to extend the domains and the clientage of the Habsburgs. He achieved that brilliant match between his son, the future Emperor Maximilian I *(r.1493–1519)*, and Mary, heiress of Charles the Bold of Burgundy. Nevertheless in 1485 the Hungarian King Matthias Corvinus captured Vienna and Frederick went to beg his bread from neighboring princes. From this point his duties were largely assumed by Maximilian, a lover of soldiering and the chase, a striking personality with chivalrous ideals and pretentions to literary culture. Yet Maximilian's own prowess failed to solve his financial problems, while he constantly overestimated his military resources. Like his ancestors he entertained splendid plans for enlarging the Habsburg possessions by marriage and conquest, and saw the family lands as an instrument for reviving the Holy Roman Empire and making it hereditary. More intelligent than his father, he understood the need for administrative and fiscal reform, even though his concept of reform differed from that of the Electors. When at the Diet of Worms in 1495 he demanded money to oppose the French invasion of Italy and to defend the Empire against the Turks, he found himself faced by a series of demands from a group headed by Berthold of Mainz and Frederick the Wise of Saxony. They proposed to erect a standing Council of Regency under princely control, to staff the Imperial Chamber (the central court) with their own nominees, to proclaim a public peace and place all who broke it under the ban of the Empire. In return they proposed to establish the "Common Penny," a tax on all property, coupled with a poll-tax on people of small means: the expenditure of the yield should be allocated by the Diet, which would be summoned annually.

The demand for a Council of Regency Maximilian naturally liked least, yet by the Augsburg Diet of 1500 he was reduced to accepting even this, for his Italian expeditions and campaigns against the Swiss had foundered hopelessly. The Council, it was arranged, should meet under the presidency of the Emperor or his deputy, but should share with him the daily executive power. Yet when after a few months the new taxation fell far short of the estimates, Maximilian announced that as Emperor he had experienced only mortification, and that he would in future act as an Austrian prince. Accordingly in 1502 he withdrew recognition from the Council of Regency and set up a standing court of his own, the Aulic Council, referring to it not only cases concerning the Habsburg territories but cases subject to Imperial jurisdiction. The Electors then drew closer together by the Compact of Gelnhausen and sought to conduct an independent foreign policy: they even discussed the possibility of deposing Maximilian and electing the French King as Emperor. These moves nevertheless proved to be the climax of the Electoral movement, a cause which the rest of German society was not prepared to take at its face value. The lesser princes and the knights feared the growing pretensions of the Electors, while the humanists encouraged by Maximilian had helped to popularize a romantic faith in the ideal of a German monarchy.

From 1504 events began to move in Maximilian's favor. The Elector Palatine, a prominent reformer, disputed the succession of the Duchy of Landshut with the Dukes of Bavaria, but he was defeated in battle by Maximilian, who then shared the disputed lands with the Dukes. In the same year both Berthold of Mainz and the Elector of Trier died, while new and brilliant dynastic acquisitions seemed about to fall to the Habsburgs. Henceforth, though Maximilian failed to reap most of these gains or to recover his influence in Italy, little of the reform plan survived. The Council of Regency did not function: the Emperor kept his Aulic Council; the "Common Penny" gave way to a tax collected by each ruler for his territory. Certain items of the Electoral program survived after a fashion, notably the division of the Empire into ten regions, known as "Circles," each with an organization for finance, police, and military levies. No method of operating this system was agreed during Maximilian's reign, and even when in 1521 many obstacles were cleared, no effective Imperial fighting force or treasury in fact emerged. Before long almost every Circle fell under the dominance of the most powerful local prince, while elsewhere the situation was rendered even worse by the disputes of rival rulers. Thus, while many individual princely states functioned with ever-increasing efficiency, the Empire failed to develop a federal administration or any other means of coordinating the political life of the German nation. The most effective national organ remained the Diet, which continued to meet periodically, to discuss common problems, and prevented some of the petty wars always threatening to erupt. Yet amid the growth of princely powers it had little contact with the people, and it came to resemble an inter-state congress rather than a governing parliament.

The future of the German princedoms was by no means everywhere determined during the century preceding the Reformation. The old practice of dividing a territorial inheritance between two or more sons had resulted in the proliferation of pygmy-states. Even in the later fifteenth century some of the major powers were continuing to follow this debilitating custom. For example, in 1485 the Saxon lands were divided between the Ernestine and the Albertine branches of the House of Wettin. The former received the office of Elector, the lands north of the Elbe, and most of Thuringia: the latter, calling themselves Dukes of Saxony, were assigned the area around the little cities of Dresden, Leipzig, and Meissen. Since the Albertines had the university of Leipzig, the Ernestines under Frederick the Wise founded that of Wittenberg in 1502; and in terms of world history we might well regard this as the most significant result of the division. A new university on the lands of a favorable and relatively strong German prince was to prove one of the very few possible bases for a movement of religious revolution.

By way of contrast, Albert Achilles, Elector of Brandenburg *(r.1470-86)* issued in 1472 his *Dispositio Achillea,* which became the law of succession for the later generations of the House of Hohenzollern. It stipulated that his eldest son should become Elector and receive the Mark of Brandenburg with its dependent territories. Henceforth this unit should remain indivisible and descend by primogeniture. Two other sons were to divide the family's small Franconian lands, yet in future each of their shares was also to remain indivisible. In such cases younger sons could henceforth receive little except money bequests and preferment to ecclesiastical benefices. In many other respects both Albert Achilles and his father Frederick *(r.1440-70)* may be regarded as progenitors of the Brandenburg-Prussian state which four centuries later came to dominate and unify Germany. They attracted the nobles to their service, diminished the privileges of their towns, set up a supreme court for the Mark, and purchased neighboring lands. Albert Achilles in addition overcame the military threats presented by Poland, the Dukes of Silesia, the Hansa towns, and Matthias Corvinus of Hungary. More clearly than the Habsburgs, the Hohenzollerns perceived that in a nonfeudal world the strength and security of any state must depend upon the capacity of its people to pay taxes. Insofar as German rulers contributed to the theory and practice of the modern state, their contributions tended to be upon this realistic, mundane level. Long before they became "enlightened" autocrats and military aggressors, the Hohenzollerns, with their poor lands, small towns, limited trade and industry, had to assume the functions of improving landlords and industrial promoters.

The politically dynamic sections of central and eastern Europe in the later Middle Ages were Switzerland and Bohemia, both of them countries wherein the common people sought to take a direct hand in shaping their own destinies. As the Swiss in a series of struggles throughout the fourteenth century threw off the rule of their Habsburg overlords, they erected and gradually enlarged their Confederation. The original example of the peasant-farmers in the Forest Cantons proved attractive even to Zürich, hitherto a free Imperial city. The experiment is one of unique interest for its period, because it produced so durable a constitution and because it comprised people of several different languages and cultures. It also demonstrated how simple men could, under favorable geographical conditions, act in rational cooperation to set up and defend in arms an orderly commonwealth free from monarchy, from feudalism, and eventually from ecclesiastical overlordship. In criticizing the many ill-directed peasant risings of late medieval and early modern Europe, we should not forget that here in Switzerland a successful rural rebellion gave rise to a viable and permanent state. Certainly the people of neighboring lands tried to draw the moral. Outlying groups of insurgents like those in the Grisons continued to join the Confederation, while the many peasant revolts of southern and central Germany took courage from the Swiss example. On the other hand, a historian of Switzerland must consider other factors apart from the long pikes and the stout hearts of the farmers from the Alpine valleys. The cohesion of central Switzerland largely depended on the trade route over the St. Gotthard pass which bound together so many towns and country districts. Even before 1300 the men of Uri had become transport workers. Again, the adherence of the big cities of Zürich and Bern became vital to the success of the Confederation and in turn this adherence depended upon the pressures of working-class and bourgeois citizens upon their city governments.

It is obvious that the Swiss enjoyed good fortune during the earlier stages of their common enterprise, which might well have been nipped in the bud had the Habsburgs been able to concentrate upon the repression of the Forest Cantons and their associates. But in the end the decision lay with the great companies of Swiss pikemen, who defeated and killed Leopold of Habsburg in 1386 at the battle of Sempach. During the succeeding century the Confederation entertained an aggressive program of expansion, one based far more upon economic calculations than were the territorial accumulations of the Habsburgs and Burgundians. To confirm their hold on the St. Gotthard the Swiss occupied Valais; to hold the northern outlets they seized Aargau and sought to reach Mulhouse. On the upper Rhine they collided with the ambitious Charles the Bold of Burgundy, whose overthrow in 1477 allowed them to incorporate Fribourg and Soleure. And when Maximilian I tried to tax them as members of the Empire, they took up arms and in 1499 forced him to rescind all measures against them. In effect the Habsburgs recognized their independence from this time onward, even though in legal theory the Swiss Confederation remained part of the Empire. Joined in 1501 by Basle and Schaffhausen, the Confederation dreamed of more glorious advances, perhaps even upon Milan or Strassburg. It nevertheless faced perils that arose less from foreign forces than from internal divisions, especially those obtaining between the poor free farmers and the prosperous capitalists of the big cities, who not only ruled within their walls but aspired to surround themselves with subservient rural districts. The insecurities of a confederation without a capital, without a common law or coinage, were underscored by further differences of interest between the cities themselves, with their varying social structures and trading connections. Moreover the great majority of the Swiss were kept poor by a steadily unfavorable balance of trade. From the time of the French invasions of Italy, thousands offered their services as mercenaries to France and to others of the contending powers. The need to limit this degrading national industry was soon to occupy the minds of Zwingli and other idealists.

To the northeast of the main Habsburg territories the peoples of Bohemia and Moravia also sought to break free from the toils of foreign dynasticism. Here national consciousness acquired an even sharper edge, since it embraced religious nonconformity and arose from a desire to cast off an alien yoke. But the Bohemians were not simply champions of a vernacular Czech culture. Their men of learning had mastered the subtleties of scholastic philosophy and from the mid-fifteenth century they embraced classical humanism as swiftly as scholars anywhere outside Italy. In the front rank of European academies stood the Caroline University of Prague, founded in 1348 by the ruler whom we have already encountered as author of the Golden Bull. Becoming Emperor Charles IV in 1355, he strove consistently to make Prague the leading capital of central and eastern Europe. Not only did he give the city its university and archbishopric; he also legislated in order to concentrate upon it the whole foreign trade of Bohemia. In addition to the Golden Bull of the Empire he devised the so-called *Majestas Carolina,* a constitution and a legal code for the Bohemian kingdom. Though this proved unacceptable to the Estates, Charles nevertheless erected an efficient bureaucracy, established a uniform coinage, kept the nobles under control, attracted to his court a host of scholars and artists, including both Czechs and Germans.

Within this Caroline golden age lay forces of disruption. Among the preachers encouraged by Charles to reform the slack Bohemian Church were men like Milíč of Kroměříže *(d.1374),* whose tirades against clerical abuses caused him to be repeatedly charged with heresy at Rome. During the subsequent quarter-century academic circles in Prague became increasingly torn by altercations between the rival scholastic systems, Realism and Nominalism. Into this intellectual struggle nationalism was soon projected, for nearly all the German scholars were Realists and the Czechs Nominalists. In addition, the intercourse with England which followed the marriage of Richard II with Anne of Bohemia *(1382)* promoted the spread of Wycliffe's doctrines among the Czech theologians. With equal enthusiasm the Germans condemned these doctrines. From this *mêlée* arose John Huss *(c.1370-1415),* who took his bachelor's degree in 1393, lectured in philosophy from 1398, and regularly preached in the Bethlehem Chapel to distinguished audiences. He began to copy and annotate the works of Wycliffe, and in 1399 his associate Jerome of Prague *(d.1416)* went to spend two years in Oxford, returning thence with further works of the English heresiarch. Later on, other Czechs went on similar errands to Oxford, some of the English Wycliffite tracts having been preserved for us only through this process of transmission to Bohemia. Meanwhile the Czech faction Huss led was favored so markedly by King Wenzel that in 1409 the Germans staged an exodus leading to the foundation of the university of Leipzig. Later that year the reappointment of Huss as rector at Prague failed to settle the struggle, since his ecclesiastical enemies remained powerful. In 1410 he was excommunicated by the Pope and by the following year the city of Prague lay under an interdict. Returning to southern Bohemia under the protection of noblemen, Huss continued to preach and write, his chief work *On the Church (1413)* having its first ten chapters taken almost bodily from Wycliffe. He then rashly accepted a safe-conduct from the Emperor Sigismund *(r.1411-37)* to attend the Council of Constance, where he soon found himself imprisoned and condemned for heresy. If he did not seek martyrdom, he accepted it. "If my death serves God's glory and your advantage, may he allow me to undergo it without base fear." Had his enemies foreseen the strength brought to the Czech national movement by his heroic death, they might well have adopted milder methods.

Huss suffered condemnation on account of the heresies contained in his book *On the Church,* especially those which envisaged the Church as the congregation of the elect, and the hierarchy of bishops and priests as unnecessary to salvation. In his view the headship of the pope was unscriptural, and papal Bulls wholly lacking in force unless clearly founded upon the Scriptures. Catholics, even reforming Catholics like Gerson, believed Huss to be perniciously claiming that no man in a state of mortal sin had any lordship or jurisdiction over Christian people. During his absence his collaborators at home laid special stress upon his eucharistic doctrine: they proclaimed that the laity should be permitted to communicate *sub utraque specie,* that is not only in bread but also in wine, hitherto reserved to the priesthood. Known as *Utraquism,* this teaching achieved rapid acceptance throughout Bohemia, where the communion chalice *(calix)* became not merely a religious but a national symbol, binding together all classes of the nation. The Four Articles of Prague in 1419 demanded Utraquism, the free preaching of the Gospel, the forfeiture by the clergy of temporal possessions, and the punishment of offences against the word of God and slanders against the kingdom of Bohemia. Faced by this defiance, the Emperor Sigismund organized four crusades *(1420–31)* against his rebellious and heretical Bohemian subjects. Under their brilliant military leaders Jan Žižka *(d.1424)* and Prokop the Bald *(d.1434),* the outnumbered Czechs made skillful use of their wagons to form mobile fortresses, and on every occasion they defeated the hosts of Germans and crusaders from other parts of Europe. In the end, invading forces simply fled on hearing in the distance the hymns of an approaching Bohemian army. And so far from standing on the defensive, the Hussites sent out their agents into Germany and Poland: others made contact with the Waldensian heretics in Italy, and one of them was burned in 1433 as far afield as Scotland.

At the moment when the Hussites could have conquered neighboring territories and when their leaders were already negotiating at the Council of Basle, a longstanding internal quarrel came to a head. They had divided into two parties: a conservative, largely middle-class group known as Calixtines or Utraquists, and the more radical group of Taborites, among whom workmen and peasants were led by a small element of clerics and scholars. Both sides sent representatives to Basle, but while the negotiations proceeded, they fought each other in May 1434 at the battle of Lipany, where victory went to the Utraquists. In 1436 the latter signed with the royal Council the *Compactata,* a treaty which purported to restore the Bohemians to the Catholic Church and yet accord them the privileges demanded by the Four Articles of Prague. Nevertheless the fragility of this peace remained clear. Radicalism did not vanish with the overthrow of the Taborites, while on the other side a strong party of Catholic noblemen demanded the restoration of lands taken from the Church.

During the middle forties there emerged as leader of the Hussites George of Poděbrady, who first served as regent and was then *(1458)* unanimously elected king by the Bohemian Estates. For some thirteen years he maintained general tolerance, despite the denunciation *(1462)* of the *Compactata* by Pope Pius II. The Papacy, which had already inspired the anti-Hussite campaigns, remained the implacable foe of the Hussites, and was further antagonized by Poděbrady's far-reaching plans to pacify and unite Europe by purely secular agencies. He did indeed plan a European league of princes to provide for arbitration in their disputes and for common defense against the Turks. The reactions of the European sovereigns were predictably varied. Respected by Emperor Frederick III and by Louis XI of France, Poděbrady found a bitter enemy in the Catholic Matthias Corvinus of Hungary. Not long before his sudden death in 1470, he sought to outbid Corvinus by choosing as his own successor a Catholic: the young Polish prince Ladislas (Vladislav I), who then ruled Bohemia from 1471 to 1516. When in the event Ladislas proved less tolerant toward his Hussite subjects than Poděbrady had designed, he had to be compelled by force to recognize that Catholics and Utraquists enjoyed equal rights in Bohemia. And though in 1490 Ladislas succeeded also to the Hungarian throne, a period of class divisions and the growing power of the oppressive Bohemian nobles augured ill for the future both of Hussitism and of the nation at large.

To the economic rivalries of lords, serfs, and townsmen were added continuing religious divisions, since the main attitudes of the Taborites had reappeared in the Unity of Bohemian Brethren, a powerful movement whose first leader was the layman Peter Chelčický *(d.c.1460)*. These Brethren separated from the Utraquists in 1467, demanding a simple, unworldly Christianity. They disliked all forms of ecclesiastical hierarchy and wanted to abase the power of the nobles and the cities: they rejected private property, military service, and the taking of oaths. Around 1500 there appeared also the Amosites, an even more deeply puritanical sect, which not only refused to accept townsmen and aristocrats, but sought to establish a society based literally upon the Sermon on the Mount.

Nearly two centuries before Bossuet denounced the divisive character of Protestantism, Catholic preachers were able to enlarge upon the same theme and to draw upon the chaotic spectacle of Hussite Bohemia. Meanwhile the German humanists, their patriotism offended by the memory of recent defeats, strove to depict the Bohemians as a nation of untutored boors. These hostile traditions spread throughout Europe and lingered on into the age of the Reformation. In 1529 bishop John Fisher, noting with alarm the rise of heresy in England, cried out in Parliament, "For God's sake, see what a realm the Kingdom of Bohemia was, and when the Church went down, then fell the glory of the kingdom." But the truly catastrophic downfall was to come a century later still, when after the battle of the White Mountain *(1621)* the victorious Habsburgs sought to wipe out both heresy and Bohemian nationhood by a brutal persecution.

Toward the end of the fifteenth century the complex of dynastic marriages between the royal houses of Poland, Bohemia, and Hungary might have given eastern Europe an alliance strong and wide enough to promote economic prosperity, to reveal common interests, and to safeguard those nations against predators both Christian and Turkish. That these advantages failed to materialize cannot solely be blamed upon incapable and unfortunate rulers. Ever since that day, these three geographically exposed but gifted peoples have paid a cruel price for their rooted political individualisms. But in 1500 no external power—except perhaps the Turks—

was capable of swallowing them whole. The Teutonic Knights and the Hansa were powerful only in the Baltic area, while the manifold involvements of the Habsburgs bade them embrace Bohemia and Hungary by dynastic marriages rather than by conquest. At this time the future pressures from the east could hardly have been foreseen, for the Principality of Moscow was still fighting for survival against the Tartar hordes and had not yet unified Russia. On the other hand the Ottoman Turks moved throughout the first quarter of the new century toward new triumphs. In 1526 the young and childless King Louis of Hungary and Bohemia, last of the Jagiellon kings, fell on the tragic field of Mohács. His kingdoms descended to his brother-in-law, Ferdinand of Habsburg, brother of the Emperor Charles V, but the victorious Turks swept on to occupy the great central plain of Hungary, leaving Ferdinand only a narrow strip of territory to the west.

By position, size, and population, the kingdom of Poland might well have seemed best fitted to lead the way toward a great alliance or even a confederation in eastern Europe. The heavy German infiltration of the Middle Ages had not prevented the growth of a vernacular culture, and had helped to keep Poland in close touch with western and central Europe. The Catholic Church had meanwhile differentiated Poland from her Orthodox neighbors, and had supplied a real bond of unity. The dynastic union with Lithuania in 1386 had added weight to the Polish resistance to the Teutonic Knights of Prussia, who suffered defeats about the same time as those of the German-led crusades against Bohemia. In 1466 Prussia became a fief of the Polish kingdom. In stark contrast with these achievements the origins of subsequent failure are also apparent in the fifteenth-century history of Poland. While Ivan the Great, Prince of Moscow *(d.1505)* was laying the foundations of the Russian Tsardom, Poland entered upon a long process of division and decline, though seemingly facing lesser problems and greater advantages. To explain her failure, the phrases "elective monarchy" and "lawless nobility" do not wholly suffice. The weakness of the state lay less in disorders and feuds in the countryside than in the weakness of the *Sejm* or Diet. Originally a Council of State composed of the magnates, prelates, and highest officers, this body had now a lower house representing the lesser nobility *(szlachta)* and the towns. Once assembled, however, the deputies were rigidly bound by the instructions of their provincial Diets, and they were hence unable to coalesce into an effective organ of legislation and government. The resultant paralysis at the center was indeed worsened by an elective monarchy all too prone to bargain away privileges on each election, again by the vast landed wealth and local powers of the great nobility. All these features, which combined to provide the perfect formula for a weak state, contrast markedly with the trend in western Europe. That medieval estates might survive to be a source of strength was well exemplified in England. But this could happen only when such representative bodies lay, not under the mandate of their local communities but under the firm guidance of a centralizing monarchy, alert to national needs and armed with well-staffed administrative, fiscal, and legal institutions. Even in the most efficient hereditary kingdoms there could be disastrous minorities, driving the preachers to that favorite text: "Woe be to thee O land, whose King is a boy." But in Poland with her hundreds of would-be kings, the situation resembled that of a permanent royal minority. Rarely henceforth, and then under great perils and exceptional leadership, could the chivalry and courage of the Polish nation shine forth.

When all is said and done, the tragedies of the eastern nations should not in the main be attributed to the errors of their leaders, or to their ramshackle constitutions, since in addition they were so clearly doomed to recurrent disaster through their geographical and ethnic backgrounds. On account of their inability to rival the major leaders of European progress, historians of Western civilization would not be justified in ignoring these nations over long periods. Then as since, they continued to make interesting and attractive contributions to the common stock, and all of them—even poor Hungary with the Ottoman Turks in the heart of the land—played active supporting roles in the unfolding dramas of Renaissance and Reformation.

THREE

*High
Renaissance
Europe*

1. Europe and the Italian Wars

The years following the death of Lorenzo the Magnificent saw Italy plunged into a period of invasion and warfare which lasted until the Peace of Cambrai in 1529. The zenith of Italy's cultural triumph became also the abyss of her political tragedy. For Europe as a whole, the quest of the nations for dominance over Italy involved sterile fighting and diplomacy which subtracted from their wealth and their humanity; and one may well question the extent to which it really promoted the already striking diffusion of Italian culture throughout Europe. The Italian people lost what remained of their political freedom, not to foreign conquerors alone, but also to native autocrats. France poured great resources into the struggle but lost it. And while the European power of victorious Spain was for the time being augmented, Italy ended by adding one more burden to the many imposed upon Spain's manpower and upon her ill-balanced internal economy.

When the Turks could seize Italian ports at will and could intrigue with the *Moriscos* in Spain, the old motive of crusade could never fade from European minds, yet within this motive religious idealism had long been a declining factor. Pope Alexander VI did not scruple to oblige the Sultan by keeping the latter's troublesome brother in custody. When Francis I thought of Naples as a crusading base, he was primarily inflamed by the quest for personal glory, and he soon showed himself prepared to intrigue with the Turks against his Christian enemy, the Emperor Charles V.

A far more significant aspect of the period lies in the technical development of warfare, which within these decades advanced more rapidly than during any similar period before the twentieth century. Armies of considerable size and complexity were often involved. For example, in 1494 Charles VIII of France invaded Italy with 60,000 men, including 1600 "lances" of cavalry (each containing six horses), 8000 Gascon infantry, 8000 Swiss, and an impressive train of horse-drawn field artillery. On the other hand the narratives of the campaigns and major battles indicate that relatively little advance had been made in the communications required to integrate— either strategically or tactically—the action of these various elements. Of the effectual advances perhaps the most striking was the improvement of artillery in numbers, mobility, and rate of fire. Guns contributed to the issue in several of the greater and more decisive battles: most notably at Ravenna, but also at Marignano and Pavia. Prevailing over the prejudices of a generation still nourished upon chivalric ideals, artillery engaged the zealous study of eminent commanders and appealed to the pride of such rulers as Ercole d'Este, the Emperor Maximilian, and Henry VIII. Alongside the field gun, a serviceable hand-weapon emerged with the arquebus and by the later stages of the Italian Wars this had replaced the crossbow.

On the other hand, it could hardly be said that gunpowder had fully achieved its modern significance. Most battles were still decided in the main by pike and sword, while small arms could only be employed under the protection of these weapons. The dominance of infantry found acknowledgement when Spanish *hidalgos* fought with the pikemen, and when Francis I personally commanded his infantry at Marignano. This situation formed the climax of a long development. Alongside the earlier successes of the English archers and the Bohemian Hussites, the mastery of infantry over mounted knights had been demonstrated in most spectacular fashion by the great phalanxes of the Swiss, as at Grandson and Morat. Their tactics, based upon close squares each of 6000 well-drilled pikemen and halberdiers, were imitated by the German *Landsknechte* and by successful Italian mercenaries like the brothers Vitelli. The Swiss model was improved upon by Gonzalo de Córdoba and other Spanish commanders in the Italian Wars. Without doubt, the Spaniards developed during this period the finest infantry of the sixteenth century, a force mainly composed of tough and agile volunteer peasants from the Castilian plateaux. Their methods were based upon the *tercio,* the unit probably so called on account of its three elements: the protective hedge of 1500 pikemen; the 1000 swordsmen who rushed through when fighting developed at close quarters; the 500 arquebusiers who gave supporting fire. These *tercios* dominated the battlefields of Europe until they were decimated by French and Swedish firepower and mobile tactics during the period of the Thirty Years War *(1618–48).*

The lack of a native infantry of this caliber sometimes hampered the French, whose standing army consisted of cavalry, and who, apart from some Gascon contingents, commonly employed Swiss mercenaries or German *Landsknechte* in the infantry role. Machiavelli's apothesis of native troops and his sweeping condemnation of mercenaries were based upon his warm admiration for the armed citizens of the German cities; yet he did not consistently attack the mercenary principle, since he also accorded admiration to the Swiss. Indeed, his attitudes seem hardly justified in the light of an unprejudiced examination of the behavior of the Italian *condottieri* during the Italian Wars. Treachery or sudden transfers of allegiance proved rare on their part. The Swiss themselves were capable of such actions, while even Spanish armies sometimes proved mutinous when their wages went unpaid. In fact many Italian mercenary captains were men of conspicuous honor and professional devotion. Few responded solely to motives of gain, while employers who failed to pay them or afford them adequate experience could hardly complain if they went elsewhere. At Agnadello and on other fields some of them proved that they could train Italian infantry capable of fighting with success against strong French forces.

The military and political problems which troubled Machiavelli went deeper than the composition of armies. That Italy failed to organize herself against invaders was due to the selfish policies of princes and the localism of outlook which marked Italians in general. Outside the kingdom of Naples, Italy remained essentially a land of city-states and civic patriotisms, while in Naples a backward-looking feudalism still obstructed the emergence of a "modern" state. Everywhere, it is true, the word *Italia* could move many hearts. Despite the cynical counsels offered in *The Prince*, Machiavelli ended his book with an emotional plea for the unification of Italy. Even the more sardonic and detached historian Guicciardini could take patriotic pride in the individual prowess of Italians, as when at Barletta a group of Italian champions vanquished their French opponents in personal combat. On the other hand, it must be conceded that a feeling for Italy as a whole underlay singularly few political decisions. When Pope Julius II raised the cry "out with the barbarians!" he coined a political slogan with appealing cultural overtones, yet he was not seriously proposing to subordinate his own political ends to an all-Italian policy.

The state-building Papacy of these years did nothing to condemn the evils of warfare, while the old ecclesiastical approval of a "just war" could easily be cited by rulers with exiguous claims to a righteous cause. The somewhat rare protests against war in general came mainly from a few north Europeans, from the uprooted internationalist Erasmus, from Thomas More in his utopian phase, from a disillusioned statesman like Archbishop Warham. Yet even these men did not hesitate to serve rulers who accepted warfare as a normal means of enforcing their claims. The dynastic war-makers could always—outside Italy at least—appeal with confidence to naïve patriotisms. Seldom if ever could they be credited with waging war in order to benefit their subjects, to secure economic gains, or even to attain "natural" boundaries. While diplomacy, military planning, and finance displayed an increasing sophistication, the Italian Wars cannot be understood in the simple terms of modern nationalism.

Below this level, war was in some sense a career for a minority. Every country contained many thousands of poor nobles and gentry trained from youth to martial exercises, still capable of knightly gestures, yet nevertheless embracing war as a profitable calling. From their profession they expected plunder as well as wages, hoped for prisoners to ransom, even for estates in conquered territories. Some of Charles V's commanders like Antonio de Leyva and Fernando de Alarcón made large fortunes. At the lower end of the scale, countless young men were driven by poverty and boredom from the less flourishing, more overcrowded areas of Europe, driven as easily to the Italian campaigns as to distant mines, or to overseas trade and adventure. For the stay-at-home peasantry, war was a recurrent hazard like the plague, though even in Italy its miseries were by no means everywhere continuous. When a city was threatened with siege, the peasants of its *contado* might hasten in to labor on the fortifications, but in course of time the general hatred of a bullying and plundering soldiery grew stronger. The Vicentine writer da Porto relates that on numerous occasions in 1508-9 north Italian peasants ambushed bodies of soldiers and slew them pitilessly, without regard to the cause for which they stood.

The technical advances promoted by the Italian Wars were not limited to the military art. The period was one of exceptionally involved and intensive diplomacy, which required rapid but comprehensive political information and analysis. It also demanded the best possible diplomatic machinery. Such needs were most felt by relatively weak states like Florence and Venice, the latter of which supplied Europe's leading model in the techniques of diplomacy. Having hitherto relied on short-term missions, the chief states now maintained a steadily growing number of permanent representatives at foreign courts. To supplement the ever more elaborate reports of their ambassadors they paid numerous spies and informers, making full use of their own merchants abroad.

What languages should be used for all this diplomatic intercourse? The medieval employment of learned clerical diplomats fluent in Latin had by no means ceased in the earlier sixteenth century, but the rise of the layman seems as striking in this sphere as in many others. In any event, though utilized in treaties and formal instruments, humanist Latin was hardly the ideal instrument for everyday communication, and as the century advanced the need for men of affairs to acquire modern languages became much more widely recognized. That even insular Englishmen made themselves fluent in Italian and French marked a change with cultural as well as political implications. To serve this more efficient diplomacy, most governments improved their courier services both at home and abroad: information and orders were transmitted more rapidly than during the medieval centuries. A Venetian ambassador in Rome could now send a letter home in three days or less; another in Paris took well under a fortnight to contact his masters in Venice. Where, however, sea voyages were involved, long and unpredictable delays remained common. Yet in their ease of communication as in their professionalism, their secular spirit and independence of the

Church, their sense of pattern and balance in Europe, their strong common interest in Italian affairs and Italian culture, the statesmen and diplomats of Europe now formed an international community more coherent than that of their medieval predecessors.

2. The Wars to the Death of Julius II

It may well seem a harsh if necessary assignment to traverse in twenty pages a series of episodes over which Francesco Guicciardini *(1482–1540)* in his great *History of Italy* took a thousand. In truth the great contemporary Florentine found even this space none too ample for his exhaustive purposes; and in later times a story was current that a criminal once went to the galleys rather than accept a sporting offer from his judges that he should instead read the whole of Guicciardini! Followed into all their ramifications, these political and military affairs have as sublime a complexity as that of any game of chess. And while so many European states became entangled, the greatest complexities arose from the Italian microcosm, where numerous states were guided or misguided by opportunist rulers through a dense jungle of motives and calculations.

At the death of the peacemaker Lorenzo in 1492 the leading Italian states were five in number: Florence, Milan, Venice, the Papacy, and Naples. None was big enough to devour the rest, but to the Medicean balance of power the patrician republic of Venice seemed to present the chief menace. During the earlier decades of the fifteenth century Venice had added to her far-flung mercantile empire a new state on the Italian *terra firma* extending as far west as the Adda. It afforded the city an independent grain supply and control of the neighboring Alpine passes: it was administered with moderation and ability, the major subject-cities of Padua, Vicenza, and Verona being accorded a high measure of self-government. While her wealth enabled Venice to buy the services of the most reputable *condottieri,* her gains had been made at a high price in terms of fear and suspicion on the part of other governments, which believed in Guicciardini's words, that the Venetians "were embracing with their thoughts the rule of all Italy." Inevitably her trading connections outside Italy and her lonely struggle at sea against the Turks and corsairs made Venice an individualist power, one held only with difficulty to any league of states.

The duchy of Milan, rendered wealthy by artificial irrigation and of late by the rise of the silk industry, was efficiently administered by the Sforza dukes, who kept a strong standing army and blocked the further westward expansion of the Venetian empire. On her other flank Milan faced the passes through which a French or a Swiss invasion would be most likely to come. Southward across the Apennine passes lay Florence in the rich valley of the Arno, the mouth of which was controlled by her restive subject-city of Pisa. Beyond Florence, the Papal States extended from the Adriatic to the Mediterranean, from the Romagna in the northeast to the frontiers with the kingdom of Naples in the south. Since its return to Rome at the end of the Great Schism, the Papacy had been intermittently attempting to forge a centralized state from this varied group of territories. The popes saw that otherwise they would remain pawns in the hands of minor neighboring powers. In 1492 considerable sections of the papal territories—the small despotisms of the Romagna and cities like Bologna and Perugia—remained virtually independent. Within and around Rome itself, the great noble factions of the Orsini and the Colonna openly disputed power with the successive popes, whose reigns were usually brief and whose efforts to build up the power and wealth of their own families could bring no lasting benefits to the Papacy. From 1492 the already tarnished moral reputation of the Papacy was being further debased by Alexander Borgia, whose love for his natural children was not the least of his indiscretions.

The kingdom of Naples lay under the harsh rule of King Ferrante *(d.1494)* and his son Alfonso of Calabria, members of an illegitimate branch of the House of Aragon, which had wrested the crown from the French claimant René of Anjou. Even under these tyrants Naples failed to shake off its ancient curse of baronial disloyalty; and while its nominal overlords, the popes, intrigued with the Neapolitan barons, the rulers of Naples repaid the compliment by encouraging the many restive interests within the Papal States.

The series of French interventions about to disturb this delicate Italian balance were based upon two dynastic claims. The dukes of Anjou asserted that the crown of Naples had been legally theirs since 1435 through the will of Queen Joanna. Nevertheless the last duke, dying in 1481, had bequeathed his claim to Louis XI of France, whose practical wisdom had warned him not to assert it by leading an actual expedition to Naples. Very different was the attitude of Charles VIII, who succeeded his father in 1483 at the age of fourteen and spent the first years of his reign under the guardianship of his sister Anne de Beaujeu. She seemed to have inherited her father's ability to the exclusion of poor Charles, whose powerful body was inhabited by a singularly weak intelligence. Achieving personal independence by 1492, Charles combined profligate habits with the romantic dream of making Naples the base for a crusade against the Turk. The second French claim upon Italy was that made to the duchy of Milan by the house of Orléans, which descended from Valentina, heiress of the Visconti. Its members naturally denounced as usurpers the Sforza dukes, whose *condottiere* ancestor Francesco had as recently as 1450 seized Milan on the extinction of the male line of the Visconti. From 1467 the French claim lay with Louis of Orléans, a cousin of Charles VIII, and in the event destined to become his successor on the French throne.

Misguided as he was, Charles VIII might nevertheless have refrained from invading Italy but for the development of a bitter quarrel between the rulers of Naples and Milan. The young duke of Milan, Gian Galeazzo Sforza, had recently married the granddaughter of King Ferrante, and the Neapolitan court desired to see the couple delivered from the oppressive tutelage of the man who had made himself actual ruler of Milan: Gian Galeazzo's uncle Lodovico Sforza, called *il Moro* because of his dark complexion. Lorenzo de' Medici had sought to pacify this feud between his two allies, but his son and successor Piero, uniquely stupid for a member of the house of Medici, vehemently took sides with Naples, thus breaking up the triple alliance on which the peace of Italy depended. When at this point Lodovico Sforza considered the idea of appealing for French help against Naples and Piero, he was bound to take into account the unpleasant Orleanist claim to Milan, and his first intention was to use the mere threat of a French invasion in order to frighten the Neapolitans into leaving him in peaceful control at Milan. This aim once secured, the French might well be induced to call off the invasion. If they insisted, they might be allowed to come as far as central Italy, to overthrow Piero de' Medici and the simoniacal Borgia pope, to force a treaty upon Naples. Then, supposed Lodovico, they could be persuaded to return home to France. Such optimism was not peculiar to him. Throughout Italy the notion persisted long after this time that in politics the French were muscular fools who could be profitably manipulated by clever Italians. In fact the second of these assumptions often proved inaccurate, and once arrived in Italy, even Charles VIII could not be made the dancing-bear of Lodovico Sforza.

At the French court various Italian visitors supported the pleas of Lodovico's envoys, notably the Cardinal della Rovere, an arch-enemy of Alexander VI, a man of great capacity and ferocious will power who became a decade later Pope Julius II. Meantime in Florence the revivalist preacher Girolamo Savonarola, Dominican prior of San Marco, foretold the doom awaiting sinful Italy at the hands of the foreign invaders about to be sent by God. On the French side, the historian Commynes remarked that the proposed Italian expedition was "by all persons of experience and wisdom regarded as a most dangerous undertaking." But opposing such doubters, the younger French courtiers wanted Italian estates and other spoils of war, while Charles's influential minister Bishop Briçonnet conjured up an attractive vision of himself in a cardinal's hat.

In September 1494 Charles crossed the Alps with his powerful and—in the eyes of Italians accustomed to careful *condottiere* methods—destructively ruthless French army. Even before he reached Florence the citizens there overthrew Piero de' Medici, but Charles came to agreement with the new Florentine republican government and, early in 1495, with the Pope. Then came the surprise: that the French were able to overrun the disaffected kingdom of Naples without having to fight a major battle. The swiftness of the whole campaign shocked all Italy, not least its sponsor Lodovico Sforza. Yet in the event Naples proved far harder to hold than to invade. Within a few weeks French maladministration offended even the hitherto pro-French Angevin partisans within the kingdom, and the resultant rebellions could not all be suppressed. Moreover the rebels found a powerful friend in Ferdinand of Aragon, who had accepted Roussillon and Cerdagne from France as a bribe to allow the invasion of Italy, yet who had no intention of leaving Charles VIII in quiet possession of Naples. Massing troops in his island of Sicily, Ferdinand did not merely plan to reinstate his relatives; he also formed the anti-French League of Venice *(March 1495)* along with the Emperor, the Pope, Venice, and Lodovico Sforza. For his part Charles VIII decided to withdraw the bulk of his army, while leaving a substantial force in Naples. In recrossing the Apennines he met the army of the League and on 6 July 1495 pushed his way past it at the drawn battle of Fornovo.

This turn of events suited Lodovico, who had been also relieved at home by the death—whether providential or by poisoning—of his nephew Gian Galeazzo. He even succeeded in making Charles restore Novara, which Louis of Orléans had seized on his own account in order to prosecute his personal claim on Milan. Nevertheless Lodovico's triumph proved short-lived. In Naples the French forces surrendered by the late summer of 1496. In April 1498 King Charles himself died suddenly as a result of violent contact with a door-lintel at the castle of Amboise. But from the Italian viewpoint the significance of this accident lay in the fact that Charles had no surviving children. He was hence succeeded by his cousin of Orléans as Louis XII, and the change obviously foreboded an early French invasion of Milan.

Despite the League of Venice, the Italian rulers had failed to learn the lesson of unity, and some strange events were happening in their midst. Inspired by the fiery sermons of Savonarola, the Florentines replaced the Medici by a new republic modeled on the constitution of Venice, while the less sophisticated among them experienced a religious revival, accompanied by a public burning of trinkets, cards, and other vanities. As an outspoken critic of the corrupt Papacy and its allies, Savonarola plunged deeply into politics, while equating his program with the will of God and prophesying the establishment of a divinely-ordered city in Florence. His career soon gave rise to bitter factions among the mercurial populace and led to the election of a Signory dominated by his enemies. Interrogated under torture and delivered to papal commissioners, Savonarola suffered burning in May 1498, leaving some indelible traces upon the more tender consciences of Italy. At the other end of the moral scale, his enemy Pope Alexander determined to erect something like a family monarchy on behalf of his son Cesare Borgia. Releasing the latter from his cardinalate, in October 1498 Alexander sent him to France armed with a dispensation which allowed Louis XII to shed his first wife and marry Anne of Brittany, widow of

Savonarola preaching to the Florentines
from a woodcut of 1495

Charles VIII. This match was indeed greatly desired by the French, since the recently acquired duchy of Brittany seemed likely to secede from the kingdom. Cesare's baggage also included a cardinal's hat for the French minister Archbishop Georges d'Amboise, who privately coveted the Papacy itself. The young Borgia, made Duke of Valentinois by the grateful Louis, then prepared to return along with the coming French invasion and thereafter to conquer the Romagna and other independent portions of the Papal States.

During these exchanges Lodovico Sforza desperately recruited Swiss mercenaries, but apart from Federigo, the new king of far-off Naples, he could find no Italian allies. Venice actually agreed to support the claims of Louis to Milan, on condition that she should receive as her share of the spoils Cremona and the fertile Ghiara d'Adda. When the French invasion began in August 1499 Lodovico fled to the Emperor at Innsbrück, upon which his commander of the Milan citadel immediately sold the place to the French. Early in 1500 Lodovico returned and briefly recovered the city of Milan, but he was betrayed by his Swiss and German mercenaries and taken to spend his last decade in the dungeons of Loches in Touraine, a sad exchange for the cultured luxury and brilliance of his earlier life.

Having won this easy success in northern Italy, Louis XII turned his thoughts southward and soon made a secret treaty with Ferdinand of Aragon to partition the kingdom of Naples. The two conspiratorial rulers gave as their justification the fact that Federigo, the new king of Naples, had betrayed Christendom by signing a treaty with the Turk. Pope Alexander, dependent for his family ambitions on the French, naturally applauded this pious retribution. After a French orgy of rape and massacre at Capua in July 1501, Federigo abdicated in order to save his country from further suffering. Though held for a time by his son, Taranto fell in March 1502 and the partition of the kingdom was consummated. Almost immediately, however, the French and the Spaniards quarrelled and began fighting over the possession of the Capitanate and other districts from which arose lucrative tolls paid on the cattle passing to and fro between their summer and winter pastures. After a series of brief campaigns and negotiations, the great Spanish general Gonzalo de Córdoba completely defeated the French at Cerignola in April and on the river Garigliano in December 1503. This latter Spanish victory proved one of the turning points of Italian and European history. It sprang not merely from the superior intelligence and unity of Gonzalo's command but from the sheer grit of the Spanish infantry under appalling weather conditions. It also arose from the dismal failure of the French to keep command of the sea, by which alone large French forces in Naples could be maintained and Ferdinand's rival base in Sicily be threatened. Even the immediate results of the Garigliano were striking. Spain could now control the Papacy and could plan from an improved base the domination of all Italy and the Mediterranean.

During these dramatic events Cesare Borgia had been given French help to crush the lords of the small Romagna states in his three campaigns of 1500–1503. Despite his deserved and perhaps counter-productive reputation for cruelty and treachery, he showed a gift for organization which with better luck might just conceivably have enabled him to carve out a personal state from the lands of the Papacy. At the time he terrified Niccolò Machiavelli, who had been sent on an unenviable mission to Cesare's headquarters; but in later years the famous Florentine began to regard the Borgia as a potential agent of Italy's unification. In view of Cesare's limited scope, the brevity of his achievements, the likelihood that future popes would gain allies to overthrow him, Machiavelli has here seemed to most observers guilty of an emotional speculation. Whatever the case, Cesare's career came to an abrupt end on the death of his father in August 1503, an event coinciding with an illness which lost Cesare control of events in Rome. After the month-long pontificate of Pius III, there succeeded on 1 November Giuliano della Rovere, Julius II, the most vehement, ambitious, and military-minded of popes. When Cesare went to Naples to seek the aid of Ferdinand of Aragon, Julius persuaded the latter to arrest him and send him to Spain.

Escaping in 1506, Cesare died in the following year, assisting his brother-in-law the King of Navarre in war against Spain. By this time Julius had not only taken over Cesare's conquests in the Romagna but had extended them by capturing the great city of Bologna from the family of Bentivoglio: he also manfully engaged in the task of bringing law, order, and food supplies to the whole of the Papal States.

Events were meanwhile building up toward a third phase of operations by foreign powers in Italy. Louis XII, who retained control of Milan, found both the Emperor Maximilian and Pope Julius II waging quarrels with the Venetians. He easily induced the two to combine with him in the League of Cambrai *(December 1508)*, which set out in detail a plan to partition the Venetian state. Though at this time fighting the Moors in Africa, Ferdinand of Aragon also joined the League, his immediate purpose being to recover Brindisi, Otranto, and other Apulian ports occupied by Venice. In the event the French alone were able to undertake in force the initial invasion of the Venetian lands. On 14 May 1509 only half the ill-coordinated Venetian army bore the brunt of the attack at Agnadello, and though the Italian infantry fought well, the French triumph was complete. The victors proceeded to occupy their share of the Venetian lands, but they innocently refrained from entering the areas assigned to their allies. Anxious to preserve their amenities from siege or rapine, Venice's subject-cities capitulated the moment their Venetian overlords withdrew, and this not only to the French but in certain comic instances to an obscure adventurer, who appeared with a small retinue and accepted surrenders as a self-styled representative of Emperor Maximilian. Pope Julius claimed and seized Ravenna, Rimini, and Faenza; Ferdinand took the Apulian ports; and other neighboring princes various frontier towns held by the Venetians. And though amid her lagoons the city of Venice lay impregnable, she appeared to have lost her land-empire once for all. Eminent Venetians did not hesitate to talk of abandoning the *terra firma* and returning once more to a maritime and trading policy.

Within a few weeks, however, the situation of Venice began to change for the better, and this partly because of the spontaneous reactions of the subject-cities. After a brief taste of foreign brutality, these civilized but easy-going communities yearned to return to their enlightened Venetian masters. Gradually the Venetian Senate recovered the confidence to return to those areas where there was still no substantial foreign occupation. In July 1509 the Senate resolved by a single vote to reoccupy Padua, and though Emperor Maximilian eventually appeared in the neighborhood, he failed either to seize Padua or to prevent Vicenza and other places from reverting to Venetian rule. At this crucial stage the League of Cambrai began to collapse under the weight of its own selfishness and cynicism. In February 1510 Julius accorded peace to Venice and later he helped to detach

Ferdinand of Aragon from the League. Needless to observe, the astute Spaniard had every reason to fear the unchecked growth of French power in northern Italy, and in addition he was seeking an opportunity to annex the frontier kingdom of Navarre. As for Julius, he now raised his famous battle cry "out with the barbarians," and devoted the short remainder of his life to the expulsion of the French from Italy.

For this purpose the Holy League was formed in October 1511, though its text spoke of defending the unity of the Church and recovering places claimed by the pope and Venice. Its members included not only the Papacy, Venice, and Spain, but also the young Henry VIII of England who, disdaining the peaceful parsimony of his father, sought to cooperate with his father-in-law Ferdinand and to win personal glory on French soil. Against this formidable combination Louis XII remained in league with the ever-impoverished and unreliable Emperor Maximilian, but he failed to build a counter-alliance of any weight. In fact he managed to quarrel with his Swiss employees, and these, led by the Cardinal of Sion, began to operate as an independent power against the French in Milan. In this emergency an able and heroic commander came to the fore on the side of France. This was Gaston de Foix, a nephew of Louis XII only twenty-three years of age, and one of the claimants to the disputed kingdom of Navarre. In a brief but brilliant campaign in northern Italy Gaston brutally sacked Brescia and hurled back the forces closing in upon Milan. On Easter Day 1512 he confronted near Ravenna a strong force of Spaniards and their allies under Cardona, Viceroy of Naples. There followed the bloodiest battle of the wars to that date, one which displayed some distinctly "modern" features, including a prolonged artillery duel in its early stages. And while under bombardment the Spanish infantry had the sense to lie prostrate, the French, led by models of chivalry like Bayard, disdained such an action as beneath their military honor. After eight hours the forces of the League were driven from the field, yet the victory of the French soon appeared illusory. Their losses in seasoned commanders were appalling. Most disastrously, Gaston de Foix himself had fallen during the closing stage of the battle, as he tried with a few companions to block the retreat of the Spaniards.

As the weakened French hesitated within a hostile countryside, the Emperor now changed sides, withdrew his troops from the French army and joined the Holy League. More important, when 20,000 Swiss poured down into the Milanese, the main French force withdrew to Asti and soon afterwards recrossed the Alps. In Italy the triumphant League settled matters at will. Though Venice had survived her peril, her trade continued to decline under the pressures of the Turks and the Portuguese. As Florence strove to maintain her integrity, she lay in a still worse position. Since the death of Savonarola, the new Florentine republic under the mediocre presidency of Piero Soderini had in Machiavelli an able secretary to its governing Council of Ten. While Florence had continued its traditional alliance with France, its subject-city of Pisa had rebelled and until 1509 had sustained a siege which had cost Florence dearly. After the battle of Ravenna, the republic had no chance of preventing the return of the Medici under Spanish control. The end came swiftly in August 1512 when the citizen-militia organized by Machiavelli fled ignominiously from a smaller Spanish force. The Spaniards then sacked Prato with a sickening brutality said to have haunted on his deathbed their companion, the Cardinal Giovanni de' Medici, later Pope Leo X. Once in command of Florence, the League restored the Medici in the person of Lorenzo II, grandson of Lorenzo the Magnificent, the constitution being remodelled to ensure effective Medicean control. Forced into retirement at his country cottage, Machiavelli gambled with the local boors at the village inn, returning home each evening to don his best clothes, enter his study, and hold intellectual converse with the great authors of classical Antiquity. In 1513 he wrote *The Prince* and began the *Discourses*. But hoping most unheroically to be recalled to office by the Medici, he dedicated the former work to Lorenzo, who probably never read it.

While in Florence the Holy League had thus found the obvious solution, in Milan a more confusing situation obtained, and it was resolved to recall the late duke's son Maximilian Sforza, who had been brought up at the Imperial court. He nevertheless returned to find himself little more than a tool of the Swiss Confederation. Indeed, to this latter were ceded those areas of the Milanese which dominated the Italian Lakes and the central Alpine passes. The survival of Venice and the reappearance of the Medici and the Sforza did not however mean that Italy had been substantially restored to the position of 1494. As Julius II lay dying in February 1513 he had ample reason to reflect upon the very limited success of his attempt to put back the clock. While he had made striking progress in reconstructing and strengthening the Papal States, his effort to expel the foreigners had lamentably failed: he had lived to see not merely Naples but all Italy passing rapidly into the dominance of Spain. Solidly established in the south, triumphant in Florence, the Spaniards prepared to establish their control in the north. Certainly they would encounter no firm opposition from the successor of Julius on the papal throne. As a Medici Leo X now belonged to a family of Spanish puppets, while his personality contrasted markedly with that of his domineering predecessor. Like Julius a patron of great artists, Leo was a pacific devotee of the cultured *dolce vita,* one without zeal to develop the political independence of the Papal States, much less to reform the Catholic Church. There succeeded one of the most disastrous pontificates in all Christian history, more disastrous even than that of Alexander Borgia, since it ended by misunderstanding the significance of Martin Luther.

3. War and Diplomacy, 1513–1530

Since no general settlement of the Franco-Spanish rivalry had been attained in 1512, there remained every likelihood that the newly-won peace of Italy would be disturbed by foreign powers. In particular, Ferdinand's ambitions were not allayed by the ousting of the French from Italy. He now pressed the claims of his second wife Germaine de Foix to Navarre, and in 1513 he conquered that portion of the little kingdom which lay on the Spanish side of the Pyrenees. The rest survived as a miniature French monarchy, and as such retained its independence until 1589, when Henry of Navarre succeeded his Valois relatives on the throne of France. Ferdinand neglected the English army which had landed at Bayonne in his support, and decimated by heat, rain, fever and wine drinking, it ingloriously departed for home. Even so, the chauvinist mood of the English was little abated by this setback, while the new minister of Henry VIII was Thomas Wolsey, a cleric with a real talent for military administration and one whose personal ambitions exceeded even those of his French parallels, Briçonnet and d'Amboise.

In the summer of 1513 there developed a new encirclement of France when Henry VIII in league with the Emperor Maximilian captured Thérouanne and Tournai, having on August 16 easily scattered a French relieving force at Guinegate, the "Battle of the Spurs." Three weeks later King James IV of Scotland attempted a diversion in favor of his French ally but was heavily defeated and slain by the English at Flodden. Already in the previous June the Swiss, without the aid of cavalry or artillery, had crushed at Novara a well-balanced and much larger French army seeking to reoccupy Milan. But as many observers began to anticipate the total defeat and even the partition of France, the members of the alliance, fearing a total collapse of the European balance, hesitated to press home the attack. Leo X perceived that both papal and Medici interests demanded an equipoise between French and Spanish power in northern Italy. For his part Ferdinand suspected that the Habsburg family would draw most benefit from the overthrow of France, and he sought to detach the feckless Maximilian from the alliance. Henry and Wolsey, hearing of this betrayal, not only made peace with Louis XII, but on the death of Anne of Brittany gave him in marriage Henry's sister Mary, a handsome girl of sixteen. The gift proved fatal to the recipient. Already somewhat senescent in his early fifties, Louis had hitherto taken care of himself, but now the round of festivities in the company of his young wife brought him to the grave within three months, and he was succeeded by his twenty-one-year-old cousin and son-in-law Francis of Angoulême.

The new king of France was a man of shallow charm and Italianate tastes, devoted no less to martial glory than to amorous intrigue. He had no intention of renouncing the claims of his predecessors and in August 1515 he crossed the Alps with a fine army, including a number of experienced foreign officers such as the renowned engineer and artillery specialist Pedro Navarra, a prisoner left unransomed by the niggardly Ferdinand. The Venetians thought it prudent to join the French as active allies: they not only pinned down the forces of the Emperor but sent a useful contingent under Alviano to aid the French invasion. On the other side Spain, the Papacy, and other states hastily sent troops to support the Swiss and Milanese forces in northern Italy. Here the situation was unhappy, since both Maximilian Sforza's extravagance and the heavy demands of the Swiss made many of the disgruntled Milanese welcome the French as liberators. Shocked by the sudden appearance of the French army from the unfrequented Col d'Argentière, the Swiss fell back on Milan, and on 13 September 1515 were brought to battle nearby at Marignano. Here a hard-fought struggle lasting for two days reached a decision when the Venetian force joined the French, while the papal troops still hung aloof at Piacenza. The Swiss were decisively worsted and though their survivors retired in good order, the legend of their invincibility was shattered. In the event this defeat at Marignano marked the end of their brief adventure as an independent power in the struggle for Italy. The peace settlement of 1516 allowed them the Ticino and most of the frontier they had won on Lakes Lugano and Maggiore: they accepted a French subsidy and henceforth preserved neutrality as a nation, while still sometimes sending contingents to serve other powers in a mercenary role. The Venetians emerged with nearly all their old territories, and continued to rule them well until struck down and stripped by Napoleon. King Francis pensioned off Maximilian Sforza and personally assumed the duchy of Milan. To this state Leo X agreed to add Parma and Piacenza, places hitherto claimed by the Papacy, and in return Francis agreed that Lorenzo de' Medici should retain power in Florence.

At the end of 1515 Leo and Francis actually met at Bologna in order to begin negotiations on the problems outstanding between the Papacy, the French Church, and the French Crown. The resultant Concordat of Bologna *(August 1516)* proved France's most signal gain from the victory of Marignano; it replaced the Pragmatic Sanction of Bourges *(1438)* and it lasted until the French Revolution. Its terms greatly favored the Crown as against the Papacy; it improved upon the Gallican Liberties hitherto allowed the French Church under the terms of Bourges. It granted the Crown nomination to the 10 archbishoprics and 83 bishoprics of France, to which were later added over 500 abbacies. While this new Corcordat limited appeals by Frenchmen to Rome, it permitted the pope to continue drawing the first fruits of benefices, and it made no claim concerning the rights of a General Council of the Church as against the Papacy. It displeased the conservative lawyers of the *Parlement* of Paris, who preferred the Gallican principles of Bourges, but King Francis had good reason to think otherwise. He and his successors now exercised full control over the leaders of the French Church, who were henceforth strongly royalist in outlook, much like the English bishops under the Tudors. On the other hand the monarchy became in relation to the Church a satisfied power, identified with the high ecclesiastical establishment and uninterested in reform. In later days this situation helped to provoke a Protestant movement arising from the lower and middle reaches of French society. Again, the medieval dichotomy between the upper and the lower clergy grew stronger still, the former being so clearly tied to the Crown while the latter remained men of the people.

In January 1516 the death of Ferdinand left his grandson Charles of Habsburg, then in his seventeenth year, sole heir to the Spanish kingdoms and colonies. The young king's lack of money and need for consolidation induced him to temporize with Francis I, and in August 1516 by the Treaty of Noyon the latter surrendered all claims to Naples, while Charles guaranteed his possession of Milan, and undertook to restore Spanish Navarre to the former ruling house of d'Albret. Charles also accepted betrothal to Louise, the infant daughter of Francis. Again, the treaty allowed the Venetians to buy back Verona and Brescia, the two cities still occupied by the Emperor Maximilian. To England the Noyon agreement proved distasteful, since Wolsey, who had retained the town of Tournai from the campaign of 1513, wished to curb France by maintaining an active alliance with Maximilian, the Venetians, and the Swiss. Yet when all these powers acceded to the treaty, Wolsey made haste to agree with Francis on the Treaty of London *(October 1518)*, whereby Tournai was returned to the French and a betrothal arranged between Henry's young daughter and the Dauphin. The betrothal was admittedly a speculative essay in dynasticism, since the combined ages of the happy couple amounted to three years! The treaty signed, Wolsey preened himself as the author of a universal peace in Christendom. Whatever his responsibility, peace suited his personal interests. This was the apogee of his career, an enviable situation for one who combined a king's chancellorship with a cardinal's hat, not to mention an overweening desire to become the second Englishman in history to occupy the papal throne.

In the event the London agreement was to prove a mere breathing-space in the European struggle. Wolsey's England mattered far less than the cardinal supposed, for there now existed only two giant powers in Europe, with Italy and many another prize lying between them. At first both Francis and Charles naturally saw an English alliance as a possible key to victory. But the balance between them could only have been upset by an England prepared to throw in resources on a scale which that increasingly prosperous nation—wanting romance but at low cost—was not prepared to concede. Since Wolsey's domestic credit and diplomatic influence were both based upon his personal commission from Rome, he was thus bound not so much to preserve a mere balance in Europe, as to remain friendly with whichever of the two great powers should gain control of the Papacy. And within a decade after the Treaty of London this motive was to become more pressing than ever, when Henry VIII called upon Wolsey to obtain from Rome an annulment of his marriage to Katherine of Aragon.

When in September 1517 the youthful King Charles sailed from Flushing to visit his Spanish kingdoms, his attitudes and his advisers remained Netherlandish. Soon after his arrival Cardinal Ximenes died neglected and dismissed, while Charles bestowed Spanish offices wholesale upon his Burgundian minister Chièvres and his other northern councillors. He could not yet address his Spanish subjects in their own tongue, and the whole atmosphere of his entourage antagonized the Spaniards. In 1518 the Cortes of Aragon and Castile made menacing demands. And as relations continued to deteriorate, the death in January 1519 of his grandfather Maximilian drew the attention of Charles to Germany, where the Electors of the Holy Roman Empire met after participating in a disgraceful campaign of bribes and counter-bribes. In the end they preferred the absent Habsburg to his chief rival Francis I, but the election of Charles in June 1519 owed much to the integrity of Frederick the Wise of Saxony, who not only refused bribes but declined a fair chance of securing the Imperial crown for himself. Charles was also much indebted to the great Augsburg banking house of Fugger, which on Netherlands securities had raised the one million gold florins needed to outbid Francis. From this time also the views of Charles

Portrait of Charles V, who wears the Burgundian order of the Golden Fleece, founded by Philip the Good a century earlier. The inscription gives his chief titles.

From the title page of *Chronicle of Flanders* (Antwerp 1531)

were broadened by his new chancellor Mercurino da Gattinara, a Piedmontese humanist who imparted the old notions that the Empire was ordained by God as a supreme world-monarchy, and that its true center lay in Italy.

In May 1520 when Charles sailed from Corunna to return to the Netherlands and Germany, the Spanish unrest came to a head. The *Comunero* rebellion under its leader Juan de Padilla was already spreading among the cities of Castile led by Toledo. Simultaneously there arose the separate revolt of the *Germanías* or brotherhoods of Valencia and Mallorca, which led to a class-war between the nobility and the lower orders of the cities. The *Comuneros* ousted Charles's regent Adrian of Utrecht and set up in his place the insane Queen Mother Juana. Quite soon, however, the Castilian nobility came to see that their fundamental interests stood nearer to those of the Crown than to those of the insurgents, who had now attracted a strange leader in the self-seeking Bishop of Zamora. At Villalar in April 1521 the *Comunero* army suffered final defeat at the hands of the royalists, and the rebel towns speedily capitulated. The *Germanías* likewise collapsed in the autumn, and on the return of Charles to Spain in 1522 the whole country had submitted to its legal sovereign. Peremptorily he ordered the Cortes to grant taxation before the hearing of grievances, and thenceforth they never refused to vote him the required funds. Charles appointed the officials and even the deputies of the Cortes, the latter being frequently bribed in order to keep them subservient to the Crown. But on his side, despite the pressure of enormous problems elsewhere, Charles was careful to stay on in Spain for the next seven years, to learn the Castilian tongue and indeed to become thoroughly imbued with the Spanish outlook. Gradually the young Netherlander became a Spaniard; and while he remained Holy Roman Emperor, at no point of his development did he pause to become a German!

During his absence from Spain in 1520–22 Charles had been by no means idle. He had visited Henry VIII at Dover and Canterbury, while after the lavish yet fruitless meeting between Henry and Francis at the so-called Field of the Cloth of Gold, Henry had moved on to see Charles again at Gravelines. From these contacts there had followed a secret treaty whereby Charles and Henry agreed that both would invade France in person, and that Charles should marry Mary, daughter of Henry and Katherine of Aragon. This match, like so many arranged during this period, did not in fact take place, yet the Anglo-Spanish-Burgundian alliance lasted for several decades, and it was to be Charles's son Philip who ultimately married Mary Tudor. Alongside these far-reaching schemes, Charles had not neglected German affairs. He had attended the Diet held at Worms from January to May 1521, and there confronted Luther and condemned his heresy. Even had his own doctrinal standpoint been more flexible, this condemnatory attitude would have been dictated by his political concept of a united Empire and a united Christendom under Imperial leadership. At the same time, Charles soon found himself developing critical attitudes toward the Papacy, since even in 1521 it was becoming painfully apparent that some radical reforms within the Church—and especially in the curia itself—must form an essential part of any plan for checking the advance of Lutheranism. On the other hand the Papacy, its independence gravely threatened by the Spaniards in Italy, could hardly be expected to accept Charles at his own high moral valuation. When Leo died and in January 1522 Charles's old tutor Adrian of Utrecht was elected pope, an austere reformer with Imperialist sympathies sat at last upon the papal throne. But in September 1523 Adrian himself died amid the undeserved execrations of the pleasure-loving Romans, and he was succeeded by another Medici, more indecisive, more elusive, more suspicious than Leo X. Lacking every quality needed to inspire confidence in the Papacy, Clement VII was to stagger on from crisis to crisis until his death in 1534.

Against the Turkish menace in Hungary even the most loyal Spaniards would not suffer Spanish troops to be used, and Charles sought to separate this problem from the rest by delegating power to his able but less patient brother Ferdinand. In February 1522 he ceded the Habsburg family lands to Ferdinand, making him Archduke of Austria and his regent in Germany. Moreover Ferdinand's marriage to the Jagiellon Princess Anne was soon to make him heir to the kingdoms of Hungary and Bohemia. In the face of Islamic pressures, the responsibilities of the Habsburg brothers did not end with the defense of eastern Europe. While the Ottoman Turks in Constantinople lacked the naval power to mount direct attacks upon Spain, they could stage landings on the Neapolitan coasts, and they could extend support to Algiers and other Moslem bases in North Africa. These latter were reinforced by Moors fleeing from Spain and they entertained hopes of linking with the disaffected *Moriscos* still living in that country. While Charles's naval strength remained weak, the Ottomans and their allies had thus outflanked his outposts in Naples and Sicily.

When in 1521–22 warfare recommenced between Francis and Charles, the former's position might well have been adjudged the stronger. Though the lands of the French king were less extensive than those of his rival, they were more compact, allowing him to operate upon interior lines. If his subjects were less numerous, they were far more united and loyal. In England Charles had a lukewarm ally by no means disposed to sacrificial effort. At the other extremity of his world, he might stir up the Shah of Persia to attack the Sultan, but the value of this diversion remained problematic. On the other hand, Francis had a wide range of actual and potential allies: the Turks, the German Protestants, the Swiss, Denmark, Scotland, most of the Italian States including Venice and even the Papacy. Of all these the most active were the Turks, who captured Rhodes in 1522 and who under their able Sultan Sulaimān the Magnificent were soon to exert massive pressures upon the eastern frontiers of the Empire. When

Francis declared war again in April 1521, he was too late to link up with the *Comuneros*, and he soon suffered a setback in Navarre. Moreover in April 1522 a Franco-Swiss army invading Milan was defeated at Bicocca, and it was not until October 1524 that Francis finally occupied the duchy, driving out the Imperial forces and besieging a large garrison at Pavia under Antonio de Leyva. Thanks largely to the efforts of the Duke of Bourbon, the great French magnate who had rebelled against Francis, the Spaniards and Imperialists obtained ample reinforcements and marched under the Marquis of Pescara to relieve Pavia. Here the garrison was not far from surrender when on 23 February 1525 the Emperor's army attacked the French besiegers, luring them from their strong positions. After a fluctuating struggle on the following day, the Spanish infantry supported by German *Landsknechte* carried the day. Francis had his horse shot under him, but was recognized by a follower of Bourbon and spared amid a slaughter which accounted for great numbers of his followers. In due course he was conveyed to comfortable captivity in Spain and consoled by a young Negress, sent as a present from his understanding sister.

The very completeness of Charles's victory at Pavia alarmed the other European governments and their fears were increased by his demand for the return of all the former Burgundian lands extorted by Louis XI from his grandmother Mary. The Italians soon sought to play a double game, especially Pope Clement and Francesco Maria Sforza, the Emperor's puppet-duke in Milan. The Turks offered France help and were soon able to give it, while Wolsey, after first trying to gain the crown of France for Henry VIII and a promise of the Papacy for himself, turned against Charles. Troubled by the great German peasant revolt of 1524–25, by the Turkish threat, by the defiance of the Lutheran princes, the Archduke Ferdinand could not support his brother by staging an attack upon France. On his deathbed less than a year after his victory at Pavia, Pescara besought his master to conclude peace. In January 1526 Charles agreed to the Treaty of Madrid, whereby Francis undertook on the Gospel and on his knightly honor to surrender not only his Italian claims but Flanders, Artois, Tournai, and the duchy of Burgundy. He also undertook to marry the Emperor's sister Eleanor, dowager Queen of Portugal. Leaving his two sons as hostages, Francis was then permitted to leave Spain, yet as Gattinara had predicted, he immediately repudiated the Treaty of Madrid. The Papacy, Venice, Florence, and Sforza formed the Holy League of Cognac against Charles and they stood on good terms with Henry VIII. For the Habsburgs even worse things were to come.

In the summer of 1526 the Turks invaded Hungary in great strength. Divided by the Protestant Reformation, by the subordination of its rich mines to Fugger finance, by a tension between the pro-German Lewis II and the patriotic Magyar nobles, Hungary presented a gallant but frail barrier to the mighty Sulaimān. On 28 August 1526 at the bloody battle of Mohács the

Turks slew the flower of the nation, including its young king. And while Archduke Ferdinand succeeded as heir to Lewis, he was able to occupy only a narrow section of Hungary to the east of Vienna. Even in Italy the position of Charles and his allies deteriorated. The Florentines made a last noble effort to retrieve their ancient liberties, expelling the Medici and setting up in May 1527 another republic. In the same month the Emperor's army in Italy ran amok and sacked Rome amid every conceivable barbarity and horror. Charles might disclaim responsibility for this appalling event, but his protestations sounded hollow since he utilized it in order to drag a reluctant Papacy, including its spiritual powers, into the service of the Habsburgs. Finally in 1528 a French army under Lautrec passed down Italy amid the general confusion and pressed back the Imperialists to Naples. Thus within three years the fruits of Pavia, ostensibly one of the most decisive battles of the age, seemed to have been wholly squandered.

The succeeding episodes are among the many which explain why writers and artists of that period so often refer to the inscrutable goddess *Fortuna,* to the uncontrollable turn of her fateful wheel. From the summer of 1528 the affairs of Italy suddenly began to run in favor of Charles. The position of Lautrec around Naples depended upon supplies transported thither by the fleet of Genoa, but Francis foolishly quarreled with the Genoese magnate and admiral Andrea Doria, who not only abandoned Lautrec but drove the French from Genoa itself. Beset by the plague, the French were worsted in August 1528 at Aversa near Naples, and later on at Landriano near Milan. They hence withdrew to the western confines of the Milanese and hostilities subsided.

Henry VIII had meanwhile taken little part in the war, but his personal affairs had become intimately dependent on its result. Desperately needing the male heir which his ageing Queen could not supply, he embarked upon his suit in Rome for a decree of nullity. Under normal circumstances he would doubtless have gained one, for he had quite a strong legal case grounded upon the invalidity of the dispensation by which Julius II had allowed Henry and Katherine of Aragon to marry, despite the latter's earlier marriage to Henry's brother Arthur. And with justice Henry could argue that several sovereigns with weaker cases had been similarly favored by the Papacy during recent times. On the other hand his plea reached Rome at the moment when the Emperor Charles, who happened to be a nephew of Katherine, was establishing full mastery over Clement VII. By the Treaty of Barcelona in June 1529 Clement promised to invest Charles with the realm of Naples and to crown him Emperor, while Charles undertook to restore papal territories lost to Venice and Ferrara, and also to establish the Medici once again in Florence. He also dropped his demands for a General Council to reform Church and Papacy. Soon afterwards Clement responded by revoking the commission granted to Cardinals Wolsey and Campeggio to try the divorce suit of Henry VIII. Thus powerless to manipulate Roman jurisdiction, Wolsey fell from office. Before many years had passed the hegemony of Charles V over Italy was thus to occasion the English Schism— ironically enough, since Henry VIII had not the faintest desire to encourage the spread of Protestantism in his kingdom.

Having recently challenged each other to personal combat, Francis and Charles were too proud to negotiate a treaty by direct contact. The Peace of Cambrai *(August 1529)* thus came to be concluded by two accomplished women: Margaret, regent of the Netherlands and aunt of the Emperor, and Louise of Savoy, the mother of Francis. This so-called "Ladies' Peace" left Francis with Burgundy and allowed him to ransom his sons. On the other hand, he surrendered all his claims in Italy as well as those to Artois and Flanders. He broke his pledge to stand by the Venetians, who soon disgorged their marginal conquests and joined Charles. The marriage arranged at Madrid between Francis and Charles's sister Eleanor was ratified, and it soon took place amid pious but ill-founded hopes that it would mark the end of the Habsburg-Valois feud. The Sforza returned to Milan, but under close Imperial tutelage. When the Florentine Republic gallantly refused to readmit the Medici even as private citizens, the old French alliance was dead. Strengthened by Michelangelo's fortifications, Florence bade a fine farewell to liberty by withstanding an eight months' siege; yet in the end she had a long line of Medici dukes imposed upon her.

Elsewhere, even in the tragic east, the affairs of the Emperor proceeded not unprosperously. The Turks had directly occupied central Hungary, leaving a Christian but anti-Habsburg prince in the great eastern province of Transylvania. When, however, Sulaimān sought to take Vienna he was driven off in October 1529 by a combined force containing both Catholic and Protestant Germans. As for Charles himself, having spent these momentous years in the relative calm of Spain, he came at last to Italy and was formally crowned Emperor by Clement VII at Bologna. The date was 23 February 1530, the anniversary of his birth in 1500 and also that of Pavia in 1525. This coronation may be regarded as the zenith of a long career beset by a multitude of trials and disappointments. Even so, it marked no definitive triumph: and its sequels soon displayed the harsh limitations placed by the European state system upon the resplendent but insubstantial dream of Gattinara.

4. Art and Letters in Italy

The term "High Renaissance" has arisen chiefly by reference to the great painters and sculptors of the first three or four decades of the sixteenth century. For most educated observers this is first and foremost the age of Leonardo, Michelangelo, and Raphael, the age of Titian, Giorgione, and Correggio, while north of the Alps it is the age of Dürer and Holbein.

When one compares the mature works of such artists with those of the *Quattrocento,* there can remain no doubt that theirs is the high summer of art. Our individual tastes may perhaps incline to the early spring of the fourteenth century, or to the late spring of Donatello's Florence, yet we could not possibly confuse the sequence of the seasons. Or to change the metaphor, one may admire the athletics of a climber on the flanks of a mountain, yet one cannot mistake them for the triumphant signal of a man standing upon the summit. By 1500 if not earlier, the spirit of ancient art and literature had been fully assimilated and subordinated to creative action, the new advances in perspective and anatomy mastered not only by innovators but by the host of professionals. Harmony, balance, proportion, confidence: these are the keynotes of the High Renaissance. Of course there remain tensions—in the case of Michelangelo overt, heroic, and tragic tensions—yet they are no longer those of the artist locked in conflict with his media and techniques. The tensions concern ideas and emotions; they occur within the artist's intellectual and spiritual world. The artist is a being of spirit who has transcended the technician and has broken free from ecclesiastical lawgivers. Whether or not he is a mathematician or expert in literary scholarship, the artist is an educated man; he assumes the right to probe the secrets of the universe, to follow the byways of history and mythology, to explore all the properties of the human body and the human spirit.

These exalted roles did not fail to reflect upon the social status of the artist. Among the neo-feudal aristocracies of northern Europe attitudes altered very slowly; even in Italy courtiers might doubt whether a gentleman should personally practice the arts, while a humanist could along with Aristotle dispute the contribution of the plastic arts to a liberal education. Nevertheless in Italy the greatest artists were now revered as semi-divine beings. Michelangelo could be rude to popes with impunity; Leonardo died in the arms of Francis I; the Emperor gladly stooped to pick up the brush of Titian. As for the many small Italian courts, they needed all the prestige they could buy. Patronage had its quirks and failures, yet rulers vied with one another to attract the famous names in both arts and letters. It has sometimes been argued that the steady drift toward despotism deprived the artist of his roots in an independent urban community, and that the corrupt princely courts cannot have provided nearly so healthy a setting. Yet if these charges did so affect art and learning—a contention by no means easy to substantiate—they were not especially characteristic of the High Renaissance decades. The autocrat-patron and the court-artist were common phenomena from the fourteenth century to the seventeenth. Mannerist and Baroque Europe, covering the two centuries after 1530, provided the most characteristic era of princely patronage, and this too proved a time of phenomenal achievement in the arts. Perhaps the modern craving for civic roots largely misrepresents the relation between artist and patron; certainly it reflects the nostalgic preoccupation of art historians with early *Quattro-cento* Florence. Yet in fact, Florence did throw off the Medici and became a real republic for the first half of the High Renaissance period. As for Venice, she remained a republic throughout the whole of those centuries, yet no art could have been more grandiose, or have gloried more boldly in the State, than the art within the Doges' Palace.

Far more meaningful than any contrast between civic and courtly art is the migration of the leadership from Florence to the Rome of Julius II and the two Medici popes. Not satisfied merely to strengthen the Papal States, the popes henceforth created a court and a monumental metropolis which would be a magnet to the whole Christian world and dwarf those of the richest prince in Europe. While this triumphalism became impressive in the High Renaissance, it was to culminate in the Baroque splendors achieved a century later by Bernini and his team. From the first the Papacy paid heavily for these successes: the fund-raising methods allowed by Leo X to create the new St. Peter's led to the revolt of Martin Luther. Yet who would now see a single building or painting of this Rome destroyed? Which of us remains so puritanical as not to suspend, at least while in Rome, our basic unbelief in the curious concept of Christianity which helped to produce these marvellous works? Even so, this is in no very deep sense ecclesiastical art. In Michelangelo it could enshrine some profoundly religious concepts, yet

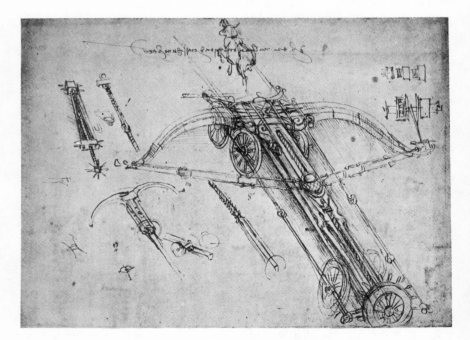

The notebooks of Leonardo contain many military inventions (such as the catapult above), expected of him by his princely patrons. (Ambrosiana, Milan)

nowhere was its expression bounded by old iconographic traditions. It has shed the gothic era for grand, generous, heroic forms, deriving first and foremost from the secular art of the Ancient World.

Of the three dominant figures of High Renaissance art, Leonardo da Vinci *(1452-1519)* must also be placed among the forerunners of modern science. He came first in time, being 23 years older than Michelangelo and 31 years older than Raphael. A Tuscan by birth, he learned painting with Verrocchio, yet he speedily outgrew the routine of the workshop. His famous letter of 1483 offering his services to Lodovico Sforza dwells in lengthy detail upon his own expertise in every aspect of military engineering, and adds almost with an afterthought:

Leonardo was fascinated by bizarre faces and is said to have followed their owners in order to portray them. (Royal Library, Windsor)

> In time of peace, I believe I can give you as complete satisfaction as anyone else in the construction of buildings both public and private, and in conducting water from one place to another. I can further execute sculpture in marble, bronze or clay. Also in painting I can do as much as anyone else, whoever he may be.

In later years he served Cesare Borgia as military engineer in the Romagna, even though he pronounced warfare "a bestial mess." A student of flight and mechanical propulsion, he sketched the principles of the helicopter and the tank. He dissected over thirty corpses and became the best anatomist and embryologist of his day. A truly scientific contemplator of the world of nature, he parted company with humanism by refusing to make man the measure of all things. On the other hand his *Last Supper* displays the artist as meditative philosopher, the psychological drama being set forth with a depth of imagination worthy of a consummate novelist. Yet that same inventiveness and contempt for tradition led him to experiment with untested methods, as a result of which the picture has almost perished. Even his *Mona Lisa* remains a ghost of the original, while there survive unimpaired portraits by hundreds of humdrum artists faithful to the old recipes. A genius so incalculable became the despair of patrons, and Leonardo's intellect cannot be measured by his surviving works. To penetrate his spirit we must study his voluminous notebooks, full of brilliant deductions and bizarre fancies. These have been adequately explored only in our own age: indeed, a mind so uniquely original and versatile could have left no immediate successors with a comprehensive grasp of its achievements.

Michelangelo Buonarroti *(1475-1564)* was more truly a son of Medicean Florence. From the patronage of Lorenzo the Magnificent and the tutelage of the painter Ghirlandaio, he turned to sculpture under the influence of Donatello and of such ancient works as he could study in the Medici collection. In their superb confidence and staggering technical powers, his early pieces—especially the *Pietà* of 1498-1500 and the *David* of 1504—form the climax of the Florentine *Quattrocento,* while at the same time foreshadowing fresh advances. With the four figures in the New Sacristy of St. Lorenzo *(1521-33)* depicting Day and Night, Dawn and Dusk, he retains this profound anatomical insight while yet subordinating the human forms to a sublime essay in poetic Expressionism. Toward the end of his long career came that monument of resignation, the *Entombment Group* in the Cathedral of Florence. Meanwhile it was the mark of a great spirit to accept and overcome the novel challenges of an unreasonable patron. From 1508 until 1512 Michelangelo turned painter at the insistence of Julius II in order to decorate the ceiling of the Sistine Chapel, a task with physical demands which might have daunted a syndicate of painters, but one which he carried through by his own hand with designs of lavish complexity. As always, Michelangelo needed nothing but the human figure to express all his concepts and emotions, yet in some of this sculptural painting—as with the *Creation of Adam*—he could convey ideas impossible to embody in marble. Such a thought applies also to the grim, Dantesque *Last Judgment* on the east wall of the Sistine Chapel, a later work *(1535-41)* heralding the earnest, tragic, defensive outlook of the Counter Reformation. Indeed, if a spirit of optimism and affirmation are to be taken as characteristic of the High Renaissance, the mature Michelangelo could scarcely typify his age.

Dying Slave
MICHELANGELO
The Louvre, Paris

Yet the sense of sin, the doubt as to his own Justification, which are so pathetically reflected in his sonnets and letters, he never allowed to interrupt the tenor of a highly concentrated life, a life in notable contrast with the many-sided, tentative, experimental career of Leonardo. Yet Michelangelo also exemplified the "universal genius." In addition to the group of masterpieces in marble and fresco, he made striking contributions to the architecture of the High Renaissance, some of them eccentric and disturbing like the Laurentian Library in Florence, some decisive and triumphant like the dome and the rear elevations of St. Peter's.

Pietà (1554–64)
MICHELANGELO
Castello Sforzesco, Milan

In 1504 when both Michelangelo and Leonardo were working in Florence, there arrived from Umbria the gentle and courtly Raphael Sanzio *(1483–1520),* hitherto a pupil of Perugino, that painter of innumerable suave and accomplished altar pieces. To this sound but limited tradition Raphael now added a thoughtful apprenticeship to the great intellectual masters Leonardo and Michelangelo. Acutely sensitive to new ideas, he absorbed some of their strength and breadth, yet he retained a personal style and an inventiveness which delivered him from the perils of plagiarism. His madonnas and portraits have a most deceptive simplicity, an art which does not reveal itself to any rapid inspection. In the course of his brief career, he stood forth as the supreme decorator, the most brilliant creator of designs to fit spaces in the whole history of painting. These gifts were exercised to most remarkable effect in the *Stanze* or state-apartments of the Vatican, rooms of no outstanding grandeur and containing some of the most intransigent spaces ever offered to a decorative artist. He began work on the *Stanze* soon after his arrival in Rome in 1508, about the time when Michelangelo was embarking nearby upon the Sistine ceiling. Though the

Reading Room, the Laurentian Library
Michelangelo
S. Lorenzo, Florence

School of Athens
RAPHAEL
Stanza della Segnatura, the Vatican

total sequence affords in itself an overwhelming experience, the great individual masterpieces are in the *Stanza della Segnatura (1508-11),* which includes the *Disputà,* the *Parnassus,* and the *School of Athens,* and in the *Stanza d'Eliodoro (1512-14),* both almost wholly by Raphael's own hand. The *Stanza dell' Incendio (1517)* and the *Sala di Constantino* were painted by pupils after Raphael's designs, the latter after his death in 1520. A design equally perfect and masterly appears in the small fresco painted by Raphael about 1514 for the banker Agostino Chigi: *The Nymph Galatea* in the Villa Farnesina, Rome.

While these three great artists may be regarded as the heirs and perfectors of the long Florentine tradition, a very different tradition had developed with singular rapidity in later fifteenth-century Venice. Previously in that eastward-facing port, architecture, mosaic, and sculpture had progressed with much splendor, though to no small extent in the wake of Byzantium. Not far away in Ravenna there remained, and still remains, a magnificent range of classical Byzantine models. While there were no ancient monuments in Venice itself, the classical heritage was handed on by Florentine artists, especially through the nearby subject-city of Padua, where Donatello executed some of his finest works. Again, the austere and

Tempesta
GIORGIONE
Accademia, Venice

monumental Mantegna *(1431–1506)* painted in the Venetian territories. In 1454 he became brother-in-law to the first great Venetian painters, Gentile and Giovanni Bellini *(c. 1429–1507; ?1431–1516)*. The lengthy and ever-developing career of the latter laid the firm foundations of the Venetian school, which already tended to withdraw from sculpturesque Florentine concepts, relying rather upon light, shade, and resonant color in order to reveal form. With Giovanni's last works, such as *Feast of the Gods (1513)* and with the earlier paintings of his pupils Giorgione *(?1478–1510)* and Titian *(?1477–1576)*, the character of the Venetian school achieved full expression. Here is painting for a leisured mercantile aristocracy which delighted in elegant buildings, rich fabrics from the Orient, all the pleasures of both city life and the country villa. In temper Venetian art is poetic and sensuous rather than scientific and intellectual. An expansionist Senate, proudly resisting its many foes, furnished patronage upon a grand scale. It was ably seconded by the churches and by the *scuole,* those wealthy clubs and charitable associations which formed a characteristic feature of the Venetian scene.

In Venice the accidents of personal genius also played a notable role. The musical, dreamlike idylls of Giorgione attained a range of experience hitherto scarcely touched by painting: such an enigmatic work as *The Tempest* breaks completely with both the literary and the spatial formulae hitherto accepted by Italian painting. At the time of Giorgione's early death in 1510, Titian had scarcely emerged from his shadow, or indeed from that of Giovanni Bellini. Yet Titian shared Bellini's infinite capacity for self-development: he never stagnated throughout the next three-quarters of a century, and even in his nineties he was producing works of a profundity and wisdom which rivalled, in a different medium, those of the aged Michelangelo. A spirit less poetically refined than Giorgione, Titian showed a boundless imagination in organizing resplendent interactions of light and color. Whether sacred or profane, his men and women display that splendid animal exuberance which was to reappear in Rubens, a true follower and kindred spirit of the great Venetian. Unlike the Florentine giants Titian made no pretences to being a polymath. He was a painter; and no other, not even Rembrandt or Velasquez, ever handled oil paint with such mastery or pursued with greater zest its immense possibilities as a medium of expression. The work of Titian led directly to that of the other two major Venetians, Paolo Veronese *(1528-88)* and Jacopo Tintoretto *(1518-94).* The latter, beginning his career under the influences both of Titian and of Michelangelo, attained certain new approaches to design and color which we must reserve for discussion in the context of Mannerism.

In the field of architecture the High Renaissance attained the same qualities of technical mastery and intellectual balance. Like the sculptors and painters, the architect had to become in some measure a classical scholar: he needed not merely to copy classical detail but to follow the mathematical proportions of ancient architecture and to grasp its innermost spirit. He was expected both to measure ancient buildings and to become familiar with theoretical treatises like that of Julius Caesar's friend Vitruvius, the architectural lawgiver who already had modern imitators like Alberti, Francesco di Giorgio, and Filarete, and who was soon to have even more authoritative successors in Sebastiano Serlio *(d.1552)* and Andrea Palladio *(d.1580).* Under these conditions, and especially in the grandiose setting of Rome, architecture became monumental rather than functional. It tended to provide stage sets rather than living accommodation, and it could on occasion lose touch with the human scale and the needs of daily life.

The first great architect of the High Renaissance, Donato Bramante *(1444–1514)* was in fact at work in Milan before 1480. A friend of Leonardo da Vinci, he evidently derived from that ever-fertile mind a number of ideas, particularly those involving centrally-planned churches. When in 1499 Bramante went on to Rome, he entered upon a phase of "correct" classicism, shown in the Damasus Court of the Vatican *(1503),* in the cloister of S. Maria della Pace *(1504),* and above all in the famous little circular temple at S. Pietro in Montorio *(1502).* In 1506 Julius II commissioned Bramante to rebuild St. Peter's, where the old fourth-century basilica of Constantine substantially survived. With his usual temerity the Pope departed from medieval precedent by ordering a centrally-planned church, and thereupon Bramante supplied an intricate design based on a Greek cross, with four apses of equal length and a huge main dome flanked by minor domes and corner towers. The fate of this project throughout the next century luridly illustrates the special problems besetting architectural patronage. From the last year of Bramante's life St. Peter's was entrusted to successive groups of architects who differed from each other and proposed many alterations. After 1547 the building came under the direction of Michelangelo, who was able to rescue the essentials of Bramante's ground plan and to design the dome, the model of its kind for all time. Nevertheless when in 1606 the church stood complete except for the façade, Paul V reverted to the notion of a Latin cross, hence lengthening the nave and adding the present inferior façade by Carlo Maderna. While by any standards the interior remained both overwhelming and harmonious, the effect of the dome upon the approaching pilgrim was lost and Bramante's great concept distinctly impaired.

Elsewhere some lesser works, such as Raphael's Palazzo Vidoni Caffarelli in Rome and even his Villa Madama, were likewise exposed to irreverent alterations. But among the more perfect examples of the period are the simple and massive Palazzo del Tè, built at Mantua by Giulio Romano in 1525–35, and the Old Library of S. Marco at Venice, designed in 1536 by Jacopo Sansovino. The latter was developed with striking subtlety from the basic idea of the Roman Colosseum, its lower Doric order surmounted by an Ionic upper story. By the 1530s architecture was progressing alongside sculpture and painting toward what modern critics have agreed to call Mannerism, that profound modification of High Renaissance principles. So far a broad fidelity to the spirit and forms of the Ancient World had been the prevalent criterion, one still splendidly exemplified in 1530 by the Palazzo Farnese, the work of the younger Antonio da Sangallo. But five years later the Palazzo Massimi by Baldassare Peruzzi disregarded the rules of the ancients, and it stands replete with the strained elegances which mark Mannerist design. Here the world of Bramante is rapidly drawing to its close. It should nevertheless be recognized that these examples refer to the

situation at the most advanced center of European design. The average
Italian town did not keep pace with Rome, and as for the rest of Europe,
even palaces and great houses commonly remained medieval buildings with
a few superficially applied classical decorations. Meanwhile, lower down the
social scale, the burghers of Dürer's Nuremberg or the London merchants of
the reign of Henry VIII continued to build old-style timber-framed houses
which usually showed trivial or negligible concessions to classical motives,
still less to classical proportions or modes of construction.

Intelligibly enough, the arts including architecture still occupy in our
day the center of most educated appreciations of High Renaissance culture,
yet historians of society and politics need to devote at least equal attention
to the contemporary world of letters. Within this field it would seem
inevitable to begin with Niccolò Machiavelli *(1469–1527)*, whose eventful
career as Florentine diplomat and official has already engaged our notice.
Since within a few years of his death, when Cardinal Pole denounced him as
a satanic influence, he has perhaps attracted even more than his due share
of attention. His literary works were the fruit of his retirement, which
sprang from the overthrow of the Florentine Republic in 1512. In his own
lifetime the best-known were his talented dramatic pieces, among which the
gay and cynical *Mandragola* is still staged, and not only in Italy. His
historical and political writings, though unprinted in his own day, can be
dated with a fair degree of precision. Machiavelli was already writing *The
Prince* in 1513 and he dedicated it to the younger Lorenzo de' Medici three

*Niccolò Machiavelli, "Writer of
Histories"*
MANNER OF BRONZINO
Palazzo Doria, Rome

years later. The *Discourses upon the First Decade of Titus Livius,* usually called the *Discorsi,* were gradually compiled between 1513 and 1519. The *Art of War* dates from 1519-20, while the *Florentine History,* begun in 1520, remained incomplete on its author's death.

According to our modern ideals of accuracy and perspective Machiavelli can hardly be pronounced a great historian. The planning of his *Florentine History* has seemed to many readers untidy and inartistic. Moreover the book lacks any original research; it abounds in factual errors, some of them in a sense deliberate, since they plainly spring from his political prejudices. For example, he would seem to falsify the whole narrative of a battle in order to justify his view that mercenary troops were cowardly and unreliable. On the other hand there appear virtues proclaiming both the man and the age. The style is terse, graphic, pungent, and readable. The *Florentine History* tells more about the author's thinking than about the history of the city, since it grapples, sometimes most perceptively, with the great political and social issues which he had already raised in *The Prince* and the *Discorsi:* the historical roles of force and fraud, war and conspiracy, political acumen and mere fortune, corruption and *virtù.* This last word is essential to the understanding of Machiavelli and of the political thought of his period. Developed from the pagan Latin *virtus,* its content had leaned ever more strongly toward boldness, cunning, decisiveness, political virtuosity, as opposed to any mere amalgam of Christian virtues. Judged by New Testament standards, *The Prince* deserves much of the criticism directed against its author by Cardinal Pole and numerous later moralists—who significantly included Frederick the Great. That recent process which seeks to depict Machiavelli as a traduced and harmless humanist—or even a mere satirist—seems an obvious over-compensation and suggests that in recent years Machiavelli has needed to be protected chiefly against his friends.

Living in an age and a country distinguished by blatant political chicanery, Machiavelli did not merely discuss power as an end in itself; he also took an obvious delight in those crude ideas and shocking phrases which stripped politics of their hypocritical veneer: that a successful prince must "learn not to be good," that he must become a great deceiver and dissembler, that he "should not keep faith when by so doing it would be against his interest." Machiavelli's attacks upon Christianity are based not simply upon the commonplace hatred of the corrupt Church and Papacy but also upon a conviction that meekness and unselfishness remain foreign to egotistic human nature, and that in any case they do not pay in the affairs of this world. On the other hand, he should not be discussed as if he were a guarded and systematic thinker, since *The Prince* is closely related to a very different literary genre: the collection of pithy, provocative aphorisms well exemplified by Guicciardini's *Ricordi.* Moreover in its last chapter *The Prince* suddenly changes key, and on a note of prophetic idealism (midway between Petrarch and Mazzini!) it summons the Italian people to throw off the toils of foreign oppressors and find unity under the great ruler who shall emerge to deliver it from slavery. Often as he cites historical examples, one does not find in Machiavelli the objective mind which coolly and fairly seeks to deduce lessons from history. Only a little below the hard surfaces there hides a literary and poetic being, a mind deeply scarred by life and displaying a mass of passionate prejudices; a mind sick of cant and led to envisage heroic and radical solutions in order to extract his countrymen from an appalling predicament.

The chief anomaly of Machiavelli's political thought is apparent rather than real. In *The Prince* he studies the erection and preservation of autocracy; but in the roughly contemporaneous *Discorsi*, his observation of ancient Rome is primarily directed to discovering the means whereby constitutional republics can be preserved. To him both problems remain significant, given the appropriate circumstances. His admiration for the immoral despot Cesare Borgia did not preclude an even deeper admiration—one much more appropriate to a Florentine—for a successful and popular republic. Indeed, he stood prepared to admit that in some places—particularly in the German lands—the moral and psychological conditions for such republics still existed in his own day. In his official capacity he had briefly visited the Tyrol and Switzerland, and in 1508–12 had composed three accounts idealizing the free cities of the Empire as frugal, brave, devout, and honest communities. Such attitudes he continued to echo in *The Prince,* the *Discorsi,* the *Art of War,* and the *Florentine History.* In Italy he proposed to revive these civic virtues by means of citizen-militias, the basis of all healthy political life. We have already observed how Machiavelli had in fact created such a militia in Florence and how its cowardice had betrayed his hopes in 1512.

By the time Machiavelli came to write *The Prince* this dream of importing Germanic virtues into Italy had been dissipated by the harsh facts of contemporary history. Amid what he regarded as corrupted Italian communities, devoid of such basic virtues, there seemed now no inconsistency in falling back upon an alternative solution, in calling upon a figure already familiar to the ancient Greeks and Romans: the autocratic lawgiver, the forceful savior or restorer of society. If in 1513 this *deus ex machina* must of necessity fulfil his task by transgressing the normal laws of morality, the fact did not entail any relaxation of those laws for his subjects. On the contrary, the purpose of the hero's ruthlessness was to provide a basis for the restoration of the people to political and personal virtue. In the later twentieth century one need hardly moralize over the apparent fallacies underlying this solution, fallacies stressed for us by the sheer corruption actually fostered by modern dictatorships, most notably by that of Machiavelli's professed pupil Benito Mussolini. In addition it might be urged that

Machiavelli misread the signs of his own day, for Europe stood in fact on the eve of a resurgence of moralism, of a period when Calvin and Loyola exacted from even the worst of rulers all the customary tributes paid by vice to virtue.

Not a few of the attitudes of Machiavelli were shared by his younger friend Francesco Guicciardini *(1483–1540),* though fundamentally the latter's mind was of a different cast, his talents of a different order. Guicciardini came of an illustrious Florentine family: his backing and brains would almost certainly have led him to a cardinalate had not his father, revolted by ecclesiastical corruption, forbidden him to accept holy orders. Thenceforth winning distinction in the law courts, Guicciardini soon became a diplomat, his despatches rivalling those of Machiavelli in their powers of analysis. From the first his ambitious and calculating mind proved admirably suited to this environment. In 1515 he entered the service of Leo X, who appointed him governor of Reggio, Modena, and other papal territories. To these the second Medici pope Clement VII added the Romagna, together with the rank of Lieutenant General, making Guicciardini virtual ruler of all the papal territories across the Apennines. By 1531 he had become governor of Bologna, but on the election of Paul III he resigned his high office in order to continue in the service of the Florentine Medici, now represented since the overthrow of the last republic by the dissolute Duke Alessandro. On the murder of this tyrant, Guicciardini aspired to become all-powerful minister to his young heir Cosimo, but with striking independence the latter suddenly dismissed his mentor. Hereby Cosimo incurred the gratitude of posterity, since it was during the three years between this event and the death of Guicciardini that the latter composed his masterpiece, the *History of Italy.*

That this distinguished career could be pursued by one who detested the papacy and found Medici rule distasteful, throws a harsh light upon the man and the period. With the uttermost frankness, though not for immediate publication, Guicciardini wrote:

> Three things I would willingly see before I die: a well-ordered republic in my native Florence; the barbarian invaders driven from Italy; the world freed from the rascal priests.

And yet he spent his life in the service of the Medicean Papacy and the Medici autocracy in Florence, the latter itself established by the foreign invaders! A believer in patrician republics of the Venetian type, Guicciardini did not with Machiavelli dream of the unity of Italy. Though not wholly immune from Italian patriotism, he could hint that the multiplicity of states had a stimulating effect upon the Italian spirit. His violent anticlericalism could boast no doctrinal motives:

> I do not know a man more disgusted than I am at the ambition, the greed, the unmanliness of the priests. . . . yet the position I held under more than one pope has compelled me for my own interest to desire their aggrandisement. But for that, I should have loved Martin Luther as myself, not that I might throw off the laws laid down in the Christian religion as commonly interpreted and understood, but in order to see this gang of scoundrels brought within due bounds—that is, either rid of their vices or stripped of their authority.

His mind was clearer and more harmonious than that of Machiavelli. In his *History of Italy* we observe this sardonic and disillusioned observer analyzing the tragedy of the years 1494–1532 with a surgical detachment, following every quirk of egotism with an unflagging zeal. His scorn for popes and princes is not counterbalanced by any trace of admiration for the long-suffering Italian people:

> Who says *people,* says in truth a foolish animal, full of a thousand errors, a thousand confusions, without taste, without discernment, without stability.

Most of such aphorisms derive from his famous anthology the *Ricordi Politici,* but similar opinions occasionally emerge amid the calm flow of the *History of Italy.* Despite a certain lack of proportion which tends to treat a small theme as fully as a major one, despite a lack of feeling for external phenomena like Luther's Reformation, Guicciardini here achieved one of the supreme monuments of the historian's craft. Upon its twenty books of narrative his fame depended almost entirely until the mid-nineteenth century, when his descendants made public a number of his manuscripts, including an able *History of Florence (1509)* which covers the period 1434–1505 and thus complements that of Machiavelli. It might well be claimed that Guicciardini's writings throw a far clearer light upon High Renaissance Italy than do those of the other great Florentine politician.

To secure a balanced grasp of this period we should recall a third and very different writer, Baldesar Castiglione *(1478–1529).* An accomplished gentleman who spent his happiest days in the service of Guidobaldo, duke of Urbino, Castiglione later became papal nuncio to Spain, where he died. Like Machiavelli and Guicciardini, he moved among great events: he saw Cesare Borgia win the friendship of Louis XII and Pope Leo actually reading Martin Luther; he worked at the excavations of ancient Rome by the side of his friend Raphael; and his epitaph was pronounced by the Emperor Charles V, "I tell you, one of the finest gentlemen in the world has died." Among the many brave spirits whose integrity emerged unscathed from the very center of the whirlwind, Castiglione stands preëminent. His famous portrait by Raphael now in the Louvre reveals the complete man, the model of equilibrium. "I am not surprised," wrote the famous bluestocking Vittoria

Baldesar Castiglione
RAPHAEL
The Louvre, Paris

Colonna, "that you have depicted a perfect courtier, for you have only to hold a mirror before you, and say what you see."

The Book of the Courtier sprang from a charming place as well as from the mind of an estimable man. Since the days of the famous *condottiere* Duke Federigo *(d.1482),* the court of the Montefeltri had attracted many admirers to its great twin-towered palace at Urbino, the center of a little state where the Apennines slope down to the Adriatic. Here Federigo, pupil of Vittorino da Feltre and employer of the biographer and book collector Vespasiano da Bisticci *(d.1498),* had created a library which he called the jewel of his crown. His son Guidobaldo *(d.1508)* spoke Greek like his native tongue, but he lived in harsher times and was excluded from his duchy for a time by Cesare Borgia. A martyr to the gout, he always retired at an early hour, leaving his court society to be governed by his duchess Elisabetta *(née* Gonzaga), who was venerated as a paragon of excellence by all who knew her. In March 1507 Pope Julius, having crushed his rebellious city of Bologna, returned to Rome through Urbino, and a number of his courtiers, charmed by the amenities of the place, lingered awhile behind. During four evenings the assembled company played a conversational game under the chairmanship of the Duchess's lady Emilia Pia: they discussed all the qualities and accomplishments, mental and physical, which went to the making of the perfect courtier. Later on Castiglione wrote up these conversations in choice but liberal Tuscan, doubtless embellishing and purifying them to no small extent. Twenty years later he published the book with

Aldus Manutius, sadly musing on the vanished scenes and companions it recalled. During the next half century it ran into scores of editions and was translated into the chief European languages. In Hoby's famous translation it dominated the minds of Elizabethan Englishmen and its presence is often felt in the works of Shakespeare. Even in the eighteenth century Dr. Samuel Johnson was still prescribing it as "the best book ever written on good breeding." Itself indebted to the Italian educators of the *Quattrocento,* it stimulated in its turn a fresh crop of courtesy books. The proverbial *Galateo* (published *1558*) by Giovanni della Casa is perhaps the most interesting of these, since it was written for the middle-class citizen rather than for the courtly aristocrat.

Ever a delight to read, *The Book of the Courtier* forms its own literary justification, and its lovers are apt to dismiss with impatience the attacks of those social historians who dislike the aristocratic tenor of early modern Europe. It does indeed accept without question gross inequalities based upon birth, and it fails to see beyond the horizons of a small *élite*. It is also pervaded by a certain unreality, since it ignores moral evil, and since it stands apart both from the grim political struggle and from the sturdy tradition of the artist-craftsman. With solemnity it discusses whether a gentleman should practice the arts, and again—in terms of an almost scholastic vacuity—whether sculpture or painting is the greater art. Many of its attractive passages prove on examination to be unoriginal, being adapted from Cicero's work *On the Orator* or from other classical sources. Needless to add, the wonderful concluding speech on Platonic love, placed in the mouth of Cardinal Bembo, is a popularization of Ficino and the still fashionable cult of neo-Platonism. Equally significant for social historians are the real-life stories of Castiglione's speakers: men like Bembo, Bibbiena, Francesco della Rovere, Giuliano de' Medici, and several lesser-known speakers, who may have uttered all these high-minded sentiments, yet who in fact committed between them all the sins and crimes in the Decalogue.

These things said, *The Book of the Courtier* remains something more than a literary fairyland, since it played its part in the modification of European society. It sought to remove crabbed pedantry and pretentious affectation from cultured living. In all the accomplishments of the courtier it demanded a certain *sprezzatura,* a "disdainful" ease, the relaxed art which conceals all the laborious practice. Again, not only did it put a woman in the chair; it devoted due space to the female courtier and raised the cultured lady to a place of equality. It brought to completion the work of the old courtesy books and the humanist educators in the concept of the gentleman, a concept which travelled well, and with all its grave limitations did useful service in the evolution of Western social ideals. On the whole the early modern gentleman seems rather less of a disembodied ideal than the medieval knight. No longer a licensed rebel, he proved assiduous in service to his prince or state. He was no mere hereditary grandee, no mere master of serfs, not even a beer-swilling warrior armed with a few perfunctory Christian superstitions. He had now to excel in his own right; he had to qualify not merely on the field but in the arts of peace, in taste and gentle manners. He was destined to extend his range of social obligations, which would one day involve the general amelioration of society. More important, the concept of the gentleman tended from the first to disrupt the rigid strata of society, for already in the sixteenth century it was being extended downward into the nonpatrician middle classes of the Italian cities. All in all this book and its many imitators have an honorable place in history, and for the social historian they supply a pleasant corrective to the somber works of the great political realists.

Needless to add, Machiavelli, Guicciardini, and Castiglione were by no means the only important Italian men of letters to flourish in the earlier sixteenth century. A historian of literature would certainly need to place alongside them at least one poet of the first rank, Lodovico Ariosto *(1474-1533),* a noble and independent spirit treated with remarkable meanness by his employers Cardinal Ippolito d'Este and the latter's brother, Alphonso duke of Ferrara. The *Orlando Furioso,* a narrative of outstanding vivacity, humor and imagination, maintains an easy superiority over the innumerable other romances of its period. Sometimes it can strike a note of genuine gravity, as when it refers to the plundering of Italy by foreign armies, but in the main it preserves a bland detachment akin to that we have observed in Castiglione. Ariosto's readers, the ladies and gentlemen, the literate citizenry, wanted diversion from the dark and problematic aspects of their age. Judging by this type of literature, their attitudes must have been secular and—beyond a chuckle over priestly sins—little concerned with the crisis facing the Church. As an Italian critic has said of Ariosto's readers: "they are obviously not very distant relatives of the characters of Boccaccio and Sacchetti, of Bandello *(d.1561),* the great storywriter of the *Cinquecento."*

Meanwhile Latin verse continued to develop an independence and imagination far exceeding any mere mimicry of the ancient classics: no finer Latin poetry has been written in modern times than that of Jacopo Sanazzaro *(d.1530),* Marcantonio Flaminio *(d.1550),* and Girolamo Fracastoro *(d.1553).* By contrast two brilliant rascals enliven the literary scene: Benvenuto Cellini *(1500-71)* goldsmith and imaginative autobiographer, and Pietro Aretino *(1492-1556),* a satirist abrasive, ruthless, and often obscene, called all too presciently by Burckhardt "the father of modern journalism." In addition there flourished a host of historical and biographical writers, among whom perhaps the most valuable in modern days is Giorgio Vasari *(d.1574),* without whose lives of the painters our knowledge of the men behind the great works of art would remain sadly deficient.

5. Humanism in Northern Europe

When and how did humanism cross the Alps and take root outside Italy? In the main, were the French, German, and English humanists mere followers, even copyists? On the other hand, can we observe independent, native movements arising in such countries? And when Italian humanism was exported elsewhere, did local conditions change its basic character? Such questions naturally spring to our minds, but most of them cannot be answered in simple terms. Some historians have regarded northern humanism as a more or less skilful process of adaptation and mimicry. At the other extreme, some have systematically minimized the debt of other nations to Italy, and (with a touch of cultural chauvinism) have envisaged new types of humanism spontaneously generated by the medieval cultures of the northern peoples. Of these two crude concepts, the latter seems to the present writer the more perilous. It has sometimes been based upon definitions of humanism so loose as to deprive the term of any historical significance. For example, there was a strong movement in the chancery of Emperor Charles IV *(r.1346–78)* to improve both Latin and German style, but those who tried to inflate this concern into an independent Bohemian humanism must have forgotten that such modest developments had occurred at various times and places throughout the central Middle Ages. Genuine humanism involved something more. It can best be defined in terms of creative classical studies and in terms of their outcome: a new outlook which made man the centerpoint and the measure of the universe. Even the enthusiastic study of ancient authors does not in itself constitute humanism. A better criterion would lie in the question whether, like most medieval students of the classics, a scholar regarded a classical text as a source of factual information, or whether with the humanists he understood it as a work of art and so assimilated its aesthetic and stylistic inspiration.

Using such exacting standards, it would be hard to name any non-Italian writer working before 1500 who advanced any aspect of humanism beyond his Italian masters. In this chapter, we shall describe the biblical humanist studies characteristic of northern Europe, yet even this movement had its precursors south of the Alps: in Valla's *Annotations on the New Testament (c.1444,* printed by Erasmus in *1505),* in Pico's *Heptaplus (1489,* a commentary on *Genesis),* and several other Italian works. And broadly speaking Italian scholarship continued more sophisticated and productive than that of northern Europe for several decades after 1500. Yet back in the fifteenth century humanism was far from extending across all the fields of achievement; it should not be equated with culture. Outside Italy numerous universities were being founded; Jan van Eyck and Hans Memling painted magnificent pictures; François Villon wrote great poetry; the *devotio moderna* flourished in the Netherlands and the Rhineland. These and many

A scanning device with which Albrecht Dürer mechanically simplified the task of reproducing an image. His model appeared through a vertical construction, her anatomical parts falling into certain of the indicated squares. Dürer's drawing sheet, divided into similar squares, matched what he saw through this device. Drawn by the artist.

other northern activities were partially or wholly independent of humanist concepts and Italian models. More important to our present purpose, the marriage of Italian humanism with the more conscience-stricken and less secular minds of the northern Europeans culminated in the birth of a hybrid usually called Christian humanism. This could boast a balance of interests and qualities different from that of the Italian *Quattrocento.*

To this situation there are obvious parallels in northern, and especially in German, art history. During the early decades of the sixteenth century there lived two German artists of surpassing stature. The mysterious painter of the Isenheim Altarpiece *(1509-11),* once called Grünewald but now thought to have been Mathis Nithardt *(d.1528),* continued to paint in gothic forms descended from those of the Flemings, and oblivious both to Italy and to the Ancient World. The other was of course Albrecht Dürer *(1471-1528),* from the first a master of line and a meticulous observer of nature; then, greeted in Venice by the aged Bellini, mastering such aspects of Italian art as he could assimilate without sacrificing his individualism and his northern independence. Their techniques apart, both Nithardt and Dürer remained men of their age and country; in modern jargon they were existentialists well aware that they stood on the edge of cataclysm. Like their more mundane contemporaries Hans Holbein *(1497-1543)* and Lucas Cranach *(1472-1553)* they accepted the Protestant Reformation when it came, but Dürer remains a tolerable equivalent of Christian humanism. His *Four Apostles* could serve as a symbol either of that movement or else of the Protestant Reformers setting forth to preach the Gospel.

A century before the time of Dürer and Erasmus, a few northerners had begun to show an intelligent interest in Italian cultural values. The French cleric Jean de Monstereul, who perished in 1418 during the massacre of Armagnacs in Paris, was a friend of Bruni and Niccoli, a worshipper of Cicero, Petrarch, and Salutati: he was the first to bring back to France manuscripts of Plautus, Vitruvius, Cato, Varro, and other ancient authors. In 1444 Aeneas Sylvius, later Pius II, praised Humphrey duke of Gloucester *(d.1447)* for introducing polite learning and fine Latin style into England. In founding at Oxford what later became known as the Bodleian Library, Duke Humphrey had in fact presented it with the writings of Dante, Petrarch, and Boccaccio, together with many classical manuscripts discovered by Italian scholars. Humphrey's protégé Thomas Beckynton, bishop of Wells *(c.1390–1465)* corresponded with several Italian humanists and headed a circle of like-minded Englishmen, several of whom left Oxford to spend long periods of study in Italy, including that of the Greek classics. Alongside these travellers went *(c.1457–60)* John Tiptoft, Earl of Worcester, who polished his Latin in Padua, translated Cicero and Caesar, visited Guarino in Ferrara and Vespasiano in Florence. In Rome Tiptoft delivered a Latin oration before Pius II which caused the latter to weep with joy at hearing such eloquence flow from the lips of an Englishman. Tiptoft was an authoritarian, credited with the desire to replace the English Common Law by Roman Law. He also figured as a commander of exceptional cruelty in the Wars of the Roses, richly meriting his execution by Lancastrian enemies in 1470. He was among the first to live up to that later proverb which conjoined the terms *inglese italianato* and *diavolo incarnato*.

A number of mid-fifteenth-century Englishmen were pupils of Guarino, including Robert Flemmyng, John Free, and John Gunthorpe; in addition William Sellyng, prior of Christ Church Canterbury, left evidence of advanced proficiency in both Greek and Latin scholarship. But apart from Gloucester and Tiptoft, nearly all the earliest English humanists were clerics who served as officials in Church and State, in particular as diplomats. Originally educated in scholastic philosophy and theology, they tended to value Greek studies less as an end in themselves than as aids to these older disciplines. Moreover they lived in a world where elegant Latin was greatly valued in official business and had become a passport to promotion in the service of kings and prelates. Oxford and Cambridge, indeed all Europe, suffered from a lack of endowed lectureships to provide for humanist teaching. In this somewhat utilitarian and clerical atmosphere there were obvious limits to the depth and the originality of humanist studies. Even so, these modest figures were true forerunners of the three major English humanists active before the end of the century: Grocyn, Colet, and Linacre.

In both France and Germany early humanism shows some parallel features, though the bureaucratic atmosphere seems less generally apparent. In 1456 the wandering scholar Peter Luder appeared in Heidelberg and announced that he would lecture publicly "on the *studia humanitatis,* that is to say, the works of the poets, orators and historians." In that same year Gregorio of Citta di Castello came to live in France and taught Greek in the university of Paris. Though his stay proved short, he instructed Robert Gaguin, who in due course led the Parisian humanist group of the 1470s. By 1473 the young Reuchlin had also arrived in Paris and learned Greek from other pupils of Gregorio. During these decades French patronage and scholarship still suffered from the results of warfare and disorder. For a time the most lively center lay not in Paris but at the great commercial and banking city of Lyons. In this tolerant cosmopolis many hundreds of Italian businessmen rubbed shoulders with northerners of all nations, while numerous German printers already labored there in the service of scholarship.

Of German humanism Rudolf Agricola *(1443-85)* is usually regarded as the founding father. Of Dutch birth, educated at Groningen under the influence of the Brethren of the Common Life, he first graduated at Erfurt around the age of fifteen. After further study at Louvain and Cologne, he spent no less than ten years in Italy, where he soon turned from law to classical studies, wrote a life of Petrarch, and became a disciple of Guarino. On his return he composed an influential tract on the humanist educational program, within which he assigned an important role to the Scriptures. More famous still became his textbook on logic, which sought to purge that subject of its scholastic framework and to make it the basis of grammar and rhetoric. Agricola followed the Italians in stressing these latter as practical subjects essential to all public life. Again like so many of the Italians, Agricola was a versatile scholar with an insatiable curiosity. A practical musician and with strong interests in the natural sciences, he also wrote a complete epitome of ancient history, subsequently lost. At the time of his early death he was learning Hebrew and planning to deepen his theological knowledge. Agricola set the tone of northern humanism by remaining a pious Christian; and the notion that he became a militant critic of the Church seems to be a wishful Protestant legend of later days.

During the reign of Emperor Maximilian I *(1493-1519)* a remarkable group of professional scholars gave German humanism those special characteristics which enabled it to make its mark upon the history of the nation. Despite some common features, these men formed a highly varied group, the older generation conservative, the younger containing pious and rebellious spirits, both capable of joining Martin Luther's revolt. Jacob Wimpfeling *(1450-1528)* was a cautious and earnest moralist, a cathedral preacher who liked to attack monks and to envisage moderate reform of the Church. Another such was Conrad Muth (Mutianus, *1471-1526)*, educated by the Brethren of the Common Life, and after his Italian travels a canon of Gotha, where he headed the most influential humanist circle in northern Germany. Some of his later followers were Luther's friends in the neighboring university of Erfurt. A neo-Platonist, Mutianus was the author of a moralistic view of Pauline Christianity, a view remote from that ultimately propounded by Luther. Another and less typical figure was Willibald Pirckheimer *(1470-1530)*, a wealthy Nuremberg patrician who studied for seven years in Italy and boasted in 1504 that he owned a copy of every Greek book published there. In later years a heavy-faced but gay widower with several mistresses and bastards, he entertained or corresponded with a host of great men, from Dürer to Erasmus, from Pico della Mirandola to Zwingli. Conrad Celtis *(1459-1508)* showed an even more deeply secular spirit, wrote erotic poetry of a frank and physical character, and died of syphilis, that scourge which had in all probability arrived from the New World.

Another victim of this disease was the anticlerical satirist Ulrich von Hutten *(1488-1523)*, the aristocrat who did so much to stir up the revolt of the German Knights in 1522. His friend, a former fellow student of Luther, was Crotus Rubeanus, author of that extremely effective satire, the *Letters of Obscure Men (1515)*. Written in deliberately vile Latin and inspired by the most obscurantist and ignorant sentiments, the letters purport to be exchanged by the clerical opponents of the older humanist Johann Reuchlin *(1455-1522)*. Both amusing and devastating, they were followed two years later by a more bitter and less attractive series, written by Ulrich von Hutten. The Reuchlin affair not only proved a climax of liberal humanism but created a link between that movement and Luther's Reformation, which many humanists at first imagined to be an offshoot of the struggle between the Dominicans and the great hebraist. In 1506 Reuchlin had published his famous work *On the Rudiments of Hebrew,* establishing that language as an essential tool of Christian theology. Within the next three years he clashed with the converted Jew Johann Pfefferkorn, who with some encouragement from the Emperor and much more from the Cologne Dominicans headed by the Rhineland Inquisitor Hochstraten, wanted to destroy all copies of the whole Jewish literature apart from the Bible. By 1512-13 the hitherto mild Reuchlin was castigating his opponents in the most violent terms, and two years later the *Letters of Obscure Men* saw the humanists and the reactionaries locked in deadly conflict. Unjustly condemned as heretical by the theological faculties of Paris, Cologne, Louvain, Erfurt, and Mainz, Reuchlin nevertheless had powerful friends. Refusing to march either with the obscurantists or with Luther, he died in his bed as the struggle rose to its climax. That the case had gone against him in Rome harmed the Papacy far more than the German humanists. By this time Rome had a genuine German heresiarch on its hands!

Classical studies apart, what links bound all these German humanists together? Despite the secular temperament of men like Celtis and Hutten, the total pagan content of the movement seems even smaller than that of Italian humanism. Like the other northerners, the Germans were actively concerned for the renovation of Christianity and their concern did not merely involve the disciplining of immoral priests or the restraint of clerical money-raising. They sought to apply new emphases in religion to the inner lives of all the social classes—new emphases beginning with Greek and Hebrew studies but ending in a Christianity based on the progressive elucidation of the Scriptures. In their aspirations, many streams of influence came together: German mysticism and the *devotio moderna,* Ficino and the Platonist interpretation of Christianity, Italian classical philology and even Jewish theosophy. This complex of ideas carried through the early decades of the sixteenth century and mingled with Luther's movement. But most significantly for the Reformation, German humanism had always contained a strong element of nationalism. It vaunted the triumphs of German arms and letters in opposition not merely to ancient Rome but also to the supercilious claims of modern Italians to be owners of a higher culture. In the face of those papal exactions which fell so heavily upon the Germans, anti-Italian sentiment could readily become anti-papal sentiment, an emotion already having some popular backing unconnected with humanism.

In more positive mood, the German humanists searched the archives for evidences of the German past. They published the sources for the early and medieval history of their nation: the *Nibelungenlied,* Otto of Freising, Einhard, and the plays of Hroswitha. They made the newly discovered *Germania* of Tacitus do heavy service on behalf of the antiquity and courage of the Germans. Johannes Nauclerus *(d.1510)* even envisaged the latter as the master-race of Europe, one which had long ago injected its vigor into the effete peoples of the late Roman Empire. Humanist chauvinism contained for a time one factor which in some measure counteracted its antipapal tendencies. Fifteenth-century Germans hated the Hussites, though less on religious grounds than in return for the appalling defeats suffered by German armies in the anti-Hussite crusades. Celtis, Wimpfeling, Trithemius, and others wrote attacks upon the Bohemians. More important, during the early decades of the sixteenth century every German humanist was bound to experience a love–hate relationship with Italy, while the obscurantism of the Dominicans and the greed of the Roman curia all helped to disseminate the prejudices so militantly expressed by Ulrich von Hutten. Until Luther spoke, the German humanists did not fully understand the implications of these prejudices, but in fact they had been laying the mental foundations both for a Scriptural, nonhierarchical religion and for a mass rejection of Rome.

The English contemporaries of the older German humanists were William Grocyn *(c.1446–1519),* Thomas Linacre *(c.1460–1524),* and John Colet *(c.1467–1519),* all three Oxford men who worked in Italy, championed Greek literature with enthusiasm, and befriended Erasmus. Grocyn studied under Poliziano and Chalcondyles from 1488 to 1490, and subsequently obtained widespread recognition as the leading English classicist of his day. It was said with some truth that after his return to Oxford, his countrymen needed no longer to visit Italy in order to learn Greek. Linacre spent the years 1486–92 in Italy and took a medical degree at Padua while ardently pursuing Greek studies. In later years he continued to follow both lines, being at once Henry VIII's physician and tutor to his daughter, the princess

Mary. Thus highly influential, Linacre regularized the practice of medicine in England by causing the King to found the Royal College of Physicians. He himself established chairs of medicine, wrote both grammatical and medical works, and translated Galen. Colet may be regarded as a figure of even greater historical interest. On his return from Italy in 1496 he delivered at Oxford an epoch-making course of lectures on Pauline Epistles. Here, long before Erasmus, Colet argued the case for a historically-minded Christianity based upon a close study of the Greek New Testament, applying humanist critiques to the Bible as boldly as to a text of Livy or Thucydides. Inevitably he attracted the dislike of those who venerated the Vulgate—and the quiet admiration of the Lollard heretics. A Platonist, he rejected not merely Aquinas and the schoolmen but the whole medieval tradition based on the thought of men trained as Roman lawyers: Tertullian, Cyprian, Augustine, and Gregory the Great. He anticipated Luther in denying that the priest-hood could absolve from sin, and he regarded the eucharist as a commemo-ration rather than a sacrifice. Colet inspired the biblical humanism of Erasmus and in addition more radical ideas. Certain of the early English Protestants, like his pupil Tyndale and his friend Latimer, doubtless derived some of their starting points from Colet as well as from Luther. Had he lived longer the charges of heresy might well have proliferated and become official. As it was, his partial immunity owed much to the fact that he had become a dignitary and benefactor. In 1504 he was appointed Dean of St. Paul's Cathedral in London, where his father (who died in that same year) was a rich mercer and twice lord mayor. Using the paternal fortune, Colet then founded St. Paul's School. Here boys were taught Greek as well as Latin, while Colet's thoughtful school regulations (which placed the school in lay hands) provided the chief model for the innumerable grammar schools founded in Tudor England.

The younger contemporary and friend of these men was Thomas More *(1478–1535)*, who inherited the classical tradition they had established at Oxford, and whose Latin novel *Utopia (1516)* asked one of the most searching questions suggested by Christian humanism. If these imaginary Utopians, acting in ignorance of Christ and led purely by the light of reason, were capable of such virtues, such excellent social organization, then how could it happen that Europe, enjoying the inestimable boon of the Christian Gospel, had to groan under the burdens of war, disease, crime, and misgovernment? In his own distinguished official career More hardly envis-aged the radical answers, since after years of close personal service to Henry VIII he became Lord Chancellor and a pillar of the establishment in Church and State. The fact that a Christian humanist had once asked this question did not necessarily make him a harbinger either of social radical-ism or of the Protestant Reformation. Not many years earlier, More had considered becoming a monk, and even now he wore a hair shirt and maintained monastic austerities in his personal life. In the early 1530s he was to figure as the chief English Catholic controversialist and to suffer a martyr's death rather than follow Henry VIII in withdrawing England from membership of the Roman Church.

With these versatile Englishmen the greatest of all the north European humanists stood for many years closely associated. The distinction of Desiderius Erasmus *(c.1466–1536)* lay in literary expression rather than in originality or depth of thought: more obviously than any of his northern compeers, he stood heir to many traditions already well developed. The illegitimate child of an obscure priest, he was fortunate to receive a good classical education in the school conducted at Deventer by the humanist Hegius under the Brethren of the Common Life. While Dutch was his mother tongue, he did not use it for literary purposes: he thought in Latin and he never appealed directly to the common people. His background left him little chance of a career except as an ecclesiastic, and in 1486 he reluctantly entered the house of Augustinian canons at Steyn. Six years later he was ordained priest, but at no time did he show signs of a monastic vocation. As for a pastoral calling, this ultimately grew in his mind, but it was directed not to a parish, or even a nation, but to the whole of Christendom.

The name of Erasmus became widely known in 1500 with the appearance of his *Adagia,* a collection of proverbs in Greek and Latin which he expanded in several later editions. Meanwhile, under the patronage of the Bishop of Cambrai he was permitted to leave his religious house, to study for some years in Paris and in 1499 to accompany his pupil Lord Mountjoy

Erasmus at Work
Quentin Matsys (a contemporary Netherlandish painter)
Galleria Corsini, Rome

to England, where Colet encouraged him in the study of the New Testament. In 1504 there appeared his *Enchiridion* or *Handbook of the Christian Soldier,* a gracious work of edification deriving not only from a direct study of New Testament Christianity but from both Platonism and the *devotio moderna.* It sought to foster a life of gentleness and love, one all too rare amid the nominal Christianity of laymen. The *Enchiridion* demanded far more than conventional piety. It discouraged not merely superstitious usages but self-seeking prayers for worldly success. By implication it disregarded the pompous hierarchy, the legalist officialdom, the mechanical observances, in favor of an inward religion of the heart. Upon the sacraments themselves it seemed to lay little stress, apart from their spiritual effects. The *Enchiridion* was followed two years later by the brilliant *Praise of Folly,* a series of homilies directed by Folly—herself a volatile, swift-changing character—against the stupidities of all classes of men and women. Erasmus did not fail to include crabbed scholars like himself, yet many readers must have drawn the harshest conclusions at the expense of worldly popes and hypocritical monks. On the other hand, with many a humorous twist the author also shows that a little folly makes the world go round; for what man or woman would marry and have a family if he rationally anticipated the pains and problems? And in the end a divine folly has saved the human race. "Christ himself became a fool when he was found in fashion as a man, that he might bring healing by the foolishness of the Cross."

Having paid a second visit to England in 1506, Erasmus went yet again in 1509 and this time he stayed for some six years. Having lived at first in More's household, he became through the influence of Bishop John Fisher a professor of Greek and theology at Cambridge. While there he completed his epoch-making edition of the Greek New Testament *(1516),* which contained his own translation into classical Latin. Though by modern standards the philological equipment of this edition shows many faults, it exercised from the first an enormous influence throughout Europe, and in due course it was to become a major weapon in the hands of the Protestant Reformers. Meanwhile the interest of Erasmus in direct propaganda had not ceased. By this time there circulated in manuscript an anonymous satire most damaging to papal prestige. Almost certainly it was the work of Erasmus, and its content is succinctly rendered by its title *Julius Exclusus* (printed *1518).* It takes the form of a dialogue at the gate of heaven between that bellicose pope and St. Peter. The damning facts of his career, elicited in light and amusing style, result in the exclusion of the confident and blustering pope. Meanwhile, with more delicate touches, with a marvellous gift for conveying human stupidity without directly attacking it, Erasmus was from this time flaying religious superstition and fraud in certain of his immensely studied *Familiar Colloquies.* He hated paganism, but equally he hated both antirational obscurantism and pharisaic religion. And more than any writer, he created an atmosphere within which the Church had to wither or else be reformed.

Having gone to Brussels in 1516 at the invitation of Emperor Charles V, Erasmus belatedly obtained papal permission releasing him from all obligations toward his religious Order. Henceforth, despite pressing invitations from various rulers, he continued to maintain his independence and his supranational status. From 1521 to 1529 he lived for the most part at Basle in the house of the famous publisher Froben. We shall shortly observe how and why he quarrelled with Luther, though during his later years his time was chiefly employed in editing for Froben the writings of the early Christian Fathers, his work ranging from the nine-volume Jerome of 1516–18 to the Chrysostom in 1530. Nevertheless after his death these ecclesiastical labors did not save him from condemnation by the Catholic Church of the Counter Reformation, which was to place his works upon the Index as those of a dangerous free-thinker, even a forerunner of the Protestant revolt. In strictly doctrinal terms it would have been difficult to convict him of heresy, but one has only to study his influence upon Reformers like Zwingli and Oecolampadius to see that he did much more than create a mere diffused atmosphere of criticism. Despite his strong fund of caution and conservatism, his feline regard for his own comfort, he deserves a place among the founding fathers of the tolerant, humane, and critical trends which foreshadowed both modern liberalism and ecumenism. His great contribution to the loosening of the bonds had been substantially made by the time of Luther's advent in 1517–18. At that point a gigantic question remained. Could Church and society be reformed by Erasmian propaganda, ironic, humorous, unheroic, international, and pacifist; or must any successful program be translated into new religious dogma and then receive the forceful backing of secular states?

In the same year as Erasmus there died Jacques Lefèvre d'Étaples (c.1455–1536), a figure in the history of Christian humanism worthy to be placed alongside those of Colet and Reuchlin. Indeed Lefèvre both anticipated and supported many of the more "advanced" positions of Erasmus, and with results not dissimilar for himself and his associates. Active among the Parisian humanists of the 1480s, he was in Italy from 1492 and mainly engaged in the study of Aristotle, though from a humanist rather than from a philosophical angle. Returning in 1507, he was appointed librarian in 1507 at the monastery of St. Germain-des-Près. Here he created a circle which aimed at the rebirth of Christianity through the study of the Bible, the Fathers, the mystics, even the recent Florentine Platonists. He urged that such study must develop through the examination of manuscripts and proceed along historical lines. Rejecting what they regarded as the arid intellectualism of the scholastics, Lefèvre and his friends took the early Fathers as their own point of departure, since they believed that the Fathers united the classical tradition with an authoritative role in interpreting the

Scriptures. In fact they exaggerated this role by attributing patristic works of the fifth and sixth centuries to the age of the Apostles. In 1512 Lefèvre published an edition of the Pauline Epistles which anticipated not only the Scriptural aspirations of Erasmus but also in considerable measure the stress which Luther was to place upon salvation through faith as opposed to good works and penances. Lefèvre thus shared responsibility with Colet and Erasmus for the plea that scholars should penetrate behind the official text of the Vulgate to the original Greek and Hebrew: it was a plea which clearly included an invitation to analyze, perhaps to redefine, words like *presbyteros, episcopos,* and *ekklesia,* to ask, for example, whether the Greek *metanoeite* should not be translated as "repent," instead of "do penance," as in the Vulgate. These were very far from being mere academic questions, for the possible answers were capable of redefining doctrine and revolutionizing the functions of the Church in society. In the end the attacks of Lefèvre upon saint worship, together with a widespread suspicion that he rejected transubstantiation, brought about the condemnation of his works by the conservative theological faculty of Paris. Withdrawing to Meaux, he and his followers remained there under the protection of his former pupil Bishop Briçonnet, and later under that of the king's sister, Marguérite of Angoulême, Queen of Navarre. Like these distinguished patrons, Lefèvre remained a liberal Catholic, a fact which entailed his rejection by both Protestants and conservative Catholics. By contrast some members of the Meaux circle like Guillaume Farel later became Protestant leaders in France and Switzerland.

Outside Italy the period 1500–1530 may thus be regarded as a watershed in the history of Western Christianity. Instead of organizing social or constitutional discontents, instead of attacking tyranny and misgovernment in the secular states, the critical forces inherent in humanism had found their targets in the Church. Moreover they developed in northern Europe a capacity for radical destruction and reconstruction. Working upon the minds of the younger generation, Christian humanism could easily pass beyond Erasmian criticism and ridicule into sterner forms of dissent: they could become an important component of the Protestant Reformation. Luther was to upbraid Erasmus for merely laughing at evil when he should have wept. On the other hand no one could yet be certain how far Rome and the Catholic hierarchy might be persuaded to accept the reasoning of the Christian humanists. These themes will soon reclaim our attention as we narrate the development of both Reformation and Counter Reformation.

The first responses of institutional Christianity were by no means wholly hostile. Throughout his lifetime Erasmus remained on excellent terms with a host of highly placed ecclesiastics. Meanwhile, following the concepts of Erasmus and Lefèvre, the "trilingual" universities and colleges—Alcalá, Utrecht, Wittenberg, Leipzig, Heidelberg, Corpus Christi at Oxford, and Bishop Fisher's two colleges at Cambridge—seemed triumphant in their defiance of the Vulgate-worshippers, the "obscure men" whose dislike of the Jews caused them to oppose Hebrew studies, the men who suspected even Greek as the language of a heretical form of Christianity. From Poland to Spain, humanists flourished under the patronage of eminent ecclesiastics. We have already observed how even Cardinal Ximenes, that fierce crusader against the Moslems, promoted biblical humanism by financing the magnificent *Complutensian Polyglot (1502–17)*, which printed the Vulgate alongside the Hebrew and Greek texts of the Bible. If the new values could flourish even in Spain, the more intelligent of the conservatives might indeed have wondered how far their arguments could be redefined, their forces regrouped, so as to arrest the seemingly irresistible forces of change. Such was the amorphous and intriguing situation when the figure of Luther suddenly loomed large throughout Christendom.

FOUR

*Reformation
and
Counter-Reformation*

1. Luther and Zwingli

Martin Luther *(1483–1546)* came from the very heart of the German nation. The son of a Thuringian miner and later mining-lessee, he knew the deprivations of working-class life. From the first his mental culture was saturated by religion, by that pious mixture of hymn singing and saint worship which then formed the religious idiom of small-town and peasant communities in central Germany. As a "poor scholar" in the St. George's School at Eisenach he learned something of the refinements and comforts of patrician life, since he was befriended here by members of the Cotta family. With the support of his father, who intended his studious son for a lucrative legal career, he entered in 1501 the famous university of Erfurt, a center of manifold cultural traditions. Here, after pursuing the usual arts course, he encountered some of the more critical approaches of late medieval philosophy and theology. From his Occamist teachers he derived a lasting impression of the majesty and omnipotence of God, and from the textbook by Nicholas of Lyra *(d.1340)* a belief in the priority of the literal sense of the Scriptures over the allegorical interpretations still widely favored by other schools of thought. Though Martin did not accompany those of his friends who joined the humanist circle of Mutianus at Gotha, he read widely in classical Latin culture, began to study Greek and Hebrew, and in later years hastened to secure all the best biblical texts prepared by the Christian humanists Reuchlin, Lefèvre, and Erasmus. In 1505 his scrupulous conscience, his vehement desire to save his soul, seem to have been intensified by the sudden deaths of certain friends. Believing his life endangered by a thunderstorm, he vowed to St. Anne to become a monk, and much to his father's chagrin honored the vow by entering the severe and highly esteemed Order of Augustinian Eremites.

Amid his subsequent efforts to deserve salvation he lay torn by a sense of sin, by the stark contrast between the exalted holiness of God and the feebleness of all human endeavor. At this point, there intervened the Vicar General of the Order, Johann von Staupitz, in his own right a commanding figure in German spiritual life. Staupitz pressed upon Luther those comforting passages of the Bible which inculcate trust in the uniqueness of Christ's reconciling mission and in the justification of men—their attainment of a saving relationship with God—by their faith, as distinct from reliance upon strenuous penances and good works. Support for this emphasis the young friar also found in the fourteenth-century German mystics, especially in Tauler and in the little *German Theology,* a tract which later on *(1516)* Luther was to publish with an enthusiastic introduction. In such writings may be seen the germ of his "theology of the cross," that consolation for troubled souls which said that if God chose a man, he would inevitably experience spiritual suffering. Even so, Luther never became a mystic. He was a biblical theologian, and to assuage his doubts he turned to the external records of Christ and St. Paul, not to any subjective visions or ineffable states of mind. Still more important for the future was his study of St. Augustine, who had based upon Paul a rigorous doctrine of justification by faith. Man was hopelessly corrupt, totally irredeemable save by a divine grace; this grace was vouchsafed to some but refused to others by an unquestionable, omnipotent Deity. In such discipleship Luther had several German and Netherlandish predecessors, such as John Pupper *(d.1475),* John of Wesel *(d.1481),* and Wessel Gansfort *(d.1489),* though he did not regard them as his own forerunners until about 1520. It also seems certain that he did not appreciate his kinship with John Huss until about this same date, when he had learned enough to shed his German prejudice against the Bohemian and to acknowledge him as an early evangelical reformer.

For a decade after his entry into the Augustinian Order Luther not only remained energetic in his monasticism but pursued a successful career as a university teacher and a preacher of revivalist sermons. In 1508 his superiors transferred him to their house in Wittenberg in order to strengthen the theological teaching at the university founded there only six years earlier by Frederick the Wise, Elector of Saxony. After a year at this poorly endowed little school—Luther himself spoke of Wittenberg as lying on the frontiers of civilization—he returned to Erfurt, and in 1510-11 was sent on the business of his Order to Rome. Though offended there by cynicism, vice, and clerical ignorance, he returned to Germany with no thought of rebellion against the Roman headship of the Church. Soon after completing this mission he was transferred once more to Wittenberg, took his doctorate, and settled down to teaching and preaching. His lecture courses of 1513-19, recovered in manuscript during the nineteenth century, mainly concern the Pauline Epistles.

They throw much light upon the gradual fashioning of his key doctrine, Justification by Faith Alone. In his autobiographical fragment of 1545 Luther dramatized this process by recalling a sudden insight he received in the tower of his monastery which elucidated the Pauline phrase "the righteous shall live by faith." This "tower-experience" modern scholars have assigned to various dates ranging from 1513 to 1518. At all events Luther's mature doctrine of justification had been attained when he wrote his *Sermon of the Threefold Righteousness,* published toward the end of 1518. This doctrine marked an advance on that of St. Augustine. Whereas the latter thought that Justification meant a gradual infusion of divine grace, whereby a man was slowly cleansed of sin, Luther held it to be a sudden imputation, a reckoning to a man's credit, of a righteousness earned simply and solely by the work of Christ. While remaining yet a sinner, a Christian could thus be delivered and put into the way of salvation by a single glorious stroke. By Luther Justification is conceived no longer as an astringent moral process, but as a cloak mercifully hung about human sin. True, a gradual process of spiritual and moral improvement must follow, but in Luther's view this secondary, incidental development contributed nothing to justify or save, and to it he applies Paul's other term, "sanctification." Here at least was an evangelical religion even more Christocentric than Augustine's, and differing still further from the gentle, moralistic *philosophia Christi* of Erasmus.

Meanwhile in 1517 Luther attained a sudden fame by bluntly attacking the papal Indulgences then being preached and sold not far from Wittenberg by the Dominican Johann Tetzel. In view of Tetzel's long experience of such fund raising, he gave vent to some amazingly incautious phrases, saying that God must forgive sins if the pope did so; and that as soon as the coin rang in the chest, the soul for which it was paid would pass immediately from purgatory to heaven. Needless to add, the notion that the Papacy could remit the guilt of sin, as opposed to a mere temporal penalty for sin, was already regarded as a highly dubious notion. Yet a number of papal Bulls had used ambiguous or misleading phraseology on this subject, while since the thirteenth century the popes had claimed to dispose of a "treasury of merits," formed by the good deeds of all Christians and offered to cancel the guilt of penitent sinners. In 1476 Sixtus IV had introduced another debatable element into the doctrine of Indulgences by extending them to the liberation of souls from purgatory. By this time even churchmen of unquestionable orthodoxy such as Cardinal Ximenes were criticizing various aspects of Indulgence selling, the doctrine of which was in due course to be more rigorously defined by the Council of Trent.

The whole background of Tetzel's campaign of 1517 looked unsavory to informed minds. With few exceptions the German bishops had long been noblemen of worldly tastes and low spiritual attainments. No exception occurred in the case of Albert of Brandenburg, with whom the Pope was in effect sharing the proceeds of this Indulgence campaign. A sybaritic, loose-living young man of twenty-four, he was already archbishop of Magdeburg,

Tetzel's Indulgence campaign: The Fugger accountant enters the receipts and the money is packed for onward transmission.

and since he wanted also the senior archbishopric of Mainz, he agreed to pay Leo X 21,000 ducats, adding some 10,000 more to obtain confirmation in all his offices. Rome agreed that he could raise all this money by the sale of Indulgences, and hence Tetzel was openly accompanied by an accountant from the banking house of Fugger, charged to collect the cash of the faithful, prior to the transfer of the necessary credits to Rome. On such occasions printed forms of receipt were available; the names of the recipients, living and dead, being inserted by hand.

Luther's revolt thus occurred as a protest against an especially obnoxious example of the long-standing tendency to reduce salvation to a business transaction. His initial protest had less to do with the theory of Indulgences than with their practical effects upon simple men and women. In accordance with academic custom, he issued his Ninety-five Theses, yet they were in effect aimed at the whole German public, for which they were rapidly translated and printed. They denied that an Indulgence could remit guilt or divine punishment for sin: it could only remit ecclesiastical penalties, and could not possibly apply to the dead. The Christian who felt true repentance did not need an Indulgence, while the "treasury of merits" had not been theologically defined and was misleading the people.

Luther himself seems to have been surprised when the Roman Inquisitor Silvester Prierias attacked his Theses with vigor. In response he further defended his positions, refusing to go to Rome, and when in October 1518 he came to Augsburg and confronted the papal legate Cardinal Cajetan, he declined to recant. The outcome now depended upon the attitude of Luther's sovereign, a famous collector of saints' relics, who might have been expected to disapprove of Luther's Theses. On the contrary, Frederick the Wise refused to deliver for punishment the man who had suddenly become the most famous figure in his university. The Church and the other princes felt reluctance to bring pressure to bear upon the Saxon Elector, since the Emperor Maximilian was old, and in the likely event of an Imperial Election, Frederick would exert great influence and might even be chosen Emperor. Meanwhile the German laity, stimulated by a generation of anti-Roman propaganda, took Luther's side with alacrity.

During the months following his clash with Cajetan, Luther carefully studied the theological and historical grounds for the papal supremacy in the Church. Again at this crucial stage, humanism entered the picture with its attack upon the Donation of Constantine and also upon the Isidorian Decretals, another late forgery still being used to strengthen the papal claims. Luther made these "discoveries" with a mixture of terror and exaltation: in this dangerous state of mind he agreed to attend a public disputation with the renowned papalist scholar Dr. Johann Eck. With elaborate ceremonies this verbal tournament was staged at Leipzig by the Catholic Duke George of Saxony, a cousin of the Elector Frederick and ruler of a substantial part of Saxony. Here in July 1519 Eck triumphed at least in the sense that he forced Luther into the open. Luther took the view that the Roman supremacy was only four centuries old in western Europe, while it had never been acknowledged by the Eastern Church. Moreover he now dared to say that there might be truth in some of the Hussite positions. Following these debates he once more made his appeal to the public with rapidity and success. For the first time in history, the power of the press decided the fate of a movement of religious dissent. The Reuchlin struggle[1] was still in progress and Luther naturally found heavy support among the humanists. But thanks to the press his case could also be accurately and swiftly presented to the mass of more or less literate citizens. And the vision presented to them by Luther was not that of their own ancient and negative anticlericalism: it was a vision based upon a positive religious message which seemed to promise a genuine renovation of the German Church.

In the epoch-making year 1520 Luther sent over twenty publications to the printer, three of which have been accounted classics by later generations. *To the Christian Nobility of the German Nation* forms a succinct but

---

[1]See p. 132.

An den Christlichen Adel deütscher Nation. von des Christlichen standes besserunng D. Martinus Luther Wittenberg.

Title page of one of the 1520 editions of *To the Christian Nobility of the German Nation* by Martin Luther. (Another edition of the same year has a picture of a knight on foot.)

capacious program of social and ecclesiastical reform. Abandoning the Papacy as doomed and irrelevant, it called upon rulers to set up evangelical churches. Vows of celibacy should be abolished, monks and nuns allowed to leave their cloisters, pilgrimages forbidden, church ceremonies simplified. Here Luther repeated his view that priests have no sacred, indelible character springing from their ordination but denied to the rest of mankind. Priests merely perform special functions in the Church, but a cobbler belongs to a spiritual estate equally with a bishop, for all Christians should be regarded as priests ministering one to another. Turning to the universities, Luther would discontinue the study of canon law and replace scholastic philosophy with languages, mathematics, history, and Bible study. Literacy he sees as an important basis of the Christian life for both sexes, and he would see established in every town a school for girls as well as for boys. He does not hesitate to attack the gluttony and ostentation of the rich; he wants a parish poor-law system and he calls upon the rulers to restrain the rapacious financiers, especially the Fuggers. To any modern observer Luther's attitude toward capitalism might seem reactionary: indeed, he regarded the rehabilitation of agriculture as the true path toward earthly happiness. But alongside such impracticable idealism, alongside its author's almost ludicrous tendency to blame all the ills of German society upon Rome, *Christian Nobility* contained a good deal of massive and compelling logic. Unlike the social pleas of Erasmus and More, it was utterly direct, unambiguous, comprehensive: it stripped the hypocrisy from a society wherein both secular class divisions and legalistic notions of priestly authority excluded human brotherliness and engendered a nominal Christianity which did not recognize its own true character. But the question remained: could a new theology make more than marginal impressions upon the European social order?

Luther's second famous tract of 1520 *The Babylonian Captivity of the Church* dealt with the sacramental system. He reduced the seven Catholic sacraments to three: baptism, confession, and the eucharist (later on he was to remove confession, as insufficiently attested by Scripture). The Bohemians and the Greeks, who granted the cup to the laity, he called orthodox: Rome which denied it he pronounced heretical. Wycliffe attacking transubstantiation had been orthodox: the scholastics who taught this novelty—based upon mere Aristotelian concepts—had fallen into heresy. Nevertheless Luther's own teaching on the eucharist maintained that the glorified body of Christ was ubiquitous and therefore present in the elements of bread and wine. As events proved, he was prepared to split the whole Protestant movement rather than question the doctrine of a real and localized presence. On the other hand he rejected with indignation the dogma that the mass was a sacrifice, or for that matter a "good work" contributing to man's salvation. He concludes *The Babylonian Captivity* by arguing that "the Church is smothered by endless regulations about rites and ceremonies," with the result that "faith in Christ is obstructed." His plea for spiritual liberty goes so far as to declare that "neither pope nor bishop nor any other person has the right to impose a syllable of law upon a Christian man without his own consent." By these words the impulsive Luther did not mean all that his wilder admirers thought he meant, yet such electrifying phrases helped to stimulate a radical spirit which would soon refuse to be comprehended within the new orthodoxies of a reformed German Church. Yet in 1520 Luther was still concerned to define the dichotomy between law and gospel, between discipline and spiritual liberty. Before the end of the year he produced *The Freedom of a Christian*. It seeks to replace discipline under the canon law with a joyful, creative liberty, expressed in willing obedience to God and in service to mankind. Every spiritual possession of a man can be traced to his faith; everything good he accomplishes must derive from that faith. Fasting, mortification, going to services should be kept in their proper places. They do not make a man good, but are mere signs of his faith: thus truly based they will be done with joy, not in a grim spirit of self-discipline. In the last resort the soul needs nothing but the word of God, and when observances become hindrances they should be abandoned.

In the autumn of 1520 when Luther was finishing *The Freedom of a Christian* he received a copy of the papal Bull which condemned forty-one beliefs attributed to him, but showed singularly little grasp of the structure of his thought. With his usual sense for theatrical gesture, he burned the Bull on December 10 outside one of the gates of Wittenberg in the presence of his faculty and students. For good measure they stoked the bonfire with works of the canon law and other monuments of papalism. And still with something approaching unanimity the German people applauded his actions. Between 1518 and the peak year 1523 a huge pamphlet literature flooded the country. In general it glorified but vulgarized Luther's conclusions, often turning them into a revival of the old anticlericalism which Luther wanted to replace with a creative gospel. This popular literature was extremely one-sided: a count for the year 1523 shows that the pro-Luther pamphlets outnumbered the Catholic pamphlets by nearly twenty to one. There also survive a host of congratulatory messages from the younger humanists. Even Wimpfeling and other elderly conservatives hoped that Luther's movement might lead to long-awaited reforms in the Church. For the moment this was also the position of Erasmus. On the other hand, Crotus Rubeanus circulated Luther's writings in Rome itself. And when the patricians of Nuremberg met as usual to celebrate the retirement of their daughters into nunneries, they also conversed approvingly of Luther's writings! Even his enemy Duke George—who at Leipzig had called his views pestilential—objected to publishing the condemnatory Bull in his dominions. As we can now see, this exultant antipapalism was bound to be followed by a process of clarification, even of disillusion. Yet for the moment the papalist minority behind Eck seems to have been small: the revolt of Martin Luther had almost become the revolt of a nation.

There followed in 1521 a dramatic sequence of events. Though now under the ban of the Papacy, Luther was given a safe-conduct by the orthodox young Emperor Charles V which enabled him to attend the Diet at Worms. Here on April 18 he made his famous refusal to recant before the distinguished assembly. Charles answered by pledging himself to wage the fight against heresy, yet he honored the safe-conduct, and as Luther left for Wittenberg the Elector Frederick found himself in a quandary. He would not surrender the person of Luther, yet he could not openly maintain him without serious consequences. He therefore resolved to make Luther disappear, and on May 4 the heresiarch was kidnapped by armed horsemen in a forest near Eisenach and taken to the Wartburg. In this romantic but lonely retreat he remained, but for one very brief excursion to Wittenberg, until March 1522. During this sabbatical year he completed his German translation of the New Testament, using Erasmus's revision *(1518)* of the Greek text. Luther's German Old Testament, unfinished until 1534, was the work of later years. The successive editions of both the New Testament and the whole Bible sold in enormous numbers; here stood Luther's most permanent literary achievement, perhaps also the most effective instrument of his cause. He based the work upon the vocabulary of the Saxon Chancery, because this would prove intelligible both to High Germans and Low Germans. More important still, he strove to put the Bible into the language of the people. "My teachers were the housewife in her home, the children at their games, the merchants in the market-places; I tried to learn from them how to express and explain myself." But among his readers—and those of earlier German Bibles—there were not a few who thought themselves vouchsafed biblical revelations more authoritative than those of Luther.

During his absence his deputies in Wittenberg, Philip Melanchthon and Andreas Carlstadt, had failed to prevent confusion arising from the advent of three sectarian prophets from the small Saxon town of Zwickau. A gifted professor of Greek and great-nephew of Reuchlin, Philip was still very young and impressionable. For his part, Carlstadt positively encouraged the radicals. This learned neurotic had supported Luther in the Leipzig debates, but he had now acquired a romantic belief in peasant wisdom which almost foreshadowed the illusions of Rousseau. Such prophets as those from Zwickau could in fact have boasted a lengthy pedigree, since they derived from a number of sources, including the twelfth-century prophecies of Joachim, abbot of Flora, and the more recent left-wing Hussite millenarian beliefs. They had flourished in Zwickau under the influence of the priest Thomas Münzer, himself an educated man with obvious Joachitic and Hussite affinities, and one who made sweeping claims to direct divine inspiration. On his return to Wittenberg Luther swiftly allayed this local outbreak. Nevertheless in due course sectarian groups headed by the Anabaptists arose in hundreds of places before the end of the decade. Having quite unwittingly helped to encourage these outbursts, Luther henceforth found himself fighting hard on two fronts. During the early twenties this prophetic idealism mingled with the agrarian discontents of the German peasantry, whose large-scale risings of 1524-25 were suppressed by the princes amid appalling bloodshed. Münzer suffered execution for his share, while Carlstadt escaped to place himself under Luther's protection.

Amid these events Luther at first appealed for moderation on both sides, but when the crisis came, he could not accept the imminent prospect of social and religious anarchy, and he called upon the princes to slay without mercy. How far this notorious outburst checked the expansion of the Lutheran movement among the defeated peasants has been inconclusively debated. In any case, from the beginning the expansion of Lutheranism owed far less to the peasants than to the populace of the German towns, a populace stimulated by preachers and pamphleteers of the new opinions. In several of these communities, especially in the two greatest Reformation centers Nuremberg and Strassburg, the records are voluminous and enable us to trace the process with considerable clarity. Neither the cities belonging to princely states nor the independent Imperial cities could boast constitutions we should call democratic. Their city councils were manned by patricians drawn from a limited group of old families, naturally cautious men desiring neither to offend the Catholic Emperor nor to encourage subversive movements among the unprivileged masses of their own citizens. Nevertheless, the predominant motive of each council was to preserve the unity and independence of its city, and hence the majority of councils followed in the wake of the people and the preachers with some hesitation; but they did not shrink from definite decisions when they judged the time ripe. Of the sixty-five main Imperial cities only fourteen never tolerated Protestantism, and most of these fourteen needed a desperate struggle to exclude the new religion. The story is not markedly different within the princely cities, many of which hastened to accept the new beliefs in advance of their rulers. Everywhere the instinct to preserve municipal solidarity—so often during recent centuries asserted by cities against their local bishops—proved a dominant factor favoring Luther's cause. To the man and to his pious supporters the assurance of divine support came from these mass movements. "The Word did it all," wrote Luther. "While I sat around drinking beer with Philip and Amsdorf, God dealt the Papacy a mighty blow."

In view of our modern knowledge concerning the early reception of Lutheranism in the cities, it would seem that undue stress has often been laid upon the initiatives of the "godly princes." Even so, during the later twenties a steadily growing group of rulers joined Electoral Saxony. The common modern presumption that they must have been wholly or almost wholly inspired by secular ambitions has little to recommend it. A prince who embraced Luther's principles ran great risks, the more especially if his state lay in the vicinity of the Habsburg lands. In Saxony that somewhat ambivalent figure Frederick the Wise was succeeded by two uncompromising Lutherans, John the Steadfast *(r.1525–32)* and his son John Frederick *(r.1532–54),* from youth an assiduous student of Luther's works. Another early convert was Philip of Hesse, a bold politician and soldier whose adulteries did not exclude a more or less genuine repentance, even a religious fervor. Already in 1525 Albert of Hohenzollern, Grand Master of the Teutonic Knights, laicized the territory of the Order, declared himself Duke of Prussia, and introduced a sweeping Lutheran Reformation. But these princes, joined by two or three lesser ones and by a powerful group of cities, did not as yet dominate even northern Germany, and at the Diet of Speyer in 1526 they still faced a distinct Catholic majority. Even so, neither side wished to plunge the Empire into civil war. For this reluctance there were several good reasons. As we have seen, in that very year the Turks followed up their victory at Mohács by occupying Hungary, with the exception of a western strip precariously occupied by the Emperor's brother Ferdinand, brother-in-law and heir to the slain King Lewis II. In 1529 the Sultan Sulaimān the Magnificent even besieged Vienna, and though the Germans stood together to drive him off, he did not concede a truce to Ferdinand until 1533. In this perilous situation the Habsburgs could hardly envisage an anti-Protestant crusade. In addition the evasive Pope Clement VII intrigued with Francis I, imperilling his own relations with the Habsburgs and incurring in May 1527 the Sack of Rome. Similar patterns recurred consistently over the next two decades, with the result that the threatened Lutheran princes and cities were granted a prolonged reprieve from Habsburg attack. Politically speaking, the Reformation owed immense debts not only to the Turks but to the Habsburg-Valois feud, since Francis I could be relied upon to place politics before religion and to back Turks or German Protestants whenever such action seemed likely to cripple the Habsburgs. The concept of a "balance of power," born in fifteenth century Italy, had now become a commonplace to the statesmen of Europe, and to many it seemed a healthier principle than a world of crusades led by the power-seeking Habsburgs and based on religious partisanship.

As the Lutheran Reformation enveloped much of the Empire, a parallel movement, owing something but by no means everything to Luther, arose within the Swiss Confederation. In some respects this unique institution seemed ill-adapted to withstand the strains of religious change and division. It comprised a number of languages and dialects; it had no head of state, no capital city, no common law or coinage. Between the poor rural cantons and the wealthy city-states of Zürich, Basle, and Berne there existed stark contrasts and tensions. The Church in Switzerland, mundane and uninspiring, exerted little intellectual or spiritual influence, while its dioceses neither corresponded territorially with the cantonal governments nor cooperated with them. During the boyhood of the Reformer Huldreich Zwingli *(1484–1531)* many Swiss were affected by both anticlerical and Erasmian opinions. Long before Luther's revolt Thomas Wyttenbach, Zwingli's teacher at Basle, had instilled into his pupils—several of them future Protestant leaders—such notions as the all-sufficiency of Christ's sacrifice and the folly of the traffic in Indulgences.

Early in 1519 Zwingli preached that series of sermons in the Great Minster at Zürich which is usually regarded as initiating the Swiss Reformation. Born of free peasant-farmers in the high Toggenburg Valley, he had acquired an enthusiasm for classical studies in his schools at Basle and Berne, and subsequently at the university of Vienna. Returning to Basle in 1502 he graduated there four years later, and was aided by his influential uncle Bartholomew, rector and rural dean of Weesen, to become parish priest at Glarus, later at Einsiedeln, and in 1518 at Zürich. During this phase his attitudes were wholly characteristic of Christian humanism, and he labored at his Greek in order "to learn the teaching of Christ from the original sources." His views derived directly from Erasmus, upon whose New Testament he based his early evangelical sermons. His was a forthright and common-sense personality; he did not share Luther's intense spiritual torments. Certainly he was sincere when he claimed to have learned his religion from the Bible and not from Luther, yet there can be no doubt that Luther's writings and popularity in the neighboring German lands lent impetus to the movement initiated by Zwingli. And in the city of Zürich is an edition *(1522)* of Luther's commentary on the Gospels and Epistles

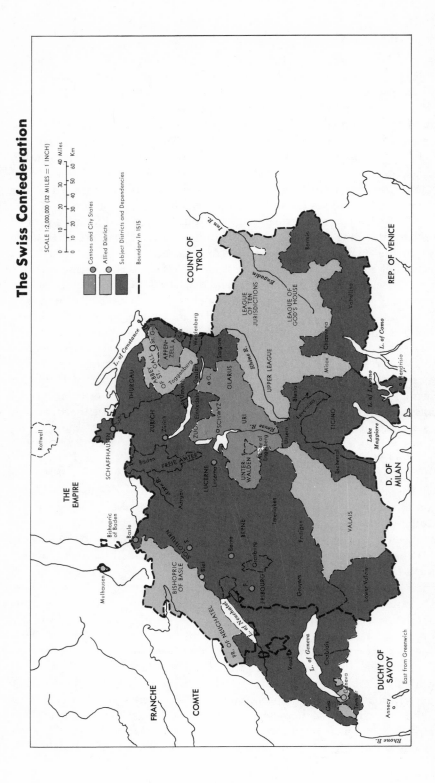

The Swiss Confederation

SCALE 1:2,000,000 (32 MILES = 1 INCH)

0 10 20 30 40 Miles
0 10 20 30 40 50 60 Km

○ Cantons and City States

○ Allied Districts

Subject Districts and Dependencies

Boundary in 1515

THE EMPIRE

Rottweil

Mulhausen

FRANCHE COMTE

Bishopric of Baden

Basle

BISHOPRIC OF BASLE

Biel

SOLOTHURN

PR. OF NEUCHÂTEL

L. of Neuchâtel

Yoverdon

L. of Geneva

Geneva

Gex

DUCHY OF SAVOY

Annecy

Lower Valais

L. of Constance

SCHAFFHAUSEN

THURGAU

ABBEY OF ST. GALL (St. G.)

APPENZELL

Toggenburg

Weesen

Walenberg

ZURICH

Zürich

Baden

FREIE AMTER

Aargau

Reuss R.

Einsiedeln

G.

OSCHWYZ

GLARUS

Sargans

URI

UNTERWALDEN

Abbey of Engelberg

LUCERNE

Lucerne

BERNE

Berne

Interlaken

Fribourg

FRIBOURG

Gruyères

Gruyère

VALAIS

UPPER LEAGUE

Rhine R.

LEAGUE OF TEN JURISDICTIONS

Engadin

LEAGUE OF GOD'S HOUSE

Bormio

Misox

Chiavenna

Valtellina

Bleno

Luvomno

Eschental

TICINO

L. of Como

Mendrisio

Lake Maggiore

L. of Lugano

COUNTY OF TYROL

Inn R.

REP. OF VENICE

D. OF MILAN

Rhone R.

East from Greenwich

covered with voluminous notes in Zwingli's neat hand. From the beginning he showed himself highly aware of practical and social problems; his first intervention in public affairs was a protest against the hiring of his countrymen as mercenaries in the Italian Wars. The degrading aspects of this traffic he observed on various visits to Italy as an army chaplain.

By 1518 Zwingli had also become known as a denouncer of superstitious pilgrimages and Indulgences, and he induced the city council of Zürich to exclude Indulgence sellers from its territories. By 1522 he and a growing party of associates were defending the eating of flesh in Lent and calling upon the Bishop of Constance to sanction clerical marriage. The resultant quarrel between the city and the Bishop—the latter actively backed by the pope—resulted in 1523 in the rejection of episcopal authority by Zürich. Moreover Zwingli went to Berne, and after a public disputation with the Catholics, persuaded that city to follow the example of Zürich. On some fronts the Swiss advance was much more gradual. Even in Zürich the mass was not abrogated until 1525, when the council consented to replace it by Zwingli's Order of Communion, a straightforward service of commemoration, with the laity partaking of both bread and wine. To Basle, now the city of Erasmus, John Oecolampadius came as university lecturer in 1522, and soon afterwards this former disciple of Luther became a firm ally of Zwingli and gradually won over the council to the latter's principles. But it was not until 1529 that Erasmus thought it prudent to avoid involvement by withdrawing to Freiburg.

By this time the social contrasts between the big cities and some of the rural areas had done much to foster religious division. The five Forest Cantons, Lucerne, Zug, Schwyz, Uri, and Unterwalden signalized their strong adherence to the Papacy and traditional Catholic doctrine. The dangerous situation of neighboring Zürich prompted her to look for friends, and the league of Swiss Protestant cities, which came into being in 1528–30, made close contacts with Strassburg. The great city of Alsace seemed in all respects a natural ally. Unlike Nuremberg and Augsburg, it lay relatively remote from the centers of Habsburg military power, and from 1523 it had been led into the Reformation by Zell, Bucer, and Capito, men who admired Luther yet leaned theologically toward Zwingli. In 1529 the divergences between the two Reformers acquired a grave practical significance. The lack of political and economic determinism throughout the next episodes is indeed striking: on both sides the governments allowed theological differences to forbid an alliance which had every political argument in its favor.

In the autumn of 1529 Philip of Hesse, ever seeking to promote united action by all the Protestant states, brought Luther and Melanchthon together with Zwingli and Oecolampadius at his castle near Marburg. At this time the Catholic pressures were growing. The Diet of Speyer had forbidden religious change; Pope and Emperor were achieving a better understanding, while Charles and Francis had at last signed a treaty which boded ill for

Memorial portrait of Zwingli. The inscription records that even while he sought the salvation of his country, he has fallen by its ungrateful sword. (The Municipal Library, Zürich)

Protestantism. Incidentally, the term "Protestant" had just come into use, following the "Protestation" signed by the Lutheran rulers and cities against the Catholic majority decision at Speyer. Nevertheless this manifest peril proved insufficient to force the two groups of Protestant divines into an agreement over the eucharist. From the beginning Zwingli had rejected as profane the notion that material objects could convey divine grace. He could not accept even Luther's doctrine of a real presence in the bread and wine; he regarded the communicant as receiving a spiritual blessing from a merely symbolic act. Luther, who had an equally closed mind since his encounter with Carlstadt's radicalism concerning the eucharist, came to Marburg refusing even to entertain Zwingli's contention that the words "This is my body" should be taken to mean "This signifies my body." Martin Bucer strove without avail to bring the two sides together. The Protestants, having inherited the ultrasensitivity of Catholicism on this particular issue, allowed it to outweigh the fact that here at Marburg they achieved agreement on all the other main issues.

On his return to Switzerland Zwingli soon renewed his conflict with the Catholic Forest Cantons, which burned a Zwinglian preacher and vetoed Zwingli's proposal that religious toleration should be allowed in the "Common Lordships," certain areas of limited independence which were ruled jointly by the whole Swiss Confederation. Rather than grant this demand, the Forest Cantons were prepared to ally with the old foe, the Habsburgs, and even before going to Marburg Zwingli had been obliged to sign a truce with them at Kappel. Now faced by their open refusal to pursue any common foreign policy, Zwingli tried to blockade their food supplies, and this failing, planned to conquer them by force of arms. Yet in the autumn of 1531 the Catholics struck first and found the Zürichers unprepared. At the battle of Kappel Zwingli bore arms and perished. For a brief space it seemed as if the Swiss Reformers had wrecked the Confederation. As for Luther, with a signal lack of generosity he rejoiced in the downfall of his rival. Nevertheless history was once again to defeat the prognostications. Among the Swiss there arose cleverer politicians and greater theologians than the gallant leader of the Zürich Reformation.

2. Lutheranism and Politics

The years of the Swiss crisis also formed a landmark in the history of the German Reformation. The return of Emperor Charles V was followed in June 1530 by the Diet of Augsburg, where Melanchthon stood confronted by a formidable list of errors drawn up by Eck, and in reply composed the Augsburg Confession. Though taken thenceforth as the standard summary of Lutheran belief, this document remains rather obviously the work of a conciliator. Melanchthon did in fact anxiously consult the Emperor's confessor and the papal nuncio in order to discover the price demanded for readmission to the Catholic fold. In the Confession of Augsburg he refrained from denying the Papal Supremacy, the seven sacraments, Indulgences, and purgatory, while the passage on the eucharist hardly excluded a Catholic interpretation. Prevented from attending the Diet by the ban of the Empire, Luther awaited the outcome at Coburg, but his fears of compromise and retreat proved needless. From the apparent pliability of Melanchthon the Pope deduced that concessions were inappropriate; he also continued to refuse the Emperor's demand for a General Council of the Church. On the other hand, the Lutheran princes stood firm against the Emperor's threats, and in February 1531 six of them joined with numerous leading cities to form the league of Schmalkalde, an association intended to prepare armed self-defense, and one which soon attracted other participants.

Faced by the need for contingents to fight the Turks, the Emperor granted the Protestants a truce at Nuremberg in 1532, and two years later he could not take revenge when Philip of Hesse defiantly reinstated the exiled Duke of Württemberg and thus set up a Protestant state in south Germany. While the Habsburgs still held the support of other southern rulers, especially that of the prince-bishops, they could count on no backing for a crusade against the Lutherans. Even the dukes of Bavaria, who staunchly excluded Protestantism from their lands, trembled at the thought of an Empire effectively ruled by Charles and his brother Ferdinand, the more so since the Habsburgs obviously intended to make the Imperial office hereditary. Meanwhile the Lutheran gains of the thirties proved spectacular. Well furnished with missionaries, Bibles, and tracts, the movement continued popular as well as princely. The winning of Württemberg encouraged the southwestern towns to declare themselves, while Protestantism won a foothold in Swabia and among the Austrian nobility and their tenants. Nevertheless its center of gravity lay in the north, outside the strategic range of the Habsburgs. Between 1529 and 1531 Goslar, Bremen, Lübeck, Rostock, Wismar, and Greifswald became Lutheran. Small princely states like Brunswick-Lüneburg and Mansfeld adhered in 1529, and they were closely followed by the secularized bishoprics of Lübeck, Schwerin, Brandenburg, and Schleswig, then rather uncertainly by the larger state of Brandenburg, where from 1535 the temporizing Elector Joachim II allowed Lutheran preachers. In 1539 Luther's enemy Duke George died, with the result that the dukes of Albertine Saxony came into line with their Ernestine cousins. In the great northeastern province of Silesia some of the princes, counts, and bishops established the new church on their lands in the early thirties, while others, influenced by the Habsburgs, delayed the change for a decade.

At the heart of the missionary effort, the university of Wittenberg now attracted students in their thousands, about one-third from north Germany, one-third from the south, and the remaining third from outside Germany. As a training center for missionaries abroad, it made its greatest impact upon the Scandinavian kingdoms. In Denmark Hans Tausen, fresh from Wittenberg, was preaching Lutheranism at Viborg in 1526, while another visitor to the Lutheran capital, the deposed King Christian II, had the New Testament translated into Danish. His uncle and successor Frederick I presented Lutheran divines to parishes and by 1530 had begun to expropriate the Danish monastic lands. After Frederick's death in 1533 a struggle for the succession was won by Luther's ardent admirer Christian III, who arranged to be crowned in 1537 by Bugenhagen, Luther's chief agent for foreign missions. With the aid of this capable divine and that of Danish scholars like Peder Palladius, Hans Tausen, and Christian Pedersen, King Christian organized an effective national church, popular in appeal, led by native clergy, but administratively controlled by the government. In Norway, then a dependency of the Danish crown, a similar situation developed, though the conservatism of the people retarded the growth of a truly national Lutheran church until the second half of the sixteenth century.

In the light of subsequent history, the most important of the Scandinavian kingdoms was Sweden; but there the initial resistance came not merely from popular immobility but from a powerful group of Catholic bishops. On the other side Lutheranism found a firm ally in King Gustavus Vasa (r.1523-60), founder of a new dynasty and leader of national resistance against the claims made by the Danish kings to the Swedish throne. Here the first native leader was Olavus Petri, who studied at Wittenberg in 1516-18 and became a thoroughgoing Lutheran by the mid-twenties, when he served as city clerk at Stockholm. Here, much as in the trading cities of Riga, Reval, and Dorpat on the eastern shores of the Baltic, the new beliefs found enthusiastic backers amongst the largely German merchant communities. Another ally intervened when Duke Albert of Prussia sent Protestant books into Sweden and encouraged his ally Gustavus to nationalize the Swedish church. More generally than in Germany, the greed of the lay nobles attracted them toward the Reformation, since the King offered to restore to them the land given to the monasteries by their ancestors since the middle of the fifteenth century. This restoration was undertaken by the Recess of Västerås in 1527, the law which not only permitted Lutheran preaching but ensured that only candidates able to preach should be ordained. It also provided that the Gospel should be taught in all Swedish schools. Four years later a national liturgy was set forth, including a communion service in the vernacular. Though they also won a fair measure of popular support, these steps were in essence a monarchical Reformation.

The sequel in Sweden revolved largely around the effects of Olavus Petri and his brother, the Lutheran archbishop Laurentius Petri, to establish by preaching and writing an authentic Evangelical Church. Despite some bitter quarrels with the heavy-handed Gustavus, they and their successors accomplished this intricate task. Again, the great territorial gains of the Swedish crown did not in the event result in the subjugation of the free peasant-farmers, the class upon which Sweden's Baltic Empire was destined to be built in the seventeenth century. In view of this coming explosion of national energy, and the fatal blow which it dealt to a later phase of Habsburg expansionism, the Swedish Reformation became an event of first-rate importance in European secular history. Again, in all these northern countries undeveloped or flagging literary cultures received a powerful impulse from biblical translations and other forms of Reformation literature. This seems especially true of Finland, where the great majority of the population spoke a language quite unrelated to that of its Swedish overlords. Even here Lutheran preaching began before 1530 and Mikael Agricola, who studied in Wittenberg from 1536 to 1539, wrote the first Finnish translation of the New Testament and became the acknowledged patriarch of the modern vernacular literature. Hence the Lutheran Reformation, like its Hussite predecessor in Bohemia, acted as midwife to the emergence of nationhoods and national cultures in northern Europe. In this respect it revivified rather than opposed the intellectual energies aroused in earlier centuries by Catholic Christianity.

Despite the advances of the thirties and early forties, these years also saw many events which foreshadowed the future division and retarding of the Lutheran movement in Germany. Its continued failure to achieve a working partnership with the Swiss was accompanied by a proliferation of radical sects and by not a little short-sightedness on the part of the Lutheran rulers and divines. In Westphalia the worldly bishop of Münster had done little to counter the spread of Protestantism, and in 1534–35 the city of Münster allowed itself to be taken over by an Anabaptist revolution, powerfully aided by immigrant groups from the nearby Netherlands. Under the prophet Jan Matthys, a communist theocracy—doubtless to be explained in part as a siege-economy—abolished all traditional institutions, even monogamy and the private family. On the death of Matthys in battle the rebel city fell under the tyranny of Jan Beukels of Leyden, a madman who demanded regal honors, practiced polygamy, and slew with his own hand a disobedient member of his harem. After a long siege aided by Catholic and Lutheran rulers, the bishop's army broke through the defenses and mercilessly slew the wretched defenders. Though untypical of sectarian religion, the Münster episode did much to convince the rest of Europe that civilization was tottering upon the brink of anarchy. Both German and Swiss Protestants adopted ever sterner measures to eradicate the sectarians, and even the tolerant city of Strassburg, where thousands of them had taken refuge, adopted a policy of repression. Yet despite the burnings and the drownings, these little "gathered churches" continued to attract the unprivileged classes in many regions of Europe.

Under the Frisian Menno Simons *(d.1561)* a pacific and moralist Anabaptism was secretly organized in the Netherlands and neighboring areas of Germany. Carried largely by the numerous emigrants who left these areas to seek prosperity elsewhere, Mennonite Anabaptism spread into the Baltic lands and also into England. A notable organizer of a more chiliastic yet nonviolent Anabaptism was the Netherlander David Joris *(d.1556)*, who lived incognito as a rich citizen of Basle, while operating an immense network of groups throughout the Rhineland, Switzerland, and the Netherlands. Yet not all the sectarians were Anabaptists and some—in our modern jargon called Spiritualists—exalted both the "inner light" of the soul and independent human will power in a manner doubly infuriating to the Scriptural and predestinarian theology of orthodox Protestantism. These Spiritualists were instructed and encouraged by several educated writers like the Bavarian scholar Hans Denck *(d.1527)*, the Swabian humanist Sebastian Franck *(d.1542)*, and the Silesian aristocrat and mystic—once a close friend of Luther—Caspar Schwenckfeld *(d.1561)*. Sectarianism thus presented a spectacle of great complexity: noble in its denunciation of religious persecution, narrow in its denial of salvation to the rest of mankind, it proved the forerunner of those many denominations which, from the seventeenth century onwards, were to play an ever-larger and increasingly respected part in European and North American religious life.

The challenge of the Swiss Reformed religion and the confusion occasioned by the sects were by no means the only trials to beset Lutheranism, even as it continued its statistical and territorial expansion. In 1538 Duke William V of Jülich-Cleves infuriated the Emperor by accepting as inheritance a large self-governing duchy within the Netherlands, while the marriage of his sisters with Henry VIII of England and the Elector of Saxony threatened to make him one of the strongest princes in the Empire. But when in 1543 William announced that he would turn Protestant, Charles intervened, defeated him in battle and forced him to abandon both his secular and his religious ambitions. Meanwhile Philip of Hesse contracted a bigamous marriage, fell foul of Imperial law, and bought his peace with the Emperor only by agreeing to renounce his plans for alliances with foreign powers. So far as concerned Saxony, the death of Duke George did not allay the family rivalry between the two branches of the House of Wettin, a rivalry soon to erupt with dire consequences. During the early forties the Emperor continued to obtain Protestant support against the Turks by condoning the half-Lutheran policy of the Elector of Brandenburg and by adopting an ostensibly moderate attitude during the conversations held at Regensburg in 1541 between Melanchthon and the devout humanist and Catholic reformer Cardinal Gasparo Contarini. These two in fact arrived at a common formula on Justification, but even this limited approach was vetoed by Rome: Contarini retired in disfavor and died the following year. When at last in 1545 Pope Paul III assembled a General Council at Trent, Charles blandly persuaded the Protestants to send representatives, yet within a few months he found himself at last in a position to use force. Allying himself with Duke William of Bavaria, he attained an understanding with the young Duke Maurice of Albertine Saxony, who was a Protestant yet willing to join the Habsburgs in the hope of being awarded the office and lands of his relative, the Elector John Frederick of Saxony. And while Charles announced that he was coming merely to punish the secular disobedience of the Elector, the Pope regarded the campaign as a crusade against heresy.

In February 1547, on the eve of the war, Luther died, worn out by incessant pamphleteering, administrative cares, and spiritual counselling. His last years had been disturbed by various doctrinal disputes between the Lutheran divines, while even Melanchthon had proposed some far-reaching changes of emphasis. While in 1520 Luther had sought to banish Aristotelian philosophy and theology, Melanchthon now reintroduced into the university curricula a revised scholasticism. Here was a neat-minded moralist, an academic teacher quite different in temperament from the volcanic man of religion whom he never ceased to venerate. He had already qualified Luther's teaching on the impotence of the human will, and on the eucharist he seemed to be moving nearer to the doctrine of Bucer. And while Melanchthon's theology had its ecumenical aspects, his views on secular affairs were anything but liberal. Though preferring oligarchic city governments, he applauded the absolutism of the princely states and even approved serfdom, the more so since he desperately feared a general relapse into moral and social anarchy. Luther had not to this degree prostrated himself before the secular state. He saw it as a sharp bridle ordained by God to tame evil men, rather than to assist in forming Christian character. He did not regard it as qualified to interfere with the spiritual lives and consciences of men, since even within this world a Christian belonged already to another and higher order of existence, to an eternal kingdom. Nevertheless in the hard political world, Luther had no practicable alternative to allowing princes, officials, and magistrates, the natural heads of congregations, a considerable share in church administration. While such people interfered little in theological matters, they appointed commissions, including both clerics and laymen, to supervise the churches withdrawn from obedience to the Roman hierarchy.

Upon this foundation Melanchthon and Luther's other successors were more than ready to build. Each of the German Protestant states now had its ecclesiastical commissioners and liturgical codes, enhancing the powers and prestige of the secular rulers but allowing little initiative to ordinary individuals and local congregations. On the other hand all men agreed that Germany desperately needed stronger states and more social-religious discipline. In the towns education made great strides under the influence of Luther and Melanchthon: the world of humanism survived, even though it was increasingly motivated by a dutiful spirit of service to Church and State. Again, the Lutheran rulers of the century following the Reformation proved for the most part pacific, responsible men; and several showed a beneficent paternalism rare in that age. Whether the Reformation changes accentuated the economic depression of the peasantry is hard to prove or to disprove. Conditions varied greatly from one region to another and in any case the evidence should not be handled in the light of some purely mythical agrarian paradise of the Middle Ages. Without doubt the major economic and political beneficiaries of this period were neither princes nor peasants, but the owners of landed estates, the families which prospered most from the general rise of food prices. Throughout central and eastern Europe, including the Slavonic nations of Poland and Bohemia, the landowners exercised even greater power in the local and national parliaments of their countries. Yet this advance of a new, money-minded feudalism occurred also in the Catholic lands, while even among the non-Catholics, many members of the rising noble classes were not Lutherans but Calvinists or Unitarians. In short, whatever its political or social results, economic change sprang from economic causes rather than from Lutheran teachings or from the conversion to Protestantism of ecclesiastical landlords.

We have momentarily glanced beyond the eight years of war and crisis which preceded the emergence of this nonmilitant but stable Lutheran world of the later sixteenth century. Though in 1547 the Protestant princes and cities mobilized on the upper Danube forces superior to those of the Emperor, they failed to concentrate their effort and hence suffered defeat in detail. When the renegade Protestant Maurice of Saxony invaded the lands of the Elector John Frederick, the latter naturally returned north, while the other contingents went home. Charles was thus enabled to make heavy financial demands upon the unprotected southern cities, though he could hardly force them to restore Catholicism. Aided by Spanish troops and generals, he then struck at Saxony, defeated John Frederick at Mühlberg in April 1547, and briefly occupied Wittenberg itself. Here he beheld the newly made tomb of Martin Luther, but refused to desecrate the remains of the heresiarch, saying "he is already before his Judge." Whatever Luther's ultimate fate, he might have felt a legitimate pride in the conduct of his disciple John Frederick, for the latter, though placed for a time under an illegal death sentence, refused to seek pardon and restoration by the surrender of his faith. Maurice was hence awarded the Electorate of Saxony, together with the territory around Wittenberg. Nevertheless he gained much less than he wanted. Charles, having used him to secure the person of his father-in-law Philip of Hesse, then to his great annoyance kept Philip captive. Soon afterwards the triumphant Emperor appeared at Augsburg with both the distinguished captives in his train. And here in the following year he promulgated the Interim of Augsburg, a personal solution intended to regulate German affairs pending the decisions of a General Council.

This Interim Pope Paul III detested, since it proposed some concessions to the Protestants, including clerical marriage and communion for the laity in both bread and wine. It also allowed a half-Protestant definition of Justification, along the lines suggested by Contarini in 1541. But the Protestant response proved even less favorable than that of the Pope. While in the southern cities the rich oligarchs accepted the Interim, Martin Bucer and hundreds of other pastors went into exile, and the common people demonstrated against the restoration of Catholic worship and religious houses. The northern princes and cities led by Magdeburg refused the conciliatory response suggested by Melanchthon; they defied the Emperor, whose growing power now inspired fear among Protestant and Catholic rulers alike. Relief from this tension came from an unexpected quarter. The disillusioned Maurice changed sides and along with other German powers concluded an alliance with the new King of France, Henry II (r.1547–59). Aided by French money, Maurice pressed southward in 1552 and almost captured the Emperor, who fled across the Brenner Pass. Even his brother King Ferdinand, who needed support against the Turks, came to an agreement with Maurice at Passau. For a time Charles himself resisted compromise and imprudently engaged the services of Albert Alcibiades of Bayreuth, a cruel rogue who had already held numerous states to ransom, irrespective of their religious allegiances. In the process of crushing this detested adventurer, Maurice lost his own life, while Charles at last retired to the Netherlands, leaving his brother to work out a German solution.

The resultant Peace of Augsburg, concluded in September 1555 after a year's negotiations, saw the virtual abandonment by the Habsburgs of their plan to achieve an autocratic, united, and Catholic Empire. The settlement had nevertheless some obvious limitations. It applied only to Catholics and Lutherans, not to sectarians or even to members of the Reformed churches, which had now fallen under the predominant influence of Calvin. It did much to discourage the Reformed Protestantism of the southwest German cities, which derived mainly from Bucer but now gradually went over to orthodox Lutheranism in order to claim the benefits of the Treaty. The basic Augsburg principle was comprehended in the phrase *cujus regio, ejus religio:* in other words, the ruler who owned a territory should decide its religion. If an individual subject found intolerable the religion of his prince or city, he would be permitted to sell off his possessions at a reasonable rate, pay a fine if he needed to gain release from any servile obligations, and then face the hardships of emigration. Having regard to those cities where some Catholic churches had recently been restored, the Peace of Augsburg stipulated that minorities should be allowed freedom of worship. Again, by the "Ecclesiastical Reservation," any ecclesiastical princes, bishops, or abbots who henceforth turned Protestant were to lose their offices, the chapters then being free to elect Catholic successors. Having insisted upon this provision, which undoubtedly did much to preserve Catholicism in Germany, Ferdinand then made a secret promise to the Lutherans that Protestant towns and the lands of noblemen within the ecclesiastical states should not be forcibly restored to Catholicism. Needless to add, these broad provisions left a multitude of intricate disputes to be settled. That they devalued men's religious convictions to the point of cynicism could not be denied. Nevertheless they were politically motivated and politically successful, if only because they spared the Empire the miseries of religious warfare for over half a century. The Peace of Augsburg represents indeed a substantial achievement for a nation so hopelessly divided, and for a period when in both France and the Netherlands the opposing religions were about to take up arms and become locked in seemingly endless conflict.

3. Calvin and the Reformed Churches

By the time of the Peace of Augsburg John Calvin *(1509-64)* was gaining a secure ascendancy within the city of Geneva and sending missionaries into France. He belonged to a generation younger than Luther's and had sprung from a very different background. His mind was as profoundly French as Luther's was German, his mission directed not merely to a Swiss city but primarily to the great French nation. Apart from creating Huguenot France he changed the political and religious configuration of Europe.

At Noyon in Picardy his father Gérard had served the cathedral chapter as solicitor and accountant: Church funds were in fact diverted to pay for the education of the promising boy at the Collège de la Marche and then from 1523 at the Collège de Montaigu in Paris. Precociously able and industrious, Calvin soon acquired an exquisite clarity in both Latin and French. He met people connected with the Meaux group of Christian humanists, together with some of those Frenchmen who since about 1518 had progressed to a study of Luther's teachings. Led by Noel Béda, head of the Collège de Montaigu, the Paris theological faculty had urged Francis I to condemn Lefèvre as well as the actual *Luthériens*. This last word was then applied indiscriminately to Reformers of various outlooks in Paris and in a number of provincial towns, but there did exist actual French disciples of Luther, such as the Augustinian Jean Vallière, burned at Paris in 1523, and the more famous Louis Berquin, who suffered a similar fate six years afterwards. During the late twenties and thirties frequent arrests and executions occurred not only in Paris but at Dijon, Beaune, Toulouse, Tours, Bordeaux, and a host of smaller southern places: in 1527 it was said of Montpellier that "the greater part of the town are Lutherans." Yet the fact that in 1528 Calvin abandoned his plan to enter the priesthood is unlikely to have been connected with these developments. It appears to have happened because of a quarrel between his father and the Noyon chapter, and the elder Calvin's shrewd conviction—once shared by the elder Luther—that money and honor sprang more readily from a legal career. Accordingly the young man went to study law at Orléans and Bourges; at the latter he studied Greek with the German jurist Melchior Wolmar, who is known to have introduced Lutheranism to receptive audiences. But during the years 1528-31 Calvin was chiefly employed in those studies of Roman Law which developed his immense capacity for orderly argument and acute definition.

On the death of his father Calvin abandoned the law for classical studies and in 1532 produced a learned commentary on Seneca's *De Clementia*. By nature a man of profound moral susceptibilities, he also shared the attraction to Seneca's stoicism felt by very different French humanists like Rabelais and Montaigne. Seneca had indeed already engaged the labors of Erasmus, whose errors Calvin did not hesitate to correct. Probably in the following year, his life was altered by a mysterious experience which he later described with a characteristic economy of words. "By a sudden conversion, God subdued and brought my heart to docility, which was more hardened against such matters than was to be expected of my youthful age." From this point he felt no doubt that his mind had become a humble instrument of the Almighty. And with almost equal suddenness he became identified with the party of Protestant reform. On All Saints' Day 1533 his friend Nicholas Cop, recently chosen rector of the university of Paris, preached what amounted to a Lutheran sermon and then fled to avoid arrest. Amongst those who judged it wise to follow him was Calvin, whose rooms were searched by authorities a few hours later. For three years he stayed in obscurity with various provincial friends; they included Lefèvre, then at Nérac under the protection of Marguérite of Navarre. Yet amid these wanderings Calvin wasted no time and within three years he had made himself a first-rate theologian.

When in 1534 an imprudent Protestant fixed a placard against the mass outside the King's bedroom, Francis gave the signal for a persecution of heretics throughout France, making the whole country dangerous for people like Calvin. The latter accordingly withdrew to Strassburg and early in 1535 to Basle, where he studied Hebrew. By something approaching a miracle of concentration he then produced in March 1536 the first edition of his *Institutio Religionis Christianae,* usually called in English the *Institutes.* In later years the successive editions of this famous work underwent considerable extensions and even structural changes before attaining its final form in 1559. Yet even in 1536 a survey of outstanding clarity, order, and penetration had been attained by a man still in his mid-twenties. Its profoundest debts are to Luther and Augustine, certainly not to Zwingli, whom Calvin never regarded as a theologian of the first rank. Calvin's basic theme is the absolute sovereignty of God within his created universe and within the mind of man. "Not only heaven and earth and inanimate creatures but also the plans and wills of men are governed so as to move precisely to the end destined by God." But the *Institutes* do not form a new Protestant scholasticism. This is a book about the Bible, both Old Testament and New, a book which seeks unflinchingly to follow the teachings of the Bible to their logical conclusions. Prominent among these, especially in the later editions, is the teaching of an absolute Predestination—acknowledged by Calvin himself as "this terrible decree"—whereby an omnipotent and inscrutable God has decided to choose some men for everlasting bliss, others for everlasting deprivation from his presence, and both without regard to their human performance.

However marvellously constructed from the Scriptures and St. Augustine, Calvin's conclusions would of course satisfy few modern Christian thinkers. To most, this exoneration of a literally omnipotent creator from all responsibility for evil seems based upon unwitting sophistries, while the decree of some men to eternal damnation has a dubious basis in the Scriptures as a whole. On the other hand, Calvin places a still heavier stress upon the redeeming mercy of Christ. No presentation of Christianity could be more Christocentric. Like Luther, he seeks to achieve utter honesty in setting forth, though not presumptuously claiming to explain, the mystifying antitheses, the apparent contradictions within the Christian faith. He takes no refuge in a sentimental or optimistic selection from the Scriptures, or for that matter in any cheap biblical fundamentalism or hell-fire evangelism. Moreover he does not for a moment maintain that Scripture study obviates the need for firm guidance by the Church. While God is free to save men outside the Church, in practice he usually saves within it. "There is no entering into life unless the Church conceives us in her womb, brings us to birth, nourishes us in her bosom and preserves us by her tutelage and discipline." Nevertheless Calvin's doctrine of the Church might by sixteenth-century standards be called liberal. He did not believe that church government need everywhere be uniform and he approved a scheme of bishops to be operated by his emissaries in Poland. With Melanchthon he

The doctrinal disputes between Lutheranism and the Reformed churches, already apparent at Marburg in 1529, grew rather than diminished after Luther's death.

believed that forms of worship could be varied according to local needs. Influenced by Martin Bucer, he mediated in a creative spirit between the eucharistic teaching of Luther and that of Zwingli. For Calvin the spiritual reality of the sacrament is not located within the physical elements of bread and wine; yet it is given to the communicant at the same moment as they are given. The spiritual action and the physical action thus occur as it were in parallel: an interpretation deeper than Zwingli's but far more readily intelligible than that of Luther. In the event, by the Zürich Agreement of 1549 Zwingli's successor Bullinger approved Calvin's doctrine of the eucharist, which attained general acceptance throughout the Reformed churches. The Lutherans nevertheless steadily refused it and this doctrine continued to provide the frontier between the Evangelical and the Reformed religion.

Returning from a brief visit to France in the summer of 1536, Calvin made for Strassburg, but found his road blocked by the opposing armies of King Francis and the Emperor Charles. Consequently he decided to make a diversion through Geneva. By this fateful chance, he met Guillaume Farel (*1489–1565*), once a member of the reforming group at Meaux and now a militant advocate of Protestantism. Seeing in Calvin an intellectual power lacking in himself and his associates, Farel urged him in the most solemn terms to stay and join the Genevan movement. The prospect seemed daunting enough. Threatened by its bishop and by the duke of Savoy, Geneva was a French-speaking city of some 16,000 inhabitants, remote from the solid German-Swiss centers of the Reformed faith, Zürich, Berne, and Basle. Internally the place was rent by factions which seemed to obviate any chance of a coherent policy. Calvin accepted Farel's charge, but after a couple of years they were both dismissed when they objected to the adoption in Geneva of a liturgy devised at Berne. Retiring to Strassburg, Calvin spent the years 1538–41 ministering to the local French congregation and learning ecclesiastical politics from the immensely experienced Martin Bucer. Recalled at last to Geneva, he obeyed with the heaviest misgivings. Though he and his party gradually built up an ascendancy, he never exercised anything resembling a dictatorship. The city council remained his master, even though during his later years it seldom rejected his advice on matters of religion. And while the council fully accepted the elaborate moral and religious code known as the Ecclesiastical Ordinances, this was often flouted by powerful families and secularist groups, which strove to avoid the replacement of Catholic discipline by Calvinist discipline. While enthusiasts like John Knox thought Geneva "the most perfect school of Christ," Calvin spoke of it on his deathbed as a perverse and stiff-necked community. In 1555 the faction headed by the Perrin family made a forceful attempt to oust Calvin and his fellow ministers but suffered a complete overthrow, followed by various sentences of death and exile. Calvin's most famous enemy and victim was not a Genevan, but a visitor already condemned by the Catholic Church. The brilliant but reckless Miguel Servetus was prosecuted by Calvin and burned by the Genevan authorities in 1553 for denying the divinity of Christ and the Holy Trinity.

Amid all these troubles a godly discipline came into being and was found acceptable by the great majority of Genevans. The influence of the ministers permeated political life, while to an extent which Luther would have disapproved they acknowledged that the secular government was divinely commissioned to enforce orthodox belief and personal morality. The Genevan Church was governed by four orders of men: pastors, doctors, lay elders, and deacons. A Consistory manned by ministers and laymen prohibited showy costume, dances, and bawdy entertainments; it also repressed superstitious usages, witchcraft, profiteering, and business frauds. Adulterers sometimes suffered the death penalty. For a time even taverns were banned, though decorous restaurants, duly furnished with bibles, failed to yield adequate profits. This crass attempt to produce a perfect Christian society by laws and by endless sermonizing had in fact some mitigating features. In Calvin's later years Geneva was regarded as the cleanest and best-ordered city in Europe. Its social services, particularly those for the sick and the aged, had few close rivals. Educational opportunity was offered on an admirable scale, especially from 1559, when Calvin played a leading part in founding a university of distinction. Not for a moment should Geneva be dismissed as a brain-washing tyranny. The system sought—and generally obtained—a willing and even enthusiastic response from the individual. Life was characterized by a sober physical and mental refinement; the element of Christian humanism coexisted with that of theocracy and when the impulse to ecclesiastical perfectionism weakened, Geneva was to occupy a high rank among the centers of secular

Calvinist iconoclasm in the Netherlands
engraving by FRANZ HOGENBERG (1579)

enlightenment. That this transition was no local accident is suggested by the parallel developments at Amsterdam and Edinburgh.

Within the Reformation period itself, the constructive enthusiasm of the movement is proved by its widespread penetration into parts of Europe where social conditions differed completely from those of a compact Swiss city-state. Whenever called upon by circumstances, the Reformed religion developed a political and military activism. So far from inducing a fatalist acceptance of God's omnipotent decrees, it provoked a disposition to effort; it impelled a man to prove to himself and others that God had indeed elected him to salvation. If the Calvinists agreed with Luther that good works availed nothing to save a man, they accepted the converse belief that such works provided an evident sign of divine grace. In a hostile environment the survival value of Calvinism was high. Moreover, once the struggle moved out of Germany, Calvin's presentation of the faith displayed features more widely attractive than those of Lutheranism. For educated laymen Calvin produced from 1541 a series of editions of the *Institutes* translated into most lucid French, while the metrical psalms of Clément Marot exercised an enormous popular appeal, attaining over fifty editions between 1543 and 1563. During the fifties and early sixties the Geneva Company of Pastors trained, examined, and sent forth hundreds of missionaries, most of them passing into France, where organized Calvinist congregations swiftly appeared in all the leading cities. In 1559 the first synod of the Reformed Church met in Paris, being attended by representatives from some 72 congregations, but two years later the Protestants were claiming that over 2000 such communities existed in France alone.

The persecution during the later years of Francis I became intensified on the accession of his son Henry II *(r.1547–59)*, who created the *Chambre Ardente,* a special court for the punishment of heretics, still inaccurately designated as *Luthériens.* But the disease-infested prisons of Paris accounted for even more victims than did the stake. Most of them were humble people, yet many leading noblemen and gentry joined the cause, among them Gaspard de Coligny, Admiral of France, Louis, Prince of Condé and his brother Antoine de Bourbon, titular King of Navarre in the right of his wife Jeanne d'Albret. Calvin inspired such magnates with a spate of letters, while their wives proved even more assiduous converts. Nobles mixed with commons in vast psalm-singing outdoor assemblies. The new creed spread into all regions of France, attaining special strength among the industrial populations of major cities like Lyons and also among the merchant classes in the seaports and maritime zones of western France. In these latter, as opposed to the old central and eastern cities, lay the new economic strength of the kingdom.

More surprising than its French successes were those of Calvinism in eastern Europe, especially in Poland and Lithuania. Even in Hungary the Turkish occupation did not greatly impede the work of missionaries. Even more pointedly than in Germany, the motto here might have been *cujus regio, ejus religio,* since the spread of the new faith depended largely on its acceptance by the nobility, who exercised almost sovereign powers within their vast estates. Such men had been Latin-educated, often in western Europe; they were alert to humanist values and Erasmian reforming aspirations. They had no affection for German literature, no affinities with the civic or monarchical aspects of Lutheranism. Though at first an urban phenomenon, Calvinism could also be readily adapted to the needs of eastern neo-feudal territories. From the fifties there rapidly arose a presbyterian system within which the gentry served as elders, appointed the ministers, and dominated the assemblies of the Calvinist Church just as they dominated their provincial and national parliaments. Needless to add, these secular motives can be exaggerated: in addition, the advances of the Reformed creed owed much to the diffusion of writings by Calvin and Bullinger, as well as to native ministers like the ex-Lutherans Jan Laski and Felix Cruciger, who by 1557–60 had set up a full-fledged presbyterian Calvinism in Little Poland and Lithuania.

France apart, in western Europe the most significant advances made by the Reformed religion occurred in Switzerland, the Palatinate, the Netherlands, and Scotland, while its influence upon the English Reformation became more powerful than might appear from the liturgy of the Anglican

Church. The Protestant areas of Switzerland can fairly be called Calvinist after the Zürich Agreement of 1549. In the Netherlands Charles V conducted a fierce persecution of Lutherans and Anabaptists, but the fifties and sixties nevertheless saw his problem made infinitely more formidable by a large influx of field-preachers trained in the Reformed faith. By 1566 a fierce popular iconoclasm was directed against the Catholic churches, while mass meetings occurred in the environs of Antwerp and other large cities. These resembled armed camps and could be dispersed only by persuasion. At this stage the Calvinist Reformation entered the field of Netherlandish politics and by gradual stages developed into a national revolt against Habsburg rule.

The long medieval dispute between England and France for influence over Scotland was soon brought to a new climax by the advent to that northern kingdom of the Protestant Reformation. In Scotland a legacy of anticlericalism and Lollardy had given way to men like Patrick Hamilton, who acquired Lutheran beliefs in Paris and at Wittenberg before his return to Scotland and his martyrdom in 1528 at St. Andrews. By 1542 expanding Protestantism became linked with a pro-English movement in opposition to the French Catholic party headed by Mary of Guise, the widow of James V and regent for her infant daughter, Mary Queen of Scots. The latter was sent to France to be educated by the Guises, while Cardinal David Beaton led the Scottish Church, and indeed for a brief space the nation itself, in the war against Henry VIII. In 1546 Beaton succeeded in capturing and burning the chief Protestant missionary George Wishart, but soon afterwards a small band of Wishart's admirers took revenge by assassinating Beaton. Besieged by a French force in the castle of St. Andrews, the rebels surrendered on a promise of early liberation, but their captors felt little obligation to keep promises made to heretics. Some among them, including Wishart's disciple John Knox, went to endure for many months the living death of galley-slaves.

Knox was a fanatic cast in a truly heroic mold. Whereas Calvin had reluctantly allowed armed resistance against oppressors of "true religion"— and then only when sanctioned by the estates and nobility of a country— Knox did not share these scruples. He belonged to the new breed of Calvinists, who in the face of the enemy neither showed nor expected forbearance. The subsequent career of Knox as a minister in the newly Protestant England of Edward VI was followed there by the Catholic reaction under Mary Tudor, which sent him into a new continental exile, and a period of close association with Calvin at Geneva. In 1555–56 he visited Scotland for a few months and was well received by many of the nobility, who formed a Protestant league called the Lords of the Congregation. The Covenant drawn up between them in strict legal terms was an instrument characteristic of the Scottish Reformation and destined to be several times repeated. Urged by the Lords to return, Knox complied in 1559 and found a powerful political organization, together with a national Church managed by lay elders. In opposition to what had by now become a national movement, the Guise family were prepared to throw in French forces, and for some years the backward little northern kingdom became a crucial front in the Reformation struggle. The key to this situation now clearly lay with Elizabeth, the new Queen of England, and her astute minister Sir William Cecil.

4. The Two English Reformations

The Reformation in England was a far less insular process than most of its historians have liked to suppose, yet it displayed so many eccentric features and had so many long-term effects. on the world history of Christianity that its leading features demand a separate account. It might be said that in England two Reformations occurred more or less contemporaneously. The one was religious, having its origins in Lollardy and Lutheranism; the other political, springing at first from anticlericalism, brought to a crisis by the nullity suit of Henry VIII, and thenceforth flourishing upon the nation's fear of the Catholic Habsburgs. Though the political and religious Reformations tended to converge, the resultant Elizabethan Settlement did not fully comprehend within the Anglican Church the most vigorous of the Protestant impulses, which, mishandled by the Stuart dynasty, helped to create the new Anglo-Scottish crisis of the seventeenth century.

Around the decade 1500–1510 English religion had not seemed destined to revolutionary change. Despite the numerous Lollard groups, despite Colet and Christian humanism, despite a few devotional writers related to the English mystics of the fourteenth century, the mass of the nation did not rise above a custom-ridden piety in which the veneration of the saints bulked very large. People went on pilgrimages much as they had done in Chaucer's day, while fine churches were still being built in the Perpendicular gothic style peculiar to the island-kingdom. The clergy formed a high proportion of educated men, yet as elsewhere in Europe, lay education was spreading, while clerical ignorance and moral laxity did not go uncriticized. More pointedly, men begrudged the payment of tithes and mortuary dues to a wealthy Church. In 1515 an enormous tumult arose in London when Richard Hunne, a merchant of known Lollard sympathies, was found with his neck broken in the bishop's prison. Yet more profoundly dangerous to the Church than the London mob were the common lawyers, a large fraternity long jealous of ecclesiastical jurisdiction and embracing not merely judges and solicitors but that considerable section of the gentry which studied the common law at the Inns of Court, in effect a legal university in London. The bishops, mostly former civil servants promoted to their sees by the King, towered remotely above the populace and systematically forbade the publication of the Bible in English. Unlike his continental neighbors, an Englishman could not read the Bible in his own language unless he consorted with heretics, who surreptitiously studied in manuscript the old translation made by Wycliffe's associate John Purvey.

The English glorify their Reformation in retrospect. Title page from Gilbert Burnet's work of 1679, still useful for its documents. Henry VIII tramples on the papal tiara; Cranmer on the papal decrees. In the background the edifice of superstition is being demolished; that of religion erected.

Though for some time the Lollard heresy had been recovering strength, it could boast organized groups in relatively few areas: London, Essex, West Kent, the Chiltern Hills, and the upper Thames Valley. With few exceptions the Lollards were manual workers, but wandering agents coordinated their activities and information. From time to time a few were burned, but without arousing more than local interest. On the other hand antisacerdotal and anticeremonial opinions—apparently of Lollard origin—seem to have circulated outside the organized Lollard communities. Most of Luther's negative criticisms had indeed been anticipated by Wycliffe, and long after the entry of Lutheranism into England numerous heretics continued to repeat Lollard teachings in the terms used a century earlier. This very gradual merging of the old and the new dissent is at present being studied in detail. Nevertheless, by no imaginable process could unaided Lollardy have occupied the seats of power. The ruling classes identified it with proletarian sedition, while it had no access to the printers, at all events until the Lutheran Reformers began to print Lollard manuscripts in order to prove the antiquity of the Reformation.

By the 1520s the greatest single source of anticlericalism was Thomas Wolsey *(c.1475-1530)*, who not only combined the offices of Papal Legate and Lord Chancellor, but amassed enormous personal wealth, invaded the jurisdictions of his fellow churchmen and gravely offended the nobility and the common lawyers. We have already observed his failure to obtain a decree of nullity for Henry VIII from Habsburg-controlled Rome. His dismissal from power in 1529 solved no problems and the King's need for a male heir now placed an immense strain upon the loyalty of English churchmen toward the Papacy. The personal nobility of Katherine, the monumental egotism and self-deception of the King, have ever since confused the real historical issue, yet eminent Catholics—even Sir Thomas More, who succeeded Wolsey as Chancellor—appreciated the necessities of the realm and the complexities of the divorce problem. The English Schism, as it now proceeded to develop from this problem, had no direct connection with religion: it arose from a clash between English national security and Habsburg family pride.

The advent of Lutheranism had meanwhile preceded the divorce crisis by a decade, the new beliefs having begun to make modest progress in English society before Henry VIII ever desired to exclude the Roman jurisdiction from his realm. About 1520 a group of scholars began meeting to discuss Luther's doctrines in the White Horse Tavern in Cambridge under the chairmanship of Dr. Robert Barnes, an Augustinian friar who later visited Wittenberg, and then acted as one of Thomas Cromwell's envoys to the Lutherans, before suffering martyrdom in the reaction of 1539-40. Some of the early Cambridge group carried the new movement to Oxford, notably into the new Cardinal College founded by Wolsey. With greater significance, during the twenties Lutheranism gained a firm footing among the London merchants, and among their fellow countrymen who were allowed to maintain a large establishment in Antwerp immune from invasion by Catholic inquisitors. No combination could have been better designed for the import of books and ideas; only a leader was needed and he soon appeared in the person of William Tyndale *(c.1494–1536)*, the greatest personality of the English Reformation. Rebuffed by English ecclesiastics in his aspiration to translate the Scriptures, Tyndale went abroad in 1524 and did most of his literary work under the protection of the English merchants at Antwerp. His pamphleteering was varied and effective, but its importance was transcended by his English versions of the New Testament and the Pentateuch. A gifted linguist and a master of English style, he created a translation which formed the dominant element in all the English Bibles (including the famous Authorized Version of 1611) until our own century. Copies of his New Testament began to flood into England in 1526, and in various editions, armed with prefaces freely translated from those of Luther, it eluded the agents of the bishops and found innumerable readers even in conservative circles. Tyndale's work upon the Old Testament was in due course carried to completion by Miles Coverdale, once a fellow Augustinian and disciple of Robert Barnes, who also fled to the Continent and in 1535 produced the first complete printed Bible in the English language. Meantime Tyndale—who drew Protestant ideas from various sources and was no mere mouthpiece of Luther—had been conducting a prolix pamphlet war with Sir Thomas More, now the official defender of the tottering Catholic establishment. In the end both of them were silenced by opponents who did not believe that the conflict should be settled by intellectual argument. Lured from the security of the English House in Antwerp, Tyndale was garrotted as a heretic by the Netherlandish government. His books continued to lay the foundations of Protestantism in English society.

By the time of Tyndale's death the English State-Reformation had reached its climax, and despite the King's personal conservatism, it had begun to develop doctrinal as well as political implications. The fall of Wolsey had been followed by two years of floundering royal expedients, but in 1531 Henry discovered a minister who could devise a purely English solution to the problem of the divorce. A former merchant with long experience in Italy and Antwerp, Thomas Cromwell *(c.1485–1540)* had studied the common law and risen to notice as Wolsey's man of business. He now found ample support in the anticlerical Reformation Parliament *(1529–36)*, a remarkable assembly in which ministers and members carried out far more legal, social and administrative changes than those hitherto accomplished in any comparable period of English history. With its ready concurrence Cromwell devised the legislation which severed the realm from papal jurisdiction and in 1534 made the King Supreme Head of the Church in England. The hitherto obscure Cambridge scholar Thomas Cranmer

Portrait of Thomas Cranmer
engraving by W. HOLL
Lambeth Palace

(1489–1556) was summoned to the archbishopric of Canterbury *(1532),* gave formal sentence upon the invalidity of Henry's marriage with Katherine, and pronounced lawful his recent marriage to Anne Boleyn.

With striking expedition Cromwell subordinated the national Church to a royal control, normally though not necessarily exercised by parliamentary statute. Moreover he organized an extensive propaganda campaign, utilizing the anticlerical arguments of Marsiglio of Padua. His domineering ecclesiastical policy should be seen alongside his striving to weaken the great feudal families as well as the Church, to build a more efficient society based upon education and the conditioning of a turbulent people to law and order. On the other hand the genuineness of Cromwell's own adherence to Protestantism, however unfervent his character, would scarcely be questioned by those familiar with the evidence. He rather than Cranmer was responsible for producing the Great Bible, an edition re-edited by Coverdale *(1539),* and for actually placing copies of it in the churches for public study. In England it was Bible reading which finally overcame the old clerical pieties, the world of saint-cults, pilgrimages, purgatory; and Bible reading which soon gave birth to a new set of problems! Though he sought to reform the secular clergy, Cromwell saw no place in the new society for the monasteries, which (with some exceptions such as the Carthusian houses) could no longer claim to be a very influential element in the devotional life of the nation. Though Cromwell obviously believed in parliamentary rule and in the common law, he also saw that the seizure of the immense monastic lands could endow the Crown in perpetuity and create a government of unshakable strength. His commissioners surveyed all clerical incomes in order to tax them more effectively, and to assess the wealth of the monasteries. In 1536, after carrying out an often unjust survey of monastic discipline, he presided over a parliamentary dissolution of those monasteries with annual incomes of less than £200: three years later the greater houses also disappeared into the maw of the State. Much fine architecture was ruined, art treasures and manuscripts lost, but in general the dissolution was not inhumanely conducted, the monks, friars, and nuns receiving modest pensions and the heads of the richer houses quite lavish ones.

These changes did not pass without arousing some opposition. In the north of England religious conservatism and feudal loyalties linked with the fear that economic disaster might follow the dissolution of the monasteries: these motives interlocked with a multitude of secular grievances to produce the Pilgrimage of Grace *(1536–37)*, the most formidable rebellion to confront any Tudor monarch. It was nevertheless dispersed without a pitched battle, while the Henrician government, anxious to win over the hesitant and half-loyal northern gentry, had the good sense to take only moderate reprisals. As for the more purely religious objectors to the Schism, they made relatively little impact upon a royalist nation which shrank fearfully from the prospect of civil war. Two eminent and virtuous Englishmen Thomas More and Bishop John Fisher went to the block *(1535)* rather than accept the severance of the realm from the Roman Catholic Church. Previously a handful of equally virtuous Carthusian monks of London had been imprisoned with barbarous cruelty and then hanged as traitors. In general, however, the English Church accepted its new headship with surprising passivity. Extremely few clerics emigrated, chief among the exceptions being the devout humanist Reginald Pole, a kinsman of the Tudors, his own suspect relatives being persecuted by Henry while Reginald denounced the King's proceedings from his cultured exile in Italy. There remained in the King's service men like Bishop Stephen Gardiner, a staunch upholder of Catholic doctrine including transubstantiation, yet prepared to abandon the papal connection and give firm support to the Royal Supremacy.

In 1539–40 the irascible King listened to Gardiner and allowed Cromwell to be condemned upon false accusations of heresy and treason. Henry then not only avoided the alliances with Lutheran rulers into which Cromwell had sought to lead him, but passed reactionary legislation, burned a few Protestants, and sought to prevent the access of the working class to the

Bible. Even so, during the last six years of the reign, Protestant literature continued to flow into the country, and the evidence distinctly suggests an uninterrupted growth of Protestantism within English society. A strong party at court, headed by the Earl of Hertford—uncle and afterwards Protector to the young heir Edward—was known to favor the new beliefs. And oddly enough, the King allowed Edward himself to be educated by tutors of similar inclinations. Again, instead of allowing Gardiner to dominate the national Church, Henry kept Cranmer in favor as a balancing force and even allowed him to plan liturgical changes along semi-Protestant lines. At the same time he ruined one of Cromwell's main contributions to the monarchy by selling off a large part of the monastic lands to pay for an expensive and avoidable war against France and Scotland. The monastic lands were eagerly bought by people of all religious persuasions, many of the most prominent being known Catholics. Land proved an excellent investment in a period when the inrush of Peruvian silver and many other causes were conspiring to produce a Europe-wide monetary inflation. In England, as in continental States where lands were detached from the Church, the gentry able to buy those lands achieved greater economic and political weight.

On Henry's death early in 1547, the group under Hertford, soon made Duke of Somerset, gave England its first openly Protestant government. At once a social idealist and a lover of personal wealth and power, Somerset was less ruthless than Henry, but could not wield the spell of an anointed King and sought to govern as leader of a small council of nobles. He permitted priests to marry and in 1549 allowed Cranmer to issue his first Book of Common Prayer. This was a masterpiece of compromise written in stately English; a revision of medieval English rites, influenced by Cardinal Quinones' reformed Catholic Breviary, by the Lutheran Church Orders, and by another scheme of compromise issued by Hermann von Wied, archbishop of Cologne. On the other hand little success attended the secular policies of Somerset. He failed to win final victory over the Scots, though his invasion with cartloads of Bibles doubtless helped to lay the foundations for the later triumph of John Knox. In England he failed to prevent outbreaks of popular discontent: an agrarian revolt in East Anglia and a rising in the western counties directed against the Prayer Book. His loss of control over country and Council in the summer of 1549 brought about his replacement by John Dudley, later Duke of Northumberland. A less scrupulous politician than Somerset, Dudley decided amid mounting financial embarrassment to continue a Protestant policy. He completed the proposed dissolution of chantries, religious guilds, collegiate churches, and other allegedly superstitious or redundant institutions; he even confiscated the "surplus" plate of the parish churches. At the same time he encouraged Cranmer to issue a revised Prayer Book *(1552)*, with brief but significant changes reducing the Communion to little more than a memorial service. During these years there entered England a stream of continental refugees headed by Martin Bucer, Jan Laski, Peter Martyr, and the renegade Vicar-General of the Capuchin Order, Bernardino Ochino. All these visitors, several of whom soon occupied important posts in the two English universities, belonged to the Reformed, not to the Lutheran religion; and they gave the young Church of England a strong push in that direction. In terms of world history the greatest error of the Lutheran Church was its failure to win England, a failure soon to be completed by the widespread rejection of English refugees by Lutherans during the coming Marian Reaction.

When the consumptive boy-king died in 1553, Dudley sought to place upon the throne his daughter-in-law Lady Jane Grey, but even the markedly Protestant counties of East Anglia rallied to the cause of the legitimate heir. Devout, virtuous, and inflexible in all matters concerning religion, Queen Mary was a true daughter of Katherine and a true granddaughter of Isabella the Catholic. From the outset of her reign she announced her intention to bring about the restoration of the Catholic faith in England. In her first Parliament she undid the Edwardian Settlement and reverted to the position which had obtained at the death of Henry VIII. The following year she directed the bishops to repress heresy and remove from their benefices the many priests who had married during the last four years. Later in 1554 the medieval legislation against heretics was revived and the antipapal statutes repealed. Cardinal Reginald Pole was received into England and, duly commissioned by the Pope, he formally absolved the realm. Despite the advances made by Protestantism under Edward VI, both the ardent Protestants and the ardent Catholics appear to have constituted smallish minorities of the population. Once again the rest of the nation preferred to accept this reversal rather than risk rebellion and anarchy. Yet from this point Queen Mary began making blunders of the first order, and by the time of her early death had alienated the sympathies of the people. In 1554 she married her cousin Philip *(1527-98),* son of Charles V and soon to be made King of Spain and many other dominions. On his arrival his large retinue of Spaniards became embroiled with the London populace, while all thinking Englishmen clearly saw that the Habsburgs would by this latest of their notorious dynastic marriages subordinate English interests to their own vast international designs. Indeed, had Mary lived longer, the harsh victimization of the Netherlands by Habsburg autocracy might well have been repeated in England.

About the same time Mary and Pole began a mass persecution of English Protestants, nearly 300 of whom perished by burning during the next four years. The great majority of the martyrs came from the common people of southeastern England, yet vitally for the prestige of the Protestant cause, several high ecclesiastics also went to the stake, including the deposed archbishop Cranmer and bishops Ridley and Latimer. At the same time some 800 men and women, mainly influential people from the upper and middle orders of society, passed into exile rather than accept Catholicism. At Frankfurt, Geneva, Strassburg, Aarau, Zürich, and other places— mainly in the Reformed countries and cities—they formed organized communities. The less fortunate English Protestants, unable or unwilling to emigrate, formed underground congregations in London and other areas, where the local magistrates often connived at their activities. In terms of the numbers burned, the Marian persecution could not compare with those current in the Habsburg territories or in the France of Henry II. But England had hitherto seen no action so concentrated, and since many of the sufferers were not lapsed Catholics but young people brought up as Protestants, the legalist inhumanity of the Marian persecution stands apparent. Its historical importance lies chiefly in the fact that it created a tenaciously unfavorable image of Catholicism in England. This image was soon to be stamped upon the national consciousness by a book second only in popularity to the Bible in pious English families: the so-called *Book of Martyrs* by John Foxe, of which many English editions appeared from 1563. Alongside this mistaken persecution may be placed the failure of the Marian Reaction to become an effective part of that European Catholic revival which we shall shortly describe. English Catholicism perhaps reached its religious nadir during the fifties. Had Mary and Pole lived longer they might well have promoted internal missions, but in fact Pole rebuffed the offer of Ignatius Loyola to train Jesuit missionaries and send them to help the Marian government.

From political blundering of another sort the hapless Mary was saved by the recalcitrance of the governing class, especially inside Parliament. For the gentry it was one thing to attend the Catholic mass again, but quite another to restore to the Church the monastic lands for which they had paid good money. In this and other matters even Philip and his father Charles urged Mary to observe moderation: while they believed in persecution wherever it paid political and religious dividends, they saw that interests of the Church and the Habsburgs would inevitably suffer from a policy which drove any considerable group of Englishmen to desperation. In November 1558 as matters were moving to this crisis Mary and her intimate adviser Pole died within a few hours of each other, all too conscious of their failure. Deserted by her unaffectionate husband, disappointed in her hope of bearing an heir to the throne, Mary passed from the scene, and amid the rejoicing of the Londoners was succeeded by the last surviving child of Henry VIII. As the daughter of the Protestant Anne Boleyn and herself suspected of Protestant sympathies, the Princess Elizabeth had occupied a perilous situation under the rule of her half-sister, and though her views were very far from radical, it was from the first accepted that she would revert to a settlement like that of her brother Edward VI. Intellectual by nature, she had enjoyed an excellent humanist education. She composed beautiful prayers and may indeed have felt a deeper personal piety than most of her biographers have allowed her. Yet certainly she was a consummate actress and knew how to conduct a love affair with the nation.

From the early days, Elizabeth received wise and cautious advice from Sir William Cecil, later Lord Burghley. But from the ecclesiastical viewpoint she succeeded to a power vacuum, since the Marian bishops stood firm by their Catholicism and had to be removed from office. The exiles returning from abroad were the only other group with a clear religious program, and though it was somewhat too Protestant for the Queen's tastes, their policy nevertheless did not prove rigidly Calvinist. Four years earlier, those exiles who accepted Cranmer's second Prayer Book had quarrelled at Frankfurt with the English Calvinists led by the fiery Scot John Knox. The latter group, having withdrawn in high dudgeon to Geneva, did not respond swiftly enough to the changes of 1558; they failed to return to England in such force as to influence the new settlement. By sheer ill luck Knox had just published a blistering attack on "the monstrous regiment [i.e. rule] of women," and an effusion meant to condemn the Catholic queens of Europe gravely offended Elizabeth. In the parliament of 1559 a distinctly Anglican settlement thus came to be hammered out in the absence of the men who would have championed a strong approach toward Geneva. By the summer of that year Parliament restored the Royal Supremacy and reinstated an amended form of Cranmer's second Prayer Book. Among the few changes were the phrases spoken at the administration of Communion which astutely left undetermined the precise nature of the divine presence. The Thirty-nine Articles of Religion, with their more distinctly Reformed tendencies, did not follow until 1563, but they have remained the basis of Anglican belief until our own day. The mild "High Church" movement of the seventeenth century and the far more pronounced one which arose in Victorian England should not be allowed to conceal the decisively Protestant character of the Elizabethan Settlement. Despite the Catholic influences upon Cranmer's Prayer Books, that Settlement was no halfway house between the Reformation and Roman Catholicism. Even its most characteristically "Anglican" theologians felt strong influences from Calvinism. And soon after the outset of the reign there arose a highly articulate Puritan party, as yet almost entirely *within* the English Church and dedicated to cleansing it from what the Puritans regarded as lingering relics of Catholicism. The Elizabethan Church thus developed a tension, yet there remained strong reasons why that tension should not be allowed to develop into instability. After the years of violent change and counter-change, the religious and political Reformations had now sufficiently fused to form a basis for the political integrity of the realm, and indeed for those intellectual developments which blossomed into the so-called Age of Shakespeare.

5.   Catholic Reform and Revival

The term Counter Reformation, commonly used to cover the religious and political revival of the Catholic Church in the sixteenth and earlier seventeenth centuries, might well be regarded as a simplification even more drastic than most such historical labels. The origins of the religious recovery long antedated the outbreak of Luther's revolt, while even in its developed stages the movement involved a spontaneous Christian revival as well as a political counter-attack upon the Protestant Reformation. That great historian Ranke, who in 1834 invented the expression Counter Reformation, conceived both Protestant and Catholic Reformations as streams arising from closely neighboring sources, but then moving apart down opposing sides of a mountain, thus becoming divided forever. In earlier chapters of our present survey we have already mentioned many of the early Catholic reformers: Ximenes in Spain, Savonarola in Florence, the Observant movements among the friars, anti-Lutheran controversialists like Eck, More, and Fisher. Another aspect of Catholic revival appears with those devotees of St. Augustine, who stressed Justification by Faith, but without carrying the implications so far as Luther. The leading heirs of this last tradition were Italians, most notably the Venetian aristocrat Cardinal Contarini, whose negotiations with the Lutherans finally collapsed in 1541 at Regensburg.

At first no country did more to stimulate religious revival than the Netherlands, with their now not-so-modern *devotio moderna.* No devotional book was more influential or more frequently reprinted in the sixteenth century than the *Imitation of Christ,* and its influence was far from being limited to the religious life of northern Europe. Just as the Netherlandish artists had fathered Portuguese and Catalan painting; just as Flemish polyphonic music had given birth to that of Italy and Spain, so did Netherlandish mysticism provide the impetus to that Spanish contemplative movement which suddenly arose in 1500, attracted very numerous devotees, and culminated in the two great Carmelite mystics St. Theresa of Ávila *(1515-83)* and St. John of the Cross *(1542-91).* Netherlandish piety also exerted marked effects upon the practical methods of a reviving faith. When around 1540 the Jesuits suggested that a religious Order should abandon the choir offices, devoting the time thus saved to education and charity, they shocked many old-fashioned people; yet a century earlier the Brethren of the Common Life had enunciated similar principles. An attractive combination of meditative prayer and humanist scholarship had also been followed in the schools of the Brethren, and this combination became a notable feature of Catholic revival in the mid-sixteenth century. A prominent connecting link between the *devotio,* Christian humanism, and early Catholic revival can be seen in the Netherlander Jean Standonck, who even in 1500 was taking practical measures to train parish priests in modern learning, Catholic theology, and personal discipline. It was Standonck who reorganized the Collège de Montaigu in Paris, where both John Calvin and Ignatius Loyola *(c.1491–1556)* studied in later years. He also founded similar colleges in Cambrai, Valenciennes, Malines, and Louvain, colleges which foreshadowed both those of the Jesuits and also the diocesan seminaries demanded half a century later by the Council of Trent.

With the exception of Adrian of Utrecht, whose would-be reforming pontificate lasted only from January 1522 to September 1523, the popes of the High Renaissance showed themselves highly reluctant to begin the work at home by rationalizing the curia and by relinquishing the financial expedients which had produced such dire results in Germany. In truth, their fears of reform at the hands of a General Council of the Church were intensified through the pressures exerted by lay rulers, and especially by the orthodox yet immensely ambitious Habsburgs. Not only did the Emperor Charles and his brother Ferdinand demand communion in both kinds for the German laity, but they threatened to assume general control of Catholic reform throughout much of Europe. While the strength of the religious revival henceforth came from the two southern peninsulas of Europe, there remained a dichotomy between the Italian Papacy and the increasingly Spanish-thinking Charles, who inherited not merely German problems but a strongly monarchical Spanish Church. This Papal-Spanish disharmony remained profound and cannot be dismissed as the mere bickering of two likeminded powers. In addition, the popes always needed to be looking over their shoulders at the power which had lost the Italian Wars. The kings of France already supported the Turkish invaders and the German Protestants: faced by any close friendship between emperor and pope, they might well proceed to imitate Henry VIII of England, splitting what remained of Catholic Christendom down the center with a Gallican schism.

Amid these confusing political forces the Catholic revival manifested itself not in Rome but locally in a host of dutiful bishops, popular missioners, and founders or reformers of religious Orders. Especially did these types of zeal manifest themselves in the Italy of 1510–40. Yet already around 1500 there had existed a number of informal religious societies called Oratories, aimed both at personal edification and practical charities. From this background arose Gasparo Contarini, Giovanni Morone, Gaetano di Thiene, and Gian Pietro Carafa, the last being bishop of Brindisi during the twenties. In 1524 Thiene and Carafa founded the Theatine Order for secular clerics, a select body which proved a school for future bishops. A similar Order was that of the Barnabites, who from the early thirties conducted open-air evangelical meetings in the north Italian cities. Closer still to the people were the reformed Franciscans known as Capuchins, patronized by the noble Vittoria Colonna but working mainly among the poor. Of the Orders for women, the most socially effective was that of the Ursulines, established in 1535 by St. Angela Merici *(d.1540),* a most attractive personality who had already for many years tended the paupers, the sick, and the young in the towns around Lake Garda. Half a century after her death the Ursulines also assumed the secular education of girls and so became the greatest of the female Orders concerned with school teaching.

The birth of new religious institutes did not in fact cease with the plethora of the twenties and thirties. One of the most influential was the Congregation of the Oratory, gradually formed in Rome between 1548 and 1564 under the leadership of St. Philip Neri *(d.1595)*, an original and gracious mystic with a characteristic none too common amid the puritanical Catholicism of this period: a sense of humor. His work, beginning in the streets of Rome, created a long chain of Oratorian houses throughout and far beyond the frontiers of Italy. His example ultimately inspired Cardinal Pierre de Bérulle to found in 1611 a French Oratory, one of the several successful Orders in the belated French stage of the Catholic Reformation. This stage lies beyond the scope of our present chapter: it is the world of St. Vincent de Paul *(c.1580-1660)*, St. François de Sales *(1576-1622)*, and the many devout lives so finely depicted in Henri Bremond's classic, *A Literary History of Religious Thought in France*. Directly and indirectly, the appearance between 1520 and 1620 of so many active—as distinct from cloistered—Orders contributed much to the image of the priesthood, the rehabilitation of which formed the most pressing task of the Catholic Church during the period of crisis. Nevertheless, the question has sometimes been asked whether too many of the choice spirits of the age were not drawn off into such Orders, leaving the inferior talent to the more prosaic yet quite basic functions of the parish priest. Yet whatever may be thought of the scale and the long-term effects of these new bodies, none of them can compare in social and political signficance with the Society of Jesus.

On the Catholic side of the great struggle Ignatius Loyola is the one figure having a historical stature comparable with those of Luther and Calvin. This Spanish nobleman might well have remained no more than a professional soldier but for a crippling leg wound sustained in 1521 during the siege of Pampeluna. During a long and agonizing convalescence his devotional reading made him decide to devote his life to propagating the faith, and he hung up his sword at the pilgrimage-shrine of Montserrat. From this stage his development became extremely deliberate; his search for a method extended over fifteen years, the years during which Protestantism was making giant strides. At Manresa he spent a year *(1522-23)* living in a hermit's cave and experiencing visions. Thereafter a brief visit to the Holy Land failed to dispel his romantic dream of converting the Moslem world. He resolved first to acquire some serious education, and after learning Latin with schoolboys at Barcelona, he progressed to the university of Paris. At the Collège de Montaigu *(1528-35)* he showed no great academic brilliance, but he broadened his outlook in this highly international society and finally in a chapel on the heights of Montmartre he and six companions founded the Society of Jesus. Of these and the three others who joined soon

Ignatius Loyola before Pope Paul III
The Gesù, Rome

afterwards, two were Savoyards, one Portuguese, and two Frenchmen, while the four Spaniards included the future missionary Francis Xavier, and Diego Laynez, destined as Loyola's successor to play a major role in the Counter Reformation.

Had not his progress to the East been obstructed by warfare between Venice and the Turks, Loyola would have led his Company back to the Holy Land, and there in all probability to an obscure and ineffective future. In the event, however, they reassembled in Rome and attracted much admiration by their labors among the poor and the sick. Contarini then came to know them and his introduction of Loyola to Pope Paul III led to the official foundation of the Society by a Bull of 1540. This slow process of gestation was followed by an expansion of remarkable speed. Despite the support of some famous nobles and clerics, lack of money always troubled the Society throughout the lifetime of its founder, yet Loyola's tenacity and trust, his almost mesmeric power over men, overcame each obstacle to expansion.

Like others of the new Orders, the Society of Jesus had essentially educational aims, the first of which was the formation of a special type of mission-priest. Then in its relation to the laity it was concerned less with fighting the new heresies than with spreading Christian knowledge among children and uninstructed people. It was a salvation army commanded by intellectuals. Its charter insisted upon the absolute obedience of its members to the Papacy and to their own superiors headed by the General of the Order. It demanded from them a vow of corporate and personal poverty and it rescinded the round of choir offices: but for the Pope's veto Loyola would have abolished musical services from his chapels and churches. Efficient, industrious, disliking pretentious religiosity, he was a thoroughly modern man despite his visions.

What made his Society unique was the methodology embodied in his *Spiritual Exercises,* the scheme he had first thought out at Manresa. From the earliest stages the *Exercises* were the basis of Jesuit discipline, though they were not printed until 1548. They took the form of a highly systematic and intensive series of meditations covering human sin; Christ's kingdom and the Passion; the glorified Lord. Originally meant to occupy a religious retreat lasting a month, they could be compressed into ten days and in later times have been widely employed in the training of priests outside the Jesuit Order. The meditations themselves called for a far more deliberate use of mental imagery than did the older modes of contemplation advocated by the mystical writers. They also aimed to develop will power, to produce active apostles as opposed to quiet contemplatives. By a paradox comparable with that in Calvinism, this systematic subordination of the individual personality ended by producing no mere dehumanized agents but instead, men of initiative and originality. In its constitution military and autocratic, the Society of Jesus attracted and inspired members of varied social backgrounds, classes, and educational attainments: the spiritual athletes were made to use common sense and take practical decisions, while the natural men of business were educated in the higher devotions.

In a world of slow communications all these capacities were soon required. By 1552 there were Jesuit houses of study in Rome, Bologna, Messina, Palermo, Valencia, Valladolid, Barcelona, Gandia, Alcalá, Salamanca, Burgos, and Paris. In Rome also was founded in that year the Collegium Germanicum, which soon became a training school for missions to combat heresies in Germany. In that country the Jesuits were popularly called "the Spanish priests," but neither here nor elsewhere can they fairly be dismissed as a religious rationalization of Spanish imperialism. Their outlook was normally supranational, their prime loyalty directed toward Rome. In Spain itself they did in fact encounter painful opposition from royal officials, from bishops, from the powerful Dominicans. In the Order at large the Portuguese element had become strong, and at the mid-century it comprised over a third of the total membership; indeed, in Portugal it threatened for a time to create a separate organization under the patronage of King John III. In France and in the Netherlands the Jesuits made slow progress for several decades, while in England they appeared far too late *(1580)* to make a decisive impact upon a Protestant, well-policed and bitterly anti-Spanish nation. By the later decades of the century they had indeed become deeply involved with politics: inevitably so, since the religious struggles of Europe had merged with the world of warfare, conspiracy, and conflicting nationalisms. The Jesuits were now widely credited with the beliefs that the end justified the means, that the pope had the right to depose kings, and that excommunicated rulers could be legitimately assassinated.

During the generalships of Loyola and Laynez *(d.1565)* the most spectacular achievements of the Jesuits took place on the German front and in overseas mission-fields. St. Francis Xavier worked in Goa, Travancore, Malacca, the Molucca Islands, and in Ceylon. Finding unscrupulous European traders the chief barrier to the extension of Christianity, he passed beyond their reach and founded a flourishing Church in the supposedly unspoiled land of Japan. After innumerable hardships and perils he died at last *(1552)* on the desolate island of St. John's at the very gate of China— which he had accepted as his next assignment! Strangely enough the Japanese Church flourished for a time, but it was decimated by the persecutions beginning in 1596-98 and ending with the exclusion of Europeans in 1640. By that time it could nevertheless glory in thousands of native martyrs and its survivors could still be recognized when in the nineteenth century Europeans returned to Japan.

A very different but equally devoted missionary was Peter Canisius *(1521-97)*, a Dutchman who joined the Society in 1543 and began preaching six years later at Ingolstadt under the patronage of the Duke of Bavaria. There in 1555 he erected a Jesuit college, and others soon followed in Cologne, Prague, Innsbrück, and Nijmegen. Under the terms of the Peace of Augsburg, Canisius could now work even in cities predominantly Protestant, and in Augsburg itself he is recorded as preaching well over 200 sermons in 1561-62. Under his leadership the Jesuit educational effort began to embrace not merely the training of priests but that of boys from aristocratic and influential families, the future pillars of the Catholic Church in Bavarian and Austrian society. Here as in other countries the Jesuits owed much of their influence to the fact that they systematized the legacy of the Renaissance educators and became known as the most efficient schoolmasters in Europe. Though it would be unjust to regard them as mainly devoted to converting the ruling classes of Europe, the fact remains that they could not and did not ignore the power structure of the society within which they had undertaken to preserve Catholicism. In the seventeenth century a Jesuit casuistry all too accommodating toward the sins of high society was to be indicted by Pascal, but in general such features should be regarded as marking a later period of decline. To the centralizing of the Church under Rome the Jesuit contribution proved crucial from the first. In licensing the Society Paul III made a wonderful bargain, for no organization fought so hard to restore the authority of the popes, and this in a period when many devout Catholics, especially in France and Spain, believed in a formal rather than in a functional Papal Supremacy. Better than any other man at the decisive Council of Trent, Laynez was to argue the case for a Roman monarchy.

Alessandro Farnese, Pope Paul III from 1534 to 1549, remained in many respects a grandee in the old Borgia-Medici tradition. He made his teen-age grandsons cardinals and elevated his undeserving son Pier Luigi to the dukedom of Parma and Piacenza. On the other hand he appointed to the cardinalate known reformers like Contarini, Carafa, Sadoleto, Pole, and Morone, and he allowed them to prepare *(1537)* a report on ecclesiastical abuses called *The Plan of the Cardinals for the Reform of the Church.* So frank did it prove that when its contents leaked out, Luther reprinted it, accompanied by his own sarcastic comments. Again, it was Paul III who fostered the Jesuits, the Ursulines, and the Barnabites. Most remarkably of all, it was he who overcame the misgivings he had hitherto shared with his predecessor Clement VII, when in 1542 he summoned to Trent *(Tridentum)* a General Council of the Church. This body did not in fact assemble until 1545, and owing to various political pressures and interruptions its work was to be spread over nearly two decades. Though it held twenty-five official sessions, these were concentrated into three periods of activity: 1545–47, 1551–52, and 1562–63. Nevertheless important canons and decrees arose from all three periods. In the end all the decisions could be embodied in one coherent code, giving a clear directive to the Roman Church, one which lasted into the twentieth century.

From any modern viewpoint many criticisms could be directed at the Tridentine Council. At all times its membership was heavily Italian. The Italian bishops outnumbered the Spaniards by six to one and the French by seven to one, while those considerable parts of the Germanic and east European world which were still Catholic remained almost unrepresented. The ambassadors of the secular rulers not only stated the views of their governments but placed heavy pressures on the ecclesiastics. Uproarious sessions, personal feuds, national intrigues, and street riots proved not infrequent in the grossly overcrowded little Alpine city. Yet the scene at Trent had its brighter aspects. The intrigues were balanced by a real sense of emergency, by much heartfelt zeal to cleanse the Church and to clarify doctrine. Many of the Italian bishops were not in fact mere papal clients, while a strong phalanx of expert theologians and canon lawyers, many of them Jesuits and Dominicans, were present as assessors to help the mere office holders. And though the success of the Council was endangered by profoundly divergent groups right up to the final sessions of 1563, its coherence was assured by an able series of papal legates, who maintained close contact with Rome. Despite the fact that the Council met under five pontificates, Rome was the one participant with well-defined objectives; it deserved by its consistency and intelligence, if not by past performance, to win the internal struggle for control of the Church.

So far as its actual decisions were concerned, the Council of Trent did not simply combat Protestant teaching: it also defined doctrines left obscure throughout earlier centuries and it decided in favor of some Catholic opinions against other Catholic opinions. Of course there existed an emotional disposition to denounce anything remotely resembling a Protestant dogma, while a liberal Catholic of the time of Erasmus might well have regarded the prevalent atmosphere as reactionary. By a rather narrow margin the Council swept aside biblical humanism and with it the Pauline-Augustinian emphases of Contarini and his admirers. In 1546 a strong party including Reginald Pole advocated that in the training of the clergy Scripture study should be given priority over the old scholastic disciplines, but this demand was thwarted by the chief Dominican representative, who stressed the delight with which the Protestants would greet such a proposal. Instead, the Council accepted St. Thomas Aquinas as the "common doctor"

The Council of Trent in session (1562–63) in S. Maria Maggiore. Within the specially erected amphitheater, the legates and cardinals faced the semicircle of bishops, the lay ambassadors sitting on their left.

of the Church and made scholastic theology the mainstay of clerical education. Quite intelligibly, during these years no provision was made to
encourage Bible reading by the laity. Needless to add, all seven sacraments
were retained; so were the doctrines of transubstantiation and the sacrificial
character of the mass. Despite the misgivings of the Emperor, the cup was
denied to the laity and the mass prohibited in languages other than Latin.
But amid the conservative theology, one creative and practical command
emerged: that a seminary to train secular clergy should be founded in every
diocese. In the event some bishops were slow to obey, but in the long run
this measure went far to rid the Church of its heaviest medieval handicap:
the bucolic and nonpreaching parish priest.

Years before the final sessions were held, concurrent steps were being
taken by the Papacy to repress Erasmian as well as Protestant propaganda.
In 1555 the former Inquisitor Gian Pietro Carafa became Pope Paul IV, and
his four-year rule became a neurotic reaction which alienated all Roman
society. The harshness of his punishments terrorized not only the heretics
but the absentee bishops, the runagate monks, and even the courtesans of
Rome. His notorious Index of Prohibited Books included by 1559 all the
works of Erasmus, all the books of more than sixty named printers, and all
translations of the Bible into vernacular languages. Thus by the sessions of
1562–63 at Trent, a full-fledged *Counter* Reformation was in full spate, all
hopes of reconciliation with the Protestants having been abandoned. It
remained for that most astute of contemporary popes Pius IV *(r.1559–65)* to
out-maneuver the warring French and Spanish factions and to bring the
Council to a triumphant conclusion. In this work he was ably backed by his
saintly nephew and secretary Charles Borromeo *(d.1584),* later so venerated
for his work among the sick and the poor in his archdiocese of Milan. Even
during the last period at Trent many members of the Council continued the
effort to curtail the financial and judicial powers of the Curia, but in the end
papal monarchy emerged even more triumphant than from the Conciliar
Movement of the previous century; more triumphant because it had shed
moral laxity, because it now had the support of many devout bishops
besides that of the Jesuits, because in a Europe rather evenly balanced
between the two main politico-religious causes, every Catholic ruler needed
the cooperation of the Papacy. The future power of Rome also sprang from
the fact that the Council left to the popes the implementation of its decrees,
together with the power to supplement them where its own work remained
incomplete. Yet even at the end, most of its members would doubtless have
been amazed could they have learned that no further General Council was
to be called until 1870.

Thus within two decades of his death, history falsified the prediction of
Martin Luther that a moribund Papacy would swiftly vanish from the scene.
Its victory had perhaps been won at a heavy price, yet although the
Inquisition and the Index hampered some thinkers, this price did not

include the atrophy of intellectual life, much less that of great art and music, within the Catholic countries. Despite such episodes as the persecution of Galileo, southern Europe continued its contribution to most branches of scientific enquiry, while the worlds of Palestrina, of Rubens and Bernini, were far from being cast into the shade by those of Rembrandt, Newton, and Bach. Yet concerning one related theme beloved by many histories of civilization, the present writer must admit to scepticism: the notion that the

Saint Ildefonso
El Greco
Convento de Illescas

Baroque art and architecture of the seventeenth century was the child of the Catholic Reformation, a "Jesuit-style," "a hymn of joy raised by the triumphant Church." The style of the middle and later decades of the sixteenth century was not of course Baroque: it was what we now call Mannerism, that somewhat cold and stilted derivative from the *maniera* of Michelangelo. The full-blooded Baroque had its origins around 1600 but did not reach its climax until a full century after the formation of the Society of Jesus. On this reckoning it seems to have taken the Church a long time to decide whether it was enjoying the Counter Reformation! In actual fact, when it did at last arrive, Baroque soon became a multi-purpose style contributing as much to the glorification of monarchs and aristocrats as to the triumph of the Church. Even in Rome, the building and decoration of the great Baroque churches came far less from the religious Orders than from the aristocracy and cardinalate, rich patrons allowed once more to rival the splendors of the High Renaissance—but in return for an adherence to dogmatic and moral purity. The great spirits of the Catholic Reformation had strangely little in common with the Baroque age: they were surely among the least pompous and flamboyant characters in the history of the Church. Reading the autobiography of Theresa of Ávila, one must believe that she would have repudiated her apotheosis in the famous marble group by Bernini. If we seek the real cultural affinities of her world, we need not go further than the poetry of her biographer Luis de Leon or that of her friend St. John of the Cross, while in the plastic arts we should turn to the strange and heightened Mannerism of El Greco *(c.1541–1614)*. Though the Catholic Reformation took the outward form of a rehabilitation of the Papacy, its inward achievement came not merely from intellectual, extroverted and theatrical Italians but from the fierce spiritual ardours of the Spanish nation.

FIVE

*The
Later
Sixteenth Century*

1. Spain and Philip II

By any reasonable criteria Spain remained Europe's strongest military and colonizing power throughout the central and later decades of the sixteenth century. At the outset of Charles's reign, the work of Ferdinand and Isabella had indeed been jeopardized by Spanish hatred of the young King's rapacious foreign advisers, by excessive taxation, by the revival of centrifugal forces always latent in the Iberian peninsula. But after the collapse of the formidable *comunero* rebellions of 1520–22, the remainder of the reign saw no further armed unrest. Under the twenty-year ministry of Francisco de las Cobos, Castilian government was steadily bureaucratized, but no attempts were made to fuse it with the institutions of Aragon. While the government secured support by judicious bribery and patronage, local administration continued amid that petty corruption satirized in later times by Cervantes. Meanwhile the habits of political obedience developed in both kingdoms. In particular the growth of Ottoman power in the western Mediterranean disposed Spaniards to loyalty, since the Emperor Charles with his foreign financiers and naval allies could make an impressive contribution toward Spain's defense. He did in fact pass over to the offensive by capturing Tunis in 1535, and his revival of the crusading spirit blinded Spaniards to the likelihood that in the last resort he would use Spanish money to pay for his world-wide designs.

For several decades the import of silver, vastly increased from 1545 by the discovery of the Potosí mines in Peru, seemed to add substance to this dream of riches and power. Seville, the gateway to the Indies, became the greatest boom-city of the age: its wealth, together with the shipbuilding of the Basques in the north and the steady Flemish demand for merino wool, stimulated both industry and agriculture throughout Andalusia and much of Castile. On the other hand, time proved that the Spanish economy was not equipped to supply the demands of the overseas colonies, or even those of the rising internal population. Arable farming did not share in the governmental favors lavished upon the Mesta, the corporation of wool-growers: it lay under the management of small peasant-farmers, who lacked the capital to expand irrigation and hence to supply the arid country's most basic need—a massive increase in corn production. Likewise the poorly organized cloth industry could not compete with its foreign rivals. Even as the Spanish weavers sought to supply the ever-growing American market, the import of foreign cloth, demanded in 1548 by the Cortes, had to be sanctioned by the government. The high prices of Spanish products in general are deplored by contemporaries, while already in 1556 a Salaman-can economic writer attributes the inflation to the huge imports of Peruvian silver—a discovery which anticipated by a decade the far better known pronouncement by Jean Bodin.

Until recently this "quantity theory" was generally held to explain the disastrous price rise which beset Spain. While the first half of the century saw moderate bullion imports and moderate price rises, in the second half a sensational advance in both imports and prices was said to have occurred. Though it gradually extended its effects throughout Europe, the silver exerted its most immediate and acute influence upon the Spanish economy. This theory, statistically enunciated in the 1930s by Earl J. Hamilton, is nowadays regarded as over-simplified. It seems clear that a large proportion of the silver recorded as entering Seville did not in fact pass into the Spanish economy, but went immediately to the king's foreign creditors or to those foreign merchants who to an ever-increasing extent supplied the colonial markets. Moreover Dr. Jorge Nadal has produced a rival set of statistics which cast doubt upon any simple "quantity theory," since they indicate a higher proportional increase of Spanish prices during the first half, as opposed to the second half of the century. Hence, while there can still be no doubt that bullion import contributed much to the inflation, the precise nature and timing of its impact, and its correlation with the price rise, remain matters for argument. It must also be recognized that the inrush of silver operated alongside other causes of inflation, such as the royal loans financed by the issue of mere credit bonds, and the lavish expenditure of the richer Spanish nobility upon luxurious building and living.

All such factors gain significance when considered in relation to the primitive Spanish economy of 1500, especially to an inelastic agriculture unable to meet large new demands. The consequent high food prices left the bulk of the people with little margin to purchase manufactured goods, and hence to create competitive industries. Moralizing historians have listed many other factors detrimental to economic health: the immense numbers of the clergy both regular and secular, the religious fanaticism which destroyed the industrious Jewish and Morisco communities, the world-wide imperialism of the Habsburg rulers, which denuded the country of young men and occasioned so great a dissipation of human effort. "A nation of

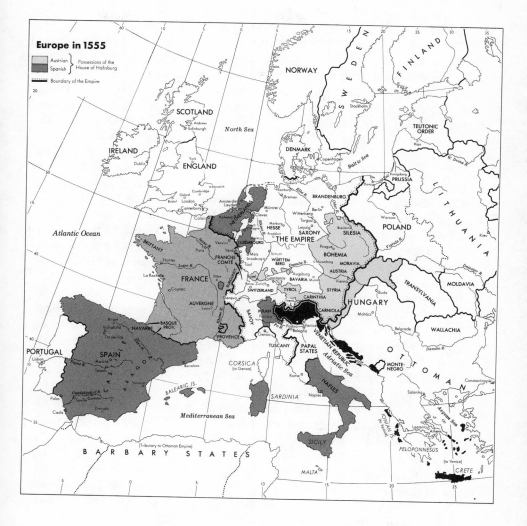

Europe in 1555

Austrian
Spanish
Possessions of the
House of Habsburg

Boundary of the Empire

NORWAY

SCOTLAND
St. Andrews
Edinburgh

North Sea

IRELAND

Dublin

ENGLAND
York
Oxford Cambridge
Bristol London
Canterbury
Calais

Atlantic Ocean

SWEDEN

FINLAND

Stockholm

DENMARK
Copenhagen

Balt'c Sea

TEUTONIC
ORDER
Riga

Lübeck
Hamburg
Bremen

BRANDENBURG

Amsterdam
Leyden
Antwerp
Münster
Cleves

Marburg
HESSE
Cologne
Frankfurt

PRUSSIA
Königsberg
W. Drina R.

Danzig

Berlin
Wittenberg
Leipzig
Torgau
SAXONY

LITHUANIA

Warsaw

POLAND

Kiev

Vistula R.

NETHERLANDS
LUXEMBOURG
Vervins
Metz
Verdun
Toul
FRANCHE
COMTÉ
Strasbourg
WÜRTEM
BERG
Speyer
Danube R.

Breslau
SILESIA
Prague
BOHEMIA
Nuremberg
MORAVIA

Dniester R.

BRITTANY
Rouen
Nantes
Seine R.
Paris
Loire R.

La Rochelle

FRANCE

Cognac

AUVERGNE
Lyons
Dijon

Bern Zurich
SWITZERLAND
Basel
Geneva
Rhone R.

Augsburg
Constance
BAVARIA
Munich
TYROL
Trent

AUSTRIA
Vienna

STYRIA

Buda
HUNGARY

Mohács

TRANSYLVANIA

MOLDAVIA

WALLACHIA

Belgrade

Danube R.

OTTOMAN

PORTUGAL
Lisbon

SPAIN
Madrid
Toledo
Valladolid
Burgos
NAVARRE
Fuenterrabia
BASQUE
PROV.
Guadalquivir R.
Palos
Seville Cordova
Cadiz
Granada

Barcelona

BALEARIC IS.

Mediterranean Sea

NAVARRE
PROVENCE

SAVOY
MILAN
Genoa
Po R.
Padua
Bologna
Venice
CARINTHIA
CARNIOLA

VENETIAN REPUBLIC

Adriatic Sea

MONTE-
NEGRO

CORSICA
(to Genoa)

TUSCANY
PAPAL
STATES
Rome

SARDINIA

NAPLES

Naples

SICILY

MALTA

Constantinople

Salonika

Lepanto
Athens
Aegean Sea

PELOPONNESUS

(to Venice)

CRETE

IONIAN
(to Venice)

(Tributary to Ottoman Empire)

B A R B A R Y   S T A T E S

soldiers and priests": this remains an exaggerated phrase. Yet Spain aspired to this ideal more ardently than the rest of her contemporaries; she had embarked upon such courses before Philip's accession and stubbornly continued in them even when their full implications were well understood by intelligent observers, Spanish and foreign alike.

Beset by illnesses and frustrated in his political schemes, Charles V began preparing for his abdication in 1555, when his sister Mary of Hungary relinquished the governorship of the Netherlands to his son Philip. The latter was also acknowledged king of Spain in January 1556, while in the September of that year a moving ceremony in Brussels saw Charles renounce the Imperial Crown in favor of his brother Ferdinand. During his remaining three years of life the former Emperor lived not very austerely in the monastery of Yuste in Estremadura, still taking a lively interest in political affairs. Henceforth the Habsburg territories lay divided between the Spanish and Austrian branches. Elected on each vacancy to the office of Holy Roman Emperor, the head of the Austrian branch ruled all the central European territories. The Spanish heirs held Castile and Aragon, the Netherlands, Franche Comté on the eastern borders of France, and the keys of Italy: Milan, Naples, and Sicily. In addition, the overseas lands all went to Philip and his Spanish successors; they included Oran and Tunis, the Canaries, and the Spanish New World collectively known as the Indies. First among these latter stood New Spain, comprising what are now Mexico, the Central American republics, the coastal areas of the Gulf as far as Florida, and the islands, including Cuba and Jamaica. The rest were New Andalusia (the northern part of modern Venezuela), New Granada (coastal Colombia), New Castile (Peru), New Estremadura (Chile), and La Plata, the areas on both banks of the Plate. On the other side of the world, the Philippines were shortly to be settled as a new colony.

To these territories Philip later made an enormous addition when he annexed Portugal and her overseas empire. In 1578 the young Portuguese King Sebastian met his death in the course of a rash campaign against the Sultan of Morocco. Asserting a claim through his mother, daughter of the former King Emanuel, Philip trampled not merely upon the rights of other claimants but upon the national sentiments of the Portuguese. The Duke of Alva occupied the country in 1581, almost rivalling the brutalities he had recently perpetrated in the Netherlands. Philip thus added to his responsibilities the extensive but vulnerable colonies of Portugal both in Brazil and in the East Indies. Altogether, despite the Habsburg partition of 1556, the complexity of his empire rivalled that of his father. He brought to the immense task of its administration an industrious and impassive temperament resembling that of Charles, yet he might be called a desk ruler as distinct from the kings of earlier days who had commonly ruled from the saddle. On his return to Spain in 1559 he established a new capital almost exactly in the center of the peninsula, choosing the small and hitherto undistinguished town of Madrid. From 1563 he increased his isolation by building the Escorial, thirty miles away in the harsh landscape of New Castile. This great pile of granite in the severest classical idiom of the day became a worthy setting for the rest of his career: at once a palace, a government office, a monastery, and a family mausoleum. Thither messengers flocked with despatches from Antwerp, Naples, Milan, Mexico City, Lima, and Manila. Too often after interminable delays, they departed from the Escorial with orders bearing the imperious signature "Yo, el Rey." Yet even when the King and his councillors acted with promptitude, it took eight months for an order to reach Peru.

Philip's remarkable memory for detail did not help him to make decisions, while his suspicious nature and his profoundly personal sense of mission prevented him from delegating important tasks. His desk thus became a bottle-neck, his actual guidance of distant subordinates cumbrous and long-delayed. "If death came from Spain," grumbled one of them, "we should all be immortal." Though he personally took—or failed to take—decisions of substance, he gained advice from a whole range of councils. Some of these were departmental, like the Councils of State, of the Inquisition, of Finance (*Hacienda*), and those which administered the Military Orders. Others were regional: the Councils of Castile, of Aragon, of the Indies, of Italy; and subsequently those of Portugal and Flanders. Amongst the latter group, the Council of Castile had nevertheless long outrun its regional character by discussing matters affecting the whole of Spain and Spanish policy. All these bodies plied the King with documents known as *consultas,* which he might then discuss at will with the Council of State or with a confidential group of ministers. This done, his decisions were returned to the appropriate council for the preparation of the necessary orders. Despite its obvious defects, here was a system of checks and balances which enabled major decisions to be based upon considered evidence and not usurped by irresponsible officials. The administration of so far-flung an empire had no precedent, and though orders were often out of date when they arrived, the Spanish system did at least ensure that in the long run the most powerful and distant proconsuls obeyed the commands of the monarchy.

Needless to add, some privileged ministers enjoyed special access to the King, yet he was controlled neither by corrupt favorites nor by men notable merely for high birth. He chose advisers of real capacity and took pains to balance one against the other. Even Spanish official thinking often saw two sides to a problem, and the King normally had both drawn to his attention. During the earlier years of the reign Alva's iron spirit stood opposed to the affable and conciliatory Ruy Gómez, prince of Eboli (*d.1573*). A third figure of consequence was Cardinal Espinoza (*d.1572*), who in the end, though President of the Councils of Castile and the Indies and also Inquisitor General, received an open reproof for his arrogance by the King, and promptly died of chagrin. After the deaths of Eboli and Espinoza, the King's mistrustful mind was for a time influenced by Antonio Pérez, the bastard son of a high ecclesiastic who had been a secretary of the Emperor Charles and then a trusted servant of Eboli. The network of espionage operated by Pérez enclosed the King's half-brother Don John, whose temporizing policy as Governor of the Netherlands *(1577–78)* soon aroused Philip's suspicions. Pérez did not scruple to procure the assassination of Don John's secretary Escovedo, and while in 1579 Philip replaced his sinister agent by the Burgundian Cardinal Granvelle *(d.1586)*, Pérez held documents so compromising that he could not be brought to justice until 1585. Escaping from captivity five years later, he fled to Aragon and sought the protection of the still powerful Justiciar of that kingdom. An attempt by the Inquisition to arrest him led to a formidable revolt in Saragossa, needing the despatch of an army for its suppression. On the surrender of his opponents the King did not merely execute the Justiciar but curtailed the powers of the Aragonese Cortes, reducing them to a subservience more nearly resembling that of the Castilian Cortes. Meanwhile the indomitable Pérez fled to France and then to England, where he betrayed Philip's state secrets to Queen Elizabeth and encouraged her enterprises against Spain. Surviving his former master, he finally sought to ingratiate himself with Philip III by betraying the secrets of his foreign protectors.

Untypical as it remains, this amazing story displays some of the weaknesses of the system and the King. A bureaucracy over-dependent upon the judgment of a single autocrat is likely to prove less efficient than a constitution which provides for the regular delegation of power, and wherein ministers are subject to scrutiny by representative institutions. This truism could be illustrated at the levels of both central and local government by a comparison between Philipine Spain and Elizabethan England. Yet in the former a profounder weakness lay in the inadequacy of the fiscal administration. Despite three ruinous bankruptcies of the state, no one had the energy to reorganize finance, much less the temerity to show the King how to devise policies within his means. Likewise the lesser men who rose to influence after Granvelle's death had no answers to the decline of Spanish industries, even though during the nineties it was frankly exposed by the Cortes of Castile. In 1598 the succession of a far less capable ruler opened even deeper abysses of administrative incapacity. To Philip and to that large body of Spaniards who shared his philosophy, economic and administrative reform mattered far less than doctrinal orthodoxy and "purity of blood." They saw religious obedience and civil order as two sides of the same coin. Despite his sexual lapses and political murders—and many contemporary rulers were equally guilty of both—Philip rigorously discharged his religious observances. From his study in the Escorial he could daily watch the celebration of numerous masses, and he fully approved the system whereby no great feast or occasion was thought complete without a ceremonial burning of heretics. Never was the Inquisition more dreaded, its spies more ubiquitous, its powers more nearly those of a state within a state.

This subordination of worldly prudence to fanaticism and racism was exemplified early in Philip's reign by the edicts of 1560-67 which drove the southern Moriscos to revolt. Whereas the Emperor Charles had not enforced the older decrees aimed against Moorish customs, Philip was prevailed upon by the archbishop of Granada and other clerical advisers to abolish their songs, dances, festivities, and public baths, to compel them to open their houses for inspection on wedding days, and force their women to relinquish the veil. The Morisco rising which began in December 1568 failed to capture the city of Granada, let alone to arouse the Moriscos of Valencia and Murcia. Its stronghold lay in the Alpujarras, the belt of hills between the Sierra Nevada and the south coast. Despite the ferocities used by the rebels against Christian villages, the revolt might have been allayed in the early stages had Philip offered the clemency suggested by his more moderate counsellors. In the event, counter-atrocities merely compelled the Moriscos to fight to the death. Despite divisions among themselves they struggled on until the early months of 1570, when they were finally overrun by an army under the leadership of Don John. There followed the forcible distribution of the Moriscos of the Granada region throughout other parts of Spain, a harsh measure but one conducted without special inhumanity. Criticized by some far-seeing Spanish laymen, this solution nevertheless avoided the supreme folly which prompted Philip III over thirty years later to attempt the complete expulsion of the Moriscos from Spain. Moreover, the episode must be seen in the context of the bitter war then in progress between Spain and the Moslem world, a war which had encouraged some Moriscos to intrigue with the Moslem powers and—at all events during the revolt—to appeal to the Sultan for an invasion of Spain.

The Morisco affair was immediately followed by a Holy League with the Pope and Venice directed against the Turks, who had recently captured the Venetian protectorate of Cyprus. In October 1571 Don John, powerfully supported by Venetian and Genoese galleys, crushed the Turkish fleet at the battle of Lepanto. Yet to this glorious victory there succeeded a host of jealousies and disagreements. In particular, Philip's desire for an African campaign clashed with the aim of the Venetians to recover their position in the eastern Mediterranean. By 1573 Venice had become sufficiently disillusioned to make a separate peace with the Turks, ceding Cyprus and paying a tribute just as if the Turks had won Lepanto. Meanwhile, though Don John captured Tunis, both this city and Goletta had fallen once again into Moslem hands by the autumn of 1574. For the sensational anticlimax Philip's narrow and suspicious diplomacy must bear a large share of the blame.

Portrait of Philip II, King of Spain
TITIAN
Galleria Corsini, Rome

In surveying the relations of Philip with the Papacy and the Catholic Church at large, we cannot rest content with the notion that he was a mere religious fanatic—or conversely regard him as a mere *politique* who consciously placed Castilian and Habsburg policy before the welfare of Catholicism. He believed his policies had divine approval, and at least until our own times their logic has been widely accepted by Spanish opinion. He was primarily maintaining the traditions of Ferdinand and Isabella, who acknowledged the spiritual supremacy of the pope while yet ascribing to the Spanish monarchy a sacred mission and a general right to manage the Church in Spain and all her dominions. Philip's special relationship with Rome appears in the story of Bartolomé de Carranza, the pious and learned archbishop of Toledo who had played a leading part at the Council of Trent and had administered at Yuste the last consolations of religion to the Emperor Charles. Carranza's trial before the Spanish Inquisition on a charge of near-Lutheran opinions began in 1559, and after seven years it needed threats of an interdict from Rome to make Philip surrender him to the papal courts. Even after securing this concession, the Pope dared not treat the case benignly. In 1576 the archbishop was compelled to abjure certain opinions discovered in his writings, to do penance, and to endure five more years of suspension from his functions, immured in the Dominican convent at Orvieto. Thus far the writ of Philip ran even in Rome itself: it was a situation which suited neither foreign Catholic states nor the prestige of the reformed Papacy.

Just charges against Philip might be to the effect that he patronized mediocrities, and that his leaden officialdom had little in common with the exalted spiritual and intellectual *élites* among his subjects. Inquisitors grievously persecuted the perfectly orthodox mystic St. John of the Cross, as they persecuted Luis de Leon, in whose superb poems the old mysticism and the newer Platonism are so attractively blended. Philip knew, but cared little for the painting of El Greco, yet he revealingly collected the bizarre fantasias of Hieronymus Bosch. Spanish humanism, already regarded with official disfavor before his time, survived at least among inoffensive classical scholars; its humane and critical spirit survived also in the fiction of Cervantes, whose warm humanity displays to perfection the more engaging traits of the complex Spanish mind. Yet such elements found no response from the patronage or the public image of the severe and inscrutable Habsburg. In his family life and private correspondence Philip occasionally emerges as a human being, yet his sense of high office, of destiny and mission, bade him conceal the fact from the world and even perhaps from himself.

A historian's balance-sheet of his worldly successes and disasters would doubtless have failed to strike Philip as significant. Yet even by modern standards the account can hardly appear as one of unrelieved tragedy. At home the false orientations can be blamed in no small part upon his preference for a Castilian as opposed to a federal concept of Spain. Yet he checked the centrifugalism of the peninsula and founded a real Spanish monarchy. He maintained loyalty and order, while the necessity for basic reforms became obvious only in his last years: he has perhaps been unduly castigated for his successors' more grievous sins of omission. Again, wiser policies on their part might have preserved his conquest of Portugal and converted it into a tolerable unification of the peninsula. And if he failed adequately to follow up his success at Lepanto, at least he defended Western Civilization in the Mediterranean. He also maintained a firm but moderate hold upon Italy, which amid its political torpor was allowed to continue in peace its great contribution to literature and the arts. While Tasso, Caravaggio, and a host of other authors and artists worked under the Spanish hegemony, many noble Italian families like the Spinolas of Genoa pursued distinguished careers in the service of their Spanish overlords.

North of the Alps, Philip's record remains a chequered one. After some disastrous first attempts to hold at bay the upsurge of Netherlandish nationalism, Philip did at least retain under his rule ten of the seventeen provinces. His failure to accomplish more must be seen in the light of his other commitments. His resources, great as they were, did not enable him to maintain a constant and simultaneous pressure upon all his enemies, who showed themselves well aware of this dilemma. Modern research has indicated that whenever Philip's Mediterranean problems became critical, he felt bound to accord them financial priority over the problem of the

Netherlands. His third major preoccupation lay in preserving the ultra-Catholic and pro-Spanish faction in the French civil wars. Here he resisted the fatal temptation to stage a full-scale invasion of France, though his judicious and successful support of the Catholic League ended by becoming inordinately expensive. Perhaps his most abysmal failure was the Armada sent in 1588 against England; and the astounding lack of any feasible plan for cooperation between his galleon fleet and Parma's troop-ferrying barges must be blamed upon Philip, whom Parma clearly warned. Even on the English side this highly experimental episode saw a fair measure of governmental ineptitude. Anglo-Dutch naval liaison proved almost nonexistent, while in the crucial engagements only the brilliant improvisation of Drake and other English commanders triumphed over a lack of ammunition which might have proved fatal. For Spain it can at least be argued that this use of an oceanic fighting fleet represented a first essay, since it had no resemblance to Mediterranean naval warfare. In the maritime struggle against England, the events of 1588 were the beginning, not the end for Spain. The remainder of the contest was less unequal and the attempts of the English to take the initiative proved in their turn inconclusive. All in all, Philip's political and military record will occasion few surprises to those familiar with the public traditions and the personal temperament inherited from his father and his forbears. In his dogged loyalty to dynastic tradition within a changing world, in his desire to shoulder personal responsibility, lay both his distinction and his errors. And could even a more profound, a more flexible and original mind have deflected Spain from the courses of self-martyrdom upon which she was set?

2.   England under Elizabeth I

As Philip is often assigned responsibility for the decline of Spain under later rulers, so the reign of Elizabeth acquires glory as the prelude to the subsequent maritime and colonial achievements of the English nation. Our present sober task is to review Elizabeth's reign in its contemporary context, an exercise apt to destroy some of the romance.

During these years there remained a marked difference of scale between the resources of Philip and those of Elizabeth. Despite its rapid growth after 1558, the population of England in 1600 cannot much have exceeded four million, little more than half the population of Castile, a third that of the Iberian Peninsula, a quarter that of France. Like Spain, England labored under severe social and economic problems, while her government, having sold off the monastic lands, lacked the financial resources to pursue an aggressive foreign policy. Elizabeth's church settlement remained insecure, her people a prey to serious religious divisions. Her northern neighbor Scotland was not yet wholly weaned of ancient pro-French traditions.

Despite the triumphant defense of English independence against Spain, even at the end of the reign a certain disillusion, less severe but somewhat resembling that of the Spaniards, clouded the minds of many English intellectuals.

Even her fervent admirers would concede that Elizabeth enjoyed an element of good fortune which so often eluded Philip's grasp. Yet without question, from the centralized medieval monarchy and from the first two Tudors, Elizabeth inherited one of the most efficient state machines of Europe. She left it stronger than she found it, though the sad experiences of her Stuart successors provide a reminder that the system could not protect monarchs less endowed with political instinct against the results of their errors.

From the first days of her reign Elizabeth convinced observers that she meant to be obeyed. While the magnificence of her court ceremonial

Elizabeth, Queen of England
ascribed to ZUCCHERO
Hampton Court

Queen Elizabeth's signature
from a manuscript in the British
Museum

stressed the divine ordination of monarchy, she knew how to make conde-
scending gestures, and in her progresses she cast her personal spell beyond
the limited circles of the Court. She kept her ministers alert by frequent
interventions into matters of detail, yet she understood the art of delegation
better than did Philip, while in William Cecil (Lord Burghley, *d.1598*) and
Sir Francis Walsingham *(d.1590)* she had faithful servants whom she sometimes infuriated and depressed, yet whom she maintained against countless
intrigues. She had favorites as well as ministers, yet only in her last years did
she tend to lose grip upon her circle, most notably in the case of the young
and popular Earl of Essex, who overestimated his ascendancy and in 1601
suffered death for open rebellion. Such miscalculations were nevertheless
rare, while the personal role of the Queen went far beyond the mere
acceptance of advice from able ministers. The basic principles of her
government were economy and moderation. Unlike Philip, she had no
illusions concerning the wealth of her government and no aspirations to
foreign conquest. For nearly thirty years she steered clear of major military
operations. She hoped to avoid direct hostilities with Spain to a point where
that hope had become a danger to her nation. Finally involved in expensive
naval warfare and Irish campaigning, she somehow managed to finance
them by rigorous retrenchment and parliamentary subsidies. At her death
her debts proved relatively small. Her hatred of fanaticism appears in her
resistance to those Protestant zealots who wanted to force the consciences of
her Catholic subjects by compelling them not merely to attend the Anglican
service but to receive the Anglican communion. Her critics inevitably fasten
upon the prevarication, the parsimony, the neuroses which appeared in
moments of crisis. And in refusing to nominate a successor she was widely
judged in her own day guilty of a vain and perilous obstinacy, whereas her
warmer admirers still defend this attitude as a hair's-breadth calculation
intended to avoid the plots which might form around both the favored
contender and his disgruntled rivals.

Under the Queen the daily government of England lay with the Privy
Council, a body she reduced from an unwieldy group of forty to twenty or
less. During the later years it comprised a round dozen members, of whom
between five and ten usually attended. Though at first it included a few
noble magnates with great territorial influence, such councillors almost
vanished later on, as the Council became ever more highly professionalized.
Unlike Philip's councils, it was a lay body, John Whitgift (archbishop of
Canterbury, *1583-1604*) being the sole ecclesiastic to play any considerable
part as a councillor. The Queen seldom attended in person. On occasion she
even took decisions without consulting the Council, or else followed the
advice of a minority. Upon certain issues the members stood divided for
years on end: a few, headed by Burghley, long dissuaded the Queen from
helping the Dutch revolt, while Walsingham and her personal favorite

Robert Dudley, earl of Leicester, led the strong group which ultimately procured the intervention of 1585.

Always the Council functioned as something more than a political advisory body. In its omnicompetence it not only investigated administrative irregularities large and small; it also adjudged suits between private persons in the manner of a court of law. If need arose it enforced its decisions by imprisonment. Repeatedly it protested against the time occupied by the hordes of private suitors, but it took no decisive action to shake off their importunities. In the later years the multitude of petitioners together with the demands of the Spanish war compelled the Council to meet daily.

Upon day-to-day government the English Parliament exerted little influence. During a reign of forty-four years, only thirteen sessions occurred, the average length of a session being less than ten weeks. In other words, Parliament was sitting for less than one-fifteenth of the period. A Tudor government could thus rule by executive action for long periods, yet ministers always conceded the need for periodic parliamentary legislation, as well as the need for parliamentary subsidies. Most sessions were called mainly for purposes of taxation, though two saw no financial demands by the Crown. In 1572, after the Ridolfi Plot to replace Elizabeth by Mary Stuart, a session was held to pass laws for the greater safety of the Queen. Again, the Parliament of 1586 assembled to review the position of Mary Queen of Scots, its strong pressure for her execution weighing heavily with Elizabeth. While some members of the House of Commons saw Parliament as presenting opportunities to discuss foreign affairs, religion and the succession to the throne, Elizabeth and her ministers gave them no encouragement. High policy and national legislation were conceived and executed by the government, not by private members. During the Parliament of 1586–87 five members with militant puritan views found themselves consigned to the Tower of London and left there for the rest of the session. In 1593 the outspoken puritan Peter Wentworth suffered a much longer term of imprisonment for persistently conspiring to introduce a bill on the succession.

Such events were nevertheless rare and untypical, and the government never needed to "pack" Parliament by interfering with elections. The Queen herself knew well how to sense the moods of the Commons, to make moderate and carefully-reasoned demands for money, to charm by personal appearances and gracious words.

Again, among the grasping Elizabethans Crown patronage past and present stimulated much heartfelt loyalty, while the recent study of parliamentary diaries has revealed the careful management by which ministers piloted bills through the Commons. The privy councillors sat on the front benches, much like cabinet ministers in a modern British parliament. They used their personal prestige, they concerted plans with the Speaker, even giving him cues during the management of debates. Moreover, after the second reading of a bill, it was usually entrusted to the detailed survey of a committee, of which all the privy councillors in the House were members. Once in committee, they naturally tended to get their own way. In the last resort the subservient House of Lords could be used to reject an unwelcome bill sent up by the Commons. In short, under Elizabeth the latter were handled by sophisticated methods: the failure of James I to continue these methods in more trying times helps to explain that gradual cessation of harmony between executive and legislature which led at last to the Civil Wars.

Alongside the Privy Council, the Tudor monarchs had developed and modified the already complex system of councils and courts inherited by them from the medieval state. In the King's Bench, the Common Pleas, and the Assizes, the old Common Law dealt with a great mass of the crimes and disputes produced by an unruly and litigious people. Yet the Tudors conspicuously failed to reform the slow and rigid procedures of the Common Law: instead they developed a speedier equitable jurisdiction in the courts of Chancery, Star Chamber, and Requests, while the distant and more feudal-minded areas of the North and of Wales (with its English border-counties) were governed respectively by the Council in the North and the Council in the Marches. These two regional councils, made immensely more effective since their early days under the Yorkist kings and Henry VII, resembled the Privy Council in wielding a combined civil and criminal jurisdiction, and in their supervision of local administration. When Elizabeth ascended the throne, William Paulet, marquis of Winchester, had very recently abolished the new financial courts erected by Henry VIII, and had recentralized the financial administration under the old court of Exchequer. This important reform was not carried further by the conservative Burghley, who failed to augment the Crown's revenues in accordance with the monetary inflation and the growing wealth of the country. To take one example, as Master of the Court of Wards—which leased out estates under Crown control during the minorities of heirs—Burghley failed to increase the takings; yet on succession to the same office his son Robert Cecil quickly doubled and then trebled them.

In the all-important sphere of finance Burghley had few ideas beyond parsimony, and Tudor government remained above all economical. The paid officials of the central government probably numbered less than one thousand. In addition, leading ministers maintained numerous secretaries out of their own pockets: Burghley's secretaries became important men in their own right and grew wealthy on the bribes offered by suitors desiring access to the great man. As with all the major European monarchies, the Crown's patronage in terms of titles, jobs, leases, and trade monopolies bound a large proportion of the ruling classes to the state, and elicited a great deal of nominally unpaid labor. In particular, local administration lay under the control of the Justices of the Peace, who worked for the local prestige and influence conferred by their office. Their judicial and administrative powers became very wide. For the guidance of these men, mostly country squires or town merchants, special treatises were published, chief among them William Lambarde's *Eirenarcha*. In its edition of 1599 this manual makes the Justices of the Peace responsible for enforcing over three hundred statutes, of which well over half had been passed under the Tudors. Within the rural communities to which most Englishmen still belonged, the relations between the governing and the working classes were at least more personal and patriarchal than in the industrial and urban societies of more recent times. On the whole, English rural society looks healthier and less static than that in most other European countries of the period. New gentry were constantly recruited from the substantial farming and merchant classes, while the varied group called yeomen formed a sizeable middle class in the countryside, their wealth often exceeding that of the poorer gentry. Beneath them ranked a peasantry of varying means. These were mainly the descendants of villeins formerly bound to perform manorial labor services, but in Elizabethan England extremely few husbandmen retained villein status or obligations.

On the other hand, trade recessions, rising prices, and a growing population had long been fostering unemployment and vagabondage. Mid-Tudor preachers, writers, and administrators had become deeply preoccupied by economic and social problems. Somewhat slowly and uncertainly, the action of the state followed this thinking by a long series of statutes. Here as elsewhere in Europe, the larger cities had taken the lead in framing practical measures, and many provisions of the national code were based upon those already adopted by the city of London or by provincial towns like Norwich and Ipswich. Earlier Tudor legislation had savagely concentrated upon the punishment of vagabondage, for "sturdy beggars" and wandering criminals remained a real social scourge. On the other hand the Elizabethans clearly distinguished other groups: the able-bodied unemployed who wanted to work, the "impotent poor" prevented from earning a livelihood by physical disability, and orphans who needed both maintenance and training. Another notable advance concerned the actual raising of funds to help these "deserving" groups. As early as 1536 an Act had encouraged the collection of voluntary alms for this purpose, but not until 1572 was a compulsory poor-rate imposed upon every householder in accordance with his ability to contribute. Finally the elaborate statute of 1598 codified the whole national system, and in its essentials lasted until the nineteenth century. Vagabonds still got no sympathy: they must be whipped, then returned to their parish of legal residence, where after a prison spell they must be placed in service and made to work. By contrast the deserving poor were put in the charge of the churchwardens and four substantial men of each parish, all the householders of which paid compulsory rates. The money thus raised went not merely to the relief of the aged and infirm, but to purchase a stock of materials upon which able-bodied paupers could work. The state had already in 1563 closely regulated the conditions of apprenticeship to trades, and now the overseers of the poor were empowered to provide for destitute young persons by placing them in legal apprenticeship to suitable masters. Thus the state evolved a moralistic and unsentimental social policy, stressing the virtues of self-help and industry, avoiding the degradation of the poor-house but combatting vagabondage by terror. Despite its obvious shortcomings, this system was probably the most advanced and effective to be applied by any national state of the period.

Though the old ecclesiastical parish thus functioned as a secular unit, and though most of the almhouses still working at the Reformation survived that process, the Church never recovered the dominance in English social and charitable policy it had exercised in medieval England, and still continued to exercise in Catholic lands. The ecclesiastics of the Anglican establishment were normally family men, and they now formed a very small element of the population. Though an increasing proportion held university degrees, the new priesthood worked amongst a better-educated laity, owing to the great increase in the number of endowed schools. Secular and practical literature, much of it aimed at the middle-class and modestly-educated reader, multiplied even more rapidly than in the England of Henry VIII. And could any range of literature have been less ecclesiastical in form and content than the Elizabethan theatre which culminated in Shakespeare? While a better-educated parish clergy with less temptation to sexual irregularities commanded increasing public respect, their economic standing did not improve so rapidly as it should have done. The Elizabethans failed to reform the ancient system of tithes, based upon the payment to the parish clergy of one-tenth of agricultural produce in the parish. Often anomalous even in country parishes, such a system became quite unworkable in the growing towns and industrial communities. As for the English bishops, they not only ceased to be leading officers of state but had to live on revenues considerably smaller than those of their predecessors. Under the pressure of the Crown, favorable leases of their estates were often granted to courtiers and officials, who could thus be cheaply rewarded. How far all these material problems helped or hampered the Christian ministry of the Anglican clergy might be long and inconclusively argued. Yet as Supreme Governor of the Church of England, Elizabeth cannot be credited with much zeal to improve or rationalize its administration. As for the church courts, they continued to act much as before the Reformation: a layman who kept a mistress or sought to dispute the will of a relative still found himself answerable to their jurisdiction.

Reconstituted after 1558 as a specifically Protestant institution, and at all times heavily influenced by Calvinist theology, the Anglican Church nevertheless developed its own devotional ethos, one largely based upon Cranmer's *Prayer Book*. Led by its famous apologist Richard Hooker (d.1600), it also developed a philosophical, broad-minded theology which did more than merely translate Calvin. Nevertheless, from the beginning of the reign highly vocal groups contended that the Church was only half-reformed. They attacked church ornaments, surplices, organ music, the sign of the cross: many of these puritans also desired to abolish episcopacy and the church courts. Their positive emphasis included more than preaching and strict Sunday observance. In a grasping and licentious world they sought the inculcation of a strict moral sensibility, and contrary to popular belief they had much more to say about practical charity than about sexual morals. In his *Second Admonition to Parliament (1572)* the Cambridge professor Thomas Cartwright (d.1603) boldly defended the pamphleteers who had advocated presbyterian as opposed to episcopal church government. Having prudently spent several years in exile, he encountered on his return heavy pressure from the Court of High Commission, a hybrid church-state body much disliked by laymen and freely compared by Lord Burghley himself with the Spanish Inquisition. In 1558-59 the surreptitiously printed satires called the *Marprelate Tracts* made scurrilous attacks upon the bishops; and though these were the work of extremists, the puritan opposition had a broad appeal among the middle classes, including many gentry and merchants in the House of Commons. It throve not merely upon Calvinist dogma but upon the plots and the fear of Spain. Despite Elizabeth's angry resistance to their demands, the puritans were patriots, indeed ultra-loyalists: the vast majority of them remained within the established Church and merely wanted to change its character. Even by 1600 the "Separatist" sectarians still formed tiny groups within English society.

In his *Treatise on the Laws of Ecclesiastical Polity* (1594-97) Richard Hooker developed a counter-view, moderate and liberal for its day. While he accepted the Protestant and reformed character of the Church of England, he also pointed to its continuity with the medieval Church. Condemning the puritan tendency to regard the Bible as a universal code of rules demanding literal application, he envisaged churches as organic and developing bodies, their structures and governments being liable to variation and change. He could distinguish good features in other Churches and accept their clergy as lawfully ordained. The legislation of a Church seemed to Hooker analogous with that of the secular state, both being—like the Scriptures themselves—subservient to the natural law, which is the supreme reason of God. This approach, too often narrowed by later and lesser Anglicans, amplified the rational foundations upon which the Church of

England was to attain to the stature of a world religion. Nevertheless the dichotomy within the Church grew apace and at Elizabeth's death, a solid phalanx of moderate puritans was concerting stronger pressures both inside and outside Parliament. Elizabeth's settlement—and her personal conservatism had done much to shape it—was to prove an uneasy resting place in the long history of the English Reformation.

The survival of Catholicism in Elizabethan England had very different social and political connotations. For a decade or more it looked as if Elizabeth might avoid any dangerous internal threat from the Romanists. All save an exiguous minority of the parish clergy retained their livings in 1559 and when, ten years later, the Earls of Northumberland and Westmorland staged a Catholic rising in the North, it was suppressed even before it could approach York. Until the papal Bull of 1570 excommunicated Elizabeth and ordered her subjects to overthrow her, she refrained from persecuting the Catholics, while in general they avoided disloyalty. After 1570 a very different situation obtained. During the seventies Catholic opposition was re-created by Cardinal Allen's seminary priests, who from 1581 were joined by the Jesuits. Both bodies consisted of English exiles trained abroad, sent into England and smuggled from one Catholic manor house to another. These heroic men made not a few converts, yet they came too late and were heavily compromised by the minority of Catholic extremists who organized the long series of murder plots and plans for a Spanish invasion. The web of conspiracy, patiently unravelled by Walsingham and his spy system, centered upon Mary Queen of Scots from her appearance in England in 1568 until her execution in 1587.

Inevitably the government found itself unable to distinguish between the plotters like the Jesuit Robert Parsons and the saints like his companion Edmund Campion. Over the years it executed as traitors more than two hundred of these priests and their direct supporters. Meanwhile the mass of the Catholic laity were most affected by the statute of 1581, which imposed the enormous fine of £20 a month upon Catholic recusants convicted of refusal to attend Anglican services. The Exchequer records show that this was a deterrent measure and slackly enforced: it could not have been otherwise, since the great majority of the English Catholics could scarcely have paid a single month's fine. The Spanish menace, including the risings in Ireland, made Protestant Englishmen see English Catholicism through a magnifying glass. Yet except in Lancashire, parts of which were heavily Catholic, the papalists formed a small section of society and one which carried little weight outside the rural backwaters of the north and the west. For the most part the Catholics remained loyalists, acutely embarrassed by the papal Bull and ready to help resist rebellion and foreign invasion. As clearly as any others of their countrymen, they realized that England could not be ruled by Mary Stuart or by Philip of Spain.

The foreign policy of Elizabeth was conditioned not merely by this menace of political Catholicism or by her need for financial economy, but also by a series of continental developments hitherto unparalleled in the experience of English statesmen. From 1562 France was weakened by a long series of civil wars between the Reformed or Huguenot minority and the Catholic majority led by the Guises. Between the two, yet normally drawn toward the Catholic side, stood the Valois dynasty under the Queen Mother Catherine de' Medici and her degenerate sons. To Elizabeth's relief the weakness of France did not make Philip master of western Europe. Her opportunity lay in the fact that Philip had not merely to support the Guises but to face an open revolt from 1567 by his own Netherlandish subjects, who lived geographically speaking upon England's doorstep. This advantageous pattern continued throughout the reign, the French wars lasting intermittently until 1598, while the truce in the Netherlands lay still six years distant when Elizabeth died in 1603.

Even before the Netherlands revolt, Philip had to remember that in one respect he was the descendant of the Burgundian rulers, whose natural ally against France had been England. While the Papacy soon sought to dethrone Elizabeth, Philip long acted as a moderating influence upon Rome. He began by the obvious maneuver: a proposal of marriage to Elizabeth, which might indeed have solved many of her problems. Yet whatever treaty safeguards Philip might have accepted, such a union would have fettered her freedom of action and have been intensely unpopular in England, where Mary Tudor's marriage and persecution had left London anti-Spanish, as well as anti-Catholic. Upon her refusal, Philip married the French princess Elizabeth of Valois *(d.1568)*. Yet this alliance did not in fact enable him to rely on France as an ally against England. He continued to view French designs upon both England and Scotland with apprehension. Until the outbreak of the civil wars in France, the Valois and the Guises depicted Elizabeth as an illegitimate usurper. They aimed to unite France, England, and Scotland under the offspring of the Dauphin Francis and his wife Mary Queen of Scots, whose grandmother Margaret Tudor had been a sister of Henry VIII. In April 1560 Elizabeth struck a shrewd blow at this plan when she despatched an army and a fleet to Edinburgh and forced the withdrawal of the French troops brought there by Mary's mother, Mary of Guise. The Protestant Lords of the Congregation and John Knox were thus put in a position to accord a daunting reception to their young Queen, when she returned to Scotland. The Dauphin, having briefly ruled as Francis II in 1559-60, died suddenly and left her to undertake this hazardous enterprise in 1561, but from the first her promises of toleration for Protestants fell upon hostile Scottish ears.

Having thus established a Reformation party in both England and Scotland, Elizabeth now sought to repeat her success—and especially to win back Calais, recently lost by her sister—in the treacherous field of French politics. In 1562 she signed a treaty with the Huguenot leader Condé, whereby she promised substantial help to his cause and obtained the right to garrison Le Havre until he should restore Calais to England. Nevertheless in the following year Condé, aided by the assassination of Francis Duke of Guise, suddenly made peace with the Queen Mother Catherine, now ruling in the name of her second son Charles IX. Both French parties then united to besiege Le Havre, where in July 1563 the English were forced into an ignominious surrender. This unlucky reverse helped to imbue Elizabeth with a marked reluctance to intervene in continental wars. In addition she regarded even her enemy Philip as a divinely-appointed sovereign, and she detested the Netherlandish rebels, who in modern eyes were fighting England's battles as well as their own. In 1568 she publicly approved the execution of their noble leader Egmont, perhaps tending to equate him and his colleague the Prince of Orange with the seditious elements among her own nobility.

What might be considered the second or middle phase of Elizabeth's foreign policy extended from the late sixties to the eve of the Armada. At home this was the period of the murder plots, which aimed to replace her by Mary Queen of Scots. The latter's struggle against her Scottish opponents had become more hopeless since her enforced marriage with Bothwell, the murderer of her second husband Lord Darnley. Defeated in 1568 at Langside, Mary fled to England, where her claims and intrigues made her far too dangerous to leave at liberty. Yet even during her imprisonment in the castles of Bolton and Sheffield, Mary could correspond with Elizabeth's enemies, thus putting herself at the head of the English Catholic extremists as clearly as Elizabeth had adopted the Scottish Protestants. Yet Mary could no longer rely on French support, since for twelve years on end Elizabeth kept the French court friendly by conducting insincere marriage negotiations, first with the Duke of Anjou (later Henry III) and then with his younger brother Alençon. When at last in 1586-87 Mary was brought to trial and found guilty, the agonized Elizabeth permitted her execution and disavowed the action too late. After this drama, finely staged by the gallant victim, a new phase of policy began to unfold, since Mary left her claims upon the English throne to Philip. The latter could now strike directly at Elizabeth, because in the event of his success, the English throne would pass to himself, not to the hitherto pro-French Mary Queen of Scots.

Already Spain and England had been gradually sliding into war, despite Elizabeth's continuing reluctance to associate herself with Orange and the Dutch patriots. As early as 1568 she had seized a treasure-ship carrying money to the Spanish troops in the Netherlands, but this blunder merely resulted in heavy reprisals against English merchants there, and in any case the money had later to be repaid to the Genoese owners. Elizabeth has often received credit for helping the Dutch privateers, the "Sea-beggars" who laid the foundations of victory in 1572 by taking Brill, and later on a whole chain of coastal bases. In actual fact she expelled the Sea-beggars from England, thus inadvertently driving them into this exploit. Meanwhile some of Philip's agents became involved in the murder plots, while others in 1579 provoked a serious Irish rebellion. Again, throughout the seventies Francis Drake and his fellow English seamen, debarred from legitimate trade with the Spanish colonies, repeatedly set sail with the explicit intention to wreck and plunder. When in 1581 Drake returned from his famous voyage around the world—distinguished by destructive attacks upon the unprotected western coasts of South America—Elizabeth made one of her few flamboyant gestures by knighting him on the deck of the *Golden Hind*. Yet not until 1585, after the death of Orange and the fall of Antwerp, did she finally agree to despatch an expedition to the Netherlands. Even then she saw the step not as a means to expel the Spaniards, but as creating a better bargaining position toward Philip. She appears to have been terrified lest on the expulsion of the Spaniards the French would unite and then invade the Netherlands.

Led by Robert Earl of Leicester, the expedition proved disastrous in quite a different manner, and Elizabeth cannot escape a share of the blame. She began by refusing to accept the sovereignty of the Netherlands, but drove a hard bargain with the Dutch leaders: that she should hold Flushing and Brill as security for the repayment of her expenses in maintaining an army of six thousand men in the country. When Leicester without her permission accepted the post of Governor General, she damaged his credit by a furious refusal; then she unwisely succumbed to the blandishments of her "sweet Robin" and allowed him to continue in office. She also maintained devious contacts with the Duke of Parma, Philip's ablest Governor, who had recently crowned his military triumphs against the patriots by taking Antwerp. Enlarging upon his previous folly, Leicester not only quarrelled with his own subordinates but became a partisan in the internal quarrels among the Dutch, backing the Calvinist and democratic elements against the hitherto pro-English party headed by the patrician burghers. Even the cautious Burghley joined with Leicester and with the ardently pro-Dutch Walsingham in pressing the Queen to increase her military commitment, yet she refused and the sorry tale was consummated by deliberate acts of treachery on the part of two English commanders during Leicester's temporary absences. His return did not arrest the tide of defeat, and amid further quarrels with his hosts Leicester was finally recalled at the end of 1587.

In her notion that she could still bargain with Philip Elizabeth was now deceiving herself, since he had already determined to stage a large-scale attack upon England. Held up by Drake's destruction of more than two hundred vessels at Cadiz and Lisbon—an act still disowned by the Queen—the Armada did not sail until May 1588, and its survivors limped back to

Spain in the autumn. In view of the inadequate training and organization of the English military levies, it seems indeed fortunate for them that the Armada failed to cover the transport of Parma's veterans across the narrow seas. On the other hand, thanks in large part to the work of John Hawkins— and other English naval administrators since the days of Henry VIII—the Spaniards met not only bad weather but a formidable English fleet which even when short of ammunition continued to fight in the seas which formed its native element.

The final phase of Elizabeth's policy took the form of continuing naval warfare, the gradual restoration of confidence on the part of the Dutch and some useful English aid given both to them and to Henry of Navarre, now rightful king of France but still locked in deadly combat with the Spanish-supported Catholic League. Thus in the end Elizabeth's hesitations were resolved by the absolute necessity to conduct a straight fight, yet it remains fair to add that without a massive increase of taxation she could not have maintained such a fight throughout her long reign. She thus saw the preservation of her country by a rare mixture of calculation and sheer good fortune. She seldom manipulated the patterns of Europe; yet obediently they shifted to cover up her mistakes. Perhaps she deserved her luck, since, unlike the grasping Habsburgs and Guises, she did not covet the lands of others. But the converse facts remain. She did not claim to be other than "mere English"; she was neither a European by outlook nor the holder of some "liberal" political philosophy aimed against the authoritarian imperialism of Spain. Those modern writers who see the Dutch rebels as standing in the forefront of the battle for modern Western ideals cannot but stress the flaws in her grasp of the situation, in her neurotic or parsimonious responses to crisis. Sir Walter Raleigh was not being wholly unjust when he wrote, "Her Majesty did everything by halves." Whatever the final judgment in this involved dispute, Elizabeth's personality and gifts were less adapted to any sort of international program than to that protracted love affair with her own people which has entitled her to be ranked among the greatest of English politicians.

3. The French Civil Wars

The monarchy of Francis I *(r.1515–47)* and Henry II *(r.1547–59)* had less solid institutional and psychological foundations than its magnificent façade suggested. Its effectiveness in the French provinces depended overmuch upon the good will, the self-interest, or the fear of the nobility. With his usual intelligence Francis himself once remarked that his nobles were dangerous in time of peace unless they could somehow be kept amused. When in July 1559 the vigorous but less intelligent Henry II was accidentally killed in a tournament with a Scotsman, there followed a series of royal minorities which displayed the profound need for a mature, legitimate, and competent king. A number of disturbing circumstances accompanied the personal tragedy. By this time the Calvinist preachers sent into France from Geneva had begun to make mass conversions and to disturb all ranks of society. Again, in April 1559 the king had been forced by bankruptcy into the Treaty of Cateau-Cambrésis with Spain, a power also bankrupted by warfare amid inflated prices. Dire need of money goes far to explain the inability of the French Crown to overcome its rivals throughout the subsequent forty years. But in 1559 it was hard to say where authority would lie. Queen Catherine de' Medici, though boasting exalted French ancestors alongside her Italian background, had hitherto been kept in political obscurity: as a possible regent she lacked credibility in the minds of the French princes and nobles. The brief rule of her eldest son Francis II lay wholly under the dominance of the Guise family, which with its Duchy of Lorraine, its immense estates in eastern France, its ambitious alliance with the Scottish royal house, its Cardinal a great figure at Trent, had suddenly come to overshadow the Valois dynasty.

Had the Guises remained unchallenged France might have been spared a collapse of authority, but there existed a host of conflicting interests, including some families scarcely less influential and ambitious. First among these stood the Bourbons, whose worldly head Antony *(d.1562)* enjoyed a royal title through his marriage to the pious Protestant Jeanne d'Albret, heiress of the little kingdom of Navarre. These were the parents of Henry of Navarre, later to become king of France upon the extinction of his Valois kinsmen. But the power of the Bourbons derived not only from their several earlier alliances with the royal house but still more from their vast lands in southwestern France, supported by the immense estates further north of their relatives the dukes of Montpensier. Antony's brother Louis Duke of Condé was another major territorial magnate and office-holder in his own right, while his acceptance of the title Protector General of the Reformed Churches sprang rather from his ambition than from deep religious convictions. A lesser family, yet seemingly big enough in 1559 to act as a balancing force, was the house of Châtillon, whose Catholic head, the duke of Montmorency, Constable of France, had served the monarchy since the battle of Marignano. His son Henry Damville, governor of Languedoc, became known during the wars as "King of the South," while his nephew Gaspard de Coligny, Admiral of France, was a Protestant of conviction and character, the man who was to come near changing the destiny of France and then to lose power and life itself in the Massacre of St. Bartholomew.

While the origin and the long continuance of the civil wars owed much to the neo-feudal character and the deep seated rivalries of those great noble families, modern research has also drawn attention to social and economic factors reaching down into the middle and lower orders of French society. Both contemporaries and later historians have depicted the squirearchy as an impoverished and restive class, waging a struggle against the general inflation, often losing lands and wealth to the growing crowds of lawyers and financiers with territorial and social ambitions. Of late, it has been forcibly argued that insofar as it became impoverished, the gentry incurred this fate through the wars themselves. Yet certainly war did produce amongst them a very numerous class which found a livelihood, a way of life, even a pleasurable romance in the prolongation of hostilities. On both sides the armies became notoriously ill-disciplined, a feature enhanced by the presence of foreign mercenaries, who terrorized large districts if they were unpaid. As a class the gentry tended to anticlericalism; a considerable proportion turned Protestant and formed the famous cavalry corps of the Huguenot armies. In some provinces they waged family feuds and fought local skirmishes having little or no relevance to the main campaigns. Even the peasantry contributed something to the gradual disintegration of French society, yet far more pardonably, since their rebellions were the inevitable outcome of hunger and distress. As for townsmen, merchants, lawyers, officials, members of the *parlements,* these became far more deeply embroiled in the religious and political issues. The *parlement* of Paris and its provincial counterparts behaved most obstructively toward the Crown and contributed little to the pacification of the realm. The lesser traders and craftsmen of many cities leaned strongly to Huguenotism, and not necessarily from economic motives, since they did so not merely in the declining cities of the interior but also in the flourishing parts of the west and the north.

In certain cases the debility of central government prompted cities and provinces to erect independent states, either separately or in groups. In 1573, for example, the Protestants of Languedoc and Upper Guienne formed republics with parliamentary assemblies at Nîmes and Montauban; they applied Presbyterian ideas to secular government and held district councils from which deputies were sent up to these assemblies. On the other side a strong democratic spirit flourished after 1589 among the ardently Catholic populace of Paris, when amid disease and starvation the city was defending itself against Henry of Navarre. A still more curious example of municipal particularism occurred in the great city of Rouen, which in 1562 offered to become subject to Queen Elizabeth, recalling the days when northern France had been ruled by Henry V! For secular as much as for religious reasons, state and society tended to disintegrate at all levels: here was a disease by no means fully eradicated from the French body politic until the final triumph of the monarchy in 1659.

While the conventional title "French Wars of Religion" must seem altogether inadequate, the contrary tendency to minimize the role of religion also endangers the truth. The severe religious persecutions by Henry II and then by the Guises made the resort to force almost inevitable. Again, the mistrust of the Huguenots and their demand for substantial guarantees of religious toleration were sharply revived by the treacherous massacre of 1572, conducted for political ends but on a religious basis. An alacrity for combat was not peculiar to the Catholics. In 1560–62 many Huguenots, both pastors and lay leaders, organized military cadres on the bases of their church congregations. They stood completely prepared for the call to arms and already in March 1560 some of them participated in the Tumult of Amboise, an unsuccessful attempt to snatch the young King from the hands of the Guises. Even before the wars began, Catherine's cool and statesman-like Chancellor Michel de l'Hôpital, founder of the *politique* party, admitted the folly of hoping for an easy religious pacification. "A Frenchman and an Englishman who are of the same religion," he added, "have more affection for one another than citizens of the same city, or vassals of the same land, who hold to different creeds."

These complex internal tensions apart, the civil wars should also be viewed in an international context. Like the Thirty Years War in the next century, like the Spanish Civil War in our own, the French struggle attracted politicians and soldiers of many other countries and became a battleground for European issues. Spain, England, the Netherlanders, and some German rulers actively intervened, while numerous organized contingents of foreigners fought on both sides. The personal, ideological, and military links with the Netherlands Revolt became ever more intimate. While a common religion and hatred of Spain united the Huguenots and the Dutch patriots, the Catholic League in Paris would have been overthrown had not the Duke of Parma brought the Spanish forces in the Netherlands to its support. Yet from one important aspect a distinction must be drawn between the two movements. The Huguenots were Frenchmen demanding toleration within a French state: the efforts of a few to found rival states were spasmodic and by no means based upon a non-French culture. On the other hand, the Netherlands Revolt marked the birth of a nation.

After repressing the Tumult of Amboise the triumphant Guises conspired with Philip to assassinate Antony of Navarre, judicially murder Condé, and exterminate both the Protestant Vaudois and the hornets' nest of Geneva. Yet before these plans came to fruition the sudden death of Francis II deprived them of full control. Catherine de' Medici with the complicity of Navarre made herself regent for her ten-year-old second son Charles IX, and she prepared to play off Bourbon against Guise. A States General called in August 1561 proposed many judicial and constitutional reforms: it also contained strong Huguenot and *politique* elements demanding religious toleration and the sale of church lands. These attitudes alienated both the lawyers and the churchmen, who resolved never to be ruled by a body so inimical to their interests. While unready to pursue policies as liberal as those of the States General, the Queen Mother in the following January accorded the Huguenots the right to worship outside walled towns. Rather than accept such proposals the Guises resolved on violent action. Seeing Huguenots assembling for worship in a barn at Vassy, Francis Duke of Guise massacred some fifty and wounded many more. He then entered Paris and seized the young King, leaving Condé, Coligny, and the Protestant leaders little alternative but to defend themselves in arms.

The first civil war *(August 1562–March 1563)* saw the brief English occupation of Le Havre, the fall of Rouen to the Catholics, the death of Antony of Navarre, an inconclusive battle at Dreux, and the assassination of the Duke of Guise. From this point political murders, by no means unknown in earlier centuries, became almost an accepted norm in western Europe. Idealized as tyrannicide, with appropriate examples from the Bible and the classics, it soon proved (like its twentieth-century equivalents) just as convenient a weapon for the tyrants themselves. For the moment, the death of Guise seemed to help the cause of reconciliation. The Peace of Amboise allowed Protestant nobles to hold services in their houses, while in each *sénéchaussée* one city was appointed, in the suburbs of which Protestant worship should be permitted. In addition, at every town where Protestantism had become established, the king might assign one or two chapels inside the walls. Paris, where Catholic feeling ran high, would be excepted from these concessions. The deal at Amboise, forerunner of many other schemes of compromise, was followed by collaboration to expel the English from Le Havre. Then came a shock to Huguenot feelings when Catherine held a consultation with the Duke of Alva at Bayonne. This event made it seem likely that she would dismiss her conciliatory adviser L'Hôpital and join Philip in a Catholic crusade. A Protestant plot to seize the King and the court was followed by the outbreak of the second war *(September 1567–March 1568)*, an inconclusive battle at St. Denis, and the Edict of Longjumeau, which reverted to the compromise of Amboise. Within a few months the refusal of both sides to implement this arrangement led to further confusion and disorder, the retirement of L'Hôpital, and the renewed ascendancy of the Guises over the Queen Mother.

In the consequent third civil war *(September 1568–August 1570)* Condé was slain in the cavalry battle at Jarnac, but a foreign force of Germans and Flemings under the Duke of Zweibrücken and the Prince of Orange penetrated deeply into France, effecting a junction with Coligny. Nevertheless Henry, the new Duke of Guise, bravely defended Poitiers, while Coligny was wounded and defeated at Montcontour. The Huguenots then displayed their usual resilience. The failure of the Catholics to follow up their victory in the field enabled Coligny to collect a large army in the south of France and to establish himself on the Loire. Still anxious to avoid Guise control, still determined to reunite the country under her feeble son Charles, the Queen Mother agreed to the Peace of St. Germain, whereby the Huguenots, in addition to the privileges hitherto offered, were allowed to worship in two cities in each province of France, while for two years they would hold as security the cities of La Rochelle, Montauban, Cognac, and La Charité.

At this juncture the Huguenots, having failed to capture the peasant masses, probably comprised less than one-tenth of the population of France, yet in terms of wealth, social status, political influence, and military organization their strength had become proportionately far greater than their numbers. Their communities lay most thickly distributed in the great rectangle between the Loire, the Rhone, and the Pyrenees, but with some strong outposts in Normandy and Dauphiné. Among the urban working classes their gains had been scattered and uncertain. Catholicism tightened its hold upon the Parisians, amongst whom the priesthood, the Jesuits, and other religious Orders were exceptionally strong. Some other cities, notably Orléans and Rouen, saw strong Catholic revivals during the later stages of the civil wars. While the Huguenots with their guarantee-towns sought a political power far beyond mere religious toleration, they could not solidly occupy great provinces and establish firm military fronts. The campaigns themselves consisted largely of raids and cavalry skirmishes: even in terms of sixteenth-century warfare, they were rendered somewhat primitive by the financial straits of both sides, which obviated the systematic use of artillery.

The Peace of St. Germain was followed by a rapid *volte-face* and then by the most sensational event of the struggle, the Massacre of St. Bartholomew. The Queen Mother at first saw the Peace as affording a new opportunity to free the Crown from the grip of the Guises, who had established their hold over her favorite son the Duke of Anjou, later to become Henry III. This prince had shown promise and played a notable part in the battles of Jarnac and Montcontour. Consequently his jealous brother Charles IX dreamed fitfully of eclipsing these deeds and uniting the French nation in a great war against Spain. Such a project seemed to demand the help of Coligny, the full recognition of Protestantism and an alliance with England and the Netherlanders. Yet as the weeks of peace passed, the Queen Mother came to view with alarm Coligny's growing influence at court, the more so in the light of her obsessive fear of Spanish arms. She also resented the personal arrogance of the Huguenot leader, who was reported as advising the King to liberate himself from her tutelage. Though Catherine had so often been compelled to work with the Guises, her attitude had hitherto deserved respect because she had sincerely aimed at the restoration of national unity and order under the Crown. Yet in August 1572 she determined to take a short cut and plotted with Anjou and Henry of Guise to assassinate Coligny amid the festivities surrounding the marriage of her daughter Margaret with the young Henry of Navarre. In the event Coligny was merely wounded and the conspirators decided, probably on the spur of the moment, to cover their traces by organizing a greater

The Massacre of St. Bartholomew in Paris, 24 August 1572. Coligny, wounded by a previous assassination attempt, is being slain in his bed.

crime and committing the nation to a new war against the Protestants. Inventing a Huguenot plot, they prevailed upon the hysterical King to authorize a general attack upon the Huguenot leaders assembled for the wedding. On the fatal day August 24 Henry of Guise personally supervised the killing of Coligny, while the Paris mob, completely out of hand, butchered a thousand or more victims. Henry of Navarre escaped only by pretending to abjure Protestantism. In other places the action depended on local circumstances. At Orléans a massacre was perpetrated by command of the city council, while at Lyons the governor sought to protect the Huguenots, yet was thrust aside by a popular revolt. At Montpellier, Bayonne, and Nîmes the authorities preserved order and no killing occurred. The total number of victims throughout the provinces cannot be closely computed, but it is generally thought to have exceeded ten thousand.

Following this depletion of their nobility, the Huguenot party developed a more urban and a more radical leadership. The inevitable outburst of antiroyalist pamphleteering extended over many years. Its conclusions, far more advanced than those of Calvin, were summarized by the systematic if unoriginal *Vindiciae contra Tyrannos (1579)* attributed to Philippe du Plessis-Mornay, an associate of Henry of Navarre. Basing his arguments upon scriptural precept and precedent, this author upholds a contractual theory of monarchy, whereby a people retains the right to depose a monarch who breaks the contract by turning tyrant. In such an event, he argues, neighboring princes are morally bound to help the oppressed. Normally the appointed magistrates of a nation are alone entitled to take the lead, but exceptions occur if the tyrant is an invader, a usurper—or a woman. As opposed to the topical approach of such tracts, the *Franco-Gallia* of François Hotman *(1573)* forms a learned interpretation of French consti-tutional history by a scholar whose view held sway until the nineteenth century. Hotman contrasts the free Germanic institutions of the Gauls and the Franks with both Roman Law and with the usurpations during recent centuries by French kings and *parlements.* On the basis of the older precedents, the French monarchy is declared elective, while the rule of women is again denounced, partly on practical grounds but partly on account of the Salic Law of the Franks, which had rigorously excluded women from the succession.

The years which followed the massacre also saw a large growth in the propaganda and influence of the *Politiques,* who remained Catholics yet in their political actions placed loyalty to the Crown above religious partisan-ship. In Languedoc Damville, and in Paris his brother the Marshal Francis of Montmorency denounced both the Guises and the Queen Mother. Among the numerous *politique* manifestos the most sustained and weighty was the *République* of Jean Bodin, who compares the ruler of a state with the steersman of a ship, who is often forced to make his way through the tempest by tacking from side to side rather than by heading straight for port. Bodin seeks the salvation of France in a legitimate and paternal monarchy. Opposing the Huguenot theorists, he rejects the arguments for tyrannicide: he embraces monarchical absolutism and a sternly imposed toleration. The same broad aims continued to be those of Catherine de' Medici, but she and her wretched progeny now lacked the moral reputation needed to restore the monarchy. The fourth and fifth civil wars *(1572-76)* continued without decisive result and during them *(1574)* died Charles IX, tormented by memories of the massacre. The Duke of Anjou had briefly accepted the elective throne of Poland, but scarcely had he arrived in that kingdom than he was recalled to succeed his brother. Belying his earlier promise, Henry III began an ineffective reign of fifteen years by spending several weeks of debauchery in Venice. His conduct was henceforth marked by strange excesses and hysterical repentances, above all by a love of greedy male favorites. A mind so ill-balanced had no chance of retrieving the prestige of the house of Valois.

The intermittent campaigning of the seventies and eighties was accom-panied, it is true, by some alluring if dubiously sincere offers to the Huguenots. That of May 1576, called the Peace of Monsieur (the title of the King's brother Alençon) appears at its face-value the most "advanced" agreement of the century. While according Catholicism a titular supremacy, it grants the Huguenots freedom of worship in all parts of the realm. Such rights are no longer limited to great nobles or specified towns, but apply to all Frenchmen, except at court and in Paris. The Peace of Monsieur does not even declare religious tolerance to be a regrettable necessity, though it expresses the hope that a General Council will at last find a way toward uniformity. Cases in which Protestants are involved must be tried by *chambres mi-parties:* courts composed of an equal number of judges from each religion. Eight towns will be garrisoned by the Huguenots, while a general amnesty will be proclaimed, together with a declaration that the Massacre of St. Bartholomew had occurred against the will of the Crown. This document need not be regarded as another trap set by the Queen Mother, for despite the Massacre she lacked religious fanaticism and now stood prepared to attempt a radical experiment along *politique* lines. Unfortunately this very effort helped to provoke a strong Catholic reaction.

Throughout much of Europe the Catholic Reformation was making steady advances: the well organized Jesuit Order preached to enthusiastic congregations and the militant Catholics planned a national organization to rival and engulf that of the Huguenots. Since the sixties they had formed local leagues in various places, but now a united Catholic League, first announced in Péronne (where the young Duke of Condé was hated as governor of Picardy), spread rapidly throughout the kingdom. In essence it was not merely Catholic but aristocratic and supranational: it openly challenged the House of Valois by naming Henry of Guise as its leader and Philip II as its protector. Yet within Paris the Guises were gradually compelled to cultivate popular enthusiasm while combatting the efforts of the citizens' Council of Sixteen to assume full control. A radical atmosphere developed which has caused some deluded romantics to compare the Paris of the League with the French Revolution. Meanwhile a substantial proportion of the aristocracy and officialdom throughout the kingdom proved equally reluctant to accept the need for compromise. In December 1576 a States General held at Blois saw no Huguenots and few *Politiques* in attendance; its members attacked the Peace of Monsieur and allowed the parties to drift into the sixth war. This soon ended in the Peace of Bergerac *(September 1577),* reverting to terms similar to those of the Peace of St. Germain. During the subsequent seven years little fighting occurred, though Henry of Navarre grew in political stature and in 1580 fought a brief campaign largely to enhance his own power in the south. At this stage the King's brother Francis (formerly Duke of Alençon and now of Anjou) seemed likely to make a greater impact upon history, for he persistently courted Queen Elizabeth and in 1580 accepted the sovereignty of the Netherlands from the rebels. Since Henry III was judged incapable of having children, it seemed far from impossible that Francis might end by ruling over all three countries. Yet while Elizabeth fooled him, he ended by stultifying himself in that graveyard of reputations the Netherlands, where his blunders culminated in an attempt to occupy Bruges and Antwerp with French forces.

Retiring from this scene, Francis died in June 1584, a month before the assassination of the Prince of Orange, whom he had so grossly embarrassed. These events heralded a new phase of the French conflict, since Henry of Navarre had now become legitimate heir to Henry III. As for the Catholic Leaguers they had been transmuted into rebels; their pamphleteers were soon at work justifying tyrannicide, and indeed borrowing the very texts and arguments hitherto used by du Plessis-Mornay and other Huguenot writers. It seemed obvious that Henry III and Henry of Navarre would now ally and make common cause against the Guises, the League and Spain: the Dutch actually offered their sovereignty to Henry III in this confident expectation. The same prospect aroused the Leaguers to frenzied military effort, resulting in their capture of many important places in northern and eastern France. Such were their successes that the opportunist Queen Mother urged her son to submit to their demands, with the effect that in July 1585 the edicts of toleration were rescinded and the Huguenots bidden to conform or go into exile. Soon afterwards the bellicose Pope Sixtus V excommunicated Henry of Navarre, yet the latter continued to attract both Huguenots and *Politiques*. Moreover Henry proved his military capacity when the eighth war *(1585-89)* broke out and he defeated the royal army at Courtras. But Henry Duke of Guise, having crushed a large invading force of Swiss and Germans, excluded the King himself from the capital and France lay disputed between the three Henries. The King was the first to break the deadlock by a *coup* worthy of both Valois and Guise. A States-General having been assembled at Blois, the King there assassinated the Duke and executed his brother the Cardinal of Guise. Nevertheless the main objective was lost, since Paris under the surviving brother, the able Duke of Mayenne, continued to defy the royal authority. Even the Sorbonne called upon the nation to throw off its allegiance to Henry III, while many towns in central and southern France also took hostile action. Amid the ever-rising confusion Catherine de' Medici died, and driven at last into alliance with Henry of Navarre, the King joined him in an advance upon Paris. But in August 1589 before they could assault the capital, the last Valois monarch fell victim to the dagger of the friar Jacques Clément, a champion of the League intent on avenging the Guises.

In the first of the Bourbon dynasty, France had at last a ruler who knew his own mind and was endowed with a realism rare in that murderous and fanatical world. Yet Henry IV could inspire a sentimental devotion; his humor and affability attracted men and women of all classes. An intrepid cavalry leader and lover of adventure, he never lost sight of France's crying need for peace. His rapid succession of mistresses detracted little from his physical vitality or from his serenity of mind. At his accession a mountainous task demanded both these qualities. In the ninth and last civil war the victories of the new ruler at Arques *(1589)* and Ivry *(1590)* left him facing a far sterner task: the capture of Paris, the greatest city of Europe. Its long perimeter made it hard to besiege, yet even so Henry's blockade reduced its population to a diet of domestic animals and vermin. The League's reign of terror could not prevent thousands from starving or more thousands from dying of fever. From military capture it was preserved when in September 1590 Philip sent Parma to its relief, but having once again intervened in masterly fashion to save Rouen in 1592, Parma died of a neglected wound. Meanwhile Mayenne could not be dislodged or the League torn asunder, Spain steadily supplying their needs from the Netherlands, from Franche Comté, and from a base in Brittany. By this time it had become obvious that Henry IV, though supported by the moderate Catholic party—and by sizeable English forces and funds—could not attain his goal by force alone. The only alternative lay in his personal reversion to the Catholic faith, since beyond question Paris and powerful groups all over France would never voluntarily accept the rule of a Protestant monarch. When Henry coined the epigram "Paris is well worth a mass," he did himself an injustice. Though his future great minister Sully refused to take this step at his side, he put the position logically enough: "You must surrender to your enemies, or defeat them, or turn Catholic." The first remained unthinkable, the second had proved impracticable; yet it had become high time to envisage the third.

When the two sides held a conference at Suresnes in April–June 1593 the Archbishop of Lyons on behalf of the League staunchly called for the imposition of religious uniformity and demanded that the Pope should have the right to decide upon the sincerity of any "conversion" professed by the King. Yet the Archbishop of Bourges insisted upon the duty of obedience even to a heretical monarch. He also proclaimed the liberties of the Gallican Church, deplored the enslavement of the Papacy by Spain, and announced that the King's heresy was only slight. Shortly afterwards Henry conferred with Catholic theologians, and though he refused to sign a declaration condemning the Reformed faith, he announced his adherence to the Catholic Church and promised religious obedience to the Papacy. On 25 July at St. Denis he submitted a signed confession of faith and heard mass. Since Rheims lay too near the Spanish forces, he was crowned at Chartres, and by observing the traditional forms undertook to banish heresy from his kingdom. Sully and the Huguenot councillors openly and with impunity refused their approval. And while in Rome Clement VIII detested the Gallican character of these events, even Mayenne told him that if Rome would not negotiate she would simply lose control of the French nation. In the event, though Henry agreed to receive in France the decrees of the Council of Trent, he refused either to hold his crown by papal permission or to undertake to frame secular policies acceptable to Rome.

The crowned and anointed King, duly in communion with Rome, still confronted some fearsome obstacles. His former Huguenot associates continued to organize a French Reformed Church with a General Assembly based upon nine provincial organizations. On the other side, the fanatical or merely seditious Leaguers included some Jesuits, whose loyalties lay neither with France, nor for that matter with Spain and the Inquisition, but with Rome. When a pupil of the Jesuits attempted to murder the King, even the orthodox *Parlement* of Paris demanded the expulsion of the Order from France, though in fact this measure was only partially executed. Meanwhile by a prolonged and unedifying blend of force and bribery Henry brought the League's leaders to terms. He ended in 1596 by appeasing Mayenne himself. The proud Guise, now made Governor of the Île de France, received payment of his enormous debts and three fortresses to hold as security.

After prolonged negotiations with the Huguenots, Henry agreed upon the Edict of Nantes in April 1598. It was a distinctly less liberal document than the Peace of Monsieur, but there was now reason to believe that the Crown would honor it. The Edict began by stating that since religious unity was not yet possible, the consciences and property of those of the "pretended Reformed religion" needed safeguards. Once more justice by *chambres mi-parties* was granted, while the Huguenots received equal rights to enter professional careers, schools, universities, hospitals, and guilds. Protestant worship was permitted in all places where it had occurred in 1577 or in 1596–97, in two places in each *bailliage* or *sénéchaussée*, and in the houses of the nobility. The Reformed Church might hold national and provincial synods, but only "by permission of the King," while political and military organizations were banned. Despite the grudging nature of these clauses, the Huguenots obtained a substantial guarantee against betrayal: the right to garrison for eight years all towns and castles held by them at the end of the previous August. Should garrisons still be kept in these "places of security" after eight years, a Protestant governor would remain in control. These guarantees, it is true, occur in a private grant by the King as distinct from the "public" portion of the treaty, but in the event they entailed the delivery to the Huguenots of nearly a hundred towns and castles, of which the most important were La Rochelle, Montauban, and Montpellier. Quite apart from any treaty provisions, one significant fact remained to buttress the agreement: that the Huguenot nobles and towns could still raise at short notice forces larger than any standing army likely to be kept by a king in time of peace.

The Edict of Nantes, though threatened and modified by Richelieu, lasted in substance until its revocation in 1685 by Louis XIV: this must surely be regarded as one of the greatest political advances of the period. The lesson had indeed been learned at a terrible cost, and on neither side did it herald a conversion to liberal optimism; yet if we except the peculiar case of Poland, the Edict created a uniquely tolerant state, conferring under effective guarantees freedom of worship and religious organization upon a dissenting minority of French citizens. Socially, economically, and culturally, the nation was to derive profound benefits from this experiment. In pleasing contrast with Spain's expulsion of Jews and Moriscos, seventeenth-century France gained wealth from her Huguenot traders, bankers, seamen and colonists. Meanwhile her foreign policy easily outmatched that of Spain, since she could decently and credibly negotiate alliances with Protestant powers. Even her great Catholic writers and preachers responded all the more brilliantly in facing the stimulus of competition. It was within this tolerant France that the last great phase—the only French phase—of the Catholic Reformation occurred. Catholic Christianity prospered alongside the Edict of Nantes and declined after the revocation of that edict. But how many contemporaries on either side even troubled to reflect upon the realities underlying this ostensible paradox?

While there followed a constructive and peaceful reign of twelve years, it would be erroneous to imagine that Henry IV had cured all the profound political and social diseases of France. To end the bloodshed and impoverishment, he was compelled to buy out the powerful neo-feudalists like Mayenne, yet the sinister lesson did not go unheeded by other ambitious magnates of that generation and the next. The spirit of privileged faction in high places survived to plague Richelieu and Mazarin until, like the far more fruitful privileges of the Huguenots, it withered under the autocracy of Louis XIV. So far as concerns France, we now leave the years of dark division for a more august age, yet neither the greatness nor the limitations of that age can be understood without some careful reflection upon its genesis amid the so-called Wars of Religion.

4. The Revolt of the Netherlands

Lutheranism, Anabaptism, and Calvinism successively swept through the seventeen provinces of the Netherlands, but political unrest during the rule of Charles V owed little to religion; indeed it owed far less to radical than to conservative sentiments. The formidable revolt of the city of Ghent in 1540 illustrates the resentment of individual communities against the erosion of ancient privileges, and still more their resistance to rising taxation. While Charles severely crushed Ghent—and also continued to burn innumerable heretics—the Netherlands maintained the most advanced economy in the world and Antwerp reached the height of its renown as the greatest trading center and money market of Europe. Charles was not unpopular; neither were the two female regents, his aunt Margaret of Savoy, who ruled until 1530, and his sister Mary of Hungary, who continued from 1530 to 1555. A true heir of the Burgundians, Charles promoted

Netherlanders in various parts of his empire. He subordinated provincial courts to a central court of justice at Mechlin and he erected a council for police and justice, a court of finance, and the Council of State. The last-named, chiefly manned by the greater nobles, exercised under the presidency of the Regent a general supervision of domestic and foreign affairs. It was also during the reign of Charles that the provinces were rounded off by the acquisition of Groningen, Guelderland, and other frontier-areas.

Ironically enough, the centralizing work of the Burgundians and their Habsburg successors contributed to that sense of unity which led to a sense of nationhood, and hence to a situation which by the accession of Philip II needed careful handling. Unlike Charles, who had been a Netherlander by upbringing, Philip had no instinctive feeling for the outlook and way of life which characterized the Low Countries. As we see it today, they had much to teach him about civilization which he would not learn. Not only did he subordinate their interests and their wealth to his world-wide schemes, but he displayed in the process neither subtlety nor patience. In taking the substance of the Netherlands, he would not even leave them the shadow of their independence. Ironically again, the insensitive methods of his quest for Catholic orthodoxy helped to destroy that greatest of the regional Catholic traditions of late medieval Europe: the *devotio moderna,* which had continued to flourish even in the mid-sixteenth century. This was a liberal and cultured Catholic tradition, pietistic yet unregimented, well suited to these outgoing citizen-communities, which had to mix with men of all nations and creeds. As a Christian tradition, it had nothing in common with Roman or Spanish legalist and inquisitorial religion. Erasmus did not teach his own countrymen a contemplative tolerance: he was himself the product of a broad-minded, unforced tradition of the inner life.

Having left the Netherlands in 1559 without paying overmuch attention to the grievances expressed by the States General, Philip appointed a third lady-regent, who had been brought up by the former two: his half-sister Margaret Duchess of Parma, illegitimate daughter of Charles V, wife to a grandson of Paul III, and mother to a boy who would become the greatest soldier of his day. Margaret was instructed to cooperate not only with the three councils but with an inner *Consulta* headed by Antoine de Granvelle *(1517–86),* like his father before him a faithful servant of the Habsburgs and one of those bequeathed by Charles to Philip. Yet in the eyes of the Netherlands nobility, Granvelle, created a cardinal in 1561, remained unpopular as a Burgundian who united smooth manners with a large appetite for power and wealth. The first stages of maladjustment involved few save members of the nobility and upper clergy, and they arose in large part from a conservative resistance to Philip's scheme of ecclesiastical reform, a scheme which in itself could claim considerable merits.

Nothing could have been more chaotic, unwieldy, and irrational than the higher administration of the Church in the Netherlands. The three sees

The Netherlands in the Period
of the Revolt

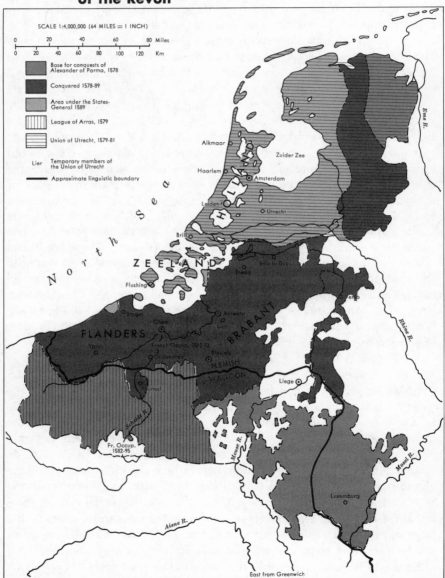

SCALE 1:4,000,000 (64 MILES = 1 INCH)

0   20   40   60   80 Miles

0   20   40   60   80   100   120 Km

Base for conquests of
Alexander of Parma, 1578

Conquered 1578-89

Area under the States-
General 1589

League of Arras, 1579

Union of Utrecht, 1579-81

Lier   Temporary members of
the Union of Utrecht

Approximate linguistic boundary

Ems R.

Zuider Zee

Alkmaar

Haarlem

HOLLAND

Amsterdam

Leiden

Utrecht

Brill

North Sea

ZEELAND

Bois-le-Duc

Breda

Venlo

Flushing

Bruges

Antwerp

BRABANT

Rhine R.

FLANDERS

Ghent

Lier

Ypres

French Occup. 1582-83

Oudenarde

Brussels

FLEMISH

WALLOON

Liege

Tournai

Schelde R.

Fr. Occup.
1582-95

Meuse R.

Mosel R.

Luxemburg

Aisne R.

East from Greenwich

of Utrecht, Arras, and Tournai were absurdly large and populous, the first-named containing three hundred walled towns. Other portions of the Low Countries lay subject to bishoprics based in foreign territories like that of Liège, while from some episcopal courts appeals could be carried to the courts of external metropolitans, such as those of Rheims and Cologne. Philip proposed to increase the number of bishoprics to fifteen, to free them from foreign controls and place them under three archiepiscopal sees at Mechlin, Cambrai, and Utrecht. The necessary new revenues were to be derived from surplus monastic estates, while the heads of religious houses would be made more closely subservient to the bishops. Finally, each bishop must appoint new prebendaries to his cathedral, two of whom in each diocese would be inquisitors charged to eradicate heresy. Even had Philip omitted this last obnoxious measure, he would still have encountered opposition, which was in fact directed far less against his antiheresy campaign than against his attack upon the vested interests of aristocracy and cities. Many monastic houses had long been appropriated by noble families and had supplied livings for younger sons. Antwerp and other towns could produce charters protecting them from more rigorous episcopal discipline. In general the scheme attracted distrust as one adopted without the consent of the States General, while Granvelle, designated to combine the archbishopric of Mechlin with the presidency of the Council of State, undeservedly received the chief share of the opprobrium. He and William Prince of Orange (1533-84, later called William the Silent) stood at loggerheads, especially when in 1561 the latter married a daughter of the former Protestant leader Maurice of Saxony. From this stage William, the wealthiest of the nobility and Stadhouder (i.e. the king's "deputy") of Holland, Zeeland, and Utrecht, incurred Philip's deep distrust.

In March 1563 Orange, Egmont, and Hoorn, the leading members of the Council of State, absented themselves from that body until Philip should remove Granvelle. A year later, when the Regent had added her voice to theirs, Philip complied, but so far from modifying his actual policy, he aroused new anger by promulgating on his own authority the decrees of the Council of Trent. Though Egmont went to Spain to represent the views of the nobility, the King issued the Edict of Segovia, which not only refused the latter any increased share in the administration but insisted afresh upon the rigorous extirpation of heresy. Even Margaret and her officialdom expressed dismay. Moreover the lesser nobility now joined the active opposition, and like their counterparts in France they formed a restive military class, though one as yet permeated only to a minor degree by Calvinism. Indeed, during the sixties and early seventies the Netherlandish national movement owed relatively little to Protestant inspiration, and many staunchly Catholic notables stood among its leaders. When fighting finally broke out in 1567, probably well under a third of the population had embraced Protestantism. As late as 1576, in a letter to the still Catholic and loyal city council of Amsterdam, the Estates of the province of Holland wrote, "we never took up arms for the sake of religion."

In modern times much misunderstanding has arisen concerning the final division of the Netherlands into a northern, mainly Protestant, Dutch Republic, and on the other hand a Catholic, Habsburg South, the predecessor of the modern Belgium. In 1560 and for long afterwards "Belgium" did not exist, even notionally or in some embryonic form. Throughout the earlier stages of the Revolt, a division along the line which divides the modern Holland[1] from the modern Belgium could not have seemed an inherently probable result. The leading opposition nobles both great and small came largely from the southern Netherlands, while as yet the chief centers of popular Calvinism lay in Antwerp and Ghent rather than in Amsterdam or in other northern cities. Likewise the final division cannot be regarded as springing from cultural patterns, since the main cultural division ran, not between the areas we now call Holland and Belgium, but across the middle of the latter. This division was linguistic, and it has survived with little change to complicate twentieth-century political problems. It runs directly westward from near Aachen, then just north of Liège and just south of Brussels, to the French border near Lille. North of this language line (except during the past century in Brussels) the people have spoken Dutch dialects for a millennium. South of the line, French and French dialects (Picard and still more Walloon) have been spoken. All in all, the basic reasons for the division were far less cultural or religious than political and military, though as we propose in due course to argue, they seem to have been less simply based upon geographical facts than some recent Dutch historians have maintained.

Certainly in the days of Margaret and Granvelle the incipient sense of nationhood embraced virtually the whole of the Netherlands. Led by a moderate government, the Provinces, with the conceivable exception of the French-speaking Walloons, would doubtless have formed a single nation. Concerning this dawn of a national consciousness, fascinating evidence recently came to light when a Dutch scholar examined the entries made by several thousand Netherlandish students and artists in the registers of Italian universities and academies. Until the years around 1560 they generally located themselves by their provinces, "Brabantinus," "Zelandus," "Hollandus," and the like. From these years onward such designations became far less usual and the students of all provinces normally described themselves as either "Belga" or "Flamengus," both of which words in that day meant no more and no less than "Netherlander." Yet one must hasten to add that this sense of national identity, when subjected to the stress of

---

[1]"Holland" has long been used by English-speaking people to mean the whole of the northern Netherlands. There, however, it has only meant the individual province of Holland.

war, did not always triumph over the old, short-sighted localism. Mere provincial thinking and municipal thinking can both be richly illustrated from the documents and annals of the Revolt.

During the year 1566 Philip turned the moderate opposition of the confederate nobility into total intransigence. In the summer the King refused to permit another session of the States-General, but he promised pardons to the obedient, undertaking to withdraw the Inquisition while leaving inquisitorial powers to the bishops. Secretly, in the presence of Alva and other witnesses he protested that he did not feel bound by these extorted concessions, and he repeated the same sentiment to the Pope. Even as the confederates were again petitioning for religious toleration, Philip was encouraged by the momentary quiescence of the Turks to despatch a punitive force under Alva. At the same time Louis of Nassau, brother of the Prince of Orange, began to prepare for the worst by recruiting mercenaries in Germany. Then throughout the central and northern provinces fanatical crowds, urged on by Calvinist preachers, suddenly began sacking the churches: the wave of iconoclasm exceeded in violence any previously seen in Europe. Of course, this event must be seen in the light of a lengthy persecution; also alongside the confessional warfare in France, which was being anxiously followed by the Netherlandish coreligionists of the Huguenots. At the same time, it disgusted moderate observers, and many Catholics and Lutherans became alienated from the national movement. Though a small group of confederates staged a rising near Antwerp, Orange and the other chief leaders stood aside, leaving the Regent's forces to recover control. Yet knowing that Philip would soon exact vengeance, Orange debated whether to remain or flee. His Catholic friend Egmont would not support armed resistance, while William despaired of obtaining any effective foreign aid. In April 1567, even as Alva marched from Spain, the Prince withdrew to his German county of Nassau.

Accompanied by a force of 10,000 Spanish veterans, Alva reached Brussels in August and upon the resignation of the Regent was invested with supreme authority, civil as well as military. Creating a special court managed by three vindictive Spaniards and known as the Council of Blood, Alva flouted all the Netherlandish liberties. This Council condemned and executed several thousand victims, driving many more into exile. Provoked by a raid by Louis of Nassau, who in May 1568 defeated a Spanish force at Heiligerlee, Alva tried and beheaded Egmont and Hoorn, against the laws of the Netherlands and against their personal privileges as members of the Order of the Golden Fleece. Torture had been freely used to secure evidence against them, but it remains impossible to see in what sense they had committed treason. In his private correspondence even Alva admitted that these executions had "hurt his soul," while European opinion, characteristically little moved by the fate of obscure sectaries or rioters, was shocked by the judicial murder of these great figures. The Netherlanders might have been even more disturbed had it ever become known that their emissary to Spain Baron de Montigny was secretly executed there on orders of Philip, who had assured him that to avoid scandal his natural death would shortly be announced. Meantime Alva easily crushed the attempts of Louis and William to invade the Netherlands, where his reign of terror discouraged any movements of sympathy. By now the oppression had become economic as well as religious and political. Immense new taxes, advised against by all expert opinion, brought trade almost to a standstill and reduced many merchants and financiers to bankruptcy. Of these taxes the most intolerable was a ten per cent charge on every sale; one far heavier in effect, since on delivery to a customer a manufactured commodity had usually incurred the tax four times over since appearing as a raw material.

Universally hated even by the loyalists, Alva was pleading to Philip for his recall when in March 1572 the Sea-beggars headed by La Marck were expelled from English harbors by Elizabeth. After capturing Brill, which commanded the Meuse, they gained control of the Scheldt by the seizure of Flushing. Though Amsterdam and Middelburg refused their demands, a long chain of towns in Holland, Guelderland, Overijssel, and Friesland soon fell into their hands, not without atrocities perpetrated against civilian Catholics. This turn of events marked a vital stage of the Revolt, which now held naval bases affording free access for arms, food, and troops. The Spaniards, having lost control of the narrow seas and the estuaries, could no longer blockade or besiege these places. Nevertheless a host of setbacks both political and military had still to be endured by the patriots. The Massacre of St. Bartholomew crushed the plans of Orange and Coligny for a Franco-Dutch alliance. Mons, captured for a few months by Louis, fell again to the Spaniards, while in capturing Mechlin Alva failed to prevent his troops from sacking churches and killing both Protestants and Catholics. Even in the north the provinces of Guelderland, Groningen, and Overijssel largely submitted, while Alva's son was sent with a large force to beleaguer Haarlem, the key to the province of Holland. After a seven-months siege, marked by much inhumanity on both sides, Haarlem fell amid sickening slaughter; yet the Spanish army, having sustained great losses, mutinied for lack of pay, while a Spanish naval force suffered a crippling defeat off Enkhuizen.

Toward the end of 1573 Don Luis de Requesens replaced Alva: lacking money and reinforcements, he pursued a conciliatory policy in the belief that Protestantism remained intrinsically weak and that a general amnesty might still elicit an orthodox and loyal response from the Netherlanders. Yet this attempt was unlikely to succeed on the morrow of Alva's atrocities. Thanks to the latter, Protestantism and bitterness had flourished together. In many cities, though the patrician councillors strove to avoid becoming the tools of a Calvinist theocracy, the Calvinist congregations and their pastors had come to form the sharp cutting-edge of the patriot cause. Even Orange, while he struggled to maintain tolerance, had to foster and use them. The fighting continued in 1574, and while Louis of Nassau was routed and slain by the Spaniards at Mooker Heyde, the Spanish blockade of Leyden was at length broken by a great flotilla of boats which slowly crossed the flooded land. Amid the triumphal celebrations Orange founded the university of Leyden, destined to play in later times so brilliant a role in European scholarship and science. The relief of Leyden having belied all his hopes, Requesens entered into negotiations with commissioners from Holland and Zeeland, yet his instructions from Spain gave him no room for maneuver. His death in March 1576 preceded an appalling mutiny by the Spanish troops, who in November sacked Antwerp with an enormous destruction of its wealth and an indiscriminate massacre of some 8,000 of its people. This "Spanish fury" stimulated patriotism even among the more provincial and parochial minds: four days later delegates from both the northern and the southern provinces signed the Pacification of Ghent, a document marking the zenith of the movement to establish a state covering the whole of the Netherlands. The Pacification agreed upon the complete expulsion of the Spaniards, the summoning of a States-General, the appointment of Orange as the Lieutenant of King Philip, the suspension of all heresy trials, and the release of political prisoners. Recognizing that in many areas Catholicism remained strong or even preponderant, it allowed freedom of Catholic worship except in Holland and Zeeland. After further successes, including the surrender of the Spanish garrison at Ghent, the Pacification was confirmed by delegates from all the provinces meeting at Brussels.

Such was the situation confronting Don John, the victor of Lepanto, still about thirty years of age when Philip sent him to try fresh methods of pacification. The new Governor found himself making no progress until he agreed upon the withdrawal of the Spanish soldiery, but when he entered Brussels in May 1577 the prospects of a settlement seemed promising to those many observers who did not understand the tenacious ruler in the Escorial. Within a few months the chivalrous and well-meaning Don John was crushed between the suspicions of two men: the Prince of Orange and his own master Philip. Duly stimulated by Antonio Pérez, Philip believed that his romantic and ambitious young half-brother sought the throne of Spain itself. As for William the Silent, he had ample reasons to suspect the good faith of any Spanish Governor—and equally to suspect inconstancy within the patriot movement, which was only too prone to fall apart as soon as Spanish pressure relaxed. The richest and most influential among the leaders of the nobility, the Croys, Lignes, Lalaings, Hennins, Lannays, Berlaymonts, were French-speaking Walloons and mostly Catholics. Such men desired the maintenance of ancient liberties and the removal of the Inquisition, yet otherwise their attitudes differed widely from those of the internationalist Orange and still more widely from those of Calvinist townspeople or Sea-beggars. A group of these southern nobles now brought about the election as Governor General—subject to Philip's approval—of the Archduke Mathias, brother of the eccentric Emperor Rudolph, and Orange found himself obliged to act the part of deputy to this new figurehead. At this stage Philip might have allowed faction its chance to ruin the patriot cause, but instead he sent back a Spanish army which in January 1578 defeated its opponents at Gemblours, driving out both Orange and the Archduke from Brussels.

This new Spanish force appeared under the command of Alexander of Parma *(1555–92),* son of the former Regent Margaret. A childhood companion of Don John, he had served gallantly under the latter at Lepanto and was now about to receive opportunities to display military and political gifts of the highest order. When in October 1578 disease and chagrin carried off the luckless Don John, Parma found himself nominated to the Governorship, and for the first time Orange was confronted by a mind as cool and subtle as his own. Admittedly the newcomer found the tide of affairs turning once again in favor of Spain, since there were now ample religious, social, and regional divisions waiting to be exploited. By outright bribery, by persuasive terms, by offers of jobs and favors, Parma rapidly built up a following among the southern nobility. Disenchanted with the Archduke, the nobles had in the previous July appealed to Francis Duke of Anjou and Alençon, who in his turn had promised to become the defender of Netherlandish liberties. Though popular with the masses and holding a secure position in the northern provinces, Orange again felt it impolitic to resist this hankering after a foreign prince; and needless to add, he well knew the many obstacles which stood in the ambitious Frenchman's path. Alençon was rejected by the Calvinists, while Elizabeth of England—whom he was still wooing—would never have tolerated a French hegemony in the Netherlands. Meanwhile Parma took advantage of this confused situation by encouraging the formation among the southern Walloons of the Union of Arras *(January 1579)* which consisted mainly of Artois and Hainault, together with Lille, Douai, and other neighboring cities. In this Union the permanent division of the Netherlands had its roots. Immediately the north responded by a rival league, the Union of Utrecht, made between Holland, Zeeland, Guelderland, and Utrecht, and subsequently joined not only by Groningen and Overijssel in the north but by Antwerp, Ghent, Bruges, Ypres, and other places ultimately destined to remain under Habsburg rule. Yet at Utrecht there was formed the matrix of the future Dutch Republic, with a General Assembly of delegates from the various provincial estates, a common executive Council, a single currency and taxation system.

There had thus come into existence two political nuclei, yet the final boundaries between their spheres of influence could not yet have been predicted with any confidence. It was Parma's historical function to establish this boundary much further north than the vast majority of the

Netherlanders desired. Having in May 1579 allied with the Union of Arras, Parma carefully prepared to detach the central areas of the Netherlands, where the leaders were still depending upon Alençon and France. In due course this prop collapsed beneath them. The absurd attempt of Alençon to seize personal power in several towns—the "French Fury" of January 1583—entailed his retirement to France, where he died in the following year. Nevertheless, at the moment when Orange, the true leader of the patriots, might have taken a firmer hold upon the destinies of the nation, he fell victim to the bullet of an assassin in the Prinsenhof at Delft. William had already earned his title *Pater Patriae,* and precisely because he had been a great *Politique* rather than a Protestant hero. He had brought to the cause virtues rare among the rulers and magnates of that generation: patience, honesty, serenity in misfortune, a readiness to spend his personal wealth in the cause, above all a capacity for moral growth and a firmness of purpose amid the confusion which beset his own compatriots. While anger at his death revitalized the Union of Utrecht, his survival could hardly have availed to arrest the steady progress of Parma toward the Scheldt. Unlike this adversary, Orange possessed no outstanding military genius and he had never commanded troops who could defeat the Spaniards in the open field.

As distinguished from the Walloon nobles and towns in the south, many places in the central provinces and in Flanders-Brabant did not readily surrender, even though Parma made this choice easier than hitherto. At least he promised to observe their privileges, to exclude the Inquisition, and to allow Protestants time to sell their property and emigrate. Without being stormed, Brussels and Ghent surrendered through starvation; Bruges was betrayed from within, while at Nymegen the Catholic citizens seized control and surrendered. Owing to the width of the Scheldt and its strong landward defenses, Antwerp presented a far tougher proposition. As Orange had planned, it could almost certainly have saved itself by flooding the country-side. Local self-interest deferred this step until too late, while Parma, who had no naval force, cut off the city from the sea by bridging the river. For a time the decision hung upon a thread and Elizabeth might have delivered Antwerp by a timely expedition. Burghley advised against such an enterprise, but even he and the Queen were shocked when in August 1585, after a siege of six months, the great city surrendered. Entering at the head of a cavalcade of Walloon nobles, Parma prevented the usual sack and slaughter; and though he imposed heavy tribute, he also announced that Protestants would be given two years to conform. Nevertheless in the longer run the fall of Antwerp became a catastrophe both for the city and for the provinces of Flanders and Brabant. Still in control of Flushing, the northern rebels blocked the entrance to the Scheldt, and their failure henceforth to recapture Antwerp simply meant the sealing off of its commerce and its speedy replacement as trading metropolis by the free city of Amsterdam. Even when the definitive peace treaty came to be signed in 1648, the Dutch Republic had no intention of reversing this situation, and it remained insistent upon the final closure of the Scheldt—final indeed until the time of Napoleon.

There followed that belated and mismanaged English expedition by the Earl of Leicester.[2] Though the resultant Anglo-Dutch quarrels were not healed until 1589, the Dutch took heart from the defeat of the Armada, while Parma's pressure lightened in 1590 and again in 1592 during his withdrawals to save Paris and Rouen from Henry of Navarre. Moreover in Maurice of Nassau (*1567–1625*), the son of William the Silent, the patriots found a new leader whose military professionalism and political acumen were truly astonishing for one in his early twenties. By 1590 he was Stadhouder in the provinces of Holland, Zeeland, Guelderland, Utrecht, and Overijssel, while a junior branch of the Orange family held that office in Groningen and Friesland, the remaining two northern provinces. Before long the Dutch had built up forces more nearly comparable with those at Parma's disposal. The fire-power of their troops and mercenaries was greatly increased, their engineers systematically trained, above all, their wages regularly paid. In 1590, before these reforms had been completed, Maurice and his advisers profitted from Parma's absence by capturing Breda. In the following year they secured Zutphen and Deventer on the Yssel front to the east and Nymegen on the Waal to the south. More important still, the fall of Gertruydenberg in 1593 gave the Dutch command of the Meuse. There followed something of a stalemate. The seven northern provinces remained free, while in the next century the Dutch were to conquer a belt of territory to the south of the estuaries of the Meuse and the Rhine. But substantially the division between the Dutch Republic and the Habsburg Netherlands had been established: the former proved unable to recover the great Dutch-speaking provinces of Flanders and Brabant.

"The outcome was determined by the great rivers." In these words the distinguished historian Pieter Geyl accounted for the division of the Netherlands. The south had been persuaded to collaborate; the center including Brussels and Antwerp had been conquered through its lack of natural defences, while the north stood free behind the river-belt. In this view, the Netherlands were divided not by race, language, culture, or even by personalities and political structures: they were divided by those brute facts of geography which dictated the course of military history. While the geographical division should never be undervalued, particularly in regard to the military career of Parma, few historians nowadays would put the matter so bluntly and simply. The premature death of Parma, the precocious ability of Maurice, the hesitations of Elizabeth, and the errors of Alençon and Leicester all suggest the weight of personal factors. Social, psychological,

[2] Above, p. 215.

and religious factors, especially those among the Walloon nobility, gave Parma that firm footing in the south without which he could not possibly have begun his great advance toward the river line. Again, we have already observed that Philip's contending problems, especially those in the Mediterranean, did much to determine the course of the struggle in the Netherlands. Furthermore, Philip repeatedly withdrew Parma's forces to support the Armada and to invade France. As for sea power, its importance for the outcome can hardly be overstressed. The line of naval bases established by the Sea-beggars formed the very backbone of the young Republic, while the events of 1588 finally excluded the possibility that a rival Spanish sea power would be created in northwestern Europe. Part of the maritime factor was a developing Dutch merchant navy and a continuing world trade which provided the northern provinces with the economic sinews of military power. As for the supposed inviolability of the river-belt, it certainly did not apply during much of the struggle. For years it was repeatedly crossed by strong Spanish forces, which had long fought around Haarlem and Leyden in the very heart of the province of Holland. Altogether, in what became essentially a war of sieges local morale often mattered more than geopolitical factors. In short, the Netherlands Revolt should not be viewed too purely through the eyes of the geographical determinist or through those of Dutch topographers. On close examination the story proves by no means the least complex of those several involved struggles extending from the Reformation to the Peace of Westphalia.

While Parma's death did not spell unrelieved tragedy for the Spanish cause, it was followed by a period of anticlimax. Philip replaced him successively by two Archdukes, sons of the Emperor Rudolph. While in 1598 the Peace of Vervins did not include the Dutch, Spain at this time agreed to confer the sovereignty—in effect, of course, the sovereignty of the conquered south alone—upon the Archduke Albert, who was to marry Philip's daughter, the Infanta Isabella. Under these mild rulers the exhausted provinces settled down, though the economy of Flanders and Brabant remained a ghost of its former self, Amsterdam wholly supplanting Antwerp. Nevertheless, the Dutch Republic could not relax, since the Spaniards, once released from combat with Henry of Navarre, were still able to grapple with the Dutch along the frontiers. In 1604 Ostend fell to that skilful commander Ambrogio Spinola, and he subsequently made further inroads into their southern positions. When in 1609 Spain at last accorded the Dutch a twelve-year truce, it was widely expected that provincial and municipal jealousies would soon cause the seven provinces to fall apart and thus make way for the return to Spanish rule. These jealousies did not fail in some measure to reappear, yet the renewal of the struggle in 1621 and its merging into the Thirty Years War did not seriously endanger the survival of the Republic. The vast prosperity, the cultural and colonizing triumphs of the Dutch served merely to underscore the enormous European importance of the Revolt. Its lasting significance did not lie in a regional victory of Calvinism over Catholicism. Begun conservatively to defend ancient privileges, the Revolt ended by creating a state and a society wherein the Calvinist restraints would soon yield to a degree of political and intellectual liberty scarcely paralleled elsewhere in Europe. The northern Netherlands were to give the seventeenth century even more than the southern Netherlands had given the fifteenth. The new Republic became a strong element in the civilization of the new age: it supplied a counterweight to that other product of the age we have just described, the revival of an autocratic and expansionist monarchy in France. William the Silent and Henry of Navarre were the common enemies of Spain, yet we can hardly forget that their respective descendants and political heirs were William III and Louis XIV!

5. Social and Intellectual Change in the Sixteenth Century

The middle and later decades of the sixteenth century afford distinct patterns of social and economic change, but in no small part they are continuations of the processes we have observed in earlier years. One widely operative influence we have considered in the aggravated but far from unique case of Spain: the impact of monetary inflation upon a society incapable of comfortable adjustments to this affliction, a society with a population growth that outstripped its capacity to increase food supplies. When confronted by a territory ravaged or under-developed, an energetic ruler found no difficulty in populating it with eager immigrants from other areas. Despite an overall growth of wealth, it is possible that for the majority of Europeans the material standard of living was in decline. In most cities an overwhelming proportion of wealth lay in a very few hands, while the last decades of the century saw a significant growth of urban slums. Yet without the steep rise of large-scale capitalism in both city and country, standards of living might have declined much further. The medieval guilds were now by-passed or taken over by enterprising private manufacturers. Socially stabilizing but economically restrictive, they met the fate deserved by their failure to stage dramatic increases of production.

In the countryside more than one process of adjustment may be observed. While in western Europe the landlord class multiplied yet had to struggle to preserve former standards, its counterpart east of the Elbe—a very lightly urbanized area—had things very much its own way and established a neo-feudal capitalism. The swift-rising prices of grain, furs, and timber gave these exporting landlords of eastern Germany and Poland-Lithuania wonderful opportunities to acquire rapid profits, provided they could retain control of cheap and plentiful labor. This meant legislation and policing to check the flight of serfs; it meant the retention or even the reimposition of labor services now shaken off by the peasantries of western Europe; it even meant that the owners of the great estates administered justice and dominated all political institutions. The princely rulers of Brandenburg, Pomerania, and Prussia had neither the riches nor the independent military force to check this process, and even the rising Brandenburg-Prussian state of the seventeenth century dared not seriously threaten its *Junker* class. In Poland-Lithuania the nobles behaved almost as sovereign princes on their estates, and after the extinction of the Jagiellon dynasty in 1572 they elected foreign kings—Henry of Anjou, Stephen Bathory of Transylvania, and Sigismund Vasa of Sweden—in order to prevent the growth of a centralized monarchical state. To the religious and cultural divisions between northern and Mediterranean Europe were thus added a certain divergence of social-economic structures along the line of the Elbe. Even within Germany itself this division left marked traces as late as 1945.

In urbanized western Europe, the situation did not entail a revival of feudal customs. Capitalist society represented a complex balance of forces and it found a measure of coherence in the creation of those international money markets at Antwerp and Lyons which for a time replaced the Fuggers and other Augsburg bankers. On this plane the tragic decline of Antwerp from the late seventies was not wholly compensated by the rise of Amsterdam, yet it did not long check the overall growth of banking, big business, and international trade. These transcended the new religious frontiers and accentuated the urban leadership of western Europe. More than ever, both cultural and economic developments were closely linked with the rapid growth of cities, often reinforced by the patronage and social magnetism of princely courts. In Brabant a third of the population became town-dwellers; in Holland, over a half. By the sixties London, Lisbon, and Seville had populations of 100,000 while Antwerp was almost as large. Amsterdam attained this same figure soon after 1600, by which date Milan had probably reached 180,000, Paris and Naples some 200,000 each. Under its Medici Grand Dukes Florence declined, yet even here the estimates point to some 60,000 inhabitants. And despite their relative economic stagnation the continental cities of Vienna, Nuremberg, and Augsburg remained far more populous in 1600 than they had been in 1500. A striking if unique case of urban growth appears in Rome, so marvellously replanned and developed by the popes. Though lacking substantial industries it grew by catering to pious tourism and by attracting ecclesiastical tribute and rents from all Italy and from other parts of Catholic Europe. Besides increasing its population from 20,000 to 100,000 during the sixteenth century, Rome managed to accommodate some half-million pilgrims in the Jubilee Year 1600. The statistical growth of cities was accompanied by the growth of urban habits on the part of Europe's aristocracies, which followed the earlier example of their Italian counterparts. *Up at a villa, down in the city:* Robert Browning's title summarizes the dual life of the classes which patronized art, letters, and the theatre from Naples to London, from Lisbon to Vienna. These classes might still spend part of the year in villas designed by Palladio, or in French châteaux, or in English Elizabethan country houses compounded strangely of gothic and classical motives. Yet their actors, musicians, authors, publishers, tailors, and milliners were essentially city-people and the modish aristocracy spent more of its time than ever before in the world of town-houses, theatres, carriages, and social assemblies.

Such patterns—and also the puritanical reactions against them—were common to Catholic and Protestant Europe. Despite the divisive intellectual and political impacts of Reformation and Counter Reformation, the theme of division can easily be overstressed in regard to the century which followed. The continuing expansion of lay education and of the publishing industry swamped all the confessional frontiers. Intellectual interests, from exacting classical scholarship to the rage for romances, from agricultural economics to astrology, were common to the whole continent. Both gentry and artists from the Protestant north completed their education and formed their tastes in Italy. Northern educators applauded and imitated Jesuit teaching methods. Translations of Italian and Spanish works abounded in England and the Netherlands. In the field of music Venice and Rome inherited the great polyphonic tradition of Flanders, but arising from these common backgrounds an original school of musicians flourished alongside Shakespeare's theatre in late Elizabethan England. Northern men of science like Vesalius and William Harvey studied in Padua. Scholastic philosophy, though not long since denounced by Luther, soon established itself in the curricula of Lutheran universities. On its higher levels even theological controversy now contained less of abuse, more of genuine dialogue. The works of Spanish Catholic mystics found many northern readers and some were adapted or plagiarised so as to provide devotional literature for Protestants. At life's other extreme, trade and finance continued to discard both religious and political allegiances. The Dutch conducted trade for their Spanish enemies. Protestant bankers were soon to tend the needs of Cardinal Richelieu and even those of the Habsburgs. Protestant kings married Catholic wives, while the perennial feud between France and Spain ensured that European war and diplomacy never developed along neat Catholic-*versus*-Protestant lines. In a word, when the Reformation had done its utmost, there remained not two Western civilizations but one.

What should we take to have been the most significant trends in European thought during the central and later decades of the century? Did they not primarily involve two phenomena: the growth of scepticism; the attainment of certain landmarks in the early history of modern natural science? If so, we shall have been justified in the emphasis earlier placed upon classical humanism, the influence of which continued all-pervasive. Humanist scholarship, often far less inspired than that of the Italian educators, remained the basis of all formal education. Even a great "natural genius" like Shakespeare, whose imagination far outran those of ancients and moderns alike, nevertheless incurred profound debts both to a modest classical education and to Italian literature of the humanist age. Similar debts stand equally evident in Lope de Vega (*1562–1635*) and the Spanish classical theatre, more evident still in the emergence of a new French literature of genius, a literature destined after a century of growth and discipline to put France at the head of the European classical tradition. The most refined sixteenth-century examples of French assimilation occur in the group of poets called the Pléiade, especially in its leading members Pierre de Ronsard (*1524–85*) and Joachim du Bellay (*d.1560*). The former, who began by publishing the first group of his sonnets and odes in 1550, attracted the favors of Henry II and Charles IX, while foreign rulers like Elizabeth vied to do him honor. Du Bellay, offspring of a notable literary family, defended with deep conviction the right of the French language to stand alongside those of Greece and Rome. He also wrote sonnets in the manner of Petrarch, one sequence *The Antiquities of Rome* being translated into English by Edmund Spenser (*d.1599*), the greatest of Elizabethan poets outside the theatre. Even du Bellay's fresh and fragile *Winnower's Song* is in fact an adaptation of a recent neo-Latin poem by a Venetian. In some of its more ambitious enterprises the Pléiade became oppressed by the weight of its classical erudition; a fact well illustrated by Ronsard's *Franciade,* an attempt at a national *Aeneid.* Here the technical skill of the poet does not save him from a certain rhetorical tedium, a lack of variety which so often arises when writers follow form as opposed to substance. Yet the genius and the language of France were to thrive upon a close discipleship to the classics, whereas from the first English poetry adopted an experimental boldness of language, style, and imagination which could produce bathos as well as originality.

For historians of Western thought the most significant figures of the new literature were perhaps not the forerunners of the age of Louis XIV but those of the eighteenth-century Enlightenment. Amongst these latter Rabelais and Montaigne may be claimed as seminal minds, as part-creators of intellectual atmospheres within which new social organisms were able to grow. It seems unhelpful to label such men "Erasmians." Though Rabelais did write to Erasmus in terms of profound admiration, even a cursory examination of his writings reveals an imaginative power, a series of radical concepts apt to make the Dutchman appear by comparison a pious and rather conservative pedagogue. What little is known of the life of François Rabelais (*?1494–c.1553*) seems to encapsulate the French society of his day. The son of a lawyer of Chinon, he joined a Franciscan convent where he was in trouble over his addiction to classical studies, even though encouraged by Guillaume Budé (*d.1540*), the leading Greek scholar of the time. Throwing off the cowl, Rabelais qualified in medicine at Montpellier and served for some years as physician at the municipal hospital of Lyons. Nevertheless in the entourage of Cardinal Jean du Bellay he visited Rome three times; in the end he gained papal absolution for his breaches of discipline and drew revenues from two French benefices. His *Pantagruel* appeared in 1533, his *Gargantua* in 1534, and the third and fourth parts of *Pantagruel* in 1546-48. These legends concerning a race of giants have a loose thread of narrative, but with their immense digressions they lack artistic unity. They purport to be written for the solace of the sick, but under the surface of buffoonery, recondite learning, and gross indecencies there lurks a radical criticism of ecclesiastical Christianity, of monks and theologians, together with secularist views on human nature and education bolder than those of the earlier generations of humanists. The later volumes display less fantasy but a more biting satire. They depict and castigate all classes of society: the peasants, artisans, monks, university students, and professors, above all the doctors and lawyers, whose foibles Rabelais knew all too well. His writing like his subject matter is protean: his immense knowledge of the classics blends curiously with his unclassical shapelessness, his verbal inventiveness, his defiant use of dialect-words and neologisms.

Needless to add, such a work aroused hatred among its victims. But for august protectors and tolerant monarchs, Rabelais would doubtless have suffered much from the Sorbonne and from the clerical and legal establishments in general. Certainly he admired Luther's attack upon ecclesiastical humbug and understood the early Protestant call to a personal religion, yet he was repelled by Calvin's austere discipline and desired to minimize dogmatic definition and liturgical niceties. He reserved a special hatred for asceticism and believed that a well-educated mind would naturally desire to make the right choices. Of all his imaginative creations, perhaps the most significant is the Abbaye de Thélème, a fashionable community of intellectual men and women practising the adage "Do what you want." Here stands a statement of human optimism, for all the major Churches the supreme heresy of modern times, the one to be most strikingly developed by Rousseau. Yet this freedom Rabelais assigns only to a qualified *élite;* and he is not irresponsibly calling for an abandonment of ethical standards. Here there emerged a serious educational theory passing well beyond that of Vittorino da Feltre and opposed to those of Loyola and Calvin alike. These notions of Rabelais were in fact too advanced to menace the disciplinary ideals of the sixteenth century. As in the Middle Ages, men still preferred to sin within the strict framework of a traditional asceticism.

A thinker of greater immediate influence was the essayist Michel Eyquem de Montaigne (*1533-92*). His father, springing of a family grown rich in the wine trade during the English rule in Guyenne, carried humanist education to extremes. He selected a German tutor who could speak no French, so that Michel could be reared exclusively upon Latin conversation. Indeed the whole parish was made to acquire a smattering of Latin for the benefit of the squire's offspring. Though in later life Montaigne became a master of the French language, in the grip of any sudden emotion he would instinctively give vent to Latin expletives. At the Collège de Guyenne he received instruction from the Scotsman George Buchanan, the first Latinist of the age. After his father's death in 1570 he abandoned a legal career and wrote his first two books of *Essais* (*1580*), living mainly among his books and growing family. Yet he also served at court in the king's chamber and in that of Henry of Navarre, on whose behalf he negotiated with the Duke of Guise. Later on he was to be present at Blois when Guise and his brother were murdered. Whilst travelling in Italy Montaigne received his recall to become mayor of Bordeaux, an unwelcome invitation which Henry III compelled him to accept. Unheroically he quitted his city during an appalling visitation of the plague. In 1588 he published a revised version of his *Essais*, together with a new third book.

Montaigne invented the Essay in all its flexibility and waywardness: in his hands it varied from three or four pages of pleasant gossip to two hundred pages of searching philosophical reflections. All his essays are bound together by the ever-present sense of an engaging personality, companionable, easy-going, never more delightful than when musing on the amenities of friendship. Even Petrarch could not reveal himself so frankly as the civilized nonhero. More important for historians, this urbane man of the world gently unveils a scepticism altogether more universal and explicit than that of Valla or Erasmus. His famous question is *Que sçais-je?* His reflections upon the uncertainty of human knowledge were bound to extend in the minds of his immense readership to the dogma of the Churches. Though outwardly such men conformed and desired to see no more religious revolutions, the Inquisition might have burned them with a far greater logic than that which impelled it to burn Protestants, those mere exponents of a rival interpretation of Christianity. Again, Montaigne's influence differed from the merely empirical tolerationism of the *politique* Catholics or that of the radical sects. Both *Politiques* and sectarians were children of a historical emergency, whereas Montaigne's tolerance sprang from his unanswered questions concerning man and the universe. This calm neutralism can be detected in many writers from his day onward, yet his importance lies less in his immediate disciples than in his ability to create an alternative intellectual *milieu* differing from that of organized religion. In short, one may well question the credentials of Erasmus as a direct ancestor of Voltaire, but one may scarcely question such credentials in the case of Montaigne.

Most prominent among those who around the turn of the century faced the stigma of free-thinking and even atheism were men like Giordano Bruno (*c.1550–1600*), Sir Walter Raleigh (*c.1552–1618*), and Galileo (*1564–1642*), men less concerned with philosophical humanism than with speculation concerning the nature of the physical universe. By their time the Churches, especially the re-armored Church of Rome, had begun to see the dangers emerging from the cosmological theories evolved by Nicolaus Copernicus (1473-1543). Of course, for centuries natural philosophy had been commonly associated with heresy and the occult. Such an association had brought much trouble to that great forerunner Roger Bacon (1214-94) of Oxford and Paris, who used the term *scientia experimentalis,* made notable advances in the science of optics, prophesied flying machines and mechanical propulsion, and understood that natural science could revolutionize the lot of mankind. More direct predecessors of Copernicus and Galileo were Jean Buridan (*d.1358*), rector of the university of Paris, and his younger contemporary Nicholas Oresme (*d.1382*), tutor to Charles V of France. The former had not only denied the need for the angelic "Intelligences" who were piously supposed to turn the celestial spheres; he had produced a forerunner of Galileo's vital concept of Inertia: the principle that a body once set in motion continues to move forever—unless actually arrested or retarded by friction or by some other counter-force. Amid his other mathematical discoveries Oresme also anticipated the seventeenth century by remarking that God had wound up the universe like a clock, and had then left it to run independently. These men started a tradition of teaching in Paris through which both Leonardo da Vinci and Galileo were to derive mechanical and astronomical concepts. Likewise at Padua there developed during the later Middle Ages a school of thought based upon the critical study of Aristotle, a school not concerned (with Aquinas) to Christianize Aristotle but to investigate his work as a natural scientist, and in due course to correct some of those many errors with which his enormous prestige had burdened medieval thought. Both Galileo and William Harvey (1578-1657) duly assimilated this methodology at Padua.

Despite such advances, even the educated minds of the sixteenth century did not swiftly discard the Aristotelian framework of cosmology, mechanics, and medicine. The textbook by Ptolemy of Alexandria (second century A.D.) still afforded the picture of a small earth-centered universe based upon a series of concentric spheres. These spheres and the celestial bodies embedded in them were all thought to consist of incorruptible matter, differing wholly from terrestial matter in structure and functions. Outermost of the spheres revolved the *primum mobile,* the "first mover," which imparted motion to the rest. Next within it there revolved a sphere in which were carried all the fixed stars. Still nearer to the earth came those concentric spheres which bore the then known planets, ranging from the furthest (Saturn) to the nearest, the moon. The orbit of the sun was thought to lie between those of Mars and Venus. As for the earth, it consisted of the four Aristotelian elements, earth, water, air, and fire; all unstable and fluctuating, in contrast with the serene and changeless heavens. The earth was conceived as spherical, yet with land emerging only in the northern hemisphere and stretching from Gibraltar to the Ganges. Yet while these terrestrial features of the Ptolemaic scheme were being rapidly outmoded by the explorers from 1492, the size of the whole universe had not been increased; the nine concentric spheres survived; so did the radical difference between celestial and terrestrial mechanics.

Dissentient propositions, it is true, had occasionally been made. Even in ancient times Aristarchus of Samos had conceived a sun-centered universe, while recently Nicholas of Cusa (*1401-64*) had entertained the possibility of a moving earth. And when at last decisive change came, it began gently and tentatively in terms of a hypothesis which no one could prove beyond doubt. In 1543, the year of his death, there appeared the work of the mild and orthodox Polish priest Copernicus, *On the Revolutions of the Celestial Spheres.* It argued that all the long-familiar data of astronomy could be explained by two suppositions: that the earth rotated daily upon its own axis, and that it was merely a planet revolving along with the rest around the sun. While Copernicus could offer no conclusive observational proof, he argued that his scheme was cleaner and simpler than that of Ptolemy, since it reduced the need for eighty spherical movements to a mere thirty-four. The objections were predictable and by no means always stupid. Admittedly, some sprang from biblical fundamentalism. "This fool wishes to reverse the entire science of astronomy," said Luther, "but sacred Scripture tells us that Joshua commanded the sun to stand still, not the earth." On the other hand it seemed not unreasonable to ask whence came the immense force needed to turn so weighty a body as the earth, a question to which Copernicus could offer no convincing reply. Again, if the earth travelled vast distances on its annual orbit around the sun, should this not produce stellar parallax, i.e. a shift every few months in the apparent positions of the fixed stars in relation to one another? That the star pattern in fact showed no observable changes throughout the year was rightly inferred by Copernicus to arise from the extreme remoteness of the stars, but distances of this order seemed merely fantastic to a sixteenth-century mind. Once again, it was argued that a rotating earth would mean that a stone dropped from a high tower must fall to a point slightly west of the vertical, since the earth below would have moved a measurable distance during the time the stone took to fall. Only long afterwards did Galileo explain why this did not happen: by the law of Inertia the falling stone retained also the rotatory speed which it (together with all other objects on earth) possessed before being dropped.

Even Copernicus did not, of course, fully detach his thoughts from the Aristotelian patterns. He continued to assume that the universe was spherical and finite. He believed the movements of the planetary bodies to be exactly circular and their velocities through space to be uniform: a sentimental attachment to the "perfection" of circularity and regularity, which was later demolished by Kepler (*d.1630*) in favor of eliptical orbits and varying velocities. The discoveries of Kepler and Galileo belong to the seventeenth century, yet between 1543 and 1600 other advances in astronomy and mechanics were continuing to occur. Tycho Brahe (*1546–1601*) with the aid of an observatory provided by his sovereign the King of Denmark spent over twenty years compiling far more extensive and accurate astronomical data than those handed down by ancient and medieval observers. From the parallax of a comet he proved that it cut through the so-called "changeless spheres" and was more distant than the moon; again, that comets had long eliptical orbits around the sun. In 1572 Brahe noticed the flare-up of a "new" star and could scarcely believe his eyes, for had not Aristotle taught that the heavens were immutable and incorruptible? Nevertheless this patient observer failed to improve upon the solar system as envisaged by Copernicus: he attempted to account for the facts by a strange scheme which made the earth still central to the orbits of sun, moon, and fixed stars. On the other hand, he concluded that the planets circled the sun, and that the sun carried them along with itself even while it circled the earth every twenty-four hours.

At another extreme of cosmology stood the renegade monk Giordano Bruno (*d.1600*), who sought to extend the Copernican picture by a process of wild but sometimes brilliant conjecture. In 1584 when in London, Bruno published three brief treatises in Italian containing a number of daring propositions: that the universe contains no fixed objects, the sun itself being mobile; that the stars are at unimaginable distances from the solar system and in themselves form centers of comparable planetary systems; that the universe is infinite and our solar system by no means at its center. More dangerously, he embraced pantheism, regarding God as the indwelling soul of the universe rather than, with Christian theology, as its external creator. After his return to Italy Bruno suffered burning for heresy, having made the contemptuous retort that the persecutors were more afraid than the victim. His career increased the alarm of the Roman Church, which had so recently affirmed the authority of Aquinas and Aristotle, and Rome proceeded at last to condemn the theories of Copernicus which had given rise to these deviations. Bruno had in fact disturbed the theologians not merely by his pantheism but also by his vision of a plurality of worlds containing other races of intelligent beings. If this were true, what happened to the doctrine of the Atonement? Must Christ be incarnated in other worlds in order to save them too? Though guiltless of such speculations, Copernicus had started revolutionary trains of thought which might end by deposing mankind from centrality in the universe. How much longer would men accept the basic Christian assumption: that God had planned the whole creation as a home for his supreme creatures, the members of the human race?

These far-reaching religious and philosophical notions intensified the atmosphere of questioning and scepticism amid which the century came to an end. But in addition some solid experiments and mathematical progress provided foundations for the great advances of the seventeenth century. In 1600 Queen Elizabeth's personal physician William Gilbert (*1540-1603*) produced a work (*De magnete*) explaining by systematic experiment the properties of lodestone and magnet, the direction and variations of the compass in relation to the poles. Gilbert accompanied his treatise by general considerations on the universe reflecting some of the beliefs of Bruno, whom he probably met in London through their patron Sir Philip Sidney. Nearly half a century after Gilbert's death, a surviving brother published a further treatise by Gilbert, which showed the respectable Elizabethan openly citing Bruno and accepting the views of that *enfant terrible* on the plurality of worlds. More important, the last decade of the sixteenth century supplied astronomy and mechanics with the mathematical tools essential to further progress. The French lawyer François Viète (*d.1603*) laid in 1591 the foundations of analytical trigonometry, while in 1586 Simon Stevin (*1548-1620*), patronized by Prince Maurice, introduced the decimal scheme of fractions. To abbreviate the immense burden of astronomical calculations, the Scots laird John Napier (*1550-1617*) invented logarithms and constructed the earliest calculating-machine for multiplication and division.

The other scientific fields to which even the briefest account of six-teenth-century change must refer are those of anatomy and medicine. Here was an advanced subject of the medieval university, one established upon the best knowledge of the Ancient World, attainable in the works of Galen (*c.130-200* A.D.). This revered tradition nevertheless inhibited original experiment. Illustrated textbooks depict the medical professor disdaining to sully his hands and sitting aloft, textbook in hand. Meanwhile below his throne a humble little figure labelled *demonstrator* conducts the dissection of a corpse, displaying in accordance with the professor's commands the organs stipulated in the sacred page. A better recipe for stagnation could scarcely have been devised. Even so, among the Italian and German artists around 1500 there had developed an increasingly exact knowledge and illustration of anatomy. This did not figure merely in works of fine art; it overflowed into the printed medical textbooks. In particular Leonardo had based his anatomical drawings upon a most careful study of materials available in the medical schools and as a result of his private dissections. From this point advances began to occur both in teaching-schools such as that of Padua and in practical surgery, for which the wars afforded ample opportunities. The French military surgeon Ambroise Paré (*1509-90*), a Protestant saved by Charles IX from the Massacre of St. Bartholomew, has been widely regarded as the father of modern surgery. He adopted a number of experimental methods outside the canon of Galen, for example sewing up instead of merely cauterising severed arteries. With a humility no doubt commoner among surgeons than among physicians, Paré stressed the need for practical craftsmanship as opposed to book-medicine.

The chief landmark in diffusion of the new knowledge was undoubtedly *The Structure of the Human Body* (*De Humani Corporis Fabrica*) published in 1543 by the Netherlander Andreas Vesalius (*1514-64*), physician to Charles V. Excellently illustrated and based in no small part upon researches conducted at Padua and Venice, this information was soon transferred to northern Europe by the Dutch disciples of Vesalius. Like Copernicus, whose work appeared in the same year, Vesalius was a cautious, even conservative worker. In later years he confessed that in his first edition he had sometimes toned down his discoveries so as not to differ too blatantly from Galen. There still remained the all-important problem concerning which Galen had misled the ages: the circulation of the blood. Even Vesalius did not know that the heart pumped out blood through the arteries to the extremities of the body, and received it back through the veins. The stalemate was first broken by Realdo Columbo (*d.1559*), a colleague of Vesalius at Padua who subsequently worked at Pisa and in Rome. In a work published in the year of his death Columbo explained the elements of the lesser or pulmonary circulation of the blood, a discovery in some degree anticipated—through mere reasoning rather than observation—by the Unitarian heretic Servetus. At least from 1578-79, another Paduan teacher Fabricius was describing the valves which check any outward flow of blood from the heart into the veins, but he failed to deduce the total relations of heart, arteries, and veins, a fact accomplished half a century later by William Harvey. Certainly the discovery of the general circulation must be credited to Harvey and not to Cesalpino (*d.1603*), one of whose obscure passages has been wrongly taken to imply his prior knowledge. Nevertheless, even by 1600 medical research had acquired a new dynamic, and just as astronomy now awaited the telescope, so anatomy, physiology, and botany awaited the microscope, an invention to be only a little longer delayed.

Not many years ago one school of historians adopted a determinist and materialist theory which credited these various scientific advances to a class of "superior artisans" as opposed to humanist men of book-learning. It remains true that ancient textbooks had sometimes inhibited experiment as well as inspiring it; again, that in medieval times lens-grinders and metalworkers could not yet fashion precision-instruments like the telescope and the microscope, upon which so many seventeenth-century advances were to depend. On the other hand, despite the sayings of Ambroise Paré, the full story will not tolerate either an indiscriminate apotheosis of the craftsman or a wholesale devaluation of the humanist. With very few exceptions the important discoveries we have so far chronicled did not in fact depend upon precision-instruments. And if one lists the agreed "leading names" in every branch of mathematics and natural philosophy, the vast majority are those of men who combined classical book-education with scientific intelligence. Even the men who did most to promote scientific navigation were educated landsmen rather than practical sailors. In short, sixteenth-century intellectuals did not choose to become either "scientists" or "humanists," a dichotomy peculiar to much more recent times. For the most part they underwent the normal academic instruction of their day, which was based upon courses concerning ancient thought and literature. Moreover it now seems clearer than ever that these humanist studies exerted favorable and stimulating effects upon scientific advance. Most scholars of that age agreed to adjudge the work of recent centuries inferior to that of Graeco-Roman Antiquity, and it was the recovery of the latter which in many cases served as a springboard to project their thought toward new concepts. They saw that a carefully edited Greek text, translated with equal care into good Latin, would prove of far greater scientific value than, for example, some old translation into bad Latin of an Arabic translation from a corrupt Greek original. Scientists had commonly been taught Greek; Greek scholars often accepted what we should call scientific assignments. Even in the fifteenth century German astronomers like Georg Peurbach and Regiomontanus had also lectured on the classics at Vienna, while later on the English physicans Thomas Linacre (*d.1524*) and John Caius (*d.1573*) spent much time on the reconstitution of Greek texts, because this labor provided their only path to a fuller knowledge of ancient Greek medicine.

It would remain misleading to proclaim the scientific triumphs of the sixteenth century as if in that age all the cobwebs were brushed away, as if scepticism and scientific logic were triumphing uniformly over superstition and customary lore. On the contrary, belief in the occult continued to flourish. The printing press was used less to make known medical discoveries than to popularize astrology, hitherto largely the perquisite of great men, who had acted on the precept that the heavens blazed forth the death of princes. Now, every comet and planetary concurrence produced a wave of printed prognostications. Likewise the concept of a hierarchical universe, so popular in the Elizabethan literary world, derived from imaginative Platonism, not from Copernican mechanism. Alchemy was assiduously practised, even by men of learning abreast of what we consider the genuine scientific achievements of the period. Meantime the persecution of witches became commoner both in Catholic and Protestant countries, perhaps more obviously in the latter, where the abolition of miracles and saint worship had left a mental void waiting to be populated by magic and counter-magic. Again, only by very slow stages did technological and medical advances contribute anything to the material well-being of the masses. Physicians often acquired much wealth by serving the rich, but their worldly success bore little relation to their medical knowledge, still less to the disinterested zeal of their labors among the public. Superstitious remedies were applied to the diseases of rich and poor alike, and only the more enlightened or well-endowed communities supported hospitals for the sick. After the mid-century the great epidemics diminished awhile, but more were still to come, while a massive infant mortality and a short average life-span defied the medical and technological measures of the period.

All in all, it remains difficult to be sure that the developing thought and administrative capacity of the sixteenth century added much to the happiness of the unprivileged classes. Feudal and ecclesiastical society had gradually yielded place to mixed aristocratic, bureaucratic, and capitalist controls, less rigidly stratified yet still based in the main upon inherited privilege. As observed, the new economic structures were more flexible than the old, yet it cannot be claimed that they triumphantly met the demands of a rising population. Largely through the growth of princely bureaucracies, order-keeping improved in some areas of Europe, but the appalling savagery of the penal codes underwent little if any mitigation. Though ecclesiastical regimentation had been shaken, it had recovered in Catholic Europe, while the future rise of liberal practices and convictions in Protestant countries could hardly have been predicted in 1600. On the other hand, from our distant vantage-point we may perhaps observe certain beacons of hope marking the way toward a less harsh future for the peoples of Europe. Humanism, Protestantism, Catholic revival had each contributed something to compassionate thought and charitable behavior. While humanists had questioned the values of a society which waged needless wars and tolerated remediable poverty, several Catholic religious Orders, and some of the puritanical ministers and councillors of Protestant cities had labored in the cause of a socially active Christianity. And while the sceptics foreshadowed the eighteenth-century Enlightenment, Rome's replanner Sixtus V might be placed among the forerunners of Enlightened Autocracy. For the most part the small traders and artisans of Europe were not yet psychologically prepared to assume a much larger share in the control of their own destinies, yet if we may judge from the immense flood of popular and bourgeois literature their mental horizons were already being rapidly enlarged. Despite the obvious limitations of both Catholic and Protestant religious thinking, Christian faith and trust continued essential to the peace, the comfort, the cohesion of society. Yet a rising proportion of Europeans had entered upon a mental world more secular, more varied, more entertaining than that of their forbears: they could live on more than one plane and find new forms of mental escape and solace. For the rapidly-expanding mass of literate men and women, the early significance of printing lay rather in its quiet enrichment of daily life than in its use by the few prophets of a coming world.

Postscript

We have chosen to conclude our survey around the year 1600, yet like any other, this terminal date cuts brutally through many organic developments. We therefore include a brief postscript which will indicate some motives stretching forward from the sixteenth century into more recent times. However inadequately performed, this exercise should illustrate the continuity of Western history and place the rest of the book in a deeper perspective.

So far as concerns political developments, we have already stressed that our period was one during which bureaucracy was consolidated, local anarchy diminished, and the authority of central governments extended. These trends were to continue throughout the seventeenth century: in old states like the France of Richelieu and Louis XIV, in new ones like Brandenburg-Prussia under its Great Elector (r.1640–88). Yet we have also detected the ambiguities concealed in that familiar formula "the rise of the nation-state." While both the boundaries and the governmental philosophies of several nation-states emerged more clearly in the sixteenth and seventeenth centuries, in Germany and Italy the host of mere regional states showed no sign of coalescing. Poland still failed to achieve internal discipline and most of Hungary did not even exchange Turkish for Imperial overlordship until 1686. Even prosperous and "advanced" Dutchmen continued to feel stronger loyalties to city and province than to the United Netherlands. For many years after 1600 the cohesion of Europe's biggest nation remained unassured. After so many decades of civil war, after the assassination of Henry IV in 1610, after lurid attempts by the nobility to exploit the minorities of both his son and his grandson, it was reasonable as late as 1655 to doubt whether the French monarchy would ever recover the powers it had enjoyed between the reign of Louis XI and that of Henry II, or whether it would continue a prey to aristocratic intrigue and remain riddled by feudal and Huguenot jurisdictions.

Moreover, for individual men and women the significance and claims of state authority continued to vary from one state to another. The state meant something perceptibly different in Spain from what it meant in England, still more so from what it meant in the new Dutch Republic. In Spain the medieval estates had dismally declined, leaving the monarchy unchallenged yet increasingly remote from both people and aristocrats. But in England and in the United Netherlands the representation of local communities in central government became ever more meaningful. Again, the functions of states had been differentiated by varying concepts of social and economic discipline; yet again by varying politico-religious notions deriving from Lutheranism, Calvinism, Anglicanism, and Catholicism. It can scarcely be claimed that during the seventeenth century this diversification declined in favor of some common pattern. On the other hand, some few of the doubtful political issues of 1600 were in fact settled, and the solutions affected not merely internal balances within states but the whole European balance of power and the pattern of alliances. During the period 1600–1660 the strength of Spain—economic, demographic, and at last military—declined to a staggering extent. At the end of the century the male line of the Spanish Habsburgs died out, leaving a grandson of Louis XIV as successor to the throne, and Spain as a *protégé* of France. Yet France herself had attained a dominant place in Europe only by arduous and gradual stages. Her great ministers Richelieu *(d.1642)* and Mazarin *(d.1661)* had waged a hard struggle to defeat the resurgent forces of anarchy and to bequeath an all-powerful government to the young Louis XIV. This they had accomplished by Mazarin's death, thenceforth leaving to the rest of Europe, led by the Dutch, the English, and the Austrian Habsburgs, the formidable task of checking the ambitions of a great and united French nation. In its essentials this precarious situation was long to endure: it lasted indeed beyond the revitalizing of France by the Revolution and until the final overthrow of Napoleon in 1815. Incidentally, this latter feat was accomplished only by the entry of Russia and Prussia into the anti-French coalition.

To return to the half-century succeeding 1600, we observe almost unredeemed tragedy in central Europe: the ruin of the political and religious compromise made in 1555 at Augsburg, and the relapse of the Empire into the Thirty Years War *(1618–48)*. Into this vortex many neighboring powers were gradually drawn. Having soon crushed rebellious Bohemia and her German supporters, the Emperor Ferdinand II appeared likely to establish his supremacy over the nerveless Lutheran states as far north as the Baltic, but from 1630 an unexpected development confounded Habsburg aspirations. Under Gustavus Adolphus and his successors, who could not afford to see the Emperor on the Baltic, hard-hitting Swedish armies drove the Catholics back southward, collected German allies, and during several campaigns operated in the heart of the Empire. This irruption, in its later stages supported by France, ensured that a new compromise was restored in

1648 by the Peace of Westphalia. It also enabled the Swedes to encircle the Baltic, though in the end their mushroom empire was destroyed by the hostility of Russia and Prussia, by its own lack of natural frontiers, and by the crazy militarism of Charles XII (*d.1718*). Yet another sequel unexpected by most observers in 1600 was the success of the Dutch Republic, which so rapidly amassed untold wealth and world-wide naval power. In a golden age which embraced the central decades of the seventeenth century, this ordered and highly urbanized society played an astonishing role in the economic, scientific, and artistic life of Europe.

Of all the European states and nations, none developed in a more surprising manner than England after the death in 1603 of Elizabeth I. The first of her Stuart successors James I held a pedantic belief in the divine right of kings, and he did not a little to alienate the monarchy from the parliamentary classes and the great city of London. The constitutional struggle, embittered by Puritan criticism of the Anglican Church, came to a head early in the reign of his son Charles I, a ruler even more rigid and incapable of maneuver. There followed the Civil Wars, the execution of Charles, and a decade (*1649–60*) of Republican government. Held together awhile by the victorious parliamentary commander Oliver Cromwell (*d.1658*), the experiment ended in the restoration of a monarchy chastened and cautious, but with its powers still largely undefined. The death of the astute Charles II in 1685 and the follies of his Catholic brother James II soon occasioned the so-called Glorious Revolution of 1688. Set upon a well-defined basis of constitutional monarchy, which was maintained by the Hanoverian dynasty after the extinction of the Stuarts in 1714, there now arose a state of outstanding stability, wealth, and naval prowess. From this stage England achieved closer integration with Scotland and became the first focus of the Industrial Revolution. Losing most of its American colonies by 1783, Britain seized or colonized a far larger world empire, much of it flimsy and short-lived, yet historically of lasting significance as a disseminator of Western ideas throughout all the continents of the world.

Looking out upon the wider world, we observe from 1600 the European maritime nations maintaining and increasing that massive outthrust which had begun in the days of Henry the Navigator and Columbus. Within a few decades Europeans had completed their chain of trading settlements around coastal Asia, though the Dutch displaced the Portuguese from the East Indies with a ruthlessness rivalling that shown a century earlier by their victims. At the same time across the Atlantic Europeans swiftly extended their hold upon a vast and under-populated Continent. Spain and Portugal lacked the demographic, administrative and economic strength to establish progressive, self-reliant states and integrated societies at so great a distance. Their slow-moving colonies were gradually overtaken in importance by those established by north Europeans in North America. In particular, English colonization began with Virginia in 1607 and New England in 1620.

Of course, despite the rapid settlement made along the coastal areas east of the Appalachians, even in 1700 it could scarcely have been prophesied that a north European culture, parliamentary and Protestant, would within a century and a half expand some 3,000 miles westward to the Pacific. Yet in long-term history the basic foundations of the United States transcended by far all the other results of that European surge across the Atlantic which had begun its confused and competitive courses under the patronage of late medieval monarchies. And the fact that the North American enterprise at first called to its aid a slave trade from Africa displays—like the Spanish exploitation of Aztec and Inca—one of the more awe-inspiring gaps in the moral code of Europeans, a code which still comprised only a portion of the Christian ethic.

So far as concerned literature, architecture, and the plastic arts, the immense achievement of the sixteenth century was to be worthily maintained in the succeeding age. France and England produced poetry and drama of the utmost brilliance. And while Italy never recovered her former cultural supremacy, she continued under Bernini and his leading patron Pope Urban VIII (*r.1623-44*) to evolve Baroque art and architecture, bequeathing them with striking success not only to Austria and Bavaria, but also to Spain, whence they passed to Mexico and there combined with native forms to produce a super-Baroque of astounding exuberance. If our former arguments can be maintained, the religious crises of the sixteenth century diversified rather than divided European culture. In any event, these crises certainly did not kill the humanist impulse, which should not be discussed as a mere recovery of the classics, but in terms of the climax and outcome of that recovery: the general enrichment of mental life which marked the sixteenth and seventeenth centuries. Humanism gave the rival Reformations their technical tools and always tended to modify the acrimony occasioned by religious zeal. Moreover, in the seventeenth century the fusion of Christian and humanist motives continued to inspire alike the poetry of Milton, the French and Spanish classical theaters, the art of both Rembrandt and Rubens, the Baroque world of southern Europe. Upon these twin pillars the greatness of early modern Western culture long continued to build.

Yet however frequently we apply the term "the Age of Reason" to the century of Bacon and Descartes, Leibniz and Newton, that century can boast only a very gradual remission of religious bigotry. Despite the continuance of tolerationist and even agnostic circles, they exerted all too little influence upon the politicians, the divines, and the mobs. Stuart England retained its morbid fear of papist plots; its government continued to persecute a Catholic minority, and sowed the seeds of lasting bitterness by maintaining a Protestant ascendancy in Ireland. On the other side, having won the Battle of the White Mountain in 1620, the Austrian Habsburgs re-catholicized Bohemia with much inhumanity, suppressing its nationhood and Hussite traditions. Far later in the century Louis XIV set aside the liberal traditions of his grandfather Henry IV, revoked the Edict of Nantes *(1685)*, and ill-treated the Huguenots as befitted his role as heir of the Spanish Habsburgs. Again, Western Christianity did not renew the attempts of the fifteenth century to establish contacts with the Orthodox Churches. It left Russia looking only to Moscow as the "Third Rome," the successor to Rome and Byzantium as the one true center of authentic Christianity. From this dream it was to be rudely awakened by its own Tsar Peter the Great, who built only superficial and secular bridges to the West. Geographically but not spiritually between the two, Catholic Poland emerged to join gloriously in the defence of Vienna against the Turks *(1683)*, but then receded into political and cultural debility, inviting the fate which befell her late in the eighteenth century: partition at the hands of her greedy neighbors.

Nevertheless when all these failures of Western religion and religious policy have been admitted, the Protestant and Catholic Reformations remain phenomena of the first importance. They founded very durable Churches; they spread education, both secular and religious; they permeated all ranks of society and won millions of converts outside Europe. Even the radical sects, having undergone many changes, found a permanent place in the more liberal countries from the seventeenth century onwards. For these and other reasons it might still be maintained that Reformation and Counter Reformation were the most profoundly significant events of the period we have surveyed. This claim would at all events have commanded assent a generation ago, when Christianity had just achieved a further great stage of world expansion. But whether these religious movements of the sixteenth century will look quite so important to historians of the twenty-first century might now be debated.

While the Reformations failed to incorporate the most liberal aspects of humanism, the latter did not fail to beget direct heirs. We have already observed those sceptical and enquiring tendencies which merged with the technological advances of the cities, and still more with the new knowledge gained through exploration, to create empires of free thinking well outside the bounds of Catholic, Lutheran, Anglican, or Calvinist theology. After 1600 even the professional ecclesiastics became in their off-duty moments ever more deeply involved in this third world of the Western spirit which was neither Catholic nor Protestant. Already there were strong indications that neither Tridentine authoritarianism nor its opponent Protestant biblicism could dominate the intellectual future of Europe, or for that matter partition it between themselves. In 1600 the great discoveries of Harvey, Gilbert, Descartes, and above all those of Galileo were about to strike the Western mind. And while the observable universe would soon be enormously enlarged by the telescope and the microscope, the new higher mathematics had arrived at just the right moment to render possible the synthesis *(1687)* of Isaac Newton, in its turn the prime foundation of both the philosophic Enlightenment and the rise of modern physical science. If alternatively we find the true keys of the kingdom not in science but in the world of poetic imagination; if we are fascinated by that influential complex of ideas known as the Romantic Movement, we should certainly look for their origins many generations before that of Wordsworth and Delacroix. In this quest, even if we discarded Petrarch and Leonardo da Vinci, we could hardly start later than du Bellay and Shakespeare, or overlook those incurable purveyors of Romantic imagery, Rembrandt, Claude, and Salvator Rosa. Perhaps, however, the most urgent task of social-intellectual history is to advance beyond the "great names," and to discover how far and how fast all these new concepts and attitudes percolated down the social scale, or again into the remoter provincial settings. The so-called "common man" has too often become the victim of those historians who see him merely in the mass, and merely as a hewer of wood and a drawer of water. Yet as the social history of the Reformation has shown us, he could in fact die readily for abstract causes; he could in some measure understand ideas which transcended his material necessities. A great deal of evidence also suggests that the swift-growing middle orders of society followed closely in the wake of intellectual change, and shared in this heightened awareness of the universe, the world, and the human race. In these problems of cultural diffusion there await new assignments still imperfectly accepted by historians.

If this Postscript should have any educational implications, they may lie in the high values of "early modern" history, in its absolute claims upon everyone desiring a historical understanding of the glory and the predicament of Western civilization. The recent flight of so many young historians into the superficial "relevance" of twentieth-century politics could result in illusion and disillusion, and this even for the cramped spirits who believe that historical study seeks merely "to account for our present world." Historical causation operates over long periods of time. The past has a place in history! Any study of the West which begins in 1900, or even in 1815 or 1776, can account for singularly little. But if, as many wise minds from Samuel Johnson to Arnold Toynbee have argued, the contemplation of history has deeper aims; if it seeks primarily to create a disinterested curiosity, a way of escape from introspective selfhood, then these aims would supply even weightier arguments for a close and curious study of the age of humanism and Reformation.

Genealogies

The Medici

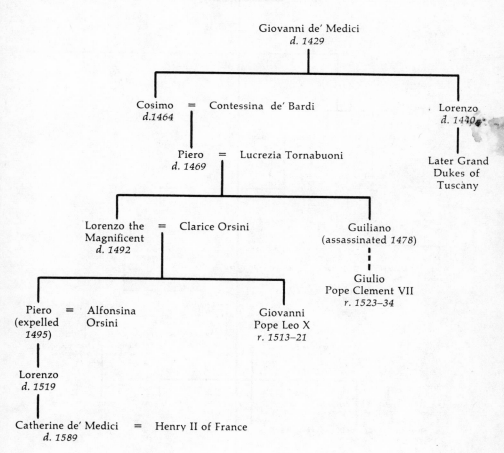

Giovanni de' Medici
d. 1429

Cosimo = Contessina de' Bardi
d.1464

Lorenzo
d. 1440

Later Grand
Dukes of
Tuscany

Piero = Lucrezia Tornabuoni
d. 1469

Lorenzo the = Clarice Orsini
Magnificent
d. 1492

Guiliano
(assassinated *1478*)

Giulio
Pope Clement VII
r. 1523–34

Piero = Alfonsina
(expelled   Orsini
1495)

Giovanni
Pope Leo X
r. 1513–21

Lorenzo
d. 1519

Catherine de' Medici = Henry II of France
d. 1589

The Houses of Valois, Orleans, Burgandy, Bourbon, and Guise

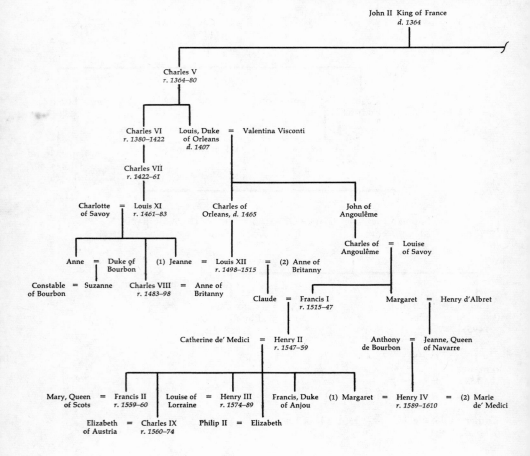

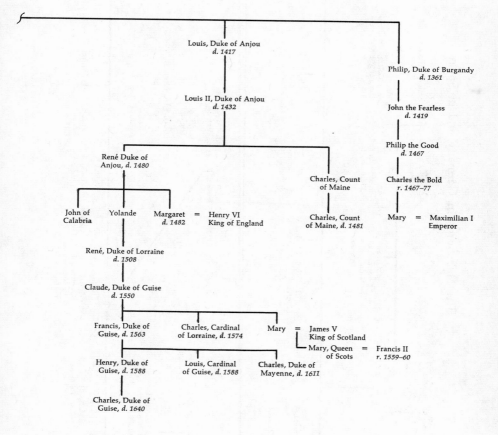

Louis, Duke of Anjou
d. 1417

Philip, Duke of Burgandy
d. 1361

Louis II, Duke of Anjou
d. 1432

John the Fearless
d. 1419

René Duke of
Anjou, *d. 1480*

Philip the Good
d. 1467

Charles, Count
of Maine

Charles the Bold
r. 1467–77

John of
Calabria

Yolande

Margaret
d. 1482

= Henry VI
King of England

Charles, Count
of Maine, *d. 1481*

Mary = Maximilian I
Emperor

René, Duke of Lorraine
d. 1508

Claude, Duke of Guise
d. 1550

Francis, Duke of
Guise, *d. 1563*

Charles, Cardinal
of Lorraine, *d. 1574*

Mary = James V
King of Scotland

Mary, Queen
of Scots

= Francis II
r. 1559–60

Henry, Duke of
Guise, *d. 1588*

Louis, Cardinal
of Guise, *d. 1588*

Charles, Duke of
Mayenne, *d. 1611*

Charles, Duke of
Guise, *d. 1640*

The Habsburgs in Germany and in Spain

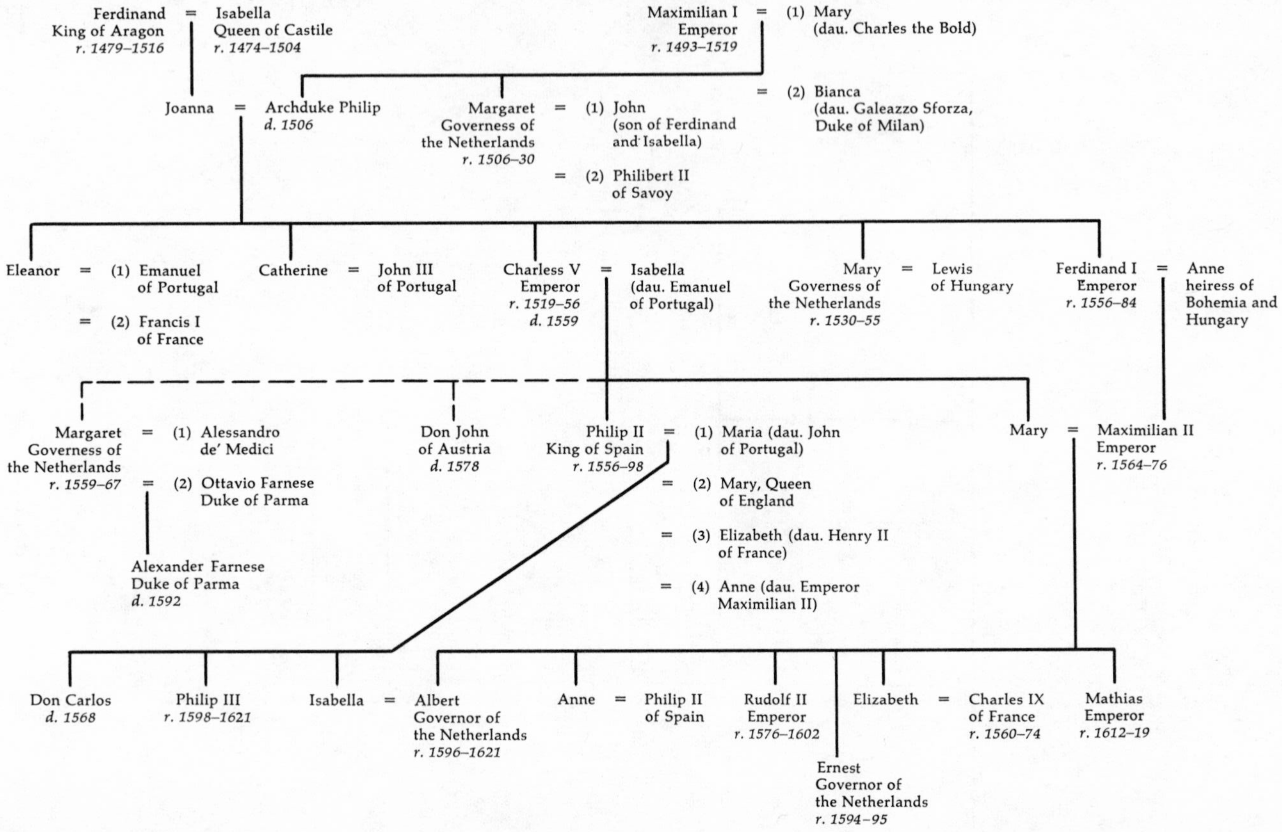

Ferdinand
King of Aragon
r. 1479–1516
=
Isabella
Queen of Castile
r. 1474–1504

Maximilian I
Emperor
r. 1493–1519
=
(1) Mary
(dau. Charles the Bold)
=
(2) Bianca
(dau. Galeazzo Sforza,
Duke of Milan)

Joanna
=
Archduke Philip
d. 1506

Margaret
Governess of
the Netherlands
r. 1506–30
=
(1) John
(son of Ferdinand
and Isabella)
=
(2) Philibert II
of Savoy

Eleanor
=
(1) Emanuel
of Portugal
=
(2) Francis I
of France

Catherine
=
John III
of Portugal

Charles V
Emperor
r. 1519–56
d. 1559
=
Isabella
(dau. Emanuel
of Portugal)

Ferdinand I
Emperor
r. 1556–84
=
Anne
heiress of
Bohemia and
Hungary

Mary
=
Lewis
of Hungary

Mary
Governess of
the Netherlands
r. 1530–55

Maximilian II
Emperor
r. 1564–76
=
Mary

Philip II
King of Spain
r. 1556–98
=
(1) Maria (dau. John
of Portugal)
=
(2) Mary, Queen
of England
=
(3) Elizabeth (dau. Henry II
of France)
=
(4) Anne (dau. Emperor
Maximilian II)

Don John
of Austria
d. 1578

Margaret
Governess of
the Netherlands
r. 1559–67
=
(1) Alessandro
de' Medici
=
(2) Ottavio Farnese
Duke of Parma

Alexander Farnese
Duke of Parma
d. 1592

Don Carlos
d. 1568

Philip III
r. 1598–1621

Isabella
=
Albert
Governor of
the Netherlands
r. 1596–1621

Anne
=
Philip II
of Spain

Rudolf II
Emperor
r. 1576–1602

Ernest
Governor of
the Netherlands
r. 1594–95

Elizabeth
=
Charles IX
of France
r. 1560–74

Mathias
Emperor
r. 1612–19

The Tudors and Stuarts

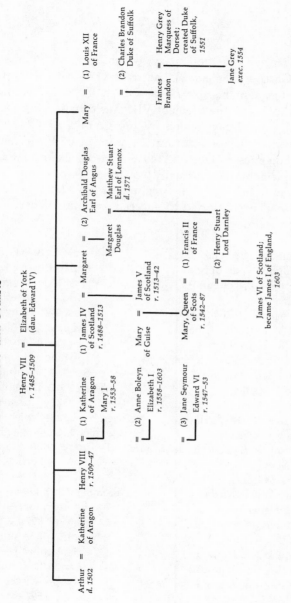

Henry VII = Elizabeth of York
r. 1485–1509 (dau. Edward IV)

Arthur = Katherine
d. 1502 of Aragon

Henry VIII
r. 1509–47

(1) Katherine =
of Aragon
Mary I
r. 1553–58

(2) Anne Boleyn =
Elizabeth I
r. 1558–1603

(3) Jane Seymour =
Edward VI
r. 1547–53

Margaret = (1) James IV
of Scotland
r. 1488–1513

= (2) Archibald Douglas
Earl of Angus

Mary = of Guise

James V
of Scotland
r. 1513–42

Margaret = Matthew Stuart
Douglas Earl of Lennox
d. 1571

Mary, Queen = (1) Francis II
of Scots of France
r. 1542–87

= (2) Henry Stuart
Lord Darnley

James VI of Scotland;
became James I of England,
1603

Mary = (1) Louis XII
of France

= (2) Charles Brandon
Duke of Suffolk

Frances = Henry Grey
Brandon Marquess of
Dorset;
created Duke
of Suffolk,
1551

Jane Grey
exec. 1554

267

The Popes

The Avignonese Captivity of the Papacy, which began in 1305 with the accession of the Gascon Clement V, ended in 1377 with the return of Gregory XI to Rome. On the election of Urban VI in 1378, rebellious cardinals elected the Anti-Pope Clement VII, thus commencing the Great Schism. This was temporarily healed by the Council of Constance in 1417. A new schism developed during the Council of Basle, which in 1439 "deposed" Eugenius IV and elected Amadeus, Duke of Savoy as Felix V. This movement had virtually collapsed before the death of Eugenius (1447), and in 1449 Felix renounced his claim in favor of Nicholas V, who had been elected to succeed Eugenius. Thereafter the succession went as follows:

NICHOLAS V (Tomaso Parentucelli)	March 1449–March 1455
CALLIXTUS III (Alphonso de Borgia)	April 1455–August 1458
PIUS II (Aeneas Sylvius Piccolomini)	August 1458–August 1464
PAUL II (Pietro Barbo)	August 1464–July 1471
SIXTUS IV (Francesco della Rovere)	August 1471–August 1484
INNOCENT VIII (Giambattista Cibò)	August 1484–July 1492
ALEXANDER VI (Rodrigo Borgia)	August 1492–August 1503
PIUS III (Francesco Todeschini-Piccolomini)	September–October 1503
JULIUS II (Giuliano della Rovere)	November 1503–February 1513
LEO X (Giovanni de' Medici)	March 1513–December 1521
ADRIAN VI (Adrian Dedel)	January 1522–September 1523
CLEMENT VII (Giulio de' Medici)	November 1523–September 1534
PAUL III (Alessandro Farnese)	October 1534–November 1549
JULIUS III (Giovanni Maria Ciocchi del Monte)	February 1550–March 1555
MARCELLUS II (Marcello Cervini)	April 9–30, 1555
PAUL IV (Gian Pietro Caraffa)	May 1555–August 1559
PIUS IV (Giovanni Angelo Medici)	December 1559–December 1565
PIUS V (Michele Ghislieri)	January 1566–May 1572
GREGORY XIII (Ugo Buoncompagni)	May 1572–April 1585
SIXTUS V (Felice Peretti)	April 1585–August 1590
URBAN VII (Giambattista Castagna)	September 15–27, 1590
GREGORY XIV (Niccolò Sfondrati)	December 1590–October 1591
INNOCENT IX (Giovanni Antonio Facchinetti)	October–December 1591
CLEMENT VIII (Ippolito Aldobrandini)	January 1592–March 1605
LEO XI (Alessandro Ottaviano de' Medici)	April 1–27, 1605
PAUL V (Camillo Borghese)	May 1605–January 1621

Reading Lists

Inevitably the following list is a somewhat arbitrary selection from an enormous literature which includes numerous other works of at least equal merit. The list is not intended for erudite specialists but for students and general readers desiring to extend their knowledge of the period and to find books which combine readable qualities with sound scholarship. In general only works in the English language are included, but a very few exceptions have been made in regard to untranslated works of special usefulness. Again, the items are for the most part recent and still readily obtainable. It so happens that for the period of Renaissance and Reformation an exceptionally large selection of pertinent books may be found in the *Torchbook* series published by Harper and Row. In these cases it has seemed most helpful to supply the Torchbook numbers, rather than particulars of the original hardback editions. Otherwise the normal places and dates are given. When no place appears, the book was published in London. The lists are arranged under the appropriate chapters, but obviously a considerable number of items must overflow these boundaries and apply to two or more chapters: several of the survey works might indeed prove useful alongside every chapter of the present book.

Chapter 1

On historiographical concepts of the period excellent guidance is afforded by
WALLACE K. FERGUSON, *The Renaissance in Historical Thought* (Cambridge, Mass.,
1948). A serviceable short guide is WILLIAM J. BOUWSMA, *The Interpretation of
Renaissance Humanism* (Service Center for Teachers of History, Washington, D.C.,
1959). On the broad themes shrewd discussion occurs in DENYS HAY's books, *The
Italian Renaissance in its Historical Background* (Cambridge, 1961) and *The Renais-
sance Debate* (1966); in MYRON P. GILMORE, *The World of Humanism, 1453–1517*
(Torchbook 3003) and in J. H. PLUMB (ed.), *The Italian Renaissance* (Torchbook 1161).
Needless to add, JACOB BURCKHARDT's classic of 1860 *The Civilisation of the Renais-
sance in Italy* (Torchbooks, 40, 41) still amply repays study.

On the earliest humanists ROBERTO WEISS, "The Dawn of Humanism in Italy,"
in *Bulletin of the Institute of Historical Research*, xlii (1969) is informative and
original. The work of Petrarch is surveyed in J. H. WHITFIELD, *Petrarch and the
Renascence* (1943). Florentine *Quattrocento* humanism has an immense bibliography, any brief selection being arbitrary. HANS BARON, *The Crisis of the Early Italian
Renaissance* (rev. ed., Princeton, 1966) is a work of first importance. For criticism of
its views on the reawakening of the ancient civic spirit, see FELIX GILBERT in *Journal of
the Warburg and Courtauld Institutes*, xii (1949) and J. E. SIEGEL in *Past and Present*,
xxxiv (1966). On Florentine government and politics see FERDINAND SCHEVILL, *Medieval
and Renaissance Florence*, vol. ii (Torchbook 1091) and NICOLAI RUBINSTEIN, *The
Government of Florence under the Medici* (Oxford, 1966). GEORGE HOLMES, *The
Florentine Enlightenment 1400–1450* (1969) gives judicious guidance on the interactions of society and culture. So does GENE A. BRUCKER, *Renaissance Florence* (New
York, 1969). MARVIN B. BECKER, *Florence in Transition* (2 vols., Baltimore, 1967) is
based on much original thought and research but is sometimes difficult reading.

Concerning the humanist educators nothing has yet supplanted the two works
by W. H. WOODWARD, *Vittorino da Feltre and other Humanist Educators* (1897) and
Studies in Education during the Renaissance (1906). On the Laurentian period and

271

Neo-Platonism the following will be found helpful: C. M. ADY, *Lorenzo de' Medici and the Italian Renaissance* (1955); NESCA A. ROBB, *Neoplatonism of the Italian Renaissance* (1925); P. O. KRISTELLER, *The Philosophy of Marsilio Ficino* (New York, 1943). For humanist philosophical thought in general, see E. CASSIRER, P. O. KRISTELLER, and J. H. RANDALL, *The Renaissance Philosophy of Man* (1948), and EUGENIO GARIN, *Science and Civic Life in the Italian Renaissance* (trans. P. Munz, New York, 1969). On the detail of classical scholarship, vol. ii of J. E. SANDYS, *A History of Classical Scholarship* (3 vols., Cambridge, 1903-8) is still standard. Note also P. O. KRISTELLER, *The Classics and Renaissance Thought* (Cambridge, Mass., 1955).

On some economic aspects see ROBERT S. LOPEZ, "Hard Times and the Investment in Culture" in a volume containing other valuable articles: *The Renaissance. Six Essays* (Torchbook 1084). Note also A. MOLHO, *The Social and Economic Foundations of the Italian Renaissance* (New York, 1969). A suggestive social analysis is ALFRED VON MARTIN, *Sociology of the Renaissance* (Torchbook 1099). For readings and extracts see G. R. ELTON (ed.), *Renaissance and Reformation 1300-1648* (2 ed., 1968); PETER BURKE, *The Renaissance* (1964).

On art and architecture general guidance should be sought in E. H. GOMBRICH, *The Story of Art* (11 ed., 1966), especially chaps. 12-18; in NIKOLAUS PEVSNER, *An Outline of European Architecture* (6 ed., 1960); and in R. WITTKOWER, *Architectural Principles in the Age of Humanism* (2 ed., 1952). From the vast body of works on Quattrocento art might be chosen: ERWIN PANOFSKY, *Renaissance and Renascences in Western Art* (Copenhagen, 1965; London, 1970); ANTHONY BLUNT, *Artistic Theory in Italy, 1450-1600* (revised ed., 1968); PETER and LINDA MURRAY, *The Art of the Renaissance* (1963); CHARLES SEYMOUR, *Sculpture in Italy, 1400-1500* (1966); CECIL GOULD, *An Introduction to Italian Renaissance Painting* (1957). Of the older works see especially BERNARD BERENSON, *Italian Painters of the Renaissance* (illustrated ed., 1952). The outstanding source book is that first published in 1550 by GIORGIO VASARI, *Lives of the Painters, Sculptors and Architects* (Everyman's Library, 4 vols., 1927).

Chapter 2

The most comprehensive single volume on fifteenth-century Europe is *The Cambridge Medieval History*, vol. viii, *The Close of the Middle Ages* (ed. C. W. PREVITÉ ORTON and Z. N. BROOKE, Cambridge, 1936). *The Cambridge Economic History of Europe*, vols. i-iii (Cambridge, 1952-66) treats many problems of the transition to modern times. A large, solid survey is S. HARRISON THOMSON, *Europe in Renaissance and Reformation* (New York, 1963). Of the shorter, suggestive books may be recommended: DANIEL WALEY, *Later Medieval Europe: from St. Louis to Luther* (1964); W. K. FERGUSON, *Europe in Transition 1300-1520* (1962); DENYS HAY, *Europe in the Fourteenth and Fifteenth Centuries* (1966); MARGARET ASTON, *The Fifteenth Century: the Prospect of Europe* (1968); HARRY A. MISKIMIN, *The Economy of Early Renaissance Europe, 1300-1460* (Englewood Cliffs, N.J., 1969).

On the French state should be consulted J. Russell Major, *Representative Institutions in Renaissance France, 1421-1559* (Madison, Wis., 1950); J. H. Shennan, *Government and Society in France, 1461-1661* (1969). A useful biography is Paul M. Kendall, *Louis XI* (1971). French and Burgundian culture could be approached through Otto Cartellieri, *The Court of Burgundy* (1929), and J. Huizinga, *The Waning of the Middle Ages* (1937; Penguin Books, 1955). On Spain see H. Mariéjol, *The Spain of Ferdinand and Isabella* (trans. B. Keen, Rutgers U.P., 1961); Henry Kamen, *The Spanish Inquisition* (1965); R. Merton, *Cardinal Ximenes and the Making of Spain* (1934). The best brief account is in J. H. Elliott, *Imperial Spain, 1469-1716* (1963, 1970, with good bibliographies). Bohemia and Hussitism are now well treated in the English language: e.g. in Matthew Spinka, *John Hus and the Czech Reform* (Chicago, 1941); Josef Macek, *The Hussite Movement in Bohemia* (Prague, 1958); R. R. Betts, *Essays in Czech History* (1969); Peter Brock, *The Political and Social Doctrines of the Unity of the Czech Brethren* (The Hague, 1957). Also on eastern Europe, consult O. Halecki, *A History of Poland* (Baltimore, Md., 1924), and vol. i of *The Cambridge History of Poland* (Cambridge, 1950).

E. F. Jacob provides a comprehensive survey of English history in *The Fifteenth Century* (Oxford, 1961), while F. R. H. Du Boulay ably synthesizes modern research in *An Age of Ambition. English Society in the late Middle Ages* (1970). On one important aspect see J. R. Lander, *The Wars of the Roses* (1965). On English economic history, the numerous books and articles of two authors are of exceptional worth: Professors M. M. Postan and E. M. Carus-Wilson.

The Church and religion are treated in a host of works, mostly suggestive of decline or tracing the roots of Protestantism. Amongst these note James Mackinnon, *The Origins of the Reformation* (1939); Gordon Leff, *Heresy in the Later Middle Ages* (2 vols., Manchester, 1966); and J. A. F. Thomson, *The Later Lollards 1414-1520* (Oxford, 1965). An introduction to the *devotio moderna* may be gained in Albert Hyma's two books: *The Christian Renaissance* (Grand Rapids, Mich., 1924) and *The Brethren of the Common Life* (Grand Rapids, Mich., 1950). An important survey of radical millenarian movements is Norman Cohn, *The Pursuit of the Millennium* (Torchbook 1037). E. F. Jacob, *Essays in the Conciliar Epoch* (Manchester, 1943) covers many aspects of church life.

Exploration and settlement overseas have an enormous bibliography: by way of introduction one might read three works by J. H. Parry: *The Age of Reconnaissance* (1964); *The Establishment of the European Hegemony, 1415-1715* (Torchbook 1045) and *The Spanish Seaborne Empire* (1966). A brief but able summary is J. H. Elliott, *The Old World and the New 1492-1650* (Cambridge, 1970). A readable introduction to problems of navigation will be found in E. G. R. Taylor, *The Haven-Finding Art* (New York, 1957).

On the rise of printing, consult S. H. Steinberg, *Five Hundred Years of Printing* (3 ed., 1966), and E. P. Goldschmidt, *The Printed Book of the Renaissance* (Cambridge, 1950). On art-history north of the Alps, note Theodor Müller, *Sculpture in Germany, France and Spain, 1400-1500* (1966), and E. Panofsky, *Early Netherlandish Painting, Its Origins and Character* (Cambridge, Mass., 1953).

Chapter 3

The standard survey of the period 1493–1520 is *The New Cambridge Modern History*, vol. i, *The Renaissance*, (ed. G. R. Potter, Cambridge, 1961). The best account of the Italian wars in English occurs in various scattered chapters of J. S. C. Bridge, *A History of France* (5 vols., Oxford, 1921–36). A general account of Italy in this period is provided by Peter Laven, *Renaissance Italy, 1464–1534* (1966). An admirable background to the political history is furnished by Garrett Mattingly, *Renaissance Diplomacy* (1955). From 1500 onwards the outstanding analytical survey is that by H. G. Koenigsberger and George L. Mosse, *Europe in the Sixteenth Century* (1968). Of the older textbooks A. J. Grant, *A History of Europe 1494–1610* (1931) remains serviceable. Among the chief political biographies of this period and of the succeeding decades is Karl Brandi, *The Emperor Charles V* (trans. C. V. Wedgwood, 1939, Cape Paperback, 1965). On Charles and his successors see the penetrating essays in H. G. Koenigsberger's *The Habsburgs and Europe* (Cornell U.P., 1971). For up-to-date guidance on Francis I consult the pamphlet by R. J. Knecht, *Francis I and Absolute Monarchy* (Historical Association, London, 1969).

J. W. Allen, *A History of Political Thought in the Sixteenth Century* (1928 and later edns.) is still probably the strongest general survey of its field. Machiavelli's two leading works are available in English: *The Discourses* (ed. Leslie J. Walker, 1950), and *The Prince* in many translations including Luigi Ricci, (revised E. R. P. Vincent, New York, 1952). A good survey of Machiavelli literature is the article by Eric Cochrane in *Journal of Modern History*, xxxiii (1961). See also, e.g. Allan H. Gilbert, *Machiavelli's 'Prince' and its Forerunners* (Duke U.P., 1938); Felix Gilbert, *Machiavelli and Guicciardini: Politics and History in sixteenth-century Florence* (Princeton, 1965); Sydney Anglo, *Machiavelli, a Dissection* (1969).

Julia Cartwright still supplies the best background to Castiglione and the court of Urbino in *Baldassare Castiglione* (2 vols., 1908). Two other important biographies are those by Roberto Ridolfi, both translated by C. Grayson: *The Life of Girolamo Savonarola* (New York, 1959), and *The Life of Francesco Guicciardini* (1967). For a translation of the latter's *Ricordi* see *Maxims and Reflections of a Renaissance Statesman* (Torchbook 1160) and for his *History of Florence* the translation by M. Domandi in Torchbook 1470. A survey of contemporary historiography is in Peter Burke, *The Renaissance Sense of the Past* (1969) and there is much of value on this theme in Myron P. Gilmore, *Humanists and Jurists. Six Studies in the Renaissance* (Cambridge, Mass., 1963).

A study of humanism outside Italy might well begin with Erasmus, though he had many predecessors north of the Alps. Among the best introductions are Margaret Mann Phillips, *Erasmus and the Northern Renaissance* (1949), and Roland H. Bainton, *Erasmus of Christendom* (New York, 1969). P. S. Allen made the greatest of all contributions with his monumental edition of the correspondence of Erasmus. Two of his briefer works still wear well: *The Age of Erasmus* (Oxford, 1924) and *Erasmus: Lectures and Wayfaring Sketches* (New York, 1934). Selections appear in *Erasmus and his Age* (trans. M. A. Haworth, Torchbook 1461) and in *Christian Humanism and the Reformation*, (ed. John C. Olin, Torchbook 1166). A substantial older book on French humanism and its background is ARTHUR TILLEY, *The Dawn of the French Renaissance* (Cambridge, 1918). A work of the first importance, as yet untranslated, is A. RENAUDET, *Préréforme et humanisme à Paris pendant les premières guerres d'Italie* (2. ed., Melun, 1953). See also WERNER L. GUNDESHEIMER (ed.), *French Humanism 1470-1600* (Torchbook 1473).

On English humanism, note ROBERTO WEISS, *Humanism in England during the Fifteenth Century* (3 ed., 1967); F. CASPARI, *Humanism and the Social Order in Tudor England* (Chicago, 1954); J. K. McCONICA, *English Humanists and Reformation Politics* (1965); W. G. ZEEVELD, *Foundations of Tudor Policy* (1948); A. J. SLAVIN (ed.), *Humanism, Reform and Reformation in England* (New York, 1969); J. R. HALE, *England and the Italian Renaissance* (1963). German humanism is less adequately treated in English, the main exceptions being the able works of LEWIS W. SPITZ. Of these note especially *The Religious Renaissance of the German Humanists* (Cambridge, Mass., 1963) and *Conrad Celtis, the German Arch-Humanist* (Cambridge, Mass., 1957). Another outstanding biography is that of HAJO HOLBORN, *Ulrich von Hutten and the German Reformation* (Torchbook 1238). F. G. STOKES (ed.), *Epistolae Obscurorum Virorum* (1909) contains Latin text and English translation; a selection is in HAJO HOLBORN (ed.), *On the Eve of the Reformation* (Torchbook 1124).

Many of the works on Italian art-history cited above under Chapter 1 also cover the art of the High Renaissance, but see also HEINRICH WÖLFFLIN, *Classic Art* (trans. P. and L. Murray, 1952); the standard survey by ANTHONY BLUNT, *Art and Architecture in France, 1500-1700* (1953); and its useful companions in the *Pelican History of Art*; G. VON DER OSTEN and H. VEY, *Painting and Sculpture in Germany and the Netherlands, 1500-1600* (1969), and G. KUBLER and M. SORIA, *Art and Architecture in Spain and Portugal and their Dominions, 1500-1800* (1959). Also valuable on Spain is BERNARD BEVAN, *History of Spanish Architecture* (1938).

Vasari (see under Chapter 1) continues even more informative on the High Renaissance masters, though his differences of emphasis from those of modern research can be assessed, e.g. by contrasting his life of Leonardo with EDWARD McCURDY, *The Mind of Leonardo da Vinci* (1928). Another attractive contemporary document is the *Autobiography* of BENVENUTO CELLINI (many eds. including that by John Pope-Hennessy, 1949). MARCEL BRION, *Albrecht Dürer, His Life and Work* (trans. J. Cleugh, 1960) is a good popular account. Dürer's writings were translated by W. M. Conway and edited by Alfred Werner (1958).

Chapter 4

The most comprehensive review of the period 1520-1610 is that provided by the second and third volumes of *The New Cambridge Modern History: The Reformation, 1520-1559,* ed. G. R. ELTON (Cambridge, 1958) and *The Counter-Reformation and Price Revolution, 1559-1610,* ed. R. B. WERNHAM (Cambridge, 1968). Relatively short surveys of the Protestant Reformation are: ROLAND H. BAINTON, *The Reformation of the Sixteenth Century* (1953); OWEN CHADWICK, *The Reformation* (1964); A. G.

Dickens, *Reformation and Society in Sixteenth Century Europe* (1966); G. R. Elton, *Reformation Europe, 1517–1559* (1963). The revised edition of Harold J. Grimm, *The Reformation Era, 1550–1650* (1965) contains remarkably capacious and well-chosen reading lists. Another substantial survey with excellent bibliographies is Émile G. Léonard, *A History of Protestantism*, vol. i (ed. H. H. Rowley, 1965). Two very stimulating collections of essays on the background and consequences of the Reformation period are H. G. Koenigsberger, *Estates and Revolutions* (Cornell U.P., 1971), and H. R. Trevor-Roper, *Religion, the Reformation and Social Change* (1967).

Introductions to Luther are provided by: Roland H. Bainton, *Here I Stand: A Life of Martin Luther* (1950 and later eds.); G. Ritter, *Luther, his Life and Work* (trans. J. Riches, 1963); E. G. Rupp, *Luther's Progress to the Diet of Worms* (1951); James Atkinson, *Martin Luther and the Birth of Protestantism* (1968); A. G. Dickens, *Martin Luther and the Reformation* (1967). A detailed account of Luther's early life appears in R. H. Fife, *The Revolt of Martin Luther* (New York, 1957); another full life with much information on the Wittenberg background is E. G. Schwiebert, *Luther and his Times* (St. Louis, Mo., 1950). Of the older accounts in English, perhaps the most solid is J. Mackinnon, *Luther and the Reformation* (4 vols., 1925–30). On Lutheran theology see J. S. Whale, *The Protestant Tradition* (1955), and E. G. Rupp, *The Righteousness of God* (1953). Wilhelm Pauck, *The Heritage of the Reformation* (revised ed., Glencoe, 1961; Oxford Paperback, 1968) has excellent analyses of Calvin, Luther, and Bucer, together with chapters on the sequels. For documents see B. J. Kidd (ed.), *Documents Illustrative of the Continental Reformation* (1911, reprinted 1967); Hans J. Hillerbrand, *The Reformation in its own Words* (1964) and *The Protestant Reformation* (Torchbook 1342); E. G. Rupp and Benjamin Drewery, *Martin Luther* (1970). The best history of the German Reformation from a Catholic standpoint is that by Joseph Lortz, *The Reformation in Germany* (trans. R. Walls, 2 vols., 1968). On two leading German cities see Miriam U. Chrisman, *Strasbourg and the Reform* (New Haven, Conn., and London, 1967) and the relevant chapters in Gerald Strauss, *Nuremberg in the 16th Century* (New York, 1966). A work most deserving of translation into English is the broad survey by Bernd Moeller, *Villes d'Empire et Réformation* (Geneva, 1966).

Possibly the best introduction to the Reformed tradition is J. T. McNeill, *The History and Character of Calvinism* (New York, 1954). Other good accounts of Calvin are R. N. C. Hunt, *John Calvin* (1933), and F. Wendel, *Calvin, The Origins and Development of his Religious Thought* (trans. P. Mairet, 1963). A first-rate pamphlet guide is that by Basil Hall, *John Calvin* (Historical Association, London, 1956). E. William Monter, *Calvin's Geneva* (New York, 1967) describes the city during and after Calvin's time. Oscar Farner's *Zwingli the Reformer* is a standard work (in German 1917; English translation, London and New York, 1952). A popular life is Jean Rilliet, *Zwingli, Third Man of the Reformation* (trans. H. Knight, 1964). A valuable documentary collection is Arthur C. Cochrane, *Reformed Confessions of the 16th Century* (1966). For the Reformed religion elsewhere see G. Donaldson, *The Scottish Reformation* (1960), and P. Fox, *The Reformation in Poland* (Baltimore, Md., 1924). The only comprehensive account of the Anabaptists and other sectarians is the elaborately subdivided and erudite work by G. H. Williams, *The Radical Reformation* (1962). Also important in these fields are E. M. Wilbur, *A History of*

Unitarianism, Socinianism and its Antecedents (Boston, Mass., 1945); E. G. Rupp, *Patterns of Reformation* (1969; chiefly on Oecolampadius, Karlstadt and Müntzer); Rufus M. Jones, *Spiritual Reformers in the 16th and 17th Centuries* (1914). A readable biography is Roland H. Bainton, *Hunted Heretic; the Life and Death of Michael Servetus* (Boston, Mass., 1953).

To understand the English Reformation demands a general knowledge of Tudor England, to be gained in such works as S. T. Bindoff, *Tudor England* (1950); G. R. Elton, *England under the Tudors* (1955); A. F. Pollard, *Wolsey* (1920, 1953); and general works cited below on Elizabethan England. The best account from a Catholic viewpoint covers all the phases in three volumes: Philip Hughes, *The Reformation in England* (3 vols, 1950-54). For the period to 1559 a more modern synthesis is A. G. Dickens, *The English Reformation* (London and New York, 1964 and later eds.). For the early phases see W. A. Clebsch, *England's Earliest Protestants 1520-1535* (New Haven, Conn., and London, 1964); E. G. Rupp, *Studies in the Making of the English Protestant Tradition* (1947); and A. G. Dickens, *Thomas Cromwell and the English Reformation* (1959; *Perennial Library,* 1969). Selected documents will be found in A. G. Dickens and Dorothy Carr, *The Reformation in England to the Accession of Elizabeth I* (1967); the best brief textbook is T. M. Parker, *The English Reformation to 1558* (1950).

Amongst the general surveys of the Catholic Reformation, the following are all useful: H. Daniel-Rops, *The Catholic Reformation* (1962); B. J. Kidd, *The Counter-Reformation* (1933, 1963); H. O. Evennett, ed. John Bossy, *The Spirit of the Counter-Reformation* (Cambridge, 1968); P. Janelle, *The Catholic Reformation* (Milwaukee, Wis., 1949); A. G. Dickens, *The Counter Reformation* (1968). On the Jesuits see especially the volumes by James Brodrick: *The Origins of the Jesuits* (1940); *The Progress of the Jesuits* (1947); *Saint Peter Canisius* (1935, 1963); *Robert Bellarmine* (rev. ed., 1961). Concerning the Papacy Leopold von Ranke's *History of the Popes* (1834-36; English trans., 3 vols., 1908) is superbly organized, in contrast with the monumental and far more detailed *History of the Popes* by Ludwig von Pastor (English trans. in numerous vols. from 1891). The great work of Hubert Jedin, *History of the Council of Trent* (2 vols., 1957, 1961) outclasses all others in this field. On St. Theresa and other mystics, see E. W. T. Dicken, *The Crucible of Love* (1963), and the various works by E. Allison Peers, especially *Studies of the Spanish Mystics* (4 vols., New York, 1927-35). The English Catholics have acquired an immense bibliography. A brief review is that by John Bossy in *Crisis in Europe, 1560-1660,* ed. T. H. Aston (1965). Useful surveys are A. O. Meyer, *England and the Catholic Church under Elizabeth* (1916; ed. J. Bossy, 1967); W. R. Trimble, *The Catholic Laity in Elizabethan England* (Cambridge, Mass., 1964).

Chapter 5

Many of the general surveys mentioned in the above lists continue serviceable for this period: e.g. *The New Cambridge Modern History,* vol. iii; Koenigsberger and Mosse; A. J. Grant, etc. A first-rate outline of the latter half of the century is J. H. Elliott, *Europe Divided, 1559-1598* (1968). On southern Europe a most opulent and erudite work has not yet (1971) been translated: FERNAND BRAUDEL, *La Méditerranée et le monde méditerranéen à l'époque de Philippe II* (Paris, 1949; greatly rev. edn., 1966). Several aspects of European economic life are covered in vol. iv. of *The Cambridge Economic History of Europe* (ed. E. E. RICH and C. H. WILSON, 1967).

On the Spain of Charles and Philip II, J. H. ELLIOTT's *Imperial Spain* (see under chap. II) remains important and it is henceforth admirably complemented by JOHN LYNCH, *Spain under the Habsburgs*, vol. i, *Empire and Absolutism, 1516–1598* (Oxford, 1965). Of the older works, perhaps the strongest survivor is R. B. MERRIMAN, *The Rise of the Spanish Empire*, vol. iv (New York, 1934). For guidance on Spanish culture see e.g. JAMES FITZMAURICE-KELLY, *A New History of Spanish Literature* (Oxford, 1926); G. BRENAN, *The Literature of the Spanish People* (Cambridge 1951); J. B. TREND, *The Civilisation of Spain* (1944); JOHN E. LONGHURST, *Erasmus and the Spanish Inquisition: the Case of Juan Valdés* (Albuquerque, N. Mex., 1950), and the books by E. ALLISON PEERS on the mystics cited under Chapter 4 above. For works on Spanish art and architecture, see under Chapter 3 above. On economic life see J. KLEIN, *The Mesta: a Study in Spanish Economic History* (Cambridge, Mass., 1920), and EARL J. HAMILTON, *American Treasure and the Price Revolution in Spain 1501–1650* (Cambridge, Mass., 1934). For criticism of the latter and further reading, see J. H. ELLIOTT, *Imperial Spain* (p. 192 ff. and pp. 395–96).

On the French Wars of Religion, it might be well to begin with a compact survey like that of J. E. NEALE, *The Age of Catherine de Medici* (Torchbook 1085) or with EDWARD ARMSTRONG's older but still useful book, *The French Wars of Religion* (2 ed., Oxford, 1904). An exceptionally useful volume in the series *Problems in European Civilization* is that edited by J. H. M. SALMON, *The French Wars of Religion* (Boston, Mass., 1967). Important articles on the origins of the wars and their Netherlandish connections are those by H. G. KOENIGSBERGER in *Journal of Modern History*, xxvii (1955) and by R. M. KINGDON in *Church History*, xxvii (1958). DR. KINGDON has also illuminated the Genevan connection in two volumes: *Geneva and the Consolidation of the French Protestant Movement* (Madison, Wis., 1967), and *Geneva and the Coming of the Wars of Religion in France* (Geneva, 1956). NICOLA M. SUTHERLAND contributes a helpful pamphlet *Catherine de Medici and the Ancien Régime* (Historical Association, London, 1966).

An indispensable yet debatable classic is PIETER GEYL, *The Revolt of the Netherlands, 1555–1609* (1937), which should nowadays be read alongside CHARLES WILSON, *Queen Elizabeth and the Revolt of the Netherlands* (1970). A briefer but well-informed account will be found in G. J. RENIER, *The Dutch Nation* (1944). Of the lives of Orange one of the most readable is that by C. V. WEDGWOOD, *William the Silent* (New Haven, Conn., 1944). An excellent interpretative essay is that by G. N. CLARK, *The Birth of the Dutch Republic* (British Academy Raleigh Lecture, 1946). JOHN LOTHROP MOTLEY's *Rise of the Dutch Republic* (3 vols., 1955 and later eds.) is most brilliantly written but its untrustworthiness can be gauged by comparing its famous chapter on the Leyden episode with the scholarly and accurate essay on the same by his contemporary ROBERT FRUIN, *The Siege and Relief of Leyden in 1574* (trans. E. Trevelyan, 1927).

The best life of Elizabeth I is that by J. E. NEALE (1934), whose volumes *The Elizabethan House of Commons* (1949), and *Elizabeth I and her Parliaments* (1953, 1957) are also essential to any understanding of Elizabethan affairs. An able short survey is that by JOEL HURSTFIELD, *Elizabeth I and the Unity of England* (1960), and much modern research is compressed by A. G. R. SMITH into *The Government of Elizabethan England* (1967). Two Americans who have contributed much to Elizabethan studies are LACEY BALDWIN SMITH, *The Elizabethan Epic* (1966), and WALLACE T. MacCAFFREY, *The Shaping of the Elizabethan Regime* (Princeton, 1968). The political and social background are admirably handled in two major volumes by A. L. ROWSE, *The England of Elizabeth* (1950) and *The Expansion of Elizabethan England* (Torchbook 1220). On Tudor foreign policy to 1588, consult R. B. WERNHAM, *Before the Armada: the Growth of English Foreign Policy 1485-1588* (1966); on Elizabeth's relations with the Netherlands, CHARLES WILSON, cited above. G. MATTINGLY, *The Defeat of the Spanish Armada* (1959) forms by far the best introduction to this episode. Puritanism is analyzed in two outstanding works: M. M. KNAPPEN, *Tudor Puritanism* (Chicago, 1939), and PATRICK COLLINSON, *The Elizabethan Puritan Movement* (1967). On religion and religious politics read also A. O. MEYER and W. R. TRIMBLE cited under Chapter 4 above. PATRICK McGURK, *Papists and Puritans under Elizabeth I* (1967) is a workmanlike survey.

To scepticism, liberalism, and tolerance the following will provide useful introductions: JOSEPH LECLER, *Toleration and the Reformation* (trans. T. L. Westow, 2 vols., New York and London, 1960; has good bibliography); WILLSON H. COATES, HAYDEN V. WHITE, and J. SALWYN SCHAPIRO, *The Emergence of Liberal Humanism*, vol. i (New York, 1966); RICHARD H. POPKIN, *The History of Scepticism from Erasmus to Descartes* (Torchbook 1391); FRANCES A. YATES, *The French Academies of the Sixteenth Century* (1947) and *Giordano Bruno and the Hermetic Tradition* (1964); WILLIAM J. BOUWSMA, *Concordia Mundi* (Harvard U.P., 1937: concerns Guillaume Postel); W. K. JORDAN, *The Development of Religious Toleration in England*, vol. i (1932).

Early modern science has now several capable general guides: CHARLES SINGER, *A Short History of Science* (Oxford, 1941); HERBERT BUTTERFIELD, *The Origins of Modern Science* (1950); A. R. HALL, *The Scientific Revolution* (1954); MARIE BOAS, *The Scientific Renaissance* (Torchbook 583); RENÉ TATON (ed.), *The Beginnings of Modern Science, from 1450 to 1800* (1964). GEORGE SARTON, *Six Wings: Men of Science in the Renaissance* (Bloomington, Ind., 1957) is mainly biographical; W. P. D. WIGHTMAN, *Science and the Renaissance* (1962) is penetrative but sometimes hard reading.

Astrology, magic and the unscientific world-view can be approached through the following: LYNN THORNDIKE, *A History of Magic and Experimental Science* (New York, 1923-41; vols. iv-vi cover the 15th and 16th centuries); D. C. ALLEN, *The Star-crossed Renaissance* (Durham, N.C., 1941); H. R. TREVOR-ROPER, *The European Witch-craze of the Sixteenth and Seventeenth Centuries* (Torchbook 1416); E. M. W. TILLYARD, *The Elizabethan World Picture* (1943); KEITH THOMAS, *Religion and the Decline of Magic* (1971). Most of the histories of art cited above continue to serve for this period, but note also Linda Murray, *The Late Renaissance and Mannerism* (1967); H. Wölfflin, *Renaissance and Baroque* (trans. K. Simon, 1964); John Pope-Hennessy, *Italian High Renaissance and Baroque Sculpture* (3 vols., 1963); H. Wethey, *El Greco* (2 vols., Princeton, N.J., 1962); James S. Ackerman, *Palladio* (1966). A serviceable introduction to the music of the period can be gained from Alec Robertson and Denis Stevens (eds.), *The Pelican History of Music,* vol. ii (1963).

Index

Achilles, Albert, 76
Achilles, Frederick, 76
Adrian of Utrecht, 104, 105, 183
Africa, colonization of, 63–65, 67
Agricola, Mikael, 159
Agricola, Rudolf, 131
Alarcón, Fernando de, 90
Albert (Archduke), 239
Albert of Brandenburg, 146
Albert of Hohenzollern (Duke of Prussia), 152, 159
Alberti, Leon Battista, 16, 18–22, 21, 118
Albertus Magnus, 5
Albret, Jeanne d', 170, 217
Alessandria, Benzo d', 7
Alexander of Parma, 236–39
Alexander VI (Pope), 62, 67, 87, 93, 94, 96
Alfonso of Calabria, 92
Alfonso I (King of Naples), 29
Allen, Cardinal William, 212
Almagro, Diego de, 68
Alphonso (Duke of Ferrara), 127
Amboise, Georges d', 95
Anabaptism, 160
Andrade, Fernan de, 67
Anne of Bohemia, 79, 105
Anne of Brittany, 94, 100
Antony of Navarre, 217, 219, 220
Aquinas, St. Thomas, 3, 5, 12, 41, 189
Aragon, 39
    merged with Castile, 60–61
Architecture
    aesthetic theory of, 19–20
    gothic, 5
    High Renaissance, 118–20
Aretino, Piètro, 127
Arezzo, Geri d', 7
Ariosto, Lodovico, 127
Ascensius, Jodocis Badus, 46
Augustine, St., 11, 12, 32, 144
Aztecs, 68

Bacon, Roger, 246
Balboa, Vasco Nuñez de, 68
Baldassare Castiglione (Raphael), 121
Barlaam (Greek teacher), 9
Barnes, Robert, 174, 175
Bathory, Stephen, 241
Battista (son of Guarino), 27
Bavaria, Counter Reformation in, 187
Beaujeu, Anne de, 92
Beaton, David, 171
Beccadelli, Antonio, 28
Beckynton, Thomas, 130
Béda, Noel, 165
Bellay, Jean du, 244

Bellay, Joachim du, 243
Bellini, Gentile, 117
Bellini, Giovanni, 117–18, 129
Bernard (Count of Armagnac), 49
Bernardino of Siena, St., 42
Bernini, Giovanni Lorenzo, 191, 192, 258
Berquin, Louis, 165
Bérulle, Pierre de, 184
Beukels, Jan, 160
Biondo, Flavio, 17
Bisticci, Vespasiano da, 125
Black Death, 39
Boccaccio, Giovanni, 3, 9, 13
Bodin, Jean, 196, 223
Bohemia
    heretics in, 41: Hussites, 78–81
    mining in, 44
Boleyn, Anne, 176, 180
Borgia, Alexander, see Alexander VI
Borgia, Cesare, 94–97, 112, 122, 124–25
Boethius, Anicius Manlius Severinus, 29, 32
Borromeo, Charles, 190
Bosch, Hieronymus, 203
Bothwell, Earl of (James Hepburn), 214
Botticelli, Sandro, 33–34
Bourbon, Antoine de, 170
Brahe, Tycho, 248
Bramante, Donato, 119
Brethren of the Common Life, 27
Briçonnet, Bishop, 93, 138
Brunelleschi, Filippo, 20–22, 21
Bruni, Leonardo, 14, 16–18, 27
Bruno, Giordano, 245, 248
Bryce, Lord, 72
Bucer, Martin, 155, 156, 161, 167, 179
Buchanan, George, 245
Budé, Guillaume, 243
Bugenhagen, Johann, 158
Bullinger, Heinrich, 167, 170
Bureau, Jean, 51
Burgundy, Hundred Years War in, 47–53
Buridan, Jean, 246
Burnet, Gilbert, 173
Byzantium, 5, 8, 26
    occupied by Ottoman Turks, 9, 65

Cabot, John, 58, 68
Cabot, Sebastian, 58, 68
Caius, John, 251
Cajetan, Cardinal, 147
Calixtus III, Pope, 65
Calvin, Gérard, 164
Calvin, John, 123, 164–71, 167, 183, 244
Campeggio, Cardinal, 107
Canisius, Peter, 187
Capito, Wolfgang Fabricius, 155

References to illustrations in *italics*.

Caraga, Gian Pietro, 183, 188, 190
Carlstadt, Andreas, 151, 156
Carranza, Bartolomé de, 202
Cartwright, Thomas, 211
Casa, Giovanni della, 126
Castiglione, Baldesar, 33, *121,* 124-27
Castile, 39
    merged with Aragon, 60-61
Catherine (Princess of France), 47
Catholic Church, 105
    attitudes on warfare of, 89
    colonization and, 69
    Conciliar Movement in, 42-43
    Counter Reformation in, 182-92: Jesuits,
        184-88; Tridentine Council, 188-90
    In Elizabethan England, 212
    Great Schism in, 14, 42
    heresies in, 40-41: Hussites, 78-81; *see
        also* Protestant Reformation
    political power of, 40
    restored to England, 179-80
    in Spain, 59-60, 62-63: Inquisition, 202-3
Catullus, Gaius Valerius, 7
Caxton, William, 46
Cecil, Robert, 208
Cecil, William (Lord Burghley), 206, 208,
    211, 215
Cellini, Benvenuto, 127
Celtis, Conrad, 132, 133
Cennini, Cennino, 23
Cesalpino, Andrea, 250
Chalcondyles, Demetrius, 133
Charles the Bold (Duke of Burgundy),
    53-54, 78
Charles I (King of England), 257
Charles II (King of England), 257
Charles V (King of France), 246
Charles VI (King of France), 47
Charles VII (King of France), 47, 50-51, 53
Charles VIII (King of France), 87, 92-94
Charles IX (King of France), 214, 219,
    221-23
Charles IV (Holy Roman Emperor), 72,
    78-79, 128
Charles V (Holy Roman Emperor), 87, 90,
    103, 124, 137, 167, 179, 195, 200-1, 250
    abdication of, 198
    accession of, 38, 64
    Counter Reformation and, 183
    Netherlands under, 228-29
    Protestant Reformation and, 150, 155,
        157, 160-61, 171
    Spain under, 102-8
Chaucer, Geoffrey, 4
Chelčický, Peter, 81
China, 67
Christian II (King of Denmark), 158
Christian III (King of Denmark), 158
Chrysoloras, Manuel, 9, 17, 26-27

Clement VII (Pope), 105-8, 125, 152, 188
Clément, Jacques, 255
Cloigny, *222*
Coeur, Jacques, 51
Colet, John, 27, 130, 133, 134, 136, 138
Coligny, Gaspard de, 170, 217, 220-22, 224
Colonna, Vittoria, 124-25, 183
Columbo, Realdo, 250
Columbus, Christopher, 65, 67-68
Conciliar Movement, 40, 42-43
Condé, Prince of (Henri II), 214
Conferma della regola (Ghirlandaio), *31*
Contarini, Gasparo, 161, 182, 183, 185, 188
Cop, Nicholas, 165
Copernicus, Nicholas, 246-48
Córdoba, Gonzalo de, 88, 96
Cordova, Gonsalvo de, 64
Correggio, Antonio Allegri da, 108
Cortés, Hernan, 68
Coster, Laurens Janszoon, 45
Council of Trent, *189*
Counter Reformation, 182-92
Coverdale, Miles, 175, 176
Cranach, Lucas, 129
Cranmer, Thomas, *173,* 175, *176,* 178, 180,
    211
Cromwell, Oliver, 257
Cromwell, Thomas, 40, 174-78
Crotus, Rubeanus, 132, 150
Cruciger, Felix, 170

Damville, Henry, 217, 223
Dante Alighieri, 3, 5, 9, 12, 14, 34
Darnley, Lord, 214
Denck, Hans, 160
Denmark, Protestant Reformation in, 158
Diaz, Bartholomew, 67
Diet of Worms, 74, 104, 150
Donatello, 23, 109, 114
Doria, Andrea, 107
Drake, Francis, 215
Duccio, Agostino di, 5, 20
Duccio di Buoninsegna, *24*
Dudley, John, 178, 179
Dudley, Robert, 207
Dürer, Albrecht, 108, 120, *129,* 132
Dying Slave (Michelangelo), *112*

Eck, Johann, 147, 157
Economic growth, 43-47
    technological developments and, 45-47
    working-class unrest and, 44
Education, 24-30
Edward II (King of England), 56
Edward III (King of England), 55
Edward IV (King of England), 53, 56-57,
    171, 178

Egmont, Lamoral, Comte d', 214, 233
Einhard, 133
El Greco, *191*, 192, 203
Eleanor (Queen of Portugal), 106, 108
Elizabeth I (Queen of England), 204–8, *205,*
    218, 224, 234, 243, 249, 257
    Netherlands and, 236–37
    Protestant Reformation and, 172, 180–81
    Spain and, 200, 212–16
Elizabeth of Valois, 213
England, 56–59
    constitutional development of, 37
    decline of feudalism in, 40
    economic development of, 70
    education in, 27
    under Elizabeth I, 204–16
    France and, 102: dispute over Scotland,
        171; French civil wars, 213–14;
        Hundred Years War, 47–53
    growth of humanism in, 130, 133–35
    heretics in, 41
    Italian Wars and, 107–8
    Netherlands revolt and, 214–16, 238
    Protestant Reformation in, 171–81:
        establishment of Church of England,
        175–76; persecution under Mary I,
        179–80
    Spain and, 64
    trade and, 44
    Wars of Roses in, 55–57
Erasmus, Desiderius, 11, 29, 89, 133, *135–39,*
    145, 165, 229, 243
    as educator, 25
    New Testament translation by, 136–37,
        143, 150, 153
Erasmus at Work (Matys), *135*
Espinoza, Cardinal, 199
Este, Cardinal, Ippolito d', 127
Este, Leonello d', 27
Este, Niccolò d', 27
Eugenius IV (Pope), 14, 29, 42

Fabricius, Hieronymus, 250
Farel, Guillaume, 138, 167
Farnese, Alessandro, *see* Paul III
Farnese, Pier Luigi, 188
Federigo (Duke of Urbino), 125
Federigo (King of Naples), 95, 96
Feltre, Vittorino da, 25–26, 125
Ferdinand of Aragon, 39, 58, *60,* 94, 96–98,
    100–2, 195
Ferdinand I (Holy Roman Emperor), 82,
    105–7, 183, 198
Ferdinand II (Holy Roman Emperor), 256
Ferdinand (King of Hungary), 152
Ferdinand and Isabella (print), *60*
Ferrante (King of Naples), 92
Ferreti, Ferreto dei, 6

Fichet, Guillaume, 45
Ficino, Marsilio, 3, 32–33
Filarete, 118
Fisher, John, 81, 136, 177
Flaminio, Marcantonio, 127
Flanders
    hostility to France of, 54
    trade with, 70
    working-class unrest in, 44
    See also Netherlands
Flemmyng, Robert, 130
Florence, 91–92
    commerce in, 44
    education in, 27
    humanism in, 6, 8, 14–24: civic, 14–16
    Medicean, 30–34
    painting and sculpture in, 22–24: High
        Renaissance, 109, 110, 114, 115
    war between Naples and, 31
    working-class unrest in, 44
Foix, Gaston de, 98
Foix, Germaine de, 64, 100
Foxe, John, 180
Fracastoro, Girolamo, 127
France
    Catholic Church in, 101–2
    civil wars in, 204, 213–14, 216–28
    conquest of marginal provinces by, 37–38
    Counter Reformation in, 187, 188
    decline of feudalism in, 40
    economic growth of, 53
    England and: dispute over Scotland, 171;
        Hundred Years War, 47–53
    growth of humanism in, 129–31, 137–38
    invasion of Italy by, 74, 87–89, 92–101:
        claims, 31–32
    literature in, 243–45
    rebellion of Burgundy, 53–55
    Protestant Reformation in, 164–66, 168–70
    rivalry between Spain and, 100, 105–8
    trade and, 44
Francesca, Piero della, 23
Francis (Duke of Anjou), 224, 225, 236, 237
Francis of Assisi, St., 42
Francis I (King of France), 87–88, 100–8,
    152–53, 165, 167, 170, 216
Francis II (King of France), 213, 217, 219
Francis (Duke of Guise), 214, 220
Francis of Montmorency, 223
Franciscan Order, 41–42
Franck, Sebastian, 160
Frederick I (King of Denmark), 158
Frederick III (Holy Roman Emperor), 54, 74,
    81
Frederick the Great (King of Prussia), 122
Frederick the Wise (Elector of Saxony), 103,
    144, 147, 150
Free, John, 130

Froben, Johann, 137
Fugger, Jacob, 72
Fuggers, the, 71, *145*

Gaguin, Robert, 131
Galateo, Antonio, 69
Galeazzo, Gian, 31
Galileo Galilei, 191, 245–47
Gama, Vasco da, 67
Gransfort, Wessel, 144
Gardiner, Stephen, 177, 178
Gattinara, Mercurino da, 104
George of Poděbrady, 80
George (Duke of Saxony), 147, 150, 158, 161
Germany, 38–39
   Counter Reformation in, 183, 186
   economic development of: banking,
      71–72; trade, 70–71
   growth of humanism in, 130–33
   painting in, 129
   Protestant Reformation in: origins,
      143–53; politics and, 157–64
Geyl, Pieter, 238
Ghiberti, Lorenzo, *22*, 23
Ghirlandaio, Domenico del, *31*, 114
Gilbert, William, 249
Giorgio, Francesco di, 118
Giorgione, Il, 108, *117–18*
Giotto di Bondone, 5, 22–23
Gómez, Ruy, 199
Gonzaga, Cecilia, 26
Gonzaga, Elisabetta, 125
Gonzaga, Giangrancesco, 25
Gonzaga, Ludovico, 26
Granvelle, Antoine de, 200, 229, 231, 232
Great Schism, 14, 42
Greek Orthodox Church, 43
Gregorio of Citta di Castello, 130–31
Grey, Lady Jane, 179
Grocyn, William, 130, 133
Guarino da Verona, 26–27, 130, 131
Guicciardini, Francesco, 32, 89, 91, 123–24
Guidobaldo (Duke of Urbino), 124, 125
Gunthorpe, John, 130
Gustavus Adolphus (King of Sweden), 256
Gustavus Vasa (King of Sweden), 158–59
Gutenberg, Johann, 45

Hamilton, Patrick, 171
Hanseatic League, 70, 71
Harvey, William, 242, 246, 250
Hawkins, John, 216
Henry of Anjou, 241
Henry IV (King of Castile), 60
Henry V (King of England), 47, 49
Henry VI (King of England), 50–52, 56
Henry VII (King of England), 53, 57–59, 64

Henry VIII (King of England), 102–4, 106–8,
   133–35, 160
   France and, 53, 98, 100
   Protestant Reformation and, 40, 171, 172,
      173, 174–80
Henry II (King of France), 170, 216, 218, 243
Henry III (King of France), 214, 223–24, 245
Henry IV (King of France) (Henry of
   Navarre), 100, 217–18, 221–22, 224–28,
   238, 240, 245, 259
Henry of Guise, 221–22, 224, 225, 227, 245
Henry the Navigator (Prince of Portugal), 65
Hochstraten (Inquisitor), 132
Hogenberg, Franz, *168*
Holbein, Hans, 108, 129
Holmes, George, 14
Holy League, 98–99
Holy Roman Empire, 38
   political structure of, 72–77
Hooker, Richard, 211
Hroswitha, 133
Hotman, François, 223
Humphrey (Duke of Gloucester), 49, 130
Hundred Years War, 47–55
Hungary
   mining in, 44
   trade and, 44
   Turkish occupation of, 82, 83, 106–7
Hunne, Richard, 172
Huss, John, 14, 41, 79, 144
Hutten, Ulrich von, 132, 133

Ignatius Loyola before Pope Paul III, 185
Inca Empire, 68
India, trade with, 67
Isabella I (Queen of Castile), 39, *60–67*, 195
Isabella (Queen of France), 47
Italy
   architecture in, 19–20: gothic, 5; High
      Renaissance, 118–20
   Counter Reformation in, 183
   invasions of, 87–101, 105–8
   literature in, 7: High Renaissance, 120–27
   painting and sculpture in, 22–24: High
      Renaissance, 108–18
Ivan the Great (Prince of Moscow), 82

James I (King of England), 208, 237
James II (King of England), 257
James IV (King of Scotland), 58, 100
James V (King of Scotland), 171
Jerome of Prague, 79
Jesuits, 184–88
Jews in Spain, 59, 60
   during Inquisition, 62–63
Joachim (abbot of Flora), 151
Joachim II (Elector of Brandenburg), 158

Joan of Arc, 49–50
Joanna (Queen of Naples), 92
John of Austria, Don, 200, 201, 235, 236
John (Duke of Bedford), 49
John the Fearless (Duke of Burgundy), 49
John (King of France), 47
John II (King of Portugal), 67
John III (King of Portugal), 187
John of the Cross, St., 182, 192, 203
John the Steadfast (Elector of Saxony), 152
John Frederick (Elector of Saxony), 152
John of Wesel, 144
Johnson, Samuel, 126
Joris, David, 160
Juana of Spain, 64, 104
Julius II (Pope), 64, 89, 93, 96–99, 110, 115, 119, 125

Katherine of Aragon, 58, 64, 103–4, 107, 174, 176
Kepler, Johannes, 247
Knox, John, 168, 171, 178, 181, 213

La Marck (head of Sea-beggars), 234
Lambarde, William, 209
Las Casas, Bartolomé de, 69
Las Cobos, Francisco de, 195
Laski, Jean, 170, 179
Latimer, Hugh, 134
Latini, Brunetto, 14
Lautrec, Vicomte de, 107
Laynez, Diego, 185, 187, 188
Lefèvre d'Étaples, Jacques, 137–38, 143, 165
Leo X (Pope), 99–101, 105, 110, 123, 124, 146
Leon, Luis de, 192, 203
Leonardo da Vinci, 24, 108–15, *110, 111*, 119, 246, 249
Leopold III (Duke of Hapsburg), 77
Lewis II (King of Hungary), 82, 106, 152
Lewis IV (Holy Roman Emperor), 40
Leyva, Antonio de, 90
L'Hôpital, Michel de, 219, 220
Linacre, Thomas, 130, 133–34, 251
Literature, 6–7
    French, 243–45
    Italian, 7: High Renaissance, 120–27
Lithuania, Protestant Reformation in, 170
Lollardy, 171, 172, 174
Louis (Duke of Condé), 170, 217, 219, 220
Louis XI (King of France), 45, 51, 53–55, 81, 92, 106
Louis XII (King of France), 49, 92, 94–98, 100, 124
Louis XIV (King of France), 227, 228, 243, 256, 259
Louis of Nassau, 233–35

Louise of Savoy, 108
Lovati, Lovato dei, 6
Loyola, Ignatius, 123, 180, 183, *185*–87
Luder, Peter, 130
Luther, Martin, 11, 110, 131–32, 137–39, 143–57, 161–63, *167*, 242, 244
    Counter Reformation and, 188, 190
    at Diet of Worms, 104, 150
    German Bible of, 38

Machiavelli, Niccolò, 38, 64, 88–89, 96, 99, *120*–24
Maderno, Carlo, 119
Madonna with Child (Masaccio), *25*
Magellan, Ferdinand, 68
Malatesta, Sigismondo, 20
Malatesta Temple (Alberti), *21*
Mannerism, 192
Mantegna, Andrea, 23
Manutius, Aldus, 46, 126
Margaret of Anjou, 51–52, 55, 56
Margaret (Princess of England), 58
Margaret (Duchess of Parma), 229, 231, 232, 236
Margaret of Savoy, 108, 228
Marguérite of Angoulême, 138
Marguérite of Navarre, 165
Marot, Clément, 169
Marsiglio of Padua, 28, 40, 176
Martin V (Pope), 42
Martyr, Peter, 179
Mary I (Queen of England), 64, 104, 133–34, 171, 179–80
Mary of Guise, 171, 213
Mary of Hungary, 198, 228
Mary (Queen of Scots), 171, 207, 212–14
Masaccio, 23, *25*
Mathias (Archduke), 236
Matocius, Giovanni de, 7
Matthias Corvinus (King of Hungary), 74, 76, 81
Matthys, Jan, 160
Matys, Quinten, *135*
Maurice of Nassau, 238
Maurice (Duke of Saxony), 161, 162, 231
Maximilian I (Holy Roman Emperor), 54, 64, 74–78, 97, 100, 103, 131
Mazarin, Jules, 256
Medici, Alessandro de', 123
Medici, Catherine de', 214, 217, 219–21
Medici, Cosimo de', 30, 32, 123
Medici, Filippo Maria de', 30
Medici, Giovanni de', 34, 99
Medici, Giuliano de', 30
Medici, Lorenzo de' (the Magnificent), 30–32, *31*, 34, 93, 101, 114
Medici, Piero de', 30, 93
Melanchthon, Philip, 151, 155, 157, 161–63

Memling, Hans, 128
Mennonite Anabaptism, 160
Merici, St. Angela, 183
Meung, Jean de, 4
Michelangelo, 24, 34, 108–15, *112–14*, 118, 119, 192
Milan, 91–92
  feud between Naples and, 93
  French claims to, 31
  humanism in, 6, 8
Milič of Kroměříže, 79
Monstereul, Jean de, 129
Montaigne, Michel Eyquem de, 69, 243–45
Montigny, Baron de, 234
More, Thomas, 69, 89, 134–35, 174, 175, 177
Morone, Giovanni, 183, 188
Moslems in Spain, 59
  during Inquisition, 62–63
Mountjoy, Lord, 135
Mussato, Albertino, 6
Münzer, Thomas, 151
Muth, Conrad (Mutianus), 131, 143

Napier, John, 249
Naples, 91–92
  feud between Milan and, 93
  feudalism in, 89
  French claims to, 31, 53
  Greek studies in, 9
  Spanish conquest of, 62, 63
  war between Florence and, 31
Nauclerus, Johannes, 133
Navarra, Pedro, 101
Neri, St. Philip, 184
Netherlands
  Catholic mystics in, 42
  Counter Reformation in, 182, 187
  economic development of, 70
  education in, 27
  growth of humanism in, 135
  Hapsburg control of, 54–55
  Protestant Reformation in, 160, 170, 171
  revolt against Spanish rule of, 228–40: England and, 214–16, 238
Newton, Isaac, 191
Niccoli, Niccolò, 14, 16, 18
Niccolò Machiavelli, "Writer of Histories," 120
Nicholas of Hereford, 41
Nicholas of Lyra, 143
Nicholas V (Pope), 29, 65
Nithardt, Mathias, 129
Nominalism, 79

Ochino, Bernardino, 179
Oecolampadius, John, 155
Oresme, Nicholas, 246
Otto of Freising, 133

Ottoman Turks, 31, 70, 82
  occupation of Byzantine Empire by, 9, 65
  invasion of Hungary by, 82, 83, 106–7
  power of, 195: naval, 105

Padilla, Juan de, 104
Painting, 22–24
  High Renaissance, 108–18
  Platonism and, 33–34
Palestrina, Giovanni, 191
Palladio, Andrea, 118
Palladius, Peter, 158
Panormita (Antonio Beccadelli), 28
Paré, Ambroise, 249
Parsons, Robert, 212
Pascal, Blaise, 187
Paul III (Pope), 123, 161, *185*, 188
Paul IV (Pope), 190
Paul V (Pope), 119
Paulet, William, 208
Pazzi Chapel (Brunelleschi), *21*
Pederson, Christian, 158
Pérez, Antonio, 200, 235
Perugino, Il, 115
Peruzzi, Baldassare, 119
Petrarch (Francesco Petrarca), 3, 6, 7, 9–13, *10*, 19, 34, 131
Petri, Laurentius, 159
Petri, Olavus, 158–59
Peurbach, Georg, 251
Pfefferkorn, Johann, 132
Philip (Archduke), 64
Philip (Duke of Burgundy), 47, 49
Philip IV (King of France), 44
Philip of Hesse, 152, 155, 157, 160
Philip II (King of Spain), 198–204, *202*, 213–15, 219, 224, 226
  marriage of Mary Tudor and, 104, 179
  Netherlands revolt against, 215, 229, 231, 233–36, 239
Philosophy
  classic, 5–6
  epicurean, 28–29
  stoic, 11–12, 28–29
Pia, Emilia, 125
Piccolomini, Aeneas Sylvius, 43
Pico della Mirandola, Count Giovanni, 34, 128, 132
Pietà (Michelangelo), *113*
Pilatus, Leontius, 9
Pisano, Niccolò, 23
Pirckheimer, Willibald, 131–32
Pius II (Pope), 43, 80, 96, 130
Pius IV (Pope), 190
Pizzaro, Francisco de, 68
Platonism, 32–34
Plautus, Titus Maccius, 26
Plethon, Gemistus, 32

Poetry, 13
  Platonism and, 34
  High Renaissance, 127
Poggio Bracciolini, Gian Francesco, 14, 16, 18, 24, 27, 30
Poland, 82–83
  Protestant Reformation in, 166, 170
  trade and, 44, 70
Pole, Reginald, 120–21, 177, 179, 188, 189
Poliziano, Angelo, 34, 133
Porto, Luigi da, 38
Portrait of Philip II (Titian), *202*
Portrait of Thomas Cranmer (Holl), *176*
Portugal, 62
  annexed by Spain, 198
  Counter Reformation in, 186–87
  exploration and colonization by, 65–67
Prierias, Silvester, 147
Primavera (Botticelli), *33*
Printing, 42, 45–47
Prokop the Bald, 80
Protestant Reformation, 40, 143–81
  in Denmark, 158
  in England, 171–81: establishment of Church of England, 175–76; persecution under Mary I, 179–80
  in France, 164–66, 168–70
  in Germany: origins of, 143–53; politics and, 157–64
  in Netherlands, 160, 170, 171
  in Scotland, 170–72, 213
  in Sweden, 158–59
  in Switzerland, 153–57, 167–71
Pupper, John, 144
Purvey, John, 41, 173

Quinones, Cardinal, 178
Quintilian, 18, 24–25

Rabelais, François, 243–44
Raleigh, Walter, 216, 245
Ranke, Leopold von, 182
Raphael, 108, 111, 115–*16*, 119, *121*, 125
Reading Room, Laurentian Library (Michelangelo), *114*
Realism, 79
Regiomontanus (Johann Müller), 251
Rembrandt van Rijn, 191
René of Anjou, 92
René (Duke of Lorraine), 54
Requesens, Don Luis de, 234, 235
Reuchlin, Johann, 131, 132, 143, 151
Richard II (King of England), 56, 79
Richard III (King of England), 57
Richelieu, Cardinal Duc de, 256
Rienzo, Cola di, 11
Robert of Anjou (King of Naples), 9, 11
Robert (Earl of Leicester), 215

Romano, Giulio, 119
Rome
  architecture in, 5
  humanism in, 18
  painting and sculpture in, 110
  popular revolution in, 11
Ronsard, Pierre de, 243
Rubens, Peter Paul, 118, 191
Rucellai, Giovanni, 20
Rudolph I (Holy Roman Emperor), 236

Sacrifice of Isaac (Ghiberti), *22*
Sadoleto, Cardinal Jacopo, 188
St. Bartholomew Massacre, *222*
S. Francesco in Gloria (Sassetta), *24*
Saint Ildefonso (El Greco), *191*
Salutati, Coluccio, 7, 14, 16–18
Salviati (Archbishop of Florence), 30
Sanazzaro, Jacopo, 127
Sangallo, Antonio da, 119
Sansovino, Jacopo, 119
Sassetta, *24*
Savonarola, Girolamo, 34, 93, 94, *95*
Savonarola preaching to the Florentines (woodcut), *95*
School of Athens (Raphael), *116*
Scientific discovery, 245–52
  cosmological theories and, 245–49
  in medicine and anatomy, 249–50
Schöffer, Peter, 45
Schwarz, Matthäus, *72*
Schwenckfeld, Caspar, 160
Scotland, Protestant Reformation in, 170–72, 213
Sculpture, High Renaissance, 108–18
Sebastian (King of Portugal), 198
Sellyng, William, 130
Serlio, Sebastiano, 118
Servetus, Miguel, 168, 250
Sforza, Francesco Maria, 106
Sforza, Gian Galeazzo, 93, 94
Sforza, Lodovico, 31, 93–95, 111
Sforza, Maximilian, 101
Shakespeare, William, 242, 243
Sigismund (Holy Roman Emperor), 79, 80
Sixtus IV (Pope), 146
Sixtus V (Pope), 225
Simons, Menno, 160
Slave trade, 65
Soderini, Piero, 99
Spain, 39, 59–69, 102–5
  colonization by, 63–69
  Counter Reformation in, 182, 186, 188
  French civil wars and, 204
  Inquisition in, 62–63, 202–3
  invasion of Italy by, 88, 97–101
  under Philip II, 195–204
  Portugal annexed by, 198
  trade and, 43

Spenser, Edmund, 243
Spinola, Ambrogio, 239
Standonck, Jean, 182–83
Staupitz, Johann von, 144
Stevin, Simon, 249
Sulaimān the Magnificent (Ottoman
    Turkish Sultan), 105, 108, 152
Swabian League, 71, 73
Sweden
    economic development of, 70
    Protestant Reformation in, 158–59
Switzerland
    military of: mercenaries, 53, 54, 95; tactics
        employed by, 88–89
    political development of, 77–78
    Protestant Reformation in, 153–57, 167–71
Sylvester I (Pope), 29
Sylvius, Aeneas, *see* Pius II

Talbot, John (Earl of Shrewsbury), 52
Tauler, Johannes, 144
Tausen, Hans, 158
Tempèsta (Giorgione), *117*
Terence, 26
Tetzel, Johann, *145,* 146
Theresa of Ávila, St., 182, 192
Thiene, Gaetano di, 183
Thirty Years War, 88
Thomas à Kempis, 42
Tintoretto, Jacopo, 118
Tiptoft, John (Earl of Worcester), 130
Titian, 108, 109, 117–18, *202*
Torquemada, Tomás de, 62–63
Trithemius, 133
Tyndale, William, 134, 175

Unity of Bohemian Brethren, 81
Urban VIII (Pope), 258
Utraquism, 80

Valla, Lorenzo, 28–30, 128
Vallière, Jean, 165
Van Eyck, Jan, 128
Vasa, Sigismund, 241
Vasari, Giorgio, 16, 127
Vega, Lope de, 243
Venice, 91
    annexations by, 38
    as center of trade, 43, 44, 65, 67

education in, 26
humanism in, 6, 8
painting and sculpture in, 116–18
Vergerio, 25
Veronese, Paolo, 118
Verrocchio, Andrea del, 111
Vesalius, Andreas, 242, 250
Viète, François, 249
Villani, Filippo, 17, 23
Villon, François, 128
Visconti, Gian Galeazzo, 14
Vitruvius, Pollio Marcus, 19
Vladislav I (King of Bohemia), 81

Walsingham, Francis, 206, 215
Warham, Archbishop William, 89
Wars of the Roses, 55–58, 130
Waurin (chronicler), 52
Welsers, the, 71–72
Wentworth, Peter, 207
Wenzel (King of Bohemia; Holy Roman
    Emperor), 79
Whitgift, John, 206
William (Duke of Bavaria), 161
William V (Duke of Jülich-Cleves), 160–61
William of Moerbeke, 9
William of Occam, 40
William (Prince of Orange), 231, 233–37,
    240
Wimpfeling, Jacob, 131, 133, 150
Wishart, George, 171
Wolmar, Melchior, 165
Wolsey, Thomas, 100, 102–3, 107–8, 174–75
Women, education of, 17–18
Woodville, Elizabeth, 57
Working-class unrest, 44
Wycliffe, John, 41, 79, 173, 174
Wyttenbach, Thomas, 153

Xavier, St. Francis, 187
Ximenes, Cardinal, 63, 103, 146

Zell (Strassburg leader), 155
Žižka, Jan, 80
Zucchero, Federigo, *205*
Zwingli, Bartholomew, 153
Zwingli, Huldreich, 78, 132, 153–57, *156,*
    166, 167

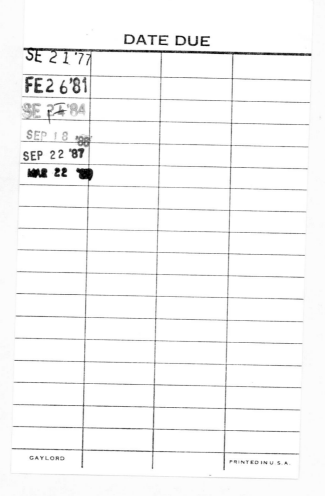

DATE DUE			
SE 21 '77			
FE 26 '81			
SE 27 '84			
SEP 18 '86			
SEP 22 '87			
MAR 22 '89			
GAYLORD			PRINTED IN U.S.A.